MEDIATION

AND THE DYNAMICS OF COLLECTIVE BARGAINING

MEDIATION
AND THE DYNAMICS OF
COLLECTIVE BARGAINING

by

WILLIAM E. SIMKIN

With a Foreword by Dr. George W. Taylor

THE BUREAU OF NATIONAL AFFAIRS, INC., WASHINGTON, D.C.

1971

Printed in the United States of America

Library of Congress Catalog Card Number: 73-161510

Standard Book Number: 87179-127-7

31

FOREWORD

A free society is founded upon the conviction that its internal conflicts can be resolved by an acceptable accommodation of diverse interests. Ours is an agreement-making society. We have long expressed a belief that by reasoning together, under our man-made systems of persuasion, people are willing and able to accommodate as between the duties which alone hold a society together and the freedom to enhance self-serving objectives by whatever means. The validity of that basic concept has always been questioned by some but perhaps never so seriously by so many as in present troubled times.

Institutional forms have been created to effect the essential accommodations, and their structures are slowly undergoing change to adjust them to the 20th Century environment. One of these institutions, collective bargaining, has been designed to bring about private agreements between representatives of employees and of management to govern the terms of employment. Despite recurrent doubts, we still hold to the proposition that the best way of resolving disputes over employment terms is by private agreement between the parties of direct interest. The costs of alternatives are still deemed to be excessive. Labor mediation thus represents an important public interest, i.e., achievement of a meeting of minds by the parties. This has been made specific in legislation, and poignantly reflected in the determined efforts of governmental agencies and the courts in critical cases coming before them to settle issues by agreement rather than by an imposed decision.

Although labor mediation is a crucial part of the national labor policy, only limited efforts have been made by researchers and others to understand or to analyze the process. Indeed, mediation has been commonly dealt with by simply asserting that it is an art which defies analysis. There is considerable substance but also a lack of depth to that observation. Each "case" has unique characteristics. They are often not easily discerned but the successful mediator must adjust his actions to them.

This pioneering study by William E. Simkin, based upon wide experience, makes a breakthrough contribution by spelling out certain principles and guideposts to assist the mediator in discerning those unique factors and then in choosing as between alternate approaches. The fortunate result could well be an enhancement of creative artistry in labor mediation.

No one has better credentials than William E. Simkin for undertaking an in-depth analysis of labor mediation. In various capacities, his professional life has been centered upon the development of third party participation as a means of assisting unions and employers in their quest for a meeting of minds. Following his distinguished service throughout the Kennedy and Johnson administrations as director of the Federal Mediation and Conciliation Service, he has drawn upon an unparalleled experience to give all of us valuable insights about mediation. The interweaving of theory and practice which he provides is of especial value in his study of a neglected phase of our striving for industrial relations grounded upon private agreements.

George W. Taylor
Harnwell Professor of Industry,
Wharton School of Finance and Commerce,
University of Pennsylvania,
Philadelphia, Pa.

PREFACE

Work occupies the largest span of our waking hours. It provides the economic base which permits other activity. Whether we work *for* or *with* others, the terms and conditions of the relationship are significant. They determine the mixture of harmony and conflict that blend to create an overall reaction of satisfaction or of frustration.

An ancient illustration of conflict is the "brick without straw" Biblical episode, recorded in the Book of Exodus. Stripped of the important religious and ethnic aspects that usually dominate our reading about that event, the story has labor relations significance.

The Israelites were working in Egypt. Pharaoh and his taskmasters had established a production standard for brickmaking, the principal occupation of the Israelite workers. A specified number of bricks were required to be produced each day. Moses and Aaron, the Israelite leaders, requested a three-day holiday for a religious observance. Pharaoh denied the request. Moreover, in retaliation, a speedup was ordered. The same daily production of bricks was demanded and the workers were required to secure their own straw or stubble, an essential ingredient. That controversy resulted in a long series of disasters, both supernatural and man-made, being inflicted on the Egyptian employers. The ultimate result was probably the longest strike of record. The children of Israel quit their jobs and left Egypt, never to return. Moreover, the descendants of the principals are not overly friendly, even today.

Conflict at the work place in the present-day world is usually channeled in different ways. Group disputes are resolved, somehow, sometime, by the process we call collective bargaining.

Collective bargaining is not readily defined. It exists in a multitude of forms. It means different things to different people. Representatives of workers and representatives of management confer, argue, and ultimately agree. But the subjects they talk about, the methods of discourse, and the ways they reach agreement are far from uniform.

Collective bargaining is essentially a two-party process. But companies and unions do not operate in a vacuum or even in an environment ringed solely by the economic and social characteristics of their own plant or industry. The public has an interest in the process, especially when conflict elements appear to dominate and a strike or lockout is threatened or occurs.

The public interest evidences itself in various ways—beyond conversation and editorial comment. Third parties are requested to assist, or they intervene in the basic two-party system under some circumstances.

This book is about mediation—a principal form of third-party participation in the bargaining process.

Mediation is not a well-known profession. A total of fewer than 500 full-time mediators work in all parts of the United States. The number of part-time practitioners is even smaller.

The philosophy and practice of mediation are often misunderstood, especially by people whose direct knowledge of collective bargaining is limited. Even some bargainers and mediators may be insufficiently aware of the underlying concepts of the process or of sound practices.

The literature about mediation is sketchy and incomplete.[1] Mediation has been characterized as an "art," the techniques of which cannot be portrayed in writing. While this notion has considerable validity, it is hoped that an attempt at articulation and analysis will be useful.

Respect for the confidential relationship between the mediator and the union and company representatives with whom he works has been a deterrent to writing about the process. To betray confidence is to destroy the future usefulness of the mediator. More important, such betrayals could do great harm to a collective bargaining relationship. For this reason, many of the best illustrations of a particular procedure or technique, especially the most readable ones, simply cannot be used even in camouflaged form. The author will not knowingly depart from this respect-for-confidence aspect of the mediator's creed.

This is not a "how to do it" book. The multiplicity of situ-

[1] Charles M. Rehmus, *The Mediation of Industrial Conflict: A Note on the Literature,* reprint by the Institute of Labor and Industrial Relations, University of Michigan-Wayne State University (1965), contains a good summary of available writings on mediation and a list of references.

ations in which a mediator functions defies any "cookbook" approach. Rather, this is an attempt to portray a basic philosophy and to suggest practices and procedures to effectuate that philosophy.

The author assumes full personal responsibility for all aspects of this book. It is not to be construed as an agency statement of policy. Mediators, in and out of government, and agency officials may well disagree either with conclusions or emphasis. Representatives of management and labor may take even greater exception to ideas expressed here.

It is hoped that the book will be useful to labor officials, management representatives, mediators, students, and interested nonparticipants. Some of the more controversial aspects of collective bargaining and mediation merit extensive study and debate. This analysis should help stimulate such discourse.

ACKNOWLEDGMENTS

The wife of a new author deserves top acknowledgment. The decision to write the book, and discussion of its contents and format have been shared experiences. Ruth's active participation has included reading and editing manuscript as well as tedious proofreading. Most of all, her keen interest and consistent encouragement have been vital at all times.

Financially, this book has been made possible by funds associated with appointments at Harvard as Kestnbaum Fellow (1969-1970) and Wertheim Fellow (1970-1971).

In 1961 Harvard University received a unique gift from the Amalgamated Clothing Workers through the Sidney Hillman Foundation, the Hart Schaffner and Marx Company, and the family and friends of Meyer Kestnbaum "to support various activities in the field of industrial relations, industrial affairs, and the problems and opportunities of industry and labor in a changing world." The terms of the gift to the University provide that "a person of experience in the field would be brought to the University for a year from management or labor organizations or government agency, or an arbitrator with capacity to write reflectively of his experiences and to participate seriously in seminars in the various schools."

The Wertheim Fellowship was established at Harvard in 1923 by the family of the late Jacob Wertheim "for support of original research in the field of industrial cooperation."

Professionally and personally, major credit is due George W.

Taylor, under whose guidance and stimulus I was fortunate enough to embark on the labor relations seas. Dr. Taylor's wisdom in the fields of collective bargaining, mediation, and arbitration is well known. Those of us who have had the privilege of intimate personal association with him can attest to the values of that experience. He has given generously of his time reading this manuscript and making important suggestions for improvement. John T. Dunlop, James J. Healy, and Joseph P. O'Donnell have been most helpful in encouragement, ideas, and suggestions. Finally, and by no means least, much of what I may know about mediation is attributable directly to the many mediators in the Federal Mediation and Conciliation Service with whom I was privileged to work over a period of eight years.

Special credit is due the officials of federal, state, and local mediation agencies and the 423 individuals who cooperated so completely in answering questionnaires. Most of the factual information in this book could have been obtained from no other sources.

Early portions of the draft manuscript were typed by Loretta Whitney in Washington, D.C.; the balance of the draft and the revisions by Marilyn Armstrong in Lexington, Mass. Both have been competent and interested assistants in the overall endeavor.

WILLIAM E. SIMKIN

March 1971

TABLE OF CONTENTS

MEDIATION PRACTICES

CRISIS BARGAINING

CHAPTER I

ABCs OF COLLECTIVE BARGAINING

Although this book is primarily about mediation, it necessarily starts by discussing a few essential ingredients and attributes of the collective bargaining process. A labor mediator works in collective bargaining environments. In a free society, it is a central notion that labor and management should fix the terms and conditions of employment by voluntary agreement. In fact, that principle is so well recognized that strikes or lockouts are usually permissible as ultimate but hopefully little-used persuaders. The intended purpose of a strike or lockout is not to produce conflict. Economic sanctions are last resort devices designed to produce agreement. When the collective bargaining process works well, as is the case in a majority of situations, the only persuaders needed are the forces of human argument and reason exercised by the two parties. Normally, it is only when the "voices of reason" within a bargaining arrangement need some assistance or a strike or lockout becomes more than a distant, hypothetical threat that a mediator enters collective bargaining. Even then, he enters to aid in the agreement-making process, not to substitute for it.

Thus, the primacy of voluntary agreement requires, first, that a mediator understand what collective bargaining is all about. Explaining it is no easy task because bargaining situations are so variable. Attempts to create models are doomed to failure because of this infinite diversity. Many books could be and have been written about various aspects of collective bargaining. Since the emphasis here is on mediation, no attempt will be made to examine or even summarize many important features. Chapters VIII and IX will outline some of the crisis variables that a mediator may encounter.

This initial chapter is restricted to examination of a few elemental considerations. How does the process of collective bargaining get started? In what forums does it operate? By what

1

methods do workers and owners effectuate the representation principle at the bargaining table? What subjects are discussed? How do results compare with objectives? How is the process appraised by the general public—by those on the outside looking in?

The sophisticated reader should be aware that some of this chapter is "old stuff" and can be scanned quickly.

ORGANIZATIONAL INGREDIENTS NECESSARY FOR COLLECTIVE BARGAINING

Collective bargaining does not begin automatically. As a matter of fact, most mass-production manufacturing industries in the United States avoided it until the late 1930s or early 1940s. Some segments of the economy are without collective bargaining today. Explanation of the nature of the collective process can begin with brief descriptions of worker-employer relationships that are outside the scope of collective bargaining.

Collective bargaining is not individual bargaining.

True individual bargaining exists only in a one-person-to-one-person relationship. An example, almost unknown in modern society, is an owner-farmer and his one hired man. The two men work together much of the time. The terms and conditions of employment are influenced by the community mores and the current economics of farm operation. The farmer talks with other farmers. The hired man talks with his counterparts in the neighborhood. But these other persons do not intervene directly, and there is little or no formality in the arrangements made between the two men about wages and working conditions.

As the size of the enterprise increases, true individual bargaining diminishes. When the farmer has even two hired hands, he must discuss many matters with the two men simultaneously. The extent of the cohesion or cooperation between the two hired men varies with the individuals.

Despite departures from true individual bargaining in other than one-person-to-one-person relationships, the essence of what is commonly called individual bargaining remains as long as the individual worker has realistic direct access to the employer or the employer's authorized representative for meaningful discussion and resolution of most of the terms and conditions of employment.

Collective bargaining is not unilateral determination.

When a business becomes huge, individual bargaining becomes impossible, except on relatively minor matters. The General Motors Corporation is at the opposite extreme to the owner-farmer. Ownership is divorced from management. The management hierarchy is itself a separate employee group or series of groups. Each successively lower tier in the management and supervisory hierarchy has responsibilities which are circumscribed by administrative policy and decisions made at higher levels. The hourly-rated employee works under a set of rules and economic arrangements not determined at the work place. Individual bargaining is greatly restricted, the opportunity for it occurring in only a few of the direct dealings between the worker and his immediate supervisor. In the absence of a union in such situations, unilateral determination by the employer is a much more apt description than individual bargaining.

In such a situation, there are restraints on the employer. Employees can quit. They can exert only enough effort to avoid discharge. For these and other reasons, a large nonunion employer establishes personnel policies and a personnel administration to attempt to promote good employee morale and preserve aspects of individual bargaining. But the size of the enterprise dictates unilateral determination of many of the most meaningful terms of employment. If the employer sees to it that these terms are at least equal to or better than those in otherwise comparable collective bargaining relationships, bargaining may be avoided. But, employees still have little or no feeling of participation and the situation can be described only as benevolent or self-serving unilateral determination.

What positive ingredients must exist to provide the foundation stones for collective bargaining?

Collective bargaining requires a formal or at least semiformal organization of employees of like status. A principal purpose of that organization must be to bargain with the employer at management levels where the discourse can be meaningful and where the employee group speaks as a group rather than on an individual employee basis. "Like status" means common interest. The employee group is technically defined as an "appropriate unit," a matter of occasional controversy that will not be explored here.

Bargaining with the employer need not be the sole purpose of the employee organization. Unions have other purposes in varying degree. They can be fraternal or professional organizations with a wide variety of social, recreational, educational, and promotional activities not related directly to the employer. They can have political objectives and interests, a factor of much lesser import in the United States than in many other countries. A few organizations, established originally with no collective bargaining objectives, have evolved into strong bargaining units. For example, many subsidiary branches of the National Education Association have acted as much like unions in recent years as the American Federation of Teachers, the AFL-CIO union having principal jurisdiction in education.

For purposes of this book, any organization of workers that "acts like a union" in its relationships with employers will be considered as engaging or seeking to engage in collective bargaining.

The union organization must be accorded some status or recognition by the employer if any real bargaining is to take place. A labor dispute can exist when the employer refuses to deal with the employee organization. In fact, the process of getting recognized, preliminary to collective bargaining, can be one of the most bitter types of disputes.

In the United States, recognition disputes have been substantially eliminated in most sectors of the economy. Title I of the Labor Management Relations Act (referred to hereafter as the Taft-Hartley Act) substitutes the ballot box for the picket line, and an important function of the National Labor Relations Board is to administer the representation portions of the Act. Whenever a majority of workers in an appropriate unit prove that they want a particular union in order to bargain collectively, the employer is required to recognize the union, and the union then represents all employees in the unit, irrespective of union membership. Earlier but somewhat similar provisions of the Railway Labor Act apply to railroads and airlines. Executive Order No. 10988, issued by President Kennedy in January 1962, provided somewhat different procedures for recognition of federal employee unions by federal agencies. Those arrangements have been supplemented and improved by Executive Order No. 11491, signed by President Nixon in October 1969, making them more comparable to those in the private sector. Some state statutes provide procedures for recognition of certain employee groups not covered by federal legislation or by executive order.

Legislation and administrative procedures, for purposes of recognition, do not cover all employee organizations. Agricultural workers in most categories are not covered by Title I of the Taft-Hartley Act. The recent organization of grape pickers in the union led by Cesar Chavez and the initial refusal of the growers to recognize that union have emphasized this fact. A number of states do not have adequate recognition protection or procedures for employees engaged in intrastate commerce. An even larger number do not have viable current procedures for recognition of employees of state and municipal agencies.

Certification by the National Labor Relations Board, signifying a formal mandatory recognition by the employer, or comparable formalities under other legislative or administrative arrangements are not the sole basis for recognition. Many unions were recognized by employers long before the passage of legislation, and some unions have been recognized informally subsequent to enactment of statutes. In a number of states and municipalities, public employee unions without any legal rights have been able to secure or force recognition.

There is no necessary identity of actual representation at any one bargaining table with the parties named in any formal certification. Employer associations (two or more separate employers who join together for purposes of bargaining) may bargain with a union or with groups of unions, the freely acknowledged coverage of the bargain being inclusive of several certifications. In fact, some employee groups not legally certified may be included in the bargain. Or, a single employer may bargain with many unions who join together for that purpose. Such differences between appropriate units for bargaining and appropriate units for initial recognition usually develop as a part of the bargaining process.

For the most part, collective bargaining will be discussed herein on a "bargaining table" basis. The management side of the table may include representatives of one or many employers. The union side may include one or many unions. How and when each side of the table acquired its specific composition will not be explored except where this composition is in dispute. When each side of the table acknowledges the representation status of the other side, bargaining can occur.

Another usual characteristic of collective bargaining is that the results of the bargain are reduced to writing. These written documents have certain legal status.

Thus far, collective bargaining can be said to have the following organizational characteristics:

1. It is not to be confused with individual bargaining or with unilateral employer determination.
2. Employees must be organized in a formal group, usually called a union, a principal objective being to bargain with one or more employers.
3. The union or group of unions must be accorded status or recognition by the employer or employers for purposes of bargaining.
4. The results of collective bargaining are usually summarized in writing and have certain legal status.

BARGAINING FORUMS

Collective bargaining may occur in three different forums. They are:

1. Crisis bargaining (bargaining of basic labor agreements)
2. Grievance procedure
3. Noncrisis dialogue

There are some who would limit use of the words "collective bargaining" to the negotiation of labor agreements, all other related activities being construed as administration of the agreements. This is quite an unrealistic notion unless intended as an exercise in semantics. The relationship between an employer and a union is the totality of the discussion and decision-making that occur (1) when basic labor agreements (contracts) are reached at periodic intervals, usually under deadline pressures; (2) during the life of these contracts as day-by-day problems are resolved by the grievance procedure; and (3) whenever discussions occur or decisions are reached on matters of mutual concern not included in the grievance procedure and in the absence of the deadline pressures of contract negotiation.

Crisis Bargaining

A typical labor contract in the United States is a written agreement setting forth the basic terms and conditions of employment for a stipulated period of time. A majority of agreements in the private sector are for a term of approximately three years. Most, but not all, of these agreements restrict or prohibit strikes and lockouts during the term of the contract. However, at the expiration date of these agreements, it is unusual for there to be any pre-agreed restriction or limitation on the right to strike or to lock out.

In substance, then, the signing of a typical three-year agreement includes a voluntary statement of intention on the part of both parties not to utilize economic sanctions (strike or lockout) during the contract term. In some instances the no-strike, no-lockout clause is not all inclusive. Economic sanctions are permitted for limited, carefully spelled-out situations.

The "no holds barred" arrangement in the private sector at the time of contract expiration necessarily creates a crisis atmosphere as that date approaches. It is for this reason that contract bargaining is sometimes referred to as crisis bargaining even though successful negotiation will avert a crisis. The deadline pressures continue unless removed by agreement.

The foregoing paragraphs assume an existing contractual relationship that is to be renewed. A variant is negotiation of an initial contract—the first contract agreed to between an employer and a union. This may occur after a period of nonunion plant operation or after one union succeeds a different union as representative of the same employees. In the case of initial contracts, there is no semi-automatic deadline date. However, the union is usually free to strike, and under some circumstances the employer may lock out. Thus, at some point in the negotiation of an initial contract, the crisis atmosphere of a deadline may be created.

Grievance Procedure

Labor agreements are not easily applied and interpreted. In the United States, in contrast to some other countries, typical agreements include at least some coverage of a multitude of terms and conditions of employment. Questions and differences of opinion arise frequently as to how a basic agreement provision is to be applied to a specific situation. Some contractual provisions are purposely generalized in language, leaving a considerable amount of latitude of application.

To provide a collective bargaining forum for resolution of these many important day-by-day operating problems, most agreements include a grievance procedure. Grievance procedures vary greatly in both form and content. At small plants a quite simple one- or two-step procedure suffices. In larger establishments and particularly for multiplant companies, there may exist as many as four or five steps. The common element is that a regularized procedure is established under which the aggrieved employee or employees together with appropriate union representatives attempt to resolve the problem with representatives of management. In the many-step procedures, representatives of both the company and the union at increasingly higher levels of authority participate if the matter is not settled at a lower step.

Except for the fact that the parties may create their own restrictions, a strike could occur whenever a grievance is unresolved. In the earlier years of collective bargaining, this is precisely what did happen in many grievance situations. In Great Britain today, grievance strikes or the equivalent constitute the great bulk of all strikes.

In the United States, approximately 95 percent of all labor agreements now contain provisions for voluntary arbitration of most grievances that remain unresolved after the last step of the two-party grievance procedure. A grievance arbitrator is typically chosen by joint agreement of the company and the union, either for one occasion (ad hoc arbitrator) or for all cases that may arise over a specified future period of time (so-called permanent arbitrator). The arbitrator hears the evidence and the positions of the parties and examines the contract. He then issues a decision, usually in writing, which the parties have agreed in advance to accept.

The grievance procedure, including voluntary arbitration when needed, represents a conscious surrender of certain rights in return for labor peace during the life of the contract. The union and the employees give up the right to strike but acquire a procedure for settlement that may include a decision by an impartial person. The employer gives up the right to lock out and embraces the possibility that a final management position may be overruled or modified.

The grievance procedure, including arbitration, creates an important body of common law in the plant, implementing and supplementing the basic agreement.

Final answers to grievance problems, whether achieved by the parties themselves prior to arbitration or by arbitration, do not necessarily resolve these matters for all time. A grievance disposition that is unsatisfactory to one or both parties may become an issue, and possibly the occasion for a strike or lockout, in the next contract negotiations.

In short, a viable grievance procedure and grievance arbitration are important integral parts of collective bargaining. Moreover, even the arbitration decisions are four-square with the principle of voluntarism. The parties have agreed to the process in return for labor peace, and any decision can be reopened at the time of the next contract negotiation.

Noncrisis Dialogue

Contract negotiation and grievance procedure represent the only collective bargaining forums in many company-union relationships. However, it is becoming increasingly evident that some common problems are not easily resolved by either of these methods. Rapid technological change frequently creates major issues during the life of a long-term agreement that the negotiators could not or did not anticipate. The grievance procedure may not be designed for or capable of resolution of such issues. Some types of problems could theoretically be resolved during the process of negotiating an agreement, but the deadline pressures do not provide the necessary time or the appropriate environment for the development of constructive solutions.

Since noncrisis dialogue will be considered fully in a subsequent chapter, no attempt will be made here to describe the process in any detail.

PRIVATE SECTOR v. PUBLIC SECTOR

For many years, most union activity and most labor disputes have involved privately owned companies and employees of such enterprises. The recent rapid growth of unions and disputes in the federal, state, and local governments and in nonprofit organizations such as hospitals and colleges now require special consideration.

Throughout most of this book, except as otherwise noted, the major discussion will be about collective bargaining and mediation in the private sector. However, a later chapter will be devoted solely to the public sector. Differences and similarities will be noted therein.

EFFECTUATION OF THE REPRESENTATION PRINCIPLE

Contract bargaining is performed by negotiating teams on both sides of the table.

A union or a group of unions select a number of persons to represent the employees. Selection may be accomplished by election or appointment. The number of members of the negotiating committee varies widely, dependent both on the size of the employee group and on custom and practice. One member is the chairman or principal spokesman. A variety of subcommittees may be created, again dependent on the size and importance of the negotiations or on past practice.

The company or the group of companies included in an employer's association designate the management negotiating team and the chairman or principal spokesman. As is the case on the union side, the composition of the management negotiating committee will vary depending on many factors. Usually the team includes industrial relations staff specialists and men directly responsible for production.

On some occasions, the principal spokesman for a company or a union, or both, is a labor relations lawyer retained for the negotiations. However, this is a practice most likely to be found in smaller bargaining relationships where full-time labor relations specialists are not employed. Normally, if an outside lawyer is present at all, he is in the negotiations as an advisor and to assist in drafting contract language after the negotiators have reached an agreement in principle.

In grievance procedure prior to grievance arbitration, both sides develop their representation in various ways. Most unions establish a continuing grievance committee composed basically of a group of shop stewards or committeemen. The chairman of the grievance committee may be an officer of the local union or a person in a special elective position. The company representatives are members of the industrial relations staff and production supervisors. Outside lawyers are seldom utilized.

If a grievance is not resolved and is to be submitted to arbitration, the local plant grievance committees are frequently supplemented at the arbitration hearings by an international union representative or a lawyer on the union side and a higher ranking company industrial relations staff specialist or a lawyer on the company side. Occasionally this type of expansion of local plant grievance committees also occurs at the last grievance step prior to arbitration.

At small or medium size companies, the composition of grievance committees may be essentially the same as the contract negotiating committees. This is much less likely to occur at larger establishments.

For purposes of noncrisis dialogue, the selection of participants is dependent on many factors, including the type of dialogue contemplated. Frequently, both company and union personnel may include individuals in the hierarchies who may not normally participate actively either in contract negotiation or grievance procedure. Special-purpose committees or procedures are usually staffed by persons selected because of their particular competence in the matter to be discussed.

The common element in all these arrangements is some realistic effectuation of the principles underlying representative forms of government.

SCOPE OF SUBJECT MATTERS INCLUDED IN BARGAINING

What are the subject matters about which companies and unions bargain? Answers to this question are so varied that it is impossible to be definitive except within the context of a specific case. However, a general framework for answers can be explored. For purposes of simplicity, this discussion will ignore very complicated and controversial questions concerning so-called mandatory subjects for bargaining, as determined by the NLRB.

When a union develops its demands preparatory to contract negotiation, it has a wide choice of potential issues. General wage increases are usually requested. But that issue may be only one among many. Additional demands may be of two varieties. Some will be requests for improvement of benefits or other provisions that already exist in the expiring contract. Some may be for new benefits or contractual arrangements about which the expiring contract was silent. Demands may be formulated in a variety of ways. Increasingly, local unions submit suggestions, thus effectuating the democratic principle. Sometimes, union officials develop the demands after only informal discussion at lower levels of the union.

Company demands are likely to be fewer in number. Normally they will be limited to requests for changes of provisions of the expiring contract that, in the company view, have been onerous or unpalatable. Sometimes a wage reduction will be requested.

A better understanding of union demands in negotiation may be gained by placing them in time perspective. We will assume a sizable manufacturing plant that was organized in the late 1930s. If it was well managed it had a unilaterally determined wage structure and many established company policies governing working conditions. A typical first agreement was what has sometimes been called a "foot in the door" contract. A wage increase was probably negotiated. In addition, the union obtained some contractual protection on matters most vital to employees, such as unjust discharge and seniority. Some type of grievance procedure was likely to have been included. The first agreement was a rather simple document. Thereafter, almost every time the agreement was renewed, new items were added and old provisions were improved or enlarged. Each time the union demands were framed, the high-priority items were the benefits or work-rule changes considered most important by employees. Obviously, all union goals were not reached, but some demands were granted by the company. Thus, the labor agreement grew in size and complexity.

As we visualize the gradual growth of labor agreements at hundreds of manufacturing plants in this general manner, we would expect great diversity to develop. Unilateral policies of Companies A, B, and C are by no means identical when the process starts. Since employees strive to improve those items they consider to be most important, the labor agreement at Company A may acquire a provision on some item not considered essential at Company B or C. Resistance to change varies among companies. Technologies and pay practices are quite different. For example, scheduled hours of work and overtime pay arrangements at a continuous-process plant that must operate seven days a week and 24 hours a day are quite different from those at a plant normally operating only five days a week on a one- or two-shift basis. Or, one plant may pay most of its employees at piece rates and another at hourly rates. In short, we would expect almost infinite variety as the many labor agreements increase their subject-matter coverage, both as to matters included in agreements and as to the specific language and intent of the various contract clauses.

But there are also factors working toward uniformity. International unions develop policies on various subjects that members attempt to obtain at all plants. Multiplant companies do not normally want widely differing policies at their several plants. Competing companies in the same industry tend to move towards uniform conditions. During World War II, National War Labor Board policies had a marked tendency to level out differences on many matters.

These opposite tendencies, one toward great diversity and the other toward uniformity, continue to operate today. Close examination of labor agreements in a variety of industries will disclose different language on almost any subject that is selected for inquiry. Substantial but somewhat lesser differences of basic intent and application will also be found.

One trend is almost universal. Labor agreements get bigger and bigger as a bargaining relationship continues over a period of years. More and more subjects creep into the agreements. The detailed coverage of any one subject is also likely to expand.

Some bargainers choose to keep their basic labor agreements relatively short and simple. In such instances the expansion occurs by way of a variety of supplemental agreements. Some bargainers attempt to put most of the agreement into a single booklet. The result may rival a telephone book for size. In all instances, the operation of the grievance procedure and grievance arbitration both clarifies and amplifies the agreement language.

Thus, the total scope of labor agreements between a company and a union in a mature relationship is extensive and complex.

The 1968-1971 agreements between the United States Steel Corporation and the United Steelworkers of America, covering production and maintenance employees at the company's steel-manufacturing and by-product coke plants, are examples of the results of collective bargaining over a period of about 30 years. The basic agreement, printed in a four by six and a-half inch booklet, runs 123 pages. Appendices in the same booklet total 28 pages. Separately printed supplements on important subjects such as pensions, insurance, and job evaluation increase the total bulk of all relevant agreements to many times the size of the basic agreement. Recorded grievance settlements and arbitration decisions fill many volumes.

The following list (not in order of appearance in the basic agreement and condensed by the author for present purposes) includes the more significant matters covered, in whole or in part, in these U.S. Steel agreements:

A. Economic benefits with provisions for application and effectuation.

    1. Wage rate matters
        a. General wage increases during life of agreement
        b. Job classification rates (supplemented by a very detailed Job Description and Classification Manual)
        c. Incentive pay provisions (supplemented by detailed plans at the several plants)
        d. Provisions governing new and changed jobs (hourly rated and incentive)
        e. Apprentice and learner rates

2. Pensions (separate agreement)
3. Insurance (separate agreement)
4. Supplemental unemployment benefits (supplemented by detailed booklet)
5. Savings and vacation plan (supplemented by detailed booklet)
6. Holidays and holiday pay
7. Vacations and vacation pay
8. Shift differentials
9. Definitions of normal hours of work and special pay provisions for Sunday, abnormally scheduled, or unscheduled hours of work
10. Overtime pay
11. Reporting pay
12. Jury pay
13. Funeral leave and pay
14. Severance pay (other than pensions)
15. Moving allowances for interplant transfer under certain conditions

B. Provisions generally classified as noneconomic, some of which may have cost implications:

1. No-strike, no-lockout clauses
2. Grievance procedure and arbitration
3. Reference to local working conditions at the various plants (supplemented by a variety of written and unwritten agreements at these plants)
4. Seniority (supplemented by detailed seniority arrangements at the several plants)
5. Suspension and discharge
6. General statements of management rights and responsibilities
7. General statements of union rights and responsibilities
8. Union security and check-off
9. Subcontracting of work
10. Safety and health provisions
11. Scheduling of vacations
12. Division of overtime work (primarily spelled out by local plant arrangements)
13. Supervisors' working provisions and arrangements relative to temporary foremen
14. Rules governing rights of access to plants by certain union representatives
15. Employee rights to transfer to other plants under certain conditions
16. Rights of employees who enter military service
17. Duration of agreement

Separate agreements at each plant cover a wide variety of matters, only some of which are noted specifically in the above list.

It requires only superficial examination of the list to conclude that discussion and decisionmaking by collective bargaining includes most of the subject matters of importance at the work place.

Agreements at small plants are much less complex but are likely to include at least some reference to most of the matters listed above as covered by agreements at U. S. Steel.

At the time of any one contract negotiation, a union will seek changes in only a fraction of the provisions of the expiring agreement. But it is free to propose almost anything. Thus, the potential scope of collective bargaining is very large. Appetites for changes or for entirely new benefits are curtailed initially by a union's observance of some semblance of reality and finally by what is obtainable from a company. This enlargement of the scope of bargaining is frequently a matter of serious dispute. Many companies believe that some union demands encroach on vital areas of management prerogative.

RESULTS OF COLLECTIVE BARGAINING
IN CONTRAST TO OBJECTIVES OF THE PARTIES

It is too often assumed that collective bargaining is dominated by conflict and that the interests of employees and employers are almost always mutually antagonistic. Peace and cooperation are seldom newsworthy, whereas strife and discord make headlines.

The fact is that substantial elements of mutual interest are present in almost all collective bargaining.

For a company to be profitable and "ahead of the pack" competitively is advantageous to workers as well as to the employer. As one prominent management representative noted succinctly: "It is of benefit to nobody to perform a hysterectomy on the goose that lays the golden eggs." [1]

For workers to be reasonably satisfied with terms and conditions of employment and to want to continue the employment relationship is likewise mutually advantageous. An experienced, cooperative work force is one of the best assets a company can have—more significant than many items that appear on a balance sheet. Many companies with the power to punish a union severely after a long "lost strike" do not press their advantage unduly. Short-term economic gain that might be secured thereby

[1] Virgil B. Day, Vice President, General Electric Company, in a speech at the January 1967 National Seminar of the Federal Mediation and Conciliation Service.

would be outweighed by the deterioration of employee morale.

Moreover, especially as respects many so-called noneconomic issues—the rules applicable to day-by-day plant operation at the workplace level—mutual interest may be paramount.

Conflict does arise. Interests are sharply divergent on many subjects. These are the portions of the collective bargaining iceberg that emerge from the surface for all to see. But the hidden portion of the iceberg—the mutual-interest portion—may be even more important.

To carry the analogy one step further, there is no uniform density or specific gravity of collective bargaining icebergs. In some relationships, conflict is minimal and mutual interest overwhelming. At the other extreme, conflict is dominant and mutual interest hard to find.

It may be useful to list qualitative and somewhat subjective results of collective bargaining in contrast to the objectives of the parties. The borderlines between the four categories to be noted below are not clean-cut, but an attempt to differentiate may point out the range of the collective bargaining spectrum. Bargaining results in:

1. Codification and clarification of items subject to easy agreement.
2. Discovery of creative solutions to matters initially thought to be sources of serious conflict.
3. Achievement of viable compromise in real and persistent conflict-of-interest issues.
4. Acceptance by one or both parties of the advisability or necessity of complete capitulation on some issue or issues in view of the alternatives.

These four categories can be explained within the context of a typical contract-renewal negotiation. The union usually enters the first conference with a long "laundry list" of demands. The company counters with a shorter list of contract changes that it seeks to achieve. What happens to these initial demands?

Easy Solutions

At a reasonably early date in the negotiations, some of the union requests and perhaps a few of the company requests have been "disposed of." The changes sought are so obviously reasonable or mutually advisable that these issues are settled quickly. Specific new or amended contract language may be written and initialed to remove the issues from further discussion. Sometimes the understanding is informal and the writing is deferred to the final-agreement stage. The important point is that these matters are realistically removed from controversy and everybody at the bargaining table knows it. These solutions are not necessarily confined to trivial matters; sometimes they are quite important.

Creative Discovery

The second category is similar to the first in that mutually satisfactory answers are found. It is dissimilar in that very genuine conflict appeared to exist at the outset of negotiations. Long, labored, and sometimes profane discussion gradually discloses the real objectives of both parties. An inventive answer finally emerges. It may come in painful steps. More rarely, it "bursts forth," sometimes from a most unlikely source. All members of the negotiating group are likely to contribute something to the evolutionary process. Sometimes the source of the solution cannot even be traced. More often there is strong leadership on both sides of the table, leadership which is ready and willing to acknowledge and digest even the smallest contribution from others.

This is the most creative aspect of bargaining. It is a process of discovery. Something quite new has been added, something that simply would not have happened in the absence of sharp intelligence and good will directed towards resolution of a difficult common problem.

The so-called M & M (Mechanization and Modernization) Agreement, negotiated in 1960 by the Pacific Maritime Association and the International Longshoremen's and Warehousemen's Union, is an illustration. For many years, longshore workers on the Pacific Coast had insisted upon and obtained work practices geared to an older technology. As machines and equipment improved, the old rules persisted or even were tightened in some respects. The obvious motivation was workers' fear of loss of jobs due to new methods and machines. Management became increasingly restive. The restrictions were onerous and were preventing technological advance. Moreover, numerous disputes on the docks were causing "quickie" strikes and loss of production. The negotiators faced up to the problem candidly and fearlessly but not painlessly. The union gave up most of the restrictions. The employers paid substantially, notably in a 35-hour-per-week work guarantee for regular men and numerous pension and other benefits. These benefits were assured by a sizable fund created by employer payments.

In crass terms, it was a "buy-off." In realistic terms, it was industrial statesmanship. The agreement has been described pictorially and candidly in a book, *Men and Machines,* published jointly by the PMA and the ILWU. A part of the joint statement of the parties reads:

> "In this bargain both sides gained: the worker a new form of security, the employer a new latitude in operations.

> "The important point is that the turn was made. If it develops that one side or the other got the better part of the bargain, then this will be a subject of future collective bargaining. Both the ILWU and the PMA are strong enough in their own right. They can take care of themselves.

> "The decision to launch the M & M program is irreversible; the change has been made.

> "Old work rules cannot be restored; employer contribution to the M & M fund cannot be returned.

> "It is too early to tell whether the agreement itself may have to be modified, but it will not be abandoned.

> "Meanwhile, this pioneering effort in the field of Men and Machines is working, and working well on the West Coast waterfront." [2]

At the expiration of the five-year agreement, the M & M Agreement was modified in some particulars. In 1969, a containerization dispute threatened temporarily to disrupt the relationship seriously. In a rapidly changing technology, few things are static. But the M & M Agreement was and is a solid framework for solution of both old and new problems.

Other examples of this "discovery" aspect of collective bargaining are many and varied. They belie the common impression that collective bargaining is not creative.

Viable Compromise

Viable compromise differs from creative discovery in a qualitative or psychological sense. An acceptable answer is found that differs from the initial position of either party. But it is not agreed to with much enthusiasm by the negotiators. It is less than the union really wants and more than the company really wants to give, even after full and complete discussion. It is not a truly creative discovery. It is something that both can live

---

[2] Louis Goldblatt (ed.), MEN AND MACHINES, International Longshoremen's and Warehousemen's Union and Pacific Maritime Association, San Francisco, 1963, p. 128.

with, at least for the duration of the agreement, and it may be acceptable only because the alternative strike costs are too great. Compromise of a wage demand is often a good illustration.

Compromise is not a dirty word. It is a necessary ingredient of the decisionmaking process in a democratic society.

Capitulation

Capitulation—giving up completely to a union or company demand or complete withdrawal by a union or a company of one of its demands—is a frequent result of collective bargaining. It too can be considered as a spectrum. At one end of the band are those union or company demands that were not very meaningful or important even when they were made. They were "window dressing" items. At the other end are issues where capitulation may be accompanied by great bitterness. In the middle of the spectrum are "trade-off" capitulations, not desirable to the party that acquiesces but acceptable by reason of capitulation by the other party on other issues.

Summary

The final agreement between the parties in each of the many thousands of contracts negotiated each year is some mix of this easy agreement-creative discovery-compromise-capitulation range.

Many mixes include little or no unhappy capitulation. Both union and company negotiators honestly believe that a good job has been done. Such negotiations are seldom accompanied by strikes and mediation is not often needed. The basic relationship between the parties is cordial and productive.

In-between mixes occupy various positions within the range and may or may not be accompanied by strikes or lockouts. Mediation is often required. Some unhappiness with the final agreement may exist on the union or company side, or on both sides, but the normal reaction at the time of settlement is that the contract is something that can be lived with for its duration. Little real bitterness has been created by the new agreement. Acquiescence in the total result overrides disappointment about a few specific segments.

In a limited number of negotiations, the result is almost complete capitulation by a company or by a union on the important issues. This can occur after a long strike. Or, it can take place without a strike where the power factors are so unequal that the weak side realizes the futility of a struggle. In either event, negotiations characterized by almost total capitulation are likely to leave scars that may not fade for many years. The weak party nurses its wounds. Acquiescence is only temporary. Hope remains that the power factors will be reversed the next time. Or, frustrations may seek release during the term of the agreement in the grievance procedure and otherwise by less than cooperative and productive behavior. Fortunately, these reactions are not typical. However, they do occur, in response to either union or company power that is overwhelming. A mediator may be powerless to prevent them, but he may be able to help avoid more serious consequences.

BASIC GOVERNMENT POLICY ABOUT COLLECTIVE BARGAINING

The basic policy of the Federal Government as respects collective bargaining is summarized in the last paragraph of Title I, Section 101, Section 1 of the Taft-Hartley Act which reads:

> "It is hereby declared to be the policy of the United States to eliminate the causes of certain substantial obstructions to the free flow of commerce and to mitigate and eliminate these obstructions when they have occurred by *encouraging the practice and procedure of collective bargaining* and by protecting the exercise by workers of full freedom by association, self-organization, and designation of representatives of their own choosing, *for the purpose of negotiating the terms and conditions of their employment* or other mutual aid or protection." [3]

It is significant that this section of the Taft-Hartley Act, passed in 1947, is substantially identical to an earlier provision of the 1935 Wagner Act. This is so despite substantial changes made in 1947 which were openly designed to add weight to the employer side in the bargaining power balance.

Moreover, Title II, Section 201 (a), new in 1947, reads in part as follows:

> "(a) sound and stable industrial peace and the advancement of the general welfare, health, and safety of the Nation and of the best interest of employers and employees can most satisfactorily be secured by the *settlement of issues between employers and employees through the processes of conference and collective bargaining* between employers and the representatives of their employees." [4]

---

[3] Italics supplied.
[4] Italics supplied.

Thus, it is clear that the Congress decided in 1935 not to be neutral about collective bargaining as a process and reaffirmed this decision in 1947. The clearly expressed national policy was to encourage it. No event has occurred since 1947 that would indicate any basic congressional change of this national policy.

Despite firm public support for collective bargaining, as evidenced by the statutory provisions noted above, critics of the process abound. The participants in the process cannot afford to relax and assume that basic public support will continue indefinitely. Over the long pull, all democratic procedures are "on trial." Collective bargaining is no exception.

FACTS ABOUT MEDIATION

CHAPTER II

WHAT IS MEDIATION?

Critics of collective bargaining seldom attack the institution directly. Unions and union members have substantial political power. The bargaining process works sufficiently well that only a management minority would honestly and solidly support return to unilateral determination by all companies of the terms and conditions of employment, even if that were possible. The principle of voluntarism is so deeply ingrained in our democratic society that frontal attacks on it have little political acceptability even outside the ranks of labor and management persons directly or indirectly involved in bargaining. For all these reasons, criticism usually takes the form of proposals for regulation or reform. In all instances, external assistance, regulation, or reform boils down to intervention by third parties, usually government personages of the executive or judicial branch or other individuals acting under governmental appointment.

What are the principal types of third party intervention, now in existence or proposed? For present purposes, attempts to answer that question will be limited primarily to discussion of intervention in contract negotiation disputes, the most visible form of actual or potential conflict in collective bargaining.

It has been common practice to apply a variety of descriptive words to the work of impartial third parties in labor disputes. A typical sequence is: conciliation, mediation, fact-finding without recommendations, fact-finding with recommendations, voluntary arbitration, and compulsory arbitration. In this word-use ladder, conciliation is considered to be the least affirmative and least potent function. Compulsory arbitration is by all odds the strongest. Since these words will be used hereafter, they should be described briefly. The following facetious definitions suggest frequently held ideas.

Conciliation is conceived of as a mild form of intervention limited primarily to scheduling conferences, trying to keep the disputants talking, facilitating other procedural niceties, carrying messages back and forth between the parties, and generally being a "good fellow" who tries to keep things calm and forward-looking in a tense situation.

Mediation is frequently thought of as a slightly more affirmative function. The mediator may make suggestions. He may even make procedural or, on rare occasions, substantive recommendations. But since he has no power and authority, these somewhat more aggressive tactics are considered to be without significant potency.

Fact-finding without recommendations is sometimes depicted as a masterful analysis of statistics, arguments, and contentions—so skillfully presented in written form that all sensible disputants should readily see the way to a mutually agreeable solution.

Fact-finding with recommendations is thought to embody all the preceding virtues normally associated with facts plus a very specific recipe for settlement that the parties should adopt and around which public sentiment will rally if the disputing parties should be so presumptuous as to raise questions.

Voluntary arbitration goes one more step toward potency. It is fact-finding plus. Since the arbitrator will be impressively wise after his fact-finding, the parties will agree in advance to accept his decision. This is a right and proper thing to do. The judgment will certainly resolve the issues in a satisfactory way, and all doubts about continuation of the dispute will be removed by the commitment to accept the decision.

Compulsory arbitration, by individual arbitrators or by a court, is admittedly a last resort and a somewhat repugnant device. It is imposed on a union and a company, usually by government decree, when one or both of the parties are very stubborn. They will not yield either to the logic of facts or to the public interest and agree to arbitrate voluntarily. The public need being paramount, it must prevail in the face of the irrational behavior exhibited by the disputants.

The definitions noted above are not taken from any textbook. They have a touch of irony that is not often stated. However, boiled down to the essentials, this is what the usual definitions mean to say.

Frequently there is ambiguity about the meaning of conciliation and mediation. As far back as 1913, when the Department of Labor was created, the enabling Act stated:

". . . the Secretary of Labor shall have power to act as *mediator* and to appoint *commissioners of conciliation.*" [1]

There is some doubt as to whether the Congress intended that the commissioners, as they came to be called, should be limited strictly in accordance with the definition noted earlier and that only the Secretary could mediate. It is much more probable that the drafters of the Act were wise men, that they did not quite know what the words meant and therefore decided to use both. Undoubtedly, they were aware that they could not give less authority to the Secretary than to his subordinates.

Similarly, when the Taft-Hartley Act was being written in 1947, the House version described the new independent agency as the Federal Conciliation Service; the Senate version called it the Federal Mediation Service. In conference, the redrafters set an example for all good compromisers and the result was the Federal Mediation and Conciliation Service. Thereby, in accord with the occasional results of some other compromises, a modest continuing job security was created for secretaries and typists all over the United States.

In a more serious vein, the various words do have somewhat different intrinsic meaning. *However, it is a central thesis of this book that both in the practical world of collective bargaining and in the best conceptual sense, the only viable distinction is between mediation and arbitration.* The word "mediation" will be used hereafter to mean a continuum of possible functions of an impartial person in the collective bargaining relationship, beginning with the common notions about conciliation and going across the scale to, but not including, arbitration.

Finally, lest any false impressions have been created by my facetious definitions, *this book is an attempt to erase any idea that mediation lacks potency.* In many respects, it plays a more powerful role than conventional arbitration. Mediation and voluntary arbitration are the only forms of third-party intervention that are fully consistent with the basic premise of voluntary agreement-making.

Having said these things, it remains to the author to attempt to demonstrate their validity.

CONTRAST WITH ARBITRATION

There is a fundamental difference between mediation and arbitration. An arbitrator has the responsibility and authority

1. Italics supplied.

to decide one or more disputed issues. The decision is binding on the parties. A mediator has no such authority. No decisions can be made by him. The parties make all the decisions by agreement. The mediator must rely on persuasion. He may suggest; he may cajole; he may even recommend, but the parties always have the right to say "no," even on most procedural matters.

Most unions and companies in the United States have agreed generally to arbitration of grievance matters—issues involving effectuation and application of written agreement terms. They sometimes agree to arbitration of other day-to-day problems, complete answers to which cannot be found in the written agreements. On rare occasions, a company and a union may agree to arbitrate one or more disputed issues of a new labor contract.

In all such instances, the agreement to arbitrate is voluntary. Normally the parties have substantial control over many aspects of the voluntary process. They select the arbitrator. They influence the procedural aspects of the hearings. They outline the issue or issues to be decided. During the proceedings, they attempt to persuade the arbitrator to decide in a particular way or ways. But the power and authority to decide has been transferred, by agreement, from the parties to the arbitrator they have selected.

The voluntary characteristics of the arbitration process are not foreign to collective bargaining concepts. When the parties agree to the process, they have "bought' an unknown answer. At its worst it may be a "pig in a poke" transaction, but it is an agreement preferable to the risks of a strike.

By contrast, any contribution, procedural or substantive, that may be made by a mediator to collective bargaining is exposed fully for the negotiators to see and appraise before they decide to accept or reject.

Compulsory arbitration is relatively rare in the United States. When it does arise, it is a result of an external force, usually government, requiring a company and a union to arbitrate. It is one feature of laws in a few states for disputes involving policemen or firemen. It has been used elsewhere in ad hoc situations under very special circumstances. The parties may or may not have a voice (1) in the selection of the arbitrator, (2) in the determination of the procedures, and (3) in the definition of the issue or issues to be decided. In any event, they have "bought" nothing. The transaction has been imposed. Thus, mediation is even further removed from compulsory arbitration than from voluntary arbitration.

BASIC PHILOSOPHY OF MEDIATION

A philosophy of mediation cannot be separated from practice and tactics. Practices will be discussed later in considerable detail. But here are a few of the basic considerations that underlie the work of a mediator.

Belief in Collective Bargaining

A mediator cannot begin to be useful unless he maintains a strong belief in the values and strengths of the collective bargaining process. This means more than being neutral between disputants. It means that the mediator must believe quite sincerely that collective bargaining is the best known method for determining the terms and conditions of employment in American industry. It means that the mediator must believe there is an underlying mutual-interest aspect of collective bargaining, that the process can be creative and laden with the possibilities of discovery. It means that he knows that compromises can be viable and constructive and that capitulation on specific issues may be a necessary feature of the process.

The mediator must recognize that he is a servant of the public that employs him and that his primary purpose is to assist in the collective bargaining process. In a very direct sense, he is a servant of the parties with whom he works.

These beliefs are not readily maintained on a consistent basis. By the very nature of his work, the mediator is exposed to and works in the current trouble segments of the total collective bargaining scene. It is when the process breaks down or threatens to break down that he is needed and utilized most. While the intelligence, morality, and integrity quotients of both management and union negotiators generally are high, the mediator must work with a few of the less well-endowed members of the human family as to some or all of these qualities.

Repeated exposure to the sour—yes, occasionally rotten—apples in the collective bargaining barrel requires a strong stomach. It is necessary, now and then, to pause and take a good look at the preponderant good apples—situations in which the process is working well.

Fortunately, the understandable tendency towards cynicism is ultimately avoided. A dispute may seem hopeless. It is fraught with frustration. But it is settled. More important, it may be settled in such a way that the negotiators on both sides are elated. The proverbial "bleary-eyed and dog-tired but happy negotiators" at a 6:00 a.m. settlement is not a figment of some reporter's imagination. Moreover, it may well be that the most unpromising human being at the bargaining table has made a key contribution to the result. Accomplishment by the parties of a sound agreement after a most difficult negotiation is a greater tribute to the validity of the process than an easy settlement. The apple comparison, noted earlier, is inadequate, like most analogies. Sour collective bargaining apples can have a regenerative quality not found in the orchard product.

The mediator who contributes to a settlement finds his faith restored.

Maximize Collective Bargaining, Minimize the Mediator Role

Inclusion of a mediator among the participants at a bargaining table does not alter the fundamental fact that it continues to be essentially a two-party process. The intervention adds a new element. That is unavoidable. But the new element is a person whose function is to assist, not supplant, the parties and the process.

When the mediator appears at the table for the first time, especially when the parties are not accustomed to an outsider, it is almost inevitable that there is an initial hiatus in the bargaining. For days, perhaps weeks, the representatives have been trying to convince the other side of the table of the validity of their positions. Arguments have been made and may have been repeated *ad nauseam*. Now there is a new face. The likely result is the attempt to convince the new person.

If this hiatus is brief it may be constructive. A silly argument made to an old foe may suddenly be shown up for what it is worth when the speaker realizes that he is talking to a knowledgeable neutral. Inconsistencies may be more apparent to all. But if the process of trying to "sell" the mediator continues too long, it is more than a waste of time. It may be quite irrelevant whether the mediator is or is not convinced. It is the other party that must agree. The sooner all the negotiators realize that the mediator's role is limited to assistance and persuasion in their various forms, the better for the process.

It is imperative that the mediator understand his function. If he does not demonstrate that he understands it, a great disservice can be done. The mediator who attempts to create the impression that he is the most important person at the bargaining table is of no help to anybody.

Proper understanding of the subsidiary nature of the mediation role must continue to and include the announcement of a settlement. Who "takes credit" when the settlement is achieved?

Mediators as a group probably have more than an average allotment of ego. They need a reasonable amount in order to survive. In shop talk among mediators, it is common to hear the expression "I settled the case," even from the most modest individual in the group. The fact, of course, is that no mediator ever "settled" any case. The parties "settled" the case. The mediator may have contributed and assisted substantially in the process, but that is quite a different thing.

It is especially important that the mediator observe a subsidiary posture in the announcement of the settlement. The negotiators have made the agreement. They are the people who will live with it. Especially in view of frequent instances of refusal of the union membership to ratify an agreement, it is essential that the negotiators take both the credit and the responsibility.

In most circumstances the negotiators are more than gracious about the mediator's contributions to the process. Frequently they say so to the public. If they do not do so it is not necessarily an indication that the mediator has made no contribution. It may be a practical political necessity. A firm handshake and a quiet, sincere "thank you" is much better compensation than a few lines in some newspaper.

Sympathetic Understanding

It is almost an axiom that the mediator must truly understand the issues if he is to be of assistance. Moreover, he must arrive at that understanding quickly. Understanding does not mean full knowledge of all details of all issues. That would be an impossibility in view of the limited time usually available, even if the mediator has done his homework before arriving at the bargaining table. No matter how much time is available, no outside person is ever likely to know the totality of an issue with which the parties may have struggled for years.

Understanding does mean that the basic elements of both sides of a contested issue must be appreciated. This need is not confined to bare facts. Quite frequently the strong emotional background of an issue and the personalities involved may be more significant than the facts.

Understanding has limited utility unless the mediator can somehow convey to the parties the fact that he knows the essence of the problem. At that point, and only then, can he expect to be accorded confidence and respect.

Sympathy with each party's position is a part of understanding. Even the most ridiculous position on an issue usually has some motivating source, sometimes quite obscure. Elimination of the issue may well require exposure of the underlying source.

Sympathetic understanding is not to be confused with approval. In conferring with one side separately, it is easy for the inexperienced mediator to make the mistake of leaving a strong impression, by word or by attitude, that he supports a quite unobtainable demand.

"Grasping the Nettle"

Collective bargaining can be a tough, hard, even brutal game. Sizable sums of money and strong emotions may be involved in difficult issues.

Once a mediator becomes reasonably convinced of the true positions of the parties, the differences may be so great that they appear to be insurmountable. Appraisals of what is and what is not obtainable must be made. At such a point, a mediator cannot properly be just a "good fellow who understands." He may be required to pull no punches in suggesting the differences between the desirable and the attainable. On some hard-fought issues he may even be required to advise capitulation. .

A risk of making himself *persona non grata* with one or both parties is frequently present. Sometimes that happens. Mediators have an expression for it, derived from coal mining—"he broke his pick."

Despite such dangers, real as they are, observation of and participation in mediation convinces the author that the parties really respect only the mediator who will "grasp the nettle" when such action is clearly required.

Confidential Relationship

Under some but not all arbitration arrangements, it would be considered improper for one party to say anything substantive to the arbitrator about a case that is not said in the presence or with the full knowledge of the other party. The premise is that anything that might influence the decision should be subject to comment and answer by both parties. Since the mediator has no decision-making powers in any event, this notion does not prevail in mediation. To the contrary, unless the parties are willing to confide in the mediator, his usefulness is limited.

Some one-party observations to a mediator are confidential only temporarily. After the case or the issue has been settled, the matter is no longer confidential by reason of the settlement itself. Something that the mediator "had in his pocket," as the expression goes, appears in due course and with full approval of the party involved. But many confidences can never be disclosed to the other party for a variety of reasons.

A second aspect of the confidential relationship concerns disclosure to the public or even informal disclosure to friends during or after a case. Mediators usually clear any statement to the press about a case with both parties, either as to precise content or in general terms. Reports of mediators to their agency are not available to others, even for research purposes, long after the case has been closed, except as specific approval may be granted after appraisal of the purpose and nature of intended use. Mediators do not testify in court in unfair labor practice and other types of cases on any matters occurring during negotiations that could be considered confidential. Mediators who teach classes or write books, like this one, must exercise great care not to disclose confidential information or anecdotes.

These confidential characteristics of the mediator's relationship with the parties are critical to useful performance. To violate a real confidence would destroy the mediator's effectiveness with the persons involved. Moreover, the labor relations grapevine is effective. A mediator with a reputation for careless conversation could become useless anywhere. An even more important consideration is that important violations of confidence could do serious harm to a collective bargaining relationship.

IS MEDIATION AN EFFECTUATION OF THE PUBLIC WILL?

Congressional approval of collective bargaining cannot be disassociated from other provisions of the same Act. The Congress did not say that two-party collective bargaining should be left solely to its own devices and that the economic sanctions of the strike and the lockout should be the only factors assisting in the agreement-making process.

Title II of the Taft-Hartley Act created the Federal Mediation and Conciliation Service. It also established provisions for national emergency disputes. The Railway Labor Act created the National Mediation Board and outlined provisions for emergency disputes. Some states have established mediation agencies.

The congressional policy statement about mediation in Section 301 (b) of Title II of the Taft-Hartley Act reads:

> "It is the policy of the United States that: . . . the settlement of issues between employers and employees through collective bargaining *may be advanced by making available full and adequate governmental facilities for conciliation, mediation,* and voluntary arbitration to *aid and encourage* employers and representatives of their employees to reach and maintain agreements . . . ." [2]

The public interest in collective bargaining, expressed other than through legislation, is most vocal about strikes. There is little doubt but that public intolerance to strikes is increasing despite the long-run decline of strike frequency. This is especially so when a nationwide or very large strike is a real national emergency (a rare event) or when substantial inconvenience is felt by large numbers of people. The cumulative effect of smaller strikes also influences overall public reaction.

The primary public purpose prompting the establishment and operation of every governmental mediation agency is the public desire (1) to prevent strikes and (2) to terminate those that do get started. A less obvious point about collective bargaining is the notion that there is a public interest in the quality of settlements. Are labor agreements in full conformance with the law? Do contracts continue, maintain, or promote racial or sex discrimination? Do wage settlements cause or promote inflation? These and related questions are being asked with increasing frequency. They are appropriate questions. No segment of the economy can or should avoid public scrutiny, criticism, and regulation, if necessary.

At least in theory, one way to assure observance of public policy in these various respects would be to have a government representative at the bargaining table with several functions. One function would be to assist in the development of bargains

---

[2] Italics supplied.

that are foursquare with laws and with public policy. Another function would be to report violations or departures from sound public policy to other governmental agencies when they do occur. In short, a government representative at the bargaining table could be a combination of (1) an advisor on law and public policy matters, (2) a judge of full and adequate compliance, and (3) a policeman to report real or alleged violations.

It should be apparent that a combination of these three functions would give the representative at the bargaining table more power and authority than exists elsewhere in the economy, even if persons could be found who were competent to perform them. A government representative is not present when legal or illegal commercial transactions are made by two principals. If the transaction is illegal, the violation is discovered later, if at all. In the rate-regulated industries such as the public utilities, a contemplated rate increase is not normally ruled upon by a government observer while it is being formulated. It is proposed by the regulated utility and approved or disapproved later by the regulatory agency.

In any event, suggestions have been made from time to time that government mediators should perform all or some of these functions.

Earlier in this chapter, it was suggested that a mediator is a servant of the public that employs him and also of the parties to a dispute. Can the mediator serve both?

There is no conflict regarding prevention of strikes and assistance in early settlement of those strikes that do commence. With rare exceptions, the public and the parties have the same objectives in this respect. But it is equally clear that few companies or unions would welcome a mediator if there were any reason to believe that he would be wearing a second hat as a legal advisor-judge-policeman. Few mediators would be qualified for the second hat, and probably no mediators would relish wearing it. There are some obvious inconsistencies between the mediator role and this other hypothetical combination of functions. Among other things there would be a direct conflict with the confidential aspect of a mediator's work. One answer to the potential dilemma is that a careful search of the legislation creating mediation agencies fails to disclose any aspect of the suggested legal advisor-judge-policeman role. Certainly, it is not a mandatory legal responsibility.

All this having been said, it does not follow that the mediator's function is to encourage and assist in any settlement that will prevent or terminate a strike without regard for the content of that settlement. A mediator's presence at the bargaining table may even provide some aura of government approval of a settlement, even if that is not the purpose of his participation. In short, contrary to a frequent assumption, the mediator does not play a "peace at any price" role.

How can a mediator avoid the "peace at any price" stigma, prevent his presence from being construed as governmental sanction of illegal or clearly improper results, and at the same time steer clear of undesirable and unwanted functions of legal advisor-judge-policeman? Answers are not easily supplied, but a few illustrative problem situations may suggest partial answers.

Preliminary to these illustrations, it should be emphasized that companies and unions are seldom venal. It is infrequent that they deliberately agree on an illegal act. On disputed or controversial matters of law or public policy, they are usually curious as to what that law or policy is and how it would apply to their case. In the larger and more sophisticated relationships, the negotiators themselves are knowledgeable about such matters and they are advised by their own lawyers and experts. In such situations, the potential questions that might be posed to a mediator are rarely, if ever, questions that could be answered with authority or precision. In the smaller, less sophisticated relationships the practical situation may be quite different. On occasion the parties may be contemplating a course of action that is clearly unlawful or in opposition to unquestioned public policy. They may be doing so as a result of ignorance of all the facts rather than by intent. The mediator may perform a useful role in such circumstances.

Discussion in negotiations of a proposal that is violative of the Wage-Hour Act is an illustration of conflict with law. If the proposal is clearly contrary to law, the mediator does have a responsibility to so advise the parties. If it is probably but not certainly in conflict with the law, he should express his doubts to the parties and suggest to them that they consult Wage-Hour officials or expert advisors of their own choice. Unless he is quite certain about the matter, the mediator should not go out on a limb by stating an opinion with an air of authority. This type of problem arises, if at all, in the smaller, newer collective bargaining relationships.

A much more difficult type of problem is illustrated by the wage "guideposts," enunciated initially by the Council of Economic Advisers in 1962 as more than generalized economic theory. It will be recalled that the guideposts became even more explicit year by year until 1967, when a numerical target was abandoned. During the period from 1962 through 1966, when a percentage wage and fringe-cost increase target was explicit, this was a form of public policy. The policy was endorsed by both President Kennedy and President Johnson. Although it had no legislative sanction, it had the approval of the executive branch of the Federal Government at the highest level. The Federal Mediation and Conciliation Service and the National Mediation Board are small but integral parts of the executive branch.

The guideposts were not approved by the AFL-CIO. They were not endorsed by the U.S. Chamber of Commerce or the National Association of Manufacturers, the two largest national employers' associations. They were supported by a few individual unions or some companies only in specific disputes, largely on the pragmatic basis that endorsement would assist the approving party within the facts and circumstances of its own case.

What was a government mediator to do while participating in a wage dispute where the guideposts were cited and utilized by a company or a union in that dispute? This policy question arose early in 1962 and became even more critical subsequently.

When called upon to do so, mediators did assist the parties in attempting to clarify the guidepost arithmetic for specific cases. This was not a simple task. A number of economic benefits simply cannot be calculated precisely. Moreover, even the Council of Economic Advisers altered or clarified its own formulae for the arithmetic as various practical problems came to light.

In a few fortunate situations, clarification of the arithmetic was helpful. The result happened to coincide roughly with union expectations and new wage and benefit budgets anticipated by the employer. The "government formula" provided a basis for resolution at about the level where negotiations would have been concluded in any event. In addition, both parties could feel good about compliance with public policy.

In at least a few other situations, a union agreed to an economic package that was either somewhat less or somewhat more than its realistic goals but reasonably close to the guidepost arithmetic. The employer did likewise. The informal pressures of public policy had some leveling effect, both downward and upward. Where the realistic differences between expectations and the guideposts were not too great, negotiators had a "handle" to go back to their principals for explanation of a result. The mediator's role in such situations was not onerous.

But what about the considerable number of situations where the guideposts exacerbated a dispute? The guidepost arithmetic simply was not acceptable to one or even both parties. What was the mediator to do in such a situation? These cases arose in at least three general types of situations, the borderlines between which were understandably fuzzy.

Some situations demonstrated clearly an inherent fault in any nationwide formula. The diversity of collective bargaining customs and practices in the United States is underestimated. Normal criteria used by most parties for bargaining on economic benefits seldom utilized the economic theory of the guideposts as more than one of many factors, if at all. In many situations, exercise of criteria familiar to the parties produced results quite different from the guidepost arithmetic. As only one of many examples, let us assume that a union had accepted a "lean" settlement three years earlier to permit a company to get into a better competitive position but with an understanding that there would be some "catch up" when and if the company became profitable. The guideposts made no provision for this factor or for many others.

A second and related problem was that, at many bargaining tables, past and anticipated cost-of-living trends constituted a very common and important feature of wage determination. The guideposts assumed a stable economy. During the latter part of the guidepost period, when actual cost-of-living trends departed very substantially from stability, this was the largest single rock on which the guidepost approach foundered.

A third problem was that some unions, whatever the facts, simply would not settle for a result close to the guideposts. Moreover, they were in a power position, usually because of scarce labor supply, to secure more money. A lesser number of companies in the early guidepost period were in a power position to support successful refusal to grant as much as the guideposts would allow.

In these diverse situations, government mediators considered it to be their primary function to assist in securing settlements.

An obligation to encourage restraint in general terms was felt. Candidly, preachment had limited effectiveness in many cases when it was apparent that any likely settlement would exceed the guidepost amount. An agreement was often preferable to a futile "take a strike" company position that was reasonably certain to result only in a still higher costing settlement after a strike. This overall approach was not a hidden agency policy. As early as May 1962, in a well-publicized speech, I stated the mediator's dilemma quite bluntly and indicated the policy that would be followed by the FMCS.

Demise of the guidepost policy has not eliminated the basic problem. The size of most economic settlements has increased markedly during the 1967-1970 period. It is beyond the scope of this book to explore the causes and effects of inflation. In any event, when a mediator is involved in a dispute including a large settlement, he and the agency that he represents may be subject to some flak. It is a misunderstanding of the mediation function to assume that a mediator can exert major influence on the size of an economic settlement.

A different problem concerns the possibility of racial or sex discrimination in labor agreements. Where discrimination exists, it is seldom expressed directly in agreement language. To the contrary, in the most common case the contract contains a strong no-discrimination clause but elsewhere, notably in the seniority clauses, covertly sanctions discrimination. Or, discrimination may exist because of unwritten practices. Especially after passage of legislation relative to this subject, an important question of mediation policy arose. The FMCS established a policy for guidance of its mediators and made it public.

The first plank of that policy was that government mediators do have a responsibility to be as well informed as possible about the law and its effectuation by other governmental agencies. A basic handbook on the subject with frequent supplemental information was provided to all mediators. A mediator cannot properly regard himself as an expert authority, nor should he pose as such. However, he should be in a position to give nonauthoritative advice to the parties on quite clear matters or refer them to more knowledgeable sources of advice when so requested.

If a disputed issue has potential discriminatory aspects, the mediator has a responsibility so to advise the parties and to assist them in the negotiation of an acceptable nondiscriminatory contract provision to the best of his ability to do so.

These three problem areas show that mediators do have some public-interest responsibilities. They are not exponents of "peace at any price." They cannot be presumed to be experts in law or in all the details of public policy even though they must be generally well-informed. Nor should they assume an authoritative pose. If the parties appear to be moving in the direction of an obviously illegal solution of a disputed issue or a solution clearly contrary to public policy, the mediator has a responsibility to caution against such action, though he cannot prevent the parties from agreeing if they insist. If there is substantial doubt about a proposal but no certainty of its illegality or impropriety, the mediator's responsibility is limited to raising the question of doubt and suggesting resort by the parties to other sources of information. In the author's view, the responsibility to oppose discrimination was much greater than the responsibility to uphold the guideposts. One was a moral imperative; the other was furtherance of an executive policy with dubious practical implications.

In no event should a mediator act as a reporter to some other government regulatory agency. To do so would be contrary to the confidential character of the relationship with the parties. In an extreme situation, a mediator might be impelled to withdraw quietly from a negotiation in order to avoid the appearance of sanction stemming from his presence. That is the strongest form of action that he should take.

With these qualifications, the mediator's primary responsibility is to assist in the negotiation of a settlement that is agreeable to the parties to the dispute.

On an overall basis, there is no doubt that mediation is a channel for effectuation of the public will. The principal task is to seek to prevent serious repercussions of bargaining on that portion of the public that is not involved directly. Avoidance of strikes or lockouts and the shortening of those that occur are the primary objectives of mediation. By emphasing the meeting of minds without resort to economic sanctions, the mediator serves both the public interest and the best interests of the parties. But the mediation role is not a "peace at any price" activity. In various appropriate ways, the mediator can be an agent working to further the public interest when that interest appears to conflict with private interest. In any and all of these activities the mediator is a "voice of persuasion" without powers of compulsion. This is entirely consistent with the basic premise of voluntarism that is a key ingredient of a free society.

CHAPTER III

MEDIATION AGENCIES AND AD HOC MEDIATORS OR FACT-FINDERS

Full-time mediators are employed primarily by federal and state agencies.

Some individuals with labor relations expertise, not regularly employed by government, work part-time as mediators or fact-finders. Sometimes they receive dispute assignments from governmental agencies or private organizations, sometimes by special appointment of government officials. Occasionally, they are selected directly by the parties. Part-time activity will usually be referred to herein as ad hoc mediation or fact-finding.

MEDIATION AGENCIES AND OTHER SOURCES OF MEDIATION APPOINTMENT

Federal

The Federal Mediation and Conciliation Service, the largest such agency, was established as an independent agency in 1947. It succeeded the United States Conciliation Service, which had been a part of the Department of Labor for many years. Its jurisdiction includes all privately owned industry engaged in interstate commerce, except railroads and airlines. In recent years, it has also provided mediation assistance in a limited number of disputes in the public sector (federal, state, and local) and in a few disputes involving nonprofit organizations (hospitals, etc.).

Its central office is in Washington, D.C., where a small staff establishes basic policy and assists in the mediation of some nationwide or otherwise critical disputes. The Service is headed by a director appointed by the President and confirmed by the Senate. He has no fixed tenure of office. Seven regional offices are maintained in New York City, Philadelphia, Atlanta, Cleveland, Chicago, St. Louis, and San Francisco. Each regional office administers and supervises the work in its geographic area. Mediators stationed at the regional offices work primarily in the areas in and surrounding each regional city. Field mediators are located in 72 additional cities throughout the United States. They report directly to a regional office.

The two principal functions of the Service are to provide mediation assistance in new contract disputes and to engage in preventive mediation activities (noncrisis dialogue). The Service also assists in the promotion of conferences, seminars, and other educational endeavors related to collective bargaining and disputes resolution.

The National Mediation Board is the second and smaller federal mediation agency. It was established in its present form in 1934, succeeding the United States Board of Mediation, which had been created in 1926. Its jurisdiction is limited to railroads and airlines.

The NMB headquarters are in Washington, D.C. As indicated by the word "Board" in its name, it is headed by three board members appointed by the President and confirmed by the Senate for three-year staggered terms. Not more than two board members may be of the same political party. Board members serve alternately as chairman. Unlike the FMCS, the NMB has no regional structure. All mediation activity is directed and administered from the Washington Office.

The principal function of the NMB is to mediate disputes in the railroad and airline industries involving union or employer requests for changes of wages, benefits, or rules (so-called major disputes). It has an additional function in these industries that differs from FMCS activities. It acts in representation cases, performing a function that is administered by the National Labor Relations Board for other interstate commerce industries.

The Secretary of Labor, an under secretary of labor, and assistant secretaries of labor occasionally may engage in mediation. On rare occasions a President, cabinet members other than the Secretary of Labor, and other officials of the Federal Government may become involved in a labor dispute. They also may appoint special mediators.

The Atomic Energy Labor-Management Relations Panel was established originally in 1949 and has continued to function since that date. Its jurisdiction is limited to atomic energy installations. Its members have usually been selected by the President on the basis of recommendations by governmental labor relations officials. One member is designated as chairman. All members, including the chairman, serve on a part-time basis.

The Equal Employment Opportunity Commission performs some conciliation and mediation functions in connection with instances of alleged racial or sex discrimination. However, it is not a mediation service comparable to the FMCS or the NMB. It interprets the law and has regulatory responsibilities. Its important mediation function is one step ahead of possible enforcement through the Department of Justice. This type of persuasion is different from the mediation activity that is the primary subject matter of this book. Accordingly, subsequent data as to mediation personnel and case load will omit the EEOC. Moreover, no reference will be made to somewhat similar compliance functions exercised by the Department of Labor in connection with possible discrimination by firms doing business with the U.S. Government.

States

State legislative and administrative practices relative to mediation vary widely.

Some 18 states and Puerto Rico maintain mediation agencies, employing one or more full-time mediators. The state statutes as to jurisdiction are far from uniform. However, most state agencies can and do exercise jurisdiction in disputes involving both interstate and intrastate commerce.

Eight other states do not employ full-time mediators, but the Commissioner of Labor or other similarly titled state official performs quite limited amounts of mediation work in addition to various other functions.

The remaining 24 states have no mediation agency and perform no mediation functions.

The recent upsurge of disputes involving employees of state and local government has added materially to the work of some state and local agencies. A subsequent chapter will be concerned with public employee disputes. It suffices to say here that most of the states that do have established mediation agencies have absorbed some public disputes along with their longer established private dispute procedures. However, New York and New Jersey have created entirely new agencies.

It is not uncommon for a governor or other state official to become involved, directly or indirectly, in an occasional labor dispute. Moreover, these officials sometimes appoint ad hoc mediators or fact-finders independently of or in conjunction with the work of a state agency.

Cities and Other Governmental Units

A few local mediation agencies, sometimes tied directly or loosely to city government, are active continuously or occasionally in labor mediation work.

New York City, Toledo, Ohio, and Louisville, Ky., are cities that have maintained active mediation agencies over a period of years. In New York City the form and structure of the activity has changed with time. The current work, limited to public employee disputes, is conducted by the Office of Collective Bargaining. The Toledo Labor-Management Citizens Committee has been active continuously for many years. The Louisville Labor-Management Committee is also an established organization with years of productive work behind it. The Citizen's Committee of Greater Wilkes-Barre (Pa.) is a smaller and somewhat newer organization.

To the author's knowledge only one county in the United States maintains a mediation agency. It is the Suffolk County (New York) Department of Labor.

None of these city or local agencies employ full-time mediators. However, administrative officials of the agencies perform some mediation work along with their regular duties, and some ad hoc mediation is performed by others under the auspices of the agency.

Mayors and other officials of numerous cities and special-purpose or short-lived committees established under city auspices have participated in labor mediation activity in a more sporadic fashion. Mayors sometimes appoint special ad hoc mediators or fact-finders.

Nongovernmental Organizations

The American Arbitration Association, widely known because of its primary function of assisting parties in the selection of labor arbitrators for grievance disputes, has occasionally been called upon to aid companies and unions in the selection of mediators or fact-finders. The volume of this activity has not been great, and for a period of years the occasional requests were handled by the AAA arbitration offices maintained in a large number of major cities.

More recently, beginning in mid-1968, this function has been centralized in the National Center for Dispute Settlement. The Center has offices in Washington, D.C., and is a semi-independent AAA activity receiving some financial support from the

Ford Foundation. Its principal mediation work is in the public sector and in a number of other conflict areas not directly relevant to labor-management relations.

Other nongovernmental organizations, or private citizens' committees, have been created from time to time either to mediate specific disputes or to perform mediation functions in particular areas. Most of these groups did not long survive.

Mediation Procedures Created by the Parties

Parties to a specific collective bargaining relationship sometimes create their own mediation procedure without recourse to any governmental agency or private organization.

The most common arrangement is for the parties to select one or more persons with known mediation skills to work with them in a specific dispute situation (usually a new contract negotiation) after an impasse has been reached or is imminent. Sometimes these procedures are known publicly, sometimes not.

A variation is for the parties to select one or more persons to serve in a continuing informal or formal mediation capacity. The Kaiser Long Range Sharing Plan and the Armour Automation Committee are examples.

A third type is the mediation function frequently performed by impartial chairmen in some of the apparel trades agreements.

SIZE OF MEDIATION WORK FORCES AND CASE LOADS IN THE UNITED STATES

How many full-time mediators are employed in the United States? How much time is actually devoted to mediation and fact-finding by ad hoc mediators and fact-finders? Only partial and inconclusive answers to these questions are available from published sources. Similarly, there are no available overall data on the number of disputes in which mediators become active. This is so despite annual reports issued by some of the agencies.

In order to obtain a comprehensive factual picture of mediation activity in the United States, the author has sent questionnaires to the agencies referred to earlier in this chapter and also some individuals. Appendix A gives details as to the purposes of the research, the response to the questionnaires, the methods used to make data comparable, the general methods of analysis of the returns to the questionnaires, and summaries of the study in tabular form.

The excellent response to the questionnaires permits a conclusion that the data presented here are reasonably accurate and comprehensive. Agency response and cooperation were virtually complete. Replies were received from 423 individuals, a 90 percent return of the personal questionnaires mailed.

A few of the more significant totals from Tables A-1 to A-5, inclusive, of Appendix A are shown below.

Mediator time devoted to mediation and fact-finding in the United States in calendar year 1968 totaled 450 man-years, broken down as follows:

Federal Agencies	292.6 man-years
Nonfederal Agencies	136.5 man-years
Individuals (ad hoc)	21.0 man-years
Total	450.1 man-years

Cases in which mediators worked actively in 1968 (defined as requiring actual presence at the bargaining table) totaled 16,685, divided as follows:

Federal Agencies	9,512 cases
Nonfederal Agencies	6,515 cases
Individuals (ad hoc)	658 cases
Total	16,685 cases

The case totals for 1968, by type of collective bargaining forum in which the mediation or fact-finding occurred, were as follows:

Contract Disputes—Private Sector	12,308 cases
Grievance Disputes	1,533 cases
Public Sector Disputes	1,473 cases
Noncrisis Dialogue	1,371 cases
Total	16,685 cases

Further analysis of the case totals provides interesting information about the extent of mediation activity within each one of the four collective bargaining forums.

Contract disputes in the private sector accounted for 73.8 percent of all mediation cases. The breakdown of agency activity in this type of mediation is as follows:

FMCS	7,587 cases
NMB	300 cases
Nonfederal Agencies	4,326 cases
Ad hoc	95 cases
Total	12,308 cases

Allowing for dual mediation (active participation by a federal and a state mediator in the same dispute), the number of different contract disputes actively mediated in the private sector in 1968 is estimated at 11,300 disputes.

Mediation of grievances represented 9.2 percent of total cases. The breakdown of agency activity is as follows:

FMCS	283 cases
NMB	none
Nonfederal Agencies	1,164 cases
Ad hoc	86 cases
Total	1,533 cases

Public sector disputes accounted for 8.8 percent of the total. The breakdown of agency activity is as follows:

FMCS	20 cases
NMB	none
Nonfederal Agencies	976 cases
Ad hoc	477 cases
Total	1,473 cases

Since some state agencies and some individuals reported the same case, public sector disputes in which mediation or fact-finding, or both, occurred in 1968 are estimated to total about 1,100 disputes.

Noncrisis dialogue in which there was known active participation by third parties accounted for 8.2 percent of total mediation case load. The 1,322 preventive mediation cases reported by the FMCS represented almost all of this type of mediation.

Figure 1, on page 48, shows much of this summary data graphically.

Detailed analysis of the individual questionnaires, not fully indicated in Appendix A, justifies brief comment here. Table A-3 shows that 92 individuals, or only 22 percent of all the individuals reporting, had ad hoc mediation or fact-finding experience in 1968. Some individuals handled more than one type of case. However, the outstanding feature of the analysis is that most of the 77 individuals who reported public sector mediation or fact-finding reported no private sector or grievance mediation. In other words, in response to the upsurge of disputes in the public sector, there is emerging a new crop of ad hoc mediators and fact-finders who have had little or no prior mediation experience.

Figure 1
Mediation and Fact-Finding
Number of Cases and Mediator-Years, 1968

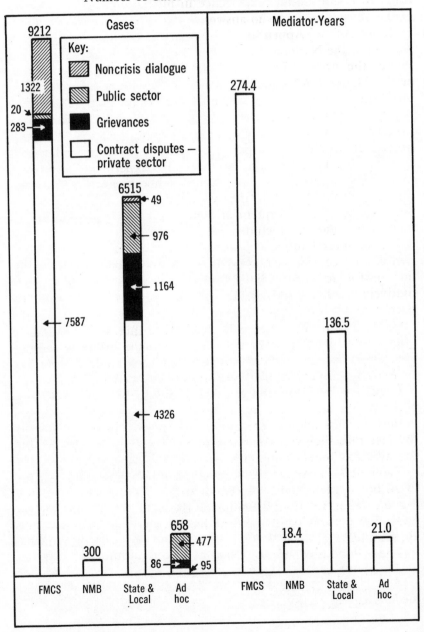

LIFETIME MEDIATION AND FACT-FINDING EXPERIENCE OF 423 ARBITRATORS

The questionnaires also were a source of valuable information about the lifetime experience in mediation and fact-finding of the 423 arbitrators who answered.

Table A-6 in Appendix A summarizes the data on disputes work with the National War Labor Board, the Wage Stabilization Board, the Atomic Energy Labor-Management Relations Panel, or the Missile Sites Labor Commission or with a federal or state mediation agency. Of the 423 individuals reporting, 123, or 29.1 percent, had some period of full-time service or continuing part-time employment with one or more of these agencies. More will be said about this in a separate chapter on wartime and special agencies. It suffices to note here that this experience has proved to be of great value in subsequent ad hoc mediation and fact-finding work. Most but not all of the 123 individuals have been selected for subsequent or concurrent ad hoc mediation appointments and are included in the data shown in Table A-7.

It is of special interest that National War Labor Board experience, once considered to be a common requirement for arbitration or for ad hoc mediation appointment, is declining quantitatively. Only 63 individuals, or 14.9 percent of the total reporting, had NWLB experience. This is due, in part, to the ravages of time. It is also evidence of the increasing volume of grievance arbitration work that has caused the influx of persons with other backgrounds. No attempt has been made to correlate these data with Table A-7, that follows in Appendix A. However, it is evident by inspection that the individuals with NWLB experience are still called upon for a preponderance of the appointments for ad hoc mediation in the private sector, despite the fact that they represent less than 15 percent of the arbitrators available for such appointments.

Table A-7 in Appendix A shows the summary data relating to ad hoc appointments to mediation and fact-finding posts during the labor relations lifetime of the 423 individuals. Of the total, 200 persons or 47 percent had received at least one such appointment.

The over-all breakdown by type of cases is as follows:

Contract Disputes—Private Sector	932	cases
Grievance Mediation	786	cases
Public Sector Disputes	839	cases
Total	2,557	cases

This fairly even distribution among the three types of cases is not likely to continue. Of the grand total of 839 public sector cases, 318 were completed in the one year of 1968. In 1968, public sector cases were 68 percent of all ad hoc cases. The rapid growth of public sector disputes undoubtedly means that if a similar labor relations lifetime analysis should be made five years hence, ad hoc work in public sector disputes would be far ahead quantitatively.

EXTENT OF MEDIATOR PARTICIPATION IN BARGAINING

It has been concluded that mediators participated actively in 1968 in about 11,300 private sector contract disputes and in about 1,100 public sector disputes.

A next logical question is the extent to which mediation is used in relation to the total numbers of bargains made. In other words, how often do the parties make their own agreements without any use of third parties at the bargaining table, and how often are mediators needed or at least used? To answer that question requires information about the total size of the bargaining universe in the United States.

Private Sector Contract Bargaining

For private sector contract bargaining, reasonably reliable estimates can be made. In fiscal year 1968, 88,926 30-day notices were filed with the Federal Mediation and Conciliation Service as required by the Taft-Hartley Act. Such notices are needed to avoid illegality if a strike or lockout should occur as well as to alert the FMCS and the state agency, if any, that crisis bargaining is occurring or is about to start.

Despite this legal requirement, it is common knowledge that some bargainers do not file notices. They may be ignorant of the law or forget about the requirement or are certain that a strike will not occur. Quite frequently, even in serious disputes, the parties and the mediator become aware that a timely notice has not been filed. It is a reasonable estimate that notices are not filed in as many as 5 percent of all negotiations. This would suggest the addition of 4,446 "missed notices."

Also in fiscal 1968, the National Labor Relations Board notified the FMCS of 3,954 certifications of new bargaining units. Negotiations usually begin soon after certification. The Taft-Hartley 30-day notices are not required for negotiation of initial contracts.

Nor are notices required in the case of enterprises not engaged in interstate commerce. Since state mediation agencies are often active in such cases an estimate should be made. No reliable basis exists for an estimate, but the nationwide annual total of intrastate negotiations is not likely to be less than 3,000 cases each year.

Finally, there are probably about 2,000 railroad and airline negotiations each year. The National Mediation Board estimates that there are about 6,000 agreements in effect. The 2,000 figure assumes that these will be reopened every three years on the average.

Summing up this approach, the actual and estimated figures for 1968 are as follows:

Taft-Hartley notices (actual)	88,926
Taft-Hartley notices not filed (estimate)	4,446
New certifications, NLRB (actual)	3,954
Intrastate commerce (estimate)	3,000
Railroads and airlines (estimate)	2,000
Total	102,326

This means that in 1968 there were at least 100,000 private sector collective bargaining situations in the United States subject to negotiation of renewal or initial agreements. It also means that 100,000 strikes or lockouts potentially could have occurred. On that basis, the 11,300 disputes requiring active mediation were 11.3 percent of the total. Or, stated in reverse, 88.7 percent of negotiations required no mediation.

However, that type of calculation includes a major error. In many negotiations, including major ones such as over-the-road trucking as well as a variety of employer association and coalition bargaining situations, many agreements are negotiated at the same bargaining table. In these situations most mediation agencies (the FMCS, in particular) consolidate more than one Taft-Hartley notice into a single mediator assignment. Thus, under the FMCS assignment and reporting system, one active case can develop out of a single Taft-Hartley notice, or several notices may result in only one case. It has not been possible to determine precise reporting methods of all the state agencies. In any event, the state agency reports would not be influenced as much as the FMCS by this factor because the state cases are typically smaller.

The real figure we seek to find here is a percentage indicating how frequently a mediator is required to participate at the bargaining table. The 11.3-percent figure does not meet the requirement.

In the absence of precise data, it can be estimated that the 100,000 bargains referred to earlier are negotiated at about 75,000 bargaining tables. *Mediation services were required, then, at about 15 percent of the private sector bargaining tables in the United States in 1968.* At the remaining 85 percent of the bargaining tables, the parties negotiated without any outside assistance.

Quite incidentally, this line of inquiry discloses what appears to be a significant error in estimates of private sector labor agreements in the United States. A figure of 150,000 has been used widely by many authors as the approximate total of labor agreements in effect. If the annual total of agreements renegotiated or signed initially in the United States in 1968 was about 100,000 agreements, the total of private sector agreements in effect was about 250,000. This is so because the weighted average duration of private sector agreements in 1968 was about two and one-half years.

The new-certification data from the NLRB, less some attrition, would suggest that agreements in the private sector are increasing at a rate of about 1 percent per year.

Public Sector

There appears to be no reliable basis for making comparable estimates for the public sector. Some data—probably incomplete—are available on the number of agreements in effect in various parts of the Federal Government. Estimates have been made in a few states. In any event, overall estimates that might be made here would be incomplete and also out of date by the time this book is in print.

A reasonable estimate is that there were 1,100 public sector disputes in which mediation or fact-finding, or both, were utilized in 1968. The total for 1971 undoubtedly will be higher. No reliable estimate can be made as to the percentage of all public sector negotiations in which mediators or fact-finders are involved. It is probable that the percentage is somewhat higher than the 15-percent figure for the private sector.

CHAPTER IV

MEDIATOR SELECTION, RETENTION, BACKGROUND AND TRAINING

In a semifacetious moment while preparing a speech [1] in 1962, the author listed the following combination of qualities sought in a mediator:

1. the patience of Job
2. the sincerity and bulldog characteristics of the English
3. the wit of the Irish
4. the physical endurance of the marathon runner
5. the broken-field dodging abilities of a halfback
6. the guile of Machiavelli
7. the personality-probing skills of a good psychiatrist
8. the confidence-retaining characteristic of a mute
9. the hide of a rhinoceros
10. the wisdom of Solomon

In a more reflective mood, one could extend the list to include:

11. demonstrated integrity and impartiality
12. basic knowledge of and belief in the collective bargaining process
13. firm faith in voluntarism in contrast to dictation
14. fundamental belief in human values and potentials, tempered by ability to assess personal weaknesses as well as strengths
15. hard-nosed ability to analyze what is available in contrast to what might be desirable
16. sufficient personal drive and ego, qualified by willingness to be self-effacing.

It is obvious that even a close approach to all 16 characteristics is not to be found in any human being. An equally obvious

---

[1] William E. Simkin, unpublished speech at Swarthmore College, Swarthmore, Pa., April 5, 1962.

fact is that these qualities do not fit any conventional job description and are not subject to objective measurement.

MEDIATOR SELECTION AND RETENTION

How are mediators selected? How well do the selection processes work? By examination and analysis of existing mediation staffs and agency requirements, can any conclusions be reached as to requisite educational or experience background?

Politics in Selection and Tenure of Mediators?

In our two-party form of government, all agencies are potentially subject to political influence in the selection and retention of personnel. Though not lucrative by comparison with jobs of equal responsibility in private industry, mediation jobs are not unattractive financially.

For the most part, mediation is a "solo" job. Direct supervision is and must be minimal. Objective measurement of performance is difficult if not impossible. This means that it is one of the fast-disappearing types of work in which individual initiative and direct personal responsibility are dominant and can be very satisfying to a person with strong inner integrity. On the other hand, it is a type of work that could be a "soft touch." Incompetence or laziness could escape positive detection for a substantial period of time.

Since qualifications for the mediator job are essentially subjective, political motives could easily influence selection. In short, the mediator job in a government agency could be quite vulnerable to political influence. But if politics prevailed in mediator selection and retention, the results could be disastrous.

The importance of selecting the very best persons available for employment cannot be overstated. An agency makes a very substantial financial investment in a new hire before he "earns his salt." More important, mistakes are difficult to correct. A mediator who is just good enough not to be fired can become a drain on the public purse for many years. A truly incompetent man can hurt the agency's reputation to such an extent that it requires several excellent men to offset the damage that is done.

A substantial part of a mediator's usefulness in a community depends on reciprocal knowledge of each other that is acquired by the mediator and the labor and industry representatives with whom he works. If his retention on the job or in that area should be dependent on political fortunes, important intangible assets would be thrown away when changes were made.

Finally, a mediator works day by day with members of both major parties. Labor representatives are predominantly but not universally Democrats. On the other side of the table, Republicans are much more likely to be found. The work is not partisan in any respect. The mediator cannot afford to be politically active in ways that could be detrimental to his profession.

For these various reasons, I believe very strongly that political influence either in the selection or retention of mediators should be avoided at all costs. What are the facts as to actual practice?

The author can summarize the situation candidly as to the Federal Mediation and Conciliation Service for the years 1961 to 1969. Prior to his acceptance of the directorship in 1961, in answer to his question, assurances were given by President Kennedy that political influence would not be countenanced. Those assurances were kept faithfully, and the White House gave full support in an early test case in which the Democratic National Committee exhibited a keen interest. The Service did not hire an applicant supported strongly by the Democratic National Committee even though he rated, on the merits, only slightly below a candidate who was hired and who had no political support. Thereafter there was no repetition of political pressure, and the same policy prevailed under President Johnson. When job applicants were considered, party affiliation was not discussed or, in most instances, even known. Congressional and other letters of support or referral indirectly or directly indicating party affiliation were received concerning some applicants. If an applicant stimulated a barrage of such letters, his campaign realistically hurt his chances. After a "yes" or "no" action had been taken on the merits, the Service notified the senator or congressman as a matter of courtesy. In a very limited number of cases, initial insistence was expressed by a member of the Congress but was withdrawn when he was advised of the reasons for selection based solely on relative merit.

FMCS employees below the mediator rank and some administrative positions of equal or higher rating are governed by Civil Service rules and regulations. However, mediators and some other top staff jobs are not. By the terms of the Taft-Hartley Act, the Director has discretionary authority in the hiring of mediators. In the author's judgment this is a sound provision because of the subjective qualities sought. And he can personally vouch for the fact that political influence can be avoided.

The detailed procedures utilized by the FMCS for mediator selection during the 1961-1969 period are outlined in Appendix B. Reference to that text will show how the Service sought to implement the nonpolitical search for individuals who could best fulfill the job requirements.

As respects job tenure, there is no evidence that field mediators of the FMCS have ever been discharged as a result of a change of party in the national administration. This is so despite the fact that every mediator job in the agency is technically up for grabs and is among the open jobs at the time of a change of administration. Job seekers look with hunger at these jobs, but the precedent of career tenure is so strong that no new administration has yet tampered with it.

Selection of the much smaller mediator staff of the National Mediation Board is accomplished by a different procedure. NMB mediators have Civil Service status and are selected from a roster. However, Board and staff members of the NMB conduct the examinations and interviews that determine qualifications for placement on the roster. Weight can be given to the subjective and personality characteristics that are so important. Thus, a principal realistic difference between FMCS and NMB selection methods is that the NMB cannot determine relative qualifications at the time of each selection. The Civil Service roster introduces an element of inflexibility.

The mediator selection and retention practices of the agencies of the states vary. No attempt will be made here to judge the extent, if any, to which political influence may be exercised in any particular state. It is quite certain that a majority of state agencies have been successful in avoidance of significant political influence.

The questionnaires answered by the state agencies did include questions as to the Civil Service status of full-time mediators. The data for the 18 states (and Puerto Rico) that employ one or more nonsupervisory mediators can be summarized quickly. In 12 states and Puerto Rico both mediator selection and tenure are governed by the Civil Service procedures that are applicable generally in the state. In the six other states, the head of the mediation agency has discretion as to selection, and mediators have no Civil Service tenure. However, in most of those six states there is considerable precedent for career status after a mediator completes an informal probationary period.

As respects ad hoc mediators, party affiliation has been a minor factor in the selection of labor relations experts called upon by the Federal Government and the states for occasional service in major disputes or disputes of high visibility. Some individuals of known party affiliation have been pressed into service by both Democratic and Republican administrations.

Educational Qualifications

No minimum educational requirement exists for new mediators hired by the Federal Mediation and Conciliation Service. In actual practice, the FMCS selection procedure, described in detail in Appendix B, has produced a wide range of results on this point. Table 1 shows a summary of the educational background of all mediators, excluding trainees, hired during the 1961-1969 period.

Table 1

MEDIATOR EDUCATIONAL BACKGROUND

FMCS New Hires, 1961-1969

Educational Background	Number of Mediators	Percent *
Graduate degree (Masters or Law)	20	14%
Bachelor's degree and some graduate work but no advanced degree	15	10
Bachelor's degree	22	15
High school graduate and some college work but no bachelor's degree	42	29
High school graduate	38	26
Some high school but not a graduate	10	7
Totals	147	100%

* Percentages do not total 100 because of rounding.

Source. FMCS Personnel files.

The National Mediation Board has no formal educational requirement. A bachelor's degree is considered to be desirable but not essential.

Minimum educational requirements of state agencies in the 18 states and Puerto Rico employing one or more full-time nonsupervisory mediators are shown in Table 2.

Table 2

MINIMUM EDUCATIONAL REQUIREMENTS

(All States and Puerto Rico Employing One or More
Full-Time Nonsupervisory Mediators as of January 1, 1969)

	Number of States
Master's or Law Degree	1
Bachelor's degree (occasionally qualified to permit substitution of experience for part of college work)	4
No formal requirement but preference for college graduate	3
Two years college	2
High school graduate	6
No formal requirement	3
Total	19

Source: Answers to author's questionnaires.

Tables 1 and 2 are not comparable. Table 1 is actual new hire experience of the FMCS, and Table 2 represents minimum requirements of the states. However, by inspection of the two sets of data, it could logically be presumed that in the same 1961-1969 period the states employed as new mediators individuals with somewhat stronger educational backgrounds than was true of the FMCS. No factual information has been obtained to test that presumption.

A more direct comparison on a different basis is available. What will be referred to hereafter as the Rutgers Study[2] includes data on the educational background of state mediators in 1962 and of federal mediators in 1964. That study was based on questionnaires sent to all mediators and supervisory mediators, including heads of agencies. The inclusion of supervisory mediators skews the results somewhat towards higher educational levels. If allowance is made for this difference, the Rutgers Study suggests a distribution very similar to that shown in the actual FMCS new-hire experience (Table 1). The Rutgers Study does show that mediators and supervisory mediators in the state agencies had somewhat more education than the comparable federal mediators.

It is apparent that formal education ranks relatively low on the totem pole for purposes of new-mediator selection. Moreover, this has been the case during a period of time when

---

[2] Indik, Goldstein, Chernick, and Berkowitz, THE MEDIATOR—BACKGROUND, SELF-IMAGE, AND ATTITUDES, Institute of Management and Labor Relations, Rutgers—The State University, New Brunswick, N.J., 1966.

graduation from high school was required by many private industries as a minimum qualification even for semiskilled jobs
and when many positions with lesser responsibility than is required of a mediator were open only to college graduates.

Since the author, when Director of the Federal Mediation and
Conciliation Service, assumed personal responsibility for approving the hiring of 10 new mediators who had not completed
high school and 38 additional mediators whose formal education stopped with a high school diploma, it may be appropriate
to go on record with a few personal comments.

Formal education does not rate very high at the bargaining
table. Typically, educational levels on the management side
are higher than on the union side but not invariably so. Native
intelligence comes through in the bargaining process. When
someone at the table, even the mediator, murders the King's
English, it's what he says that counts rather than the way he
says it.

Second, it is almost a truism that level of attainment in our
educational system is not a satisfactory measuring rod of ability,
especially for work requiring the qualities and characteristics
noted at the beginning of this chapter.

Third, a very great number of the better-paying white collar
jobs are quite effectively closed to individuals who have not advanced beyond high school. With limited job opportunities
ahead, there is a discernible tendency for the "cream of the
crop" of those with lower academic attainment to seek those few
good jobs that are open to them.

If all other considerations are equal when comparing two applicants, the better educated individual has a distinct advantage. Nevertheless, it is the author's strong opinion that it would
be a great mistake to make a college degree a prerequisite for
mediation work.

The general point can be illustrated by what may be a coincidence. A small number of full-time mediators known officially
as National Representatives and more commonly as "trouble
shooters" work in and out of the Washington office of the
FMCS. They rank just below the Disputes Director and the Assistant Disputes Director. They have been selected carefully
from the entire field staff of more than 260 mediators because
of their demonstrated ability in the most difficult cases. As of
January 1, 1969, two trouble shooters were college graduates or
better. The other two had no formal education beyond high

school. Experiential education can be as significant or more important than formal education.

It should be emphasized that these comments are not intended as an anti-education diatribe. To the contrary, the author believes firmly that mediator educational attainment levels should continue to rise. But this does not mean that rigid requirements are needed or desirable.

Experience Qualifications

What types of previous work experience are required or are desirable for new mediators? It might logically be assumed that the same or closely related work in an impartial capacity would be a necessary or at least desirable qualification. What are the sources of impartial experience and how extensively have they been utilized?

State mediators might be a source of experienced mediators for FMCS employment. Among the Service staff of full-time mediators and administrative and supervisory personnel who performed some mediation (295 individuals as of January 1, 1969), 15 had state or city mediation experience on a full-time basis just prior to FMCS employment.

When the National War Labor Board was discontinued after World War II and when special disputes procedures were terminated during the Korean War, one might have expected that many of the persons who served in disputes settlement would seek and obtain employment with the FMCS. A few did. However, most such persons returned to teaching, sought or resumed arbitration or consulting work, or were employed in private industry. Only four mediators still on the FMCS staff came to the Service from those sources.

National Labor Relations Board experience might appear to be qualifying. However, because of the dominant representation and regulatory functions of the NLRB, usual experience in that agency is only tangentially useful in mediation. Eight mediators on the FMCS staff as of January 1, 1969 had NLRB experience just prior to mediation employment.

A total of five FMCS mediators had experience in labor relations functions in agencies of the Department of Defense and seven in the Department of Labor. Two had labor attaché experience with the Department of State.

At each regional office of the FMCS, one individual who is not a mediator, the Administrative Assistant, acquires or can obtain substantial background knowledge of mediation procedures and methods. After special training, a few of the most promising administrative assistants have been promoted to mediation positions. Seven FMCS mediators once were administrative assistants.

Although labor arbitration is quite different from mediation, it might be expected that arbitrators would be a likely source. However, there were only two ex-arbitrators on the FMCS staff as of January 1, 1969, in addition to the author, who was then Director. Moreover, these two men had been employed by the United States Conciliation Service as arbitrators before so-called "free arbitration" was discontinued. They remained with the Service as mediators.

Only two of the FMCS mediation staff were full-time teachers just prior to FMCS employment. A fair number of mediators do have teaching experience at some earlier point in their careers.

What about graduates of specialized labor relations programs or schools at universities and colleges? Harvard, Cornell, Illinois, UCLA, Pennsylvania, California (Berkeley), Wisconsin, Michigan, and many other institutions provide special training at the undergraduate or graduate level. Several FMCS mediators had labor relations courses at these colleges or are graduates. However, only one was hired as a mediator trainee immediately after such educational experience. The others had practical bargaining experience with companies or unions after their school work and before employment by the FMCS.

There are reasons for the almost complete absence of direct hires from universities and colleges. A typical bachelor's degree recipient or even an MBA graduate between the ages of about 21 and 24 is not likely to be acceptable immediately as a solo mediator. Within labor and management ranks there exists a belief that youth should be tempered by experience. The official minimum age for new FMCS mediators (not trainees) is 32 years, but that minimum can be and has been waived in appropriate instances. A cogent reason for the paucity of new hires directly from college sources is the probability that other employment offers to the best of the MBA graduates in their late twenties have been too good financially to permit effective competition by the FMCS.

The FMCS mediator-trainee program is an attempt to assure input .of young blood to balance the larger group of new hires who fall in a bracket of about 30 to 50 years of age. In recent years, three mediator-trainee positions have been available at all times. Individuals selected for these positions lack the required amount of collective bargaining experience for mediator positions but have some qualifying experience and college labor relations training.

Over the eight-year span from 1961-1969, 14 mediator-trainees were hired by the FMCS. Appendix B includes a short section providing additional information about this program. (It should be noted that the list of 14 mediator-trainees in Appendix B does not include several individuals who were less than 32 years of age when hired or whose collective bargaining experience was less than normal requirements but who were hired as mediators (not trainees). In such cases, the individuals were considered to be sufficiently well qualified to merit waiver of normal age or experience requirements.)

A total of 25 persons on the FMCS staff came to the Service from a wide variety of other types of work just prior to FMCS employment that could properly be characterized as impartial. Of these 25, seven came from jobs that were labor relations oriented (labor law practitioner, consultant, etc.). The remaining 18 came from a wide variety of jobs not related to labor relations.

To recapitulate, 92 out of the 295 members of the FMCS staff on January 1, 1969, who mediated full time or who might mediate part time were hired by the agency or its predecessor agency from jobs that were substantially impartial. Table B-2 in Appendix B summarizes the types of prior jobs held.

The remaining 203 members of the staff, or 69 percent of the total, came to the FMCS or its predecessor agency directly from substantially full-time union or management labor relations positions. A typical successful applicant with a union background had been an international representative, or the equivalent, for considerably longer than the requisite period of time. In that capacity, he had been primarily responsible for negotiating many labor agreements with a number of companies and for presenting grievance cases to arbitrators, and had participated in many grievance meetings at the last step prior to arbitration. A typical successful applicant with a management background had been the industrial relations director, or the equivalent, of a medium-sized company or at a plant of a larger multiplant company who had comparable experience and responsibility dealing with one or, more often, several unions.

Why has so much emphasis been placed on experience at the bargaining table? The simple answer is that there is no substitute for such experience or its equivalent. Most of the impartial sources for mediators, including the mediator-trainee program, provided some equivalent experience through personal observation at the bargaining table. No mediation service can afford to turn a man loose as a mediator until he has a sort of extrasensory perception of the collective bargaining process acquired through actual participation or penetrating observation.

Does an exclusive union or management background provide a bias that will jeopardize a mediator's effectiveness? Subsequently, facts will be presented about the distribution between the two sources—labor and management. This is not an answer even if the "split' should be equal. Mediation is normally a solo operation. It would not solve any problems if half an agency's staff should have a union bias and the other half a management bias. In that type of situation, each party would "jockey" to attempt to obtain a mediator partial to its position.

Elimination of potential bias begins with the selection process. The FMCS selection procedures described in Appendix B note the importance given to informal confidential checking by a regional director in the applicant's home community. One of the questions asked most searchingly is whether the individual could be impartial.

Experience has demonstrated that bias soon disappears—if it ever existed. It is a common occurrence for a company to indicate a preference for a specific mediator with a union background. It is equally common for a union to state a preference for a specific mediator who happens to have had a management background. The FMCS retains and exercises the right to assign mediators irrespective of expressed preference by the parties. However, these frequent preferences that are volunteered and which can sometimes be accommodated are reasonable proof that prior background is not a significant factor in mediation if an agency is properly administered. The parties want the best available mediation. An individual's performance as a mediator is what counts, not his affiliation in some prior job.

A related point may be of interest. Some years ago it was a general FMCS policy not to station a new mediator in the same community or geographical area in which he had served as a union or management representative. The general notion was that he would not be acceptable "on the other side of the fence." After he had been suitably "fumigated" by working as a mediator several hundred miles away, an individual frequently would be permitted by the Service to move back to his old habitat. This policy has not been observed in recent years. It was the author's opinion that if an individual had to be "fumigated" he was not wanted in the first place. All new hires are not stationed in their home community; that would be impossible for administrative reasons. But a very substantial number of newly-employed individuals have remained at home. The known results of this change of policy have been generally good. If an individual is fair-minded, his prior associations are of value in his new work and his morale is improved by working in an area to which he and his family are acclimated. For obvious reasons, a new man is not often assigned to disputes involving his own former union or company.

Although employment with unions or companies does not stigmatize a good mediator, reasonable equality of union and management experience is desirable. If there were no other reason, the shedding of minor prejudices during initial training is facilitated by a diversity of experience.

Table 3 below is a summary of the types of jobs held just prior to employment as mediators by the FMCS or by the United States Conciliation Service, the predecessor agency. It shows the facts (1) for the entire staff and (2) for all mediators hired 1961-1969.

Table 3

PRIOR WORK EXPERIENCE
LAST JOB HELD PRIOR TO FMCS EMPLOYMENT

(as of January 1, 1969)

	All Mediators		New Mediators Hired 1961-1969	
Type of Prior Job	Number	Percent	Number	Percent
Union	125	43%	77	49%
Management (labor relations)	78	26	48	30
Impartial*				
Labor-relations-oriented	74	25	27	17
Not labor-relations-oriented	18	6	6	4
Totals	295	100%	158	100%

* See Table B-2 in Appendix B for details.
Source: FMCS Personnel Files.

The Rutgers Study,[3] referred to earlier, is the only known source of information concerning jobs held by state mediators prior to their employment by a state agency. The data presented are based on 1962 questionnaires. The same study presents 1964 data regarding prior employment of FMCS mediators. That study suggests no marked differences between federal and state mediators in employment backgrounds. There are no data in the Rutgers Study that would permit a direct comparison between Table 3 and the state agencies. The principal problem is that, for state agencies, the Rutgers Study lumps together all business employment. Table 3 shows under the "Management" heading only those management jobs that were in labor relations.

Irrespective of whether prior pertinent labor relations experience was with management, with unions, or in an impartial capacity, it is possible to compare federal (both FMCS and NMB) minimum experience requirements for initial employment with those of the state agencies. Table 4 does this.

[3] Note 2 above.

Table 4

MINIMUM LABOR RELATIONS EXPERIENCE REQUIREMENTS
FOR EMPLOYMENT TO
JOURNEYMAN* NONSUPERVISORY MEDIATOR JOBS

Federal and State Agencies

Agency	Number of States	Minimum Total-Experience Requirement (years)	Credit for Education?	Maximum Extent of Education Credit, If Any (years)
Federal (FMCS & NMB)		7	yes	3
States	1	10	yes	4
	1	7	yes	2
	2	6	yes	2
	6	5	no	
	1	4	no	
	1	3	no	
	7	No formal requirement		

* Where more than one nonsupervisory grade exists, total experience requirement is for entrance to first journeyman grade, excluding trainees and not counting probationary time at a possible lower grade.
Source: Answers to author's questionnaires.

Mediator Turnover

Data are available from the personnel files of the Federal Mediation and Conciliation Service as to turnover rates for mediators. The summary figures for the eight-year period 1961-1968 are as follows:

Reason for leaving FMCS	Numbers of Individuals	
	Eight Year Totals	Average Turnover per Year
Mandatory Retirement (age 70)	17	2.1
Early Retirement (normally after 62 years of age)	34	4.3
Discharge	1	0.1
Death	23	2.9
Resignation	25	3.1
Totals	100	12.5

Since the number of mediator and supervisory mediation jobs during the eight-year period averaged about 260, the resignation rate was approximately 1.2 percent per year. This was probably among the lowest quit rates that can be found anywhere.

No comparable data were obtained for the state agencies.

Mediator Age

No current data were obtained about mediator age distribution. However, the Rutgers Study [4] provides information for state agency mediators in 1962 and for FMCS mediators in 1964. Despite low turnover rates, the modest expansion that has taken place in the FMCS staff and in the staffs of a few state agencies probably has resulted in age distributions now that are not drastically different from the Rutgers data. In any event, Table 5 shows the 1962 and 1964 picture.

Length of Mediator Service

The Rutgers Study [5] provided information as to length of mediation service. Table 6 presents more up-to-date data for the Federal Mediation and Conciliation Service, including prior service with the United States Conciliation Service, the predecessor agency. The state agencies have not been asked to update the 1962 state data. For this reason, the federal and state figures are not fully comparable.

It may be noted, however, that the Rutgers Study showed that more than half the FMCS mediators had 10 or more years'

4 Note 2 above.
5 Note 2 above.

Table 5

MEDIATOR AGE

| | Numbers | | Percentages** | |
| | FMCS | State Agencies | FMCS | State Agencies |
Age	1964*	1962*	1964*	1962*
25-34	10	4	5%	5%
35-44	35	20	16	24
45-54	95	39	43	48
55-64	72	16	32	20
65 and Over	8	3	4	4
	220	82	100%	100%

* Source—Rutgers Study.
** Because of rounding, percentages may not total 100.

service in 1964, whereas only about 40 percent of the state mediators had comparable service in 1962. As of January 1, 1969, the FMCS picture had changed; only 35 percent of the field mediators had 10 or more years' service.

Mediator Salaries

Salaries of mediators employed by the Federal Mediation and Conciliation Service or by the National Mediation Board have increased rather dramatically over a 10-year period.

An example may suggest the effects of a number of government-wide increases that have benefited higher-rated classified employees, including mediators, more than is commonly recognized. The FMCS has two journeymen grades for mediators,

Table 6

LENGTH OF SERVICE OF MEDIATORS—PRESENT AGENCY

| | Numbers | | Percentages *** | |
Length of Service	FMCS** 1/1/69	State* Agencies 1962	FMCS** 1/1/69	State* Agencies 1962
Less Than 1 Year	25	10	9%	12%
1-3 Years	45	13	17	16
4-6 Years	52	16	19	20
7-9 Years	52	10	19	12
10-12 Years	19	12	7	15
13-15 Years	8	11	3	13
16-18 Years	28	6	11	7
19-21 Years	4	2	1	2
22 or More Years	34	2	13	2
Totals	267	82	100%	100%

* Source—Rutgers Study.
** Source—FMCS personnel files—field mediators only (excluding supervisory and administrative.)
*** Because of rounding, percentages may not total 100.

GS-13 and GS-14; promotion from GS-13 to GS-14 is on the basis of merit only. Let us assume that a mediator was promoted from GS-13 to the first step rate of GS-14 in March 1960. That promotion itself yielded a salary increase, but the effect of the promotion will be ignored. The beginning GS-14 salary was then $11,355 per year. In March 1970 the beginning GS-14 rate was $19,643, an increase of about 73 percent in the 10-year period. In addition, the mediator would have benefited from so-called in-grade increases that long have been a part of the government pay structure. These are intermediate salary rates between the minimum or first-step rate of a classification and the maximum rate. The appropriate GS-14 step rate for the mediator in our illustration would be $23,573 in March 1970. In short, the combination of general increases and in-grade increases would have resulted in more than doubling the March 1960 salary.

Mediators have fared no better than other classified federal employees in similarly rated jobs. However, it is apparent that these salary increases are part of the reason for the exceedingly low quit rate and for the sizable number of applicants for each available new job.

The 1971 salary scales for experienced federal mediators are as follows:

Grade	Minimum	Maximum
GS-14	$20,815	$27,061
GS-13	17,761	23,089

State mediator salaries also have been increasing, but the available evidence indicates that they have increased somewhat less on a percentage basis than federal salaries. Moreover, the state agency salary scales for the most part have always been lower than those of the FMCS. For this reason, even the same percentage increases as in the Federal Government would not prevent the gap from widening.

Answers to the author's questionnaires provide a basis for comparing federal and state salary scales as of January 1, 1969. Appendix B shows the method used for the comparison, and the summary results are tabulated in Table B-3 of that Appendix. In round figures, the weighted average state agency salary scale as of January 1, 1969, was about 25 percent below the federal scale. The weighted average salary scale of the four largest state agencies was about 19 percent below the federal scale. In a few instances, state agencies permit mediators to arbitrate during off-duty time. FMCS mediators are not permitted to arbitrate. The opportunities available to these few state mediators to close the earnings gap are too limited to warrant much consideration.

MEDIATOR TRAINING

Maintenance of an effective mediation staff requires major emphasis on training in two areas. New mediators must be competent enough to operate on their own before they can be assigned to actual solo cases. Experienced mediators need continually to expand their knowledge of new issues and new problems to meet the emerging challenges at the bargaining table.

New Mediator Training

The extent of formal or even informal training for new mediators is realistically dependent on the size of the agency. Small agencies must normally hire new mediators one at a time. It is almost impossible to arrange special orientation training. Only the largest agency, the Federal Mediation and Conciliation Service, can arrange its mediator selection procedure to permit simultaneous employment of a number of individuals.

FMCS training begins with a concentrated two-week orientation program, conducted at the Washington office. Classes have varied in size from six to 12 mediators. The orientation program includes limited instruction in administrative matters, such as reporting. Major emphasis is on mediation principles and techniques. Seminar-type discussion of both crisis negotiation and preventive mediation is led by experienced mediators and mediation supervisors. Extensive use is made of simulated mediation cases in which each member of the new class acts as mediator, labor representative, or management representative. Experienced mediators observe and comment as part of the teaching method.

At the conclusion of the Washington orientation program, each mediator is assigned to the regional office of the region in which he is expected to work. At that office he receives detailed instruction in office procedures, reporting procedures, and related matters. However, here again the major emphasis is on training at the bargaining table. The new man is assigned initially as an observer, working in rotation with several experienced mediators stationed at the regional office. When not in actual conferences with the parties, the experienced mediators discuss the issues, the procedures, and the mediation tactics with the new mediator. As more exposure occurs, they bring the new mediator more and more into actual participation in a mediation panel operation.

This on-the-job training at the regional office is supplemented by relatively short-term assignments to work with experienced mediators at several field offices in the region.

Throughout the training period the regional director and assistant regional director receive informal reports from the experienced mediators as to the individual's rate of progress. They also spend a considerable amount of time with the new mediator, discussing his experiences and his reactions to the handling of a variety of cases by different mediators and counseling with him.

The regional director assigns the new mediator to a case on his own when he believes the man is ready. Normally it is a smaller case or one that is expected to be of less than average difficulty. There are no firm rules as to the duration of regional office and field office training prior to the first solo assignment. The period may vary from a minimum of five or six weeks to a maximum of almost a year, depending primarily on the individual mediator's prior experience and his readiness. While working on the initial solo cases, the new mediator consults extensively with his regional director and with other experienced mediators in the office.

The first year of employment is probationary. At or before the end of the probationary year the regional director makes an appraisal and report to the Washington office. Quarterly reports have been made officially in the meantime. If at any time during the year after a fair exposure it becomes clear that the new hire will not become a satisfactory mediator, his services are terminated. In rare instances a probationary period has been extended beyond one year.

Upon satisfactory completion of the probationary year, an applicant who has been hired at GS-12 is promoted to GS-13, the first journeyman mediator grade.

Mediator-trainees, referred to in Appendix B, attend one and frequently two orientation courses during their training period in Washington. During that period they also are typically assigned temporarily to three different regional offices, where they work with experienced mediators and the regional directors. As the end of the trainee period approaches, a decision is made as to the region to which the new man will be assigned. Permanent assignment to a region terminates the trainee period, but training within that region continues in essentially the same manner as noted above for other new mediators.

All state agencies answering the questionnaire and the National Mediation Board have on-the-job training. Few details are available, but initial observation and work with experienced mediators is the usual arrangement. The much smaller size of these agencies makes it more difficult to arrange diversified assignments with experienced men.

Continued Training of Experienced Mediators

The pace of collective bargaining change as respects issues, methods of bargaining, and related matters is so rapid that no one field mediator can hope to keep fully up to date simply by handling his assigned cases. Moreover, even the most experienced mediator can and must learn continuously from other mediators and from persons who are students of or participants in the collective bargaining process. All agencies seek to facilitate this continuous learning process among the regular staff. As is the case with new mediator training, the larger the agency, the greater the possibility of accomplishment.

The Federal Mediation and Conciliation Service program can be divided into several parts: (1) FMCS annual seminars, (2) FMCS workshops, (3) FMCS regional or area conferences, (4) distribution of literature, and (5) participation in conferences and seminars planned by or with others for larger audiences.

The FMCS annual seminar program, initiated in 1957, varies somewhat in form and content. However, a typical series in recent years has consisted of two one-week seminars in January or February, the months of the year in which the work load usually is relatively low. One half of the entire mediation staff work together at one location for a week. After a pause of a week or more, to permit interchange of case assignments back home, the other half of the staff meet for a substantially identical one-week program. Top staff personnel from the Washington office attend both seminars. Some of the sessions are addressed by outstanding representatives of industry, labor, and the academic community; adequate time is allowed for group discussion. The addresses usually deal with the most pressing collective bargaining problems of the moment. The program has been enriched greatly by the outstanding cooperation of the outside leadership. It is customary for more than 80 percent of the Service's first choices as speakers to accept and appear—a record that any conference planner who invites competent and busy people would find hard to beat. Labor and industry members of the National Labor-Management Panel have been generous in assuming leadership roles as well as in attending the seminars. The balance of the sessions consist of small workshops of mediators (approximately 20 per group).

A special feature of the annual seminars, started in 1965, has been the attendance by invitation of mediators' wives. Approximately one half the potential group, primarily those who do not have young children at home, attend—though not at government expense. Wives attend some of the meetings and a special program is arranged by and for them. It is well known that the irregularities of a mediator's life are extreme. Vacations, holidays, anniversaries—all can go down the drain when an important dispute demands attention. The seminars provide an opportunity for wives to gain new appreciation of the collective bargaining and mediation processes to which their husbands devote so much of their lives.

The FMCS workshops, started in a regularized way in May 1964, are one-week meetings usually held in Washington and attended by about 15 mediators each. Outside leadership is secured for most of the meetings, again with remarkable cooperation on the part of those invited. The program is much more detailed and concentrated than the seminar program. Typical topics, each of which has been the sole subject matter of a one-week workshop, have included (1) job evaluation, (2) incentives, (3) pensions, (4) insurance, and (5) the construction industry. Several workshops have been preventive mediation clinics. The primary objective in all workshops is intensive group participation. Four workshops are scheduled each year; this permits workshop attendance by each field mediator at least once every three years.

Most of the seven regions hold a regional conference each year. These are of two or three days' duration, are held within the region, and are limited in attendance to mediators and supervisory staff of that region plus a limited number of Washington office staff and invited speakers. These conferences fulfill some of the same purposes as the larger annual seminars, but they are also designed to concentrate on problems of special importance in the region.

Attendance at all these training programs (annual seminars, workshops, and regional conferences) is confined primarily to FMCS mediators and top staff except for invited outside leadership. State mediation agency representatives have been invited to participate in the seminars and workshops. Many state mediators have attended, although the number at any one program has not been large.

These group training programs are of special importance to the mediators in the small offices. The solo nature of most mediation work makes it essential that mediators have opportunities to exchange experiences, procedures, techniques, and basic philosophy of collective bargaining and of mediation with their peers.

Throughout the year, a modest distribution of selected literature and labor-relations publications is made to field mediators. Within the confines of the budget, the purpose is to permit mediators to keep up with current developments without being swamped by a flood of material. A newsletter, produced monthly at the Washington office, is a most useful device for keeping mediators informed of the nationwide scope of the Service's activities.

Mediators participate to the extent that time permits in leadership capacities, as well as attendance, at the multitude of conferences, seminars, and meetings held each year on labor relations throughout the United States. Some are cosponsored by the FMCS.

The state agencies have one conference each year that has many of the objectives of the FMCS seminars. The Association of Labor Mediation Agencies (ALMA), an organization of the active state agencies, holds an annual meeting of three or four days' duration, usually in August. Several staff officials from the Washington office of the FMCS attend by invitation.

MEDIATION PRACTICES

Chapter V

MEDIATION FUNCTIONS IN CRISIS BARGAINING

What does a mediator do in a contract negotiation case? No answer to that question is possible on a generalized basis. It is almost literally true that the same mediator does different things in each case. Nor would any two persons serving as mediators function identically in the same case.

However, there are a sizable number of functions that are available when, as, and if needed.

Mediation functions can be classified under three headings:

1. Functions that are essentially procedural;
2. Functions intended to facilitate communications;
3. Functions that may be more affirmative and substantive as to the issues in dispute.

The borderlines are not firm or absolute. Sometimes, a move made by a mediator may include a combination of functions. However, the distinctions may be useful to an understanding of the mediation role.

PROCEDURAL FUNCTIONS

Scheduling Meetings

Once a mediator enters a case, subsequent meetings are usually arranged and scheduled by him after consultation with both parties.

Making arrangements for meetings is not necessarily difficult. Under some circumstances, all that is involved is checking with the parties and determining which times and places are acceptable to both. It may be essentially a clerical task. However, in a sizable number of instances, the timing of the next meeting or some other aspect of the arrangement can be an integral part of the strategy of the parties and therefore can present real problems.

In a stalemate situation, a request by one party for a meeting may be construed as a sign of weakness. This is especially so with less sophisticated negotiators. Or, one or both parties may indicate that they do not want to meet unless a commitment is made by the other party, in advance, that a change of position will be forthcoming on one or more important disputed issues.

When the mediator schedules the meetings, the sign-of-weakness stigma can be averted. There is no loss of face in acquiescing to a mediation request. It is a common occurrence for one party to contact the mediator and request a meeting but to accompany that request with an admonition that the source should not be disclosed. Not infrequently, both parties may so indicate their desires to the mediator in a confidential manner.

Negotiators sometimes attend a meeting called by the mediator with great reluctance. The mediator may be told in no uncertain terms by one or possibly both parties that a meeting would be fruitless and ill-advised. In the face of such opposition it is possible, indeed probable, that the objecting party will not be in a mood to advance anything constructive. The mediator must then weigh the objections and the likelihood of a futile meeting against the fact that no settlement can be achieved unless the parties meet. There is always the possibility, realized in numerous instances, that something will happen to get "reluctant dragons" started on a positive approach. If a dispute is of public importance, the outside pressures for meeting may be very great. The mediator may know, in confidence, that one side is prepared to make a concession. No experienced mediator will ignore the wishes of the parties entirely. Normally he will schedule meetings only if it appears to him that there is at least a remote hope of progress.

Recessing Meetings

Under some circumstances a mediator may take the initiative to stop or recess a joint meeting, even if the parties do not so propose. This is most likely to occur in an atmosphere of anger or retrogression. Even though a negotiation has been progressing in a reasonably satisfactory manner, some unexpected development may cause or threaten a backward movement. An unduly harsh word or careless observation may undo much that has been accomplished. However, great sensitivity to the totality of the situation is required. Explosions or displays of temper sometimes serve a very constructive purpose. In fact, they may occasionally be planned or contrived.

Another occasion for recessing a meeting can be a prolonged stalemate. The parties are simply repeating *ad nauseam* the same things that have been said dozens of times. Continued discussion is valueless; the parties are only hardening their positions.

There is a common public notion that meetings should be continued on a regularized basis in all cases. This is quite erroneous. Under some circumstances, continued meetings will only exacerbate the dispute. Or, in a long lost-strike situation, meetings may give hope to the strikers when there is no realistic reason for hope. Hard facts that must be faced should not be masked by an endless series of fruitless meetings.

A more constructive reason for a recess is the injection of a new idea that cannot be pursued productively until after each side has discussed it fully away from the bargaining table. Even better, a tentative agreement may have been reached, but some time is required for one or both negotiating teams to secure approval from a larger committee or a higher authority.

A recess called by a mediator is frequently announced by him in the following or similar words: "Negotiations between . . . . and . . . . have been recessed to be resumed at an early date. The purpose of the recess is to permit the parties to reexamine their positions." Such an announcement is not very descriptive. At one extreme, a more candid statement would be: "These people are so mad at each other that there can be no hope of settlement for a long time if they stay together. They need time to cool off." At the other extreme a more complete announcement would be: "A tentative agreement has been reached. However, it cannot be announced until full approval has been obtained from the principals." The routine type of announcement is not very helpful to the public. However, the more explicit announcement could retard or even prevent agreement.

Arranging Joint and Separate Meetings

Full agreement between the parties cannot be reached until they face each other across the table. However, a mediator normally will hold a number of meetings separately with each side.

Negotiation facilities are usually arranged with one room for joint meetings and one or more caucus rooms. The mediator may shuttle back and forth between the separate rooms, bringing the parties to joint meetings at appropriate intervals. The arrangements are normally the same for direct negotiations in the absence of a mediator. The separate rooms in that case are for internal discussion by company and union personnel as required by developments at joint meetings.

Separate meetings attended by the mediator serve several purposes. If he has the respect and confidence of the parties, he will secure at those meetings a candid appraisal of the ultimate desires and priorities of each side. He can explore tentative solutions more quickly and directly than would be possible in the presence of the other party. In general, he will gain a better feel for the realities of the bargaining situation.

Mediators are sometimes criticized for overdoing the separate meeting procedure and not stimulating enough direct confrontation. Whether this criticism is valid depends on the facts of each case. In one extreme situation in which the author participated as mediator, at least 95 percent of the meetings were separate sessions. Mutual animosity between the two principal negotiators was so great that no other course of action was possible. The dispute was concluded by a memorandum in which the parties stated explicitly that each was agreeing with the mediator but not with each other. At the signing ceremonies, the negotiators refused even to shake hands for purposes of a picture in the union newspaper. They did consent to stand on each side of the mediator and were shown in the picture shaking hands only with him. At the other extreme, and especially where negotiating committees are small, the great bulk of the time will be spent in joint meetings. There can be no hard-and-fast rules as to the ratio of separate and joint meeting time.

Influencing Duration of Continuous Meetings

Somewhat independent of scheduling or recessing meetings is the matter of duration of continuous meetings. In the early days of a typical negotiation, a negotiating day tends to be a normal work day or even shorter. The crisis pressures are not severe. Frequently, both parties need a substantial amount of time away from formal meeting time to develop their priorities and strategy.

However, as the strike deadline approaches the pressures increase and, unless there is a complete deadlock, the duration of meetings expands. Round-the-clock bargaining is quite common immediately before a deadline. There are several reasons for this intense activity. All too often, too much remains to be done within too few hours even if the desire for settlement is mutual; most people have an ingrained tendency to defer hard decisions as long as possible. Some negotiators take pride in having the physical and mental stamina to outlast their opposites at the bargaining table. Many negotiators, especially on the union side, think their constituents will not believe they have done the best job if there is not at least one all-night meeting. There is also the fear, usually on the management side, of the "nibbler." A nibbler is a negotiator who defers total acceptance until the very last moment, grasping repeatedly for one more small concession as long as any time remains.

Independent of the features just discussed is what might be called "progress momentum." Agreement on even a minor issue may create an atmosphere of optimism and drive. The parties are eager to tackle and settle another issue. Nobody wants to stop for fear that it will not be possible to recreate the spirit of progress. Meals are deferred long past normal times, and then somebody becomes sufficiently hungry to send out for coffee and hamburgers. Even when that simple fare arrives in the bargaining room, it may go cold because an important phase of the discussion must be concluded without interruption.

An incident may illustrate this almost frenzied drive for a settlement. An out-of-town mediator dropped in on a negotiation session to discuss an unrelated matter briefly with his fellow mediator. He knew nothing about the case. He entered the meeting at 8:00 p.m. and left with the active mediator at 8:10 p.m. when a very short recess was called. Before hearing anything from the resident mediator, he said, "There will be a settlement here at about 10:00 p.m." In that brief period, despite his lack of familiarity with the case, his experience enabled him to sense an atmosphere of progress. And his prediction proved to be approximately correct.

But even such an atmosphere of rapid progress can evaporate short of complete agreement. What then should be done? Should the mediator attempt to "keep feet to the fire" in the hope of surmounting the obstacle? Or, should the meeting be recessed for a few hours' sleep to consolidate gains and permit the negotiators to approach the immediate problem with refreshed minds and bodies? Much may depend on that decision It should not be presumed that the mediator has the final word.

Here, again, he is limited to persuasion, though his voice may well be a determining factor.

Because long strenuous meetings are common in crisis situations, a successful mediator must have the necessary physical and mental stamina. Of all persons at the bargaining table, the mediator must be able somehow to stay with it to the end and retain good judgment even in a state of exhaustion.

Changing Location of Meetings

For direct negotiations, most parties have developed their own habits and customs. Such practices are far from uniform. Meetings sometimes are held in company offices, particularly if facilities have been designed for the purpose. Both Ford and General Motors have specially designed negotiating rooms, including a large room with the "big table," smaller rooms for subcommittees, special caucus rooms with private telephone lines, and food facilities. Less frequently, negotiations take place at union offices. A third approach—and the most common one—is to reserve facilities at a hotel or motel for the duration of the negotiating period.

When a mediator enters a case, he will often make no attempt to alter the existing physical arrangement. However, if the arrangement is known to be inadequate or if he believes that a change of scenery would be desirable, he will offer the parties the use of the rooms maintained in that city by the cognizant mediation service or rent suitable rooms at a hotel. A change of location may or may not be desirable, depending on the facts of the specific case. As always, the mediator must be sensitive to the needs of the parties.

In recent years modest budget allotments have permitted the Federal Mediation and Conciliation Service to upgrade substantially most of its office and meeting-room facilities. At one time facilities were likely to be unsuitable and not conducive to productive meetings. An adequate physical environment for negotiations is not as important as the personalities at the table, but it is unwise economy for a governmental mediation service to be unable to provide satisfactory quarters. Hotel arrangements have some advantages over rooms in an office building: sleeping rooms and food are more readily accessible. But so are the bars; under the stress and strain of a tough negotiation, many an evening, night, or even late afternoon session has been sabotaged by the proximity of the bar.

Occasionally it may be decided to move the meetings to another city. In extreme cases negotiations may even be moved to the White House (actually the Executive Building adjoining the White House); that has happened in a few relatively recent instances such as steel, railroads, and copper. Somewhat more often negotiations have moved to the Federal Mediation and Conciliation Service or Labor Department offices in Washington. Or Washington may be avoided altogether. What are the advantages and disadvantages of a change of location?

One advantage is that the negotiators are removed from their everyday activities and are thereby able to concentrate more effectively on the major job at hand. Another probable advantage is that a move to another city at government request dramatizes the seriousness of the dispute and demonstrates public concern. Sometimes a move to another city, away from the local plant, permits easier access to additional company, union, and government personnel who may be drawn into the negotiations, directly or indirectly.

Relocation may, however, have its drawbacks. Removal of union officials from ready access to their constituents may make ratification of the final agreement more difficult. Some people function less effectively outside their natural habitat. The publicity attendant upon a so-called White House negotiation is not always beneficial to the collective bargaining process.

Mediators and mediation agencies cannot afford to have any doctrinaire or rigid ideas about the location of negotiations. In most instances, this matter is worked out by agreement with the parties. In the occasional case when a change of location proposed by the mediation agency is accepted with reluctance, the agency should act only after careful appraisal of all the pros and cons in that case.

Chairing Meeting and Maintaining Order

Direct negotiations are usually chaired by one of two methods. The principal negotiators on each side are co-chairmen of all sessions. Or, they act alternately as chairman. Experienced and sophisticated negotiators seldom encounter serious difficulty with either of these arrangements. However, it is apparent that problems can arise if the negotiations become stalemated. The co-chairmen or the alternating chairmen are not disinterested persons who can distinguish completely their roles as partisans from their roles as procedural leaders of a discussion.

When a mediator enters a case, he almost always becomes chairman of the meeting. Potentially, at least, he is in a much better position to keep the discussion going, to divert the dialogue into other channels when it bogs down, and generally to bring about a more productive tone in the proceedings. Skillful use of alternate joint and separate meetings can "keep noses to the grindstone" with purpose when the absence of a neutral chairman would result in a recess.

In a limited number of situations, especially when a stalemate has not yet developed, the mediator may not want to chair the joint meetings. His basic objective to maximize direct bargaining may be best served by concentration of his efforts in his separate meetings with the parties.

As collective bargaining has developed over the years, it is seldom necessary now for a mediator to move overtly to keep order at a meeting. Despite strong beliefs and emotions, most negotiations are reasonably orderly even without a mediator. However, the presence of a neutral chairman does help preserve order and, most important, can promote more meaningful discussion.

It should go without saying, of course, that a mediator-chairman is successful in this aspect of his task only if he is skilled in the art of leading a meeting.

Proposing Discussion Sequence or Grouping of Issues

In a typical dispute, a sizable number of issues will be in dispute when the mediator arrives, some major and some minor. If the negotiators are experienced and skilled they will already have arranged these issues into logical groupings, and their own direct negotiations will have established an orderly sequence of discussion. However, this is not always the case. Especially among inexperienced negotiators, it is common to encounter aimless or hit-or-miss conversation.

After a mediator has become acquainted with the issues and has acquired confidential information about priorities, he can do much to try to steer the negotiations in the direction of agreement. He can aid in soft-pedaling the throw-away items. He can group tradeoff items. When a logical grouping of important issues or a single major issue is being discussed, he can insist on concentration on that issue or issues. When tempers get unduly frayed, he can shift to a less controversial subject. Before an issue reaches the point of being beaten to death by words with no hope of immediate agreement, he can terminate that discussion until a more propitious time. In short, he can assist in keeping a meeting within productive bounds.

Suggesting Subcommittees

Sometimes discussion of an issue or group of issues will develop to a point of possible agreement, but much detailed work must be done to achieve final agreement. Frequently it will be most productive for the parties to create a small subcommittee to pursue the matter further and report back to the principal negotiating committee. If the parties do not initiate such a course of action on their own, the mediator may suggest it. If the idea is acceptable, two things may be accomplished. The principal committee can turn its attention to other matters. Of perhaps greater importance, the subcommittee members may obtain a greater sense of personal accomplishment than would otherwise be the case. This is particularly true if there is a large negotiating committee, of whom only a few are meeting for the major discussions. If some negotiators sit by themselves for hours with nothing to do but receive periodic reports from the principal negotiators, they quite naturally acquire a sense of futility and may even become obstructive.

This observation leads to the next likely course of events. It is almost axiomatic that a small committee can reach tentative agreement on difficult subjects more readily than a large committee can. Except in the most obstinate type of "fishbowl" negotiations, some formal or informal small principal committee must be created as the deadline approaches if the negotiations are to be fruitful. The problem is particularly acute within the union negotiating group. As practical men and women, they know that a smaller group must be created to work effectively. However, nobody likes to be left out. The internal political problem of creating a small committee may be so great that it requires a strong mediator's suggestion to accomplish what everybody knows must be done.

Whether a formal or informal top committee is created after a mediator's suggestion or without it, it is imperative that everybody be fully conscious of "the guys in the other room." It is necessary to make certain that they are kept informed adequately and are actually brought into the joint discussions as much as possible without destroying the advantages of the smaller committee.

Arranging for Orderly Record Keeping

In the more elaborate and systematic negotiating arrangements, both parties create an accurate mechanism for recording progress or lack of it. As tentative agreement is reached on each issue, one or more persons on each side make careful notes. If the agreement is reduced to exact language at the time of agreement (not a universal custom), the text may be typed and initialed within a matter of minutes. Periodically, all issues in dispute are reviewed in joint session to make sure that each side has the same understanding of the status of negotiations.

In many of the smaller or less systematic bargaining arrangements, the parties do not have a fully adequate mechanism for recording agreements or status. If this is the case, the strike deadline may approach or even pass with differing recollections. What may have seemed to be an agreement on all matters comes unstuck when it develops that the parties do not have the same impression of what has happened. Especially in an around-the-clock session where much has been accomplished, such confusion is understandable even if it may also be disastrous.

To attempt to avoid such results, a mediator can do several things. He can suggest in advance that the parties provide their own suitable mechanisms. He can and usually does keep his own notes of the proceedings, and these can be referred to for clarification. Periodically, he will review the status of issues at a joint meeting. Regardless of his procedures the mediator routinely should insist on a complete joint status review at the successful conclusion of a negotiation.

Occasionally a tape recording or stenographic transcript may be made of all negotiations. Apart from the cost problem, these are usually undesirable practices. There is too great a tendency to talk for the record, which may lead to embarrassment when the record is compared with the results. Even more significant is the probability that negotiators will be too inhibited to reach an agreement. Some of these same adverse reactions can occur if the mediator is too obvious in his note-taking or makes extensive records. The mediator's notes are intended primarily to spur his memory, not as a precise recording of the proceedings.

Proposing and Developing Procedures for Contract Extensions or Strike Postponements

As a contract deadline approaches and a strike seems likely, an obvious question is posed to the mediator. Should he attempt to secure a contract extension or other form of strike postponement?

If such a proposal is to be made, the timing is important. If it is made too early, it will tend to destroy the usefulness of deadline pressures. If the parties know that a request for postponement will be made and that both are likely to agree to it, they may seize upon this as an excuse for avoiding the difficult last-minute decisions that precede a real strike or lockout threat. Conversely, if it is made too late, the strike or lockout procedures may be so far advanced that it is almost impossible to reverse them.

These considerations are complicated further by the fact that any actual contract extension or postponement brings up new questions. What about retroactive pay? How long an extension is appropriate? Should an extension preserve all or only some of the provisions of the expiring contract? Will the company attempt to continue operations if a strike does occur? These and other questions, injected into negotiations in the most critical hours or minutes, could block a settlement.

A further complication arises in a continuous process industry such as basic steel or chemicals. In such industries, preparation for a shutdown must begin hours or days before a deadline.

In view of these complexities, a mediator must first ask himself an important question: "What would be gained by delay?" If there is some real hope and the principal problem is lack of time for agreement, a request made at the right moment may be advisable. However, if positions have so hardened that additional time is not likely to make any difference, it would be a disservice to the parties to delay the inevitable.

If the mediator concludes that an extension would be advisable, the next important question is whether both parties would agree to it. If the request is rejected, the fact that it was made will have muddied the negotiations, may even have helped cause a strike, and certainly will have served no useful purpose.

Knowing that a mediator can request an extension, the

parties will sometimes anticipate these questions. On the one hand, the mediator may be advised quietly by the principals that an extension will be acceptable, if needed, and the appropriate timing and general content will be indicated. On the other hand, one or both parties may advise the mediator in no uncertain terms that a request for an extension will be rejected under any circumstances.

If the parties do not voluntarily provide any advice to the mediator, or if what they do say is confused or uncertain, he has no alternative but to keep his own counsel, answer the critical questions in his own mind as best he can, and postpone any suggestion of an extension until the last possible moment. At that time he may want to check quietly with the principal negotiators to obtain some answers before he determines a course of action.

In short, a request for a contract extension, which may seem to an outsider to be a simple and sensible mediation tactic, is in fact a very complicated and sometimes doubtful procedure.

Proposing and Developing Procedures for Deferred Settlement of Limited Issues

Quite frequently, agreement is possible at the deadline on all but one or two issues. But the remaining items in dispute are "strike issues" to the union or "take a strike issues" to the company—sometimes both.

In such a situation the mediator should always ask himself whether there are any possible procedural arrangements under which an agreement can be concluded with a method for future resolution of the residual dispute. This is a concept that differs appreciably from a contract extension. Everything will have been "buttoned up" except the one or two items. At least some of the perplexing questions associated with a contract extension do not arise.

What are the procedural arrangements for future resolution that may be considered? Without being unnecessarily exhaustive, they are:
1. arbitration;
2. fact-finding with recommendations;
3. a new form of mediation;
4. a study committee or similar bipartite device.
Combinations of these four procedures are possible.

Arbitration of new-contract disputes is in general disfavor in American industry, usually on both sides of the table. In contrast to the growth of grievance arbitration, new-contract arbitration has declined in recent years. Despite this discouraging fact, too little attention has been directed by the parties— and by mediators—to the potential of limited arbitration. Much of the objection to contract arbitration is and has been within a framework of unlimited arbitration of a wide variety of new contract terms.

How can arbitration be limited? As noted already, it can be confined to one or two issues with all other contract terms concluded by the parties. Moreover, the parties can prescribe boundaries and establish criteria for those issues that are to be arbitrated. The fixing of boundaries and the establishment of meaningful criteria are not simple tasks. An objector can say with some validity that if the parties can agree on these matters, they could agree on the disputed issues. However, this type of arbitration has not often been approached with the imagination and inventiveness that have characterized many other aspects of bargaining. When weighed against the hazards of a strike, the notion should be explored thoroughly in many situations.

There are some indications that general aversion to voluntary arbitration of new contract terms is diminishing. Under the auspices of the American Arbitration Association, a prestigious committee of labor, management, and neutral persons has been created to examine the matter thoroughly. Creation of a committee does not necessarily herald change of attitude. However, this step has followed other encouraging indications that thoughtful persons on both sides of the table realize the limitations of the strike and lockout as primary persuaders. Voluntary arbitration is thoroughly consistent with the principle of agreement-making by the parties, particularly if the parties develop the criteria and boundaries to suit the facts of a specific case. Imaginative mediation can do much to detect the circumstances under which such arbitration is feasible and in the development of the procedures within each set of circumstances.

If the parties are unwilling to agree to arbitration, even in a limited form, fact-finding with recommendations may be considered. Fact-finding will be discussed more fully in a subsequent chapter. At this point it suffices to say that this procedural device preserves the right of either or both parties to reject recommendations. Since it lacks the element of finality, it may be necessary to preserve the right to strike or lock out if recommendations are rejected. But if the choice is a certain strike versus only a possible strike, the procedure may have merit.

Without casting aspersions on the mediator, it may be possible to conclude an agreement on all but one or two issues and proceed to a new form of mediation after the strike deadline. The Federal Mediation and Conciliation Service has experimented successfully with this device in recent years. Additional mediation concentrated on one or two remaining issues with the assistance of a troubleshooter mediator or an outside labor relations expert has averted many strikes. As is the case with fact-finding, this procedure may be unsuccessful, and a strike may occur anyway. However, the record of strike avoidance by this procedure has been sufficiently good to suggest that it should often be given careful consideration.

Another rather common procedure is to refer the few remaining issues to a special negotiating committee (sometimes called a study committee). For example, the parties may agree on a total sum of money to correct intraplant or interplant inequities. The allocation of that sum is worked out over a period of days, weeks, or even months after the contract signing. This procedure may also be applicable to extensive but necessary changes of seniority arrangements, some aspects of pension and insurance plans, revisions of incentive plans, and similar subjects.

One common criticism of this procedure is that it has too often been a device to sweep issues under the rug. Nothing gets done, and when the same or similar issues arise in subsequent negotiations, the deferral-to-a-special-committee idea is defeated by recollection of earlier sad experiences. In order to avoid this result, it is possible to put teeth in the idea by providing for a possible future strike if the issues have not been resolved within a stipulated period of time. In the 1965 Boeing-IAM negotiations, a long-festering series of seniority issues were deferred after a 14-day strike to six months' special study and mediation with preservation of the right to resume the strike if the special negotiation should be unsuccessful. At the end of six months, that potential strike pressure was needed, but an agreement was reached.

Because of his freedom to make suggestions at the appropriate time, a knowledgeable and inventive mediator is in a peculiarly good position to propose and help develop a wide variety of procedures of the general type discussed in this section.

Fending Off Other Outside Intervention

In disputes of national significance, of immediate defense impact, or even of intense local interest, many public officials and government agencies have a legitimate interest in the progress of negotiations. A very real problem faced by negotiators is that they may be interrupted at the most inopportune times by information-seeking telephone calls or personal visits or by requests for mediation intervention. The press may insist on information in a variety of ways. In some disputes, the principal negotiators would have little time to negotiate if they gave careful personal attention to this barrage of inquiry and interest.

If an established mediation agency has one or more mediators in the negotiations, one of the responsibilities of that agency may be to protect the parties from this well-intentioned interference. This can be done in a variety of ways.

The Federal Mediation and Conciliation Service maintains regular liaison with the Department of Defense, the Department of Labor, and other government agencies and offices. One purpose of such liaison is to encourage the direction of inquiries to the mediator instead of to the parties. Obviously, the mediator and the agency must respect the confidences of the parties. Nothing can be said to others that the parties would not say themselves if called. A possible exception is the sometimes hazardous prediction as to whether there will be a strike or the likely duration of a strike. Occasionally, other officials may be dissatisfied with the limited disclosure that is permissible and may attempt to make direct contact anyway. However, these exceptions do not detract materially from the fact the mediator can and does help preserve to the parties the maximum time needed for negotiation.

With respect to the press, the parties frequently request that only the mediator make announcements to the news media during the hectic days and hours before a deadline. In such instances the mediator must always check carefully with the parties to determine what, if anything, can be said. The parties may sometimes agree upon a total news blackout.

The mere fact that a mediator is involved in the negotiations minimizes the type of official inquiry discussed in the first part of this section. The public is represented by the mediation agency or agencies created by government, and that tends to discourage other intervention.

One incident that can now be told may illustrate this general function. During the 1968 basic steel negotiations, the author made a publicly known short trip to Pittsburgh. The principal purpose of that visit was not mediation. A meeting was held with the top negotiating committee, but no details of the current status of negotiations were discussed—and intentionally so. My objective was to confirm a personal hunch that an agreement would be concluded successfully by the parties without mediation or other intervention. The parties could give no assurance that my speculation was accurate, but it was evident that they had a strong mutual desire to agree and wanted to be left alone. I communicated my impression in several ways. A short, basically optimistic statement to the press and the mere fact of my immediate return to Washington emphasized the intention of the Government to rely on direct negotiation. My reports to others in Washington stressed the importance of a hands-off government policy. Fortunately for the country and the parties— and, incidentally, me—the hunch was accurate. It is reasonably certain that it was because the purpose was so limited that the visit and the surrounding circumstances contributed to successful bargaining.

Continuing Negotiations After a Strike Begins

If all prestrike negotiation and mediation efforts fail and a strike begins, negotiations usually terminate at or even before the strike hour. Mediators and negotiators once concluded almost automatically that the initiation of a strike would rule out further meetings for at least a short period of time.

Experience has shown that this is not always a necessary result. In a sizable number of known cases, negotiations have continued past the strike hour with little or no interruption, and an agreement has been reached after only a few hours. In the majority of these cases, the negotiations continued only because of mediator insistence.

No general rules can be suggested as to whether the mediator should attempt to keep the meetings in progress without a break. In a substantial majority of cases, to insist on continuation would be an error or would be futile. Nothing could be accomplished except to irritate the parties. However, if the parties are not far apart and if the atmosphere is otherwise conducive to continued meetings, a strike may spark productive discussion where the threat of a strike was ineffectual.

Creation of Alternative Deadlines

It has been noted that a strike deadline often stimulates hard bargaining. But if a strike begins and has persisted for some time, what can be done to create new deadlines or the equivalent? Costs to the parties of lost wages and lost profits build up pressures, but these elements of attrition do not terminate conflict automatically. A strike can easily degenerate into a senseless exhibition of staying power, long after the normal functions of these economic sanctions have fulfilled their intended purposes.

In an actual strike situation, both the company and the union may be reluctant to initiate resumption of negotiations. To do so may be construed as a sign of weakness. This is even more likely to be the case than with an initial request for mediation before a strike occurs, discussed in a preceding section. After confidential checking with each party, a mediator can perform a most useful function by his initiation of renewed negotiations. The sign of weakness stigma is avoided.

After meetings have been resumed, the mediator can create a new deadline by indications that he will withdraw for a time if no progress is made. One or both negotiating teams may not want to confront their constituencies with the fact that the mediator has left town with a "no progress" announcement.

If the dispute is of major public interest, the mediator may indicate to the parties his appraisal of the next step that government may take. If a Taft-Hartley injunction is predictable or if some other special procedure is likely, the threat of such developments may spur bargaining. Obviously, this tactic is useful only if the next step is less palatable to the parties than mediation. If one or both parties are simply waiting for that next step anyway, the tactic would not be a threat; it would be a promise. In that situation, the mediator would want to discount any next step if he should be in a position to do so.

A mediator should be alert to maximize the inducement-to-bargain effect of economic factors. A union's strike fund may be nearing exhaustion. A company on strike may not be in a favorable position to bid on a large contract on which bids will be taken at an early date. Seasonal industries are often subject to special deadline pressures during a strike. If the dispute is in New York or Rhode Island where unemployment compensation payments to employees begin after a fixed waiting period, that date may be very significant to the bargaining strategy.

Extraneous events may be sources of deadline pressures. For example, a segment of the news media on strike may be sensitive to a visit to the locality by an important personage or to a future significant planned event.

Although the parties are usually fully aware of many of these considerations and take them into account in formulation of their strategies, a resourceful mediator can frequently utilize such factors in the creation of alternative deadlines.

COMMUNICATION FUNCTIONS

Keeping Communication Channels Open

As long as direct negotiations are progressing in a satisfactory manner, little or no outside assistance is usually needed to facilitate communications between the parties. Experienced negotiators usually maintain effective channels in addition to the discussion at the bargaining table. However, less experienced negotiators and even the best company and union practitioners may tend to close these normal avenues of discourse in a stalemated situation and especially during a strike.

In addition to the procedural function of attempting to schedule meetings as needed, a mediator can do much to keep the normal channels open in the intervals between meetings. It is quite common practice for a mediator to check frequently with representatives of both parties. Something may be said, deliberately or otherwise, in a friendly conversation that, with permission, can be passed along to the other side in one way or another. This may pave the way for an early meeting. Or, the mediator may suggest a direct approach to the other party.

If the mediator is to retain the respect and confidence of the parties, it is obvious that such conversations, whether by telephone or in person, must be handled with great care. However, this communication function, properly exercised, can do much to facilitate bargaining.

Trying on for Size

One aspect of bargaining is not well understood by persons who have not participated in the process. At a formal joint negotiating meeting, any spokesman must exercise great care in discussing an issue. It is difficult to explore without making a commitment.

To illustrate, let us assume that the union is demanding a general wage increase of 20 cents per hour for the first year and that the company is offering 15 cents. If a company spokesman openly asks, "Would you accept 16 cents?," it will be difficult indeed ever to get that penny back. That penny was probably "spent" when the question was asked. Nobody on the union side will ever forget it. Similarly, if a union spokesman makes even a strong hint about anything less than 20 cents, the settlement is reasonably certain to be less than 20 cents.

Experienced negotiators usually are able to avoid this problem by resorting to confidential, frequently man-to-man, discussion. Possible concessions can be explored without commitment. However, even in such situations, at least one man on each side of the table knows that something other than an official position is being contemplated. A semblance of commitment, sometimes intentional, has taken place.

If a mediator is involved in the negotiations, he can "try on for size" a great variety of possible solutions. He has no money to spend and no authority to reduce a demand. This process of "trying on for size" may be one of the important features of the separate meetings with each party. Obviously, the parties must have faith in the discretion of the mediator. He would make a great and perhaps fatal error if he were to disclose confidential information meant for his ears alone. As long as he respects these confidences, he may ascertain ultimate or close to final positions even though no commitment has been made by either party to the other side.

To continue the illustration used earlier, the following question is sometimes asked of mediators early in the training period: "Suppose you should discover in confidential separate sessions that the company is prepared to pay 18 cents per hour and that the union is prepared to settle for 17 cents per hour. What would you do?" There are several possible good answers to that question, and the obvious 17½ cents per hour answer is not necessarily the best. Needless to say, a mediator seldom finds much overlap. Those cases are usually settled by the parties without assistance. If, as is usual, the confidential disclosures do not meet or overlap, the process of exploration without commitment has narrowed the real dispute and is an important step towards agreement.

Communicating Mediator's Assessment of Rigidities of Position

As a mediator develops knowledge of the real positions of both parties, it is usually quite clear that each side has a formal or informal priority list. Both the union and the company will have a "must" list including some matters that are quite definitely "strike" or "take a strike" issues. They will be less adamant about an intermediate list of issues. Finally, there will be some issues that are "throw away" items or easy to resolve.

Success in negotiations may depend on early awareness of each side of the rigidity of position of the other side's "must" items. In direct negotiations, the form of presentation, the tone of discussion, and other factors will usually make these facts known. However, a strong or lingering suspicion may exist that a sham battle is being fought on one or more "must" issues and that capitulation will occur when the chips are down. Thus, one or both parties may be battering their heads against stone walls in the mistaken belief that the other side will weaken. If a mediator is convinced that an adamant position is "for real," his personal assessment may make the doubting side aware of the "facts of life" and help avoid a fruitless strike.

This mediation function can be quite valuable, but it should be obvious that it involves dangers. Suppose the mediator goes out on a limb in trying to convince the union of the futility of one of its demands, based upon his assessment of a management position. Then the company capitulates suddenly on that issue. The mediator's face is red, and his effectiveness probably has been lessened for the balance of the case.

An illustration of an accurate mediation assessment may clarify this function. In one negotiation, the spokesman for the employer association had said in every way possible that the companies would not yield to a certain union demand. Fortunately, it was not the top-priority union demand. However, a majority of the union negotiating committee kept insisting to me as the mediator that the president of the largest company, not present in the negotiations, would yield on this issue and persuade the other companies to do likewise. That union belief, among other things, was holding up a settlement. It was not possible for the individual in question to meet the union negotiators face to face. However, with the full knowledge and approval of all the negotiators, the mediator had a candid long-distance telephone conversation with him. He became convinced that the employer position was final and so advised the union. Thereupon the union dropped the demand and a settlement was soon achieved. It is quite possible that that telephone call and the circumstances surrounding it avoided a costly and needless strike.

On the other side of the coin, personal experiences could be cited of instances where the mediator's assessment of the rigidity of a union's final position on a wage issue helped persuade a company to settle at that figure rather than take a strike and probably settle subsequently at a still higher figure.

Communicating Mediator's Assessment of Negotiators' Ability and Commitment to "Sell" Agreement to Their Constituencies

Elsewhere in this volume, problems associated with membership rejection of tentative agreements will be considered. One aspect will be noted here.

Increasingly, as a tentative agreement seems possible, management representatives are asking the question: "Can the union sell it?" Sometimes the question is: "Will the union representatives even make an honest and hard attempt to sell it?" If employers are in serious doubt about the answers to these questions, the best offers may not be forthcoming. Rejection is viewed as a foregone conclusion and a needless strike may occur.

This problem frequently requires that a mediator explore these questions in some depth with the union negotiators. If the mediator can be convinced that the employer fears are groundless or at least that all members of the negotiating committee are negotiating in good faith and will make an honest effort to convince the membership, that assessment will be communicated to the company negotiators. An available settlement may be realized.

Here, again, the mediator assumes risk. The assurances he

gives management necessarily are based only upon an appraisal of personalities and the few facts that may be available. If a rejection occurs anyway, the mediator may be blamed. Despite these hazards, communication by the mediator of his personal appraisal will usually be worth the risk.

Arranging for Top-Level Direct Communications

As a difficult case nears or reaches a climax with an agreement in sight but with important obstacles still ahead, the parties may be putting too much reliance on the mediator. He has been present for some time at all joint meetings, large and small. The negotiators may even forget that they have been in similar situations on earlier occasions and have reached agreement without assistance. Or they may be fearful that they will offend the mediator if they meet in his absence.

Despite the virtues of mediation, it is nevertheless true that some negotiators may not be as candid and uninhibited in the presence of the mediator as when they are alone. Moreover, especially at such a stage, the understandable and proper desire of the principals to "do their own thing" may be just what is needed to effect a settlement. For these reasons, and under the appropriate set of circumstances, the mediator may suggest to the top negotiators that they get together without him or figuratively "lock themselves in a room" to attempt to resolve the last remaining obstacles.

Such top-level direct communication without the mediator obviously should not be forced on unwilling persons. Nor is it a procedure applicable to all cases, for it might "blow" the negotiations completely. However, it is a suggestion that has saved many settlements. Especially when the idea originates with the mediator, it is further evidence of the fundamental principle that negotiations are the basic responsibility of the parties and that the mediation role is limited to assistance.

MORE AFFIRMATIVE AND SUBSTANTIVE FUNCTIONS

We turn now to what may be designated, for want of a better description, more affirmative or substantive functions. The procedural and communication functions may require much skill, judgment, and experience, but they do not involve mediator input with respect to the specific issues in dispute. They are manipulative functions in the best sense of the term, designed to facilitate resolution by the parties and utilizing, for the most part, the proposals and ideas on disputed issues that are advanced by the negotiators themselves.

Most of the functions to be discussed hereafter represent activities of the mediator that may contribute to the substance of dispute settlement.

Smoking Out Priorities

Mention has been made of the priority order in which each party to a negotiation groups the disputed issues. There are the must items at the one extreme and the "throw away" items at the other. In between are demands and requests, keenly desired but susceptible to compromise, postponement, or possible abandonment.

In the best organized negotiations, each team enters with carefully thought-out priorities. In other situations, especially on the union side, a multitude of demands have not been adequately sorted out and appraised, even internally, and the real priorities may emerge only gradually. In all instances, priorities change as ideas meet opposition.

A mediator's usefulness will be limited indeed if he is unable to distinguish between the substantial and the relatively trivial issues. Moreover, it may be necessary or advisable for him to seek to assist the parties in the sorting-out process. Not infrequently, a union or management committee may encounter internal disagreement in the arrangement of priorities. The principal negotiators may welcome assistance from the mediator in killing off some issue that is a pet project of one negotiator but is unattainable or even impracticable. Without being dictatorial or improperly slipping into a decision-making role, a mediator can quite properly influence the priority development by calling on his general labor relations experience, his knowledge of contractual provisions elsewhere, and his specific knowledge of negotiations elsewhere.

Since the mediator is in a position to know the priorities on both sides of the table, he may with caution attempt to influence them in the direction of settlement. If a union "must" can be matched up with a company "yes or maybe," or vice versa, it may be possible to remove some issues from controversy early in the proceedings. Or, more likely, the information will be tucked away in the mediator's mind for use when it appears likely to contribute to progress.

In short, smoking out priorities is a process by which the mediator can contribute to the substance of dispute settlement.

Deflating Extreme Positions

The difficult cases are those in which several of the same items are high on the priority lists of both sides and important objectives point in opposite directions. This situation can result in a complete deadlock. Something has to give if continued stalemate is to be avoided. At an appropriate time, a mediator may attempt a process sometimes known as "deflating extreme positions."

An extreme position is not necessarily "extreme" as an arbitrator might view it. It may have very considerable intrinsic merit. However, it can be extreme if it is almost certainly unattainable in the case at hand. For example, in the 1966 General Electric-IUE negotiations, improved grievance arbitration was a high-priority union objective — an objective that had been achieved years earlier in most other industrial plants. However, company opposition was so great that this priority had to be abandoned in order to secure an agreement. The company, for its part, had to compromise materially its longstanding and high-priority opposition to retroactive pay. The mediators in that case acted vigorously to assist the parties in retreating from these high-priority positions. Their efforts, however, were not necessarily reflective of their personal views on the two issues.

Attempts by mediators to deflate extreme positions almost always are made in separate meetings. It is ordinarily both unwise and unproductive to do or say something in a joint meeting that is, in effect, strengthening the position of one party on a particular issue.

Mediators sometimes are criticized for hard-hitting deflation activity. Unquestionably, such attempts are designed to assist one party on the issue in question. Since this is the case, is the mediator maintaining his necessary impartiality?

It would be nice to be able to say that the mediator always maintains his impartiality by balancing his attempts to deflate, offsetting efforts on one issue with efforts in the other direction on other issues. Candor does not permit that easy answer in many cases. It is clear that the mediator must be just as ready and willing to push in one direction as he is in the other direction. However, the hard facts of some cases do result in what may seem to be an imbalance.

Mediator impartiality is absolutely essential. However, impartiality cannot be judged by activity on specific issues. The costs of an unnecessary strike to the union and to employees or the costs to a company of an unwise decision to take a strike may be even more important in the total equation.

There can be no doubt that really hard-hitting deflation activities entail risks. It is even possible that the mediator may make himself *persona non grata*. If his judgments, either on the issue being discussed or on the overall aspects of the case, are in error, as they can be, it is possible for a mediator to render a disservice to the parties.

These risks dictate some caution. But it is the author's considered opinion that there are many situations in which risks must be taken if a mediator is to be truly effective. And if his judgment and persuasive ability are good, the parties will respect him for taking risks.

Offering Creative Suggestions on Specific Issues

A safer and sometimes more productive mediation function is the suggestion of alternative solutions to specific problems. If the mediator has the requisite combination of imagination and experience, he should be able to make one or more suggestions for resolution of a specific issue that have not been advanced by either of the parties. Occasionally the suggestion may appropriately be characterized as a compromise. Frequently it is more than a compromise. Sometimes the suggestion may originate out of the mediator's experience, either as a one-time bargainer or as a mediator in other cases. Not infrequently it may be a substantially new idea that he devises out of the specific facts and circumstances of the current case.

It should not be assumed that suggestions from the mediator are always welcomed. Sometimes the strategy of the parties includes adherence to firm positions on a given issue, at least until just before a deadline. A premature mediator suggestion could upset such strategy. Resultant irritation might then prevent any serious consideration of the merits of a proposal that might have been accepted if made at the right time.

For this and other reasons, mediator suggestions normally are made separately to one or the other of the parties in the first instance. If the suggestion is untimely, that fact will be apparent quickly. If the suggestion is totally unacceptable, the other side does not even need to know about it. If the suggestion does appear to be acceptable, the mediator can exercise his judgment as to when or whether it should be proposed to the other party.

Mediator suggestions on specific issues are part of the "trying on for size" process that can be of substantial assistance in ultimate resolution of a dispute.

Assessing Costs of a Strike Against Values of Remaining Issues

As negotiations approach a deadline and significant differences remain, both parties must make hard decisions. In general terms the issue then becomes: "Are the values of the remaining issues worth the costs of a strike?"

Normally the parties are fully aware of the implications of the decisions that each must make. This is the most critical time in the entire negotiating period. Positions will firm up or one or both sides will concede enough to make a settlement. This is also the time that may be most crucial for mediation activity. If the mediator has any tricks left in his bag, this may be the time to use them.

One affirmative function that a mediator can exercise is to emphasize the costs of a strike. Adequate recognition of such costs is a necessary requisite to movement on the issues. The parties should be even more aware of the costs than the mediator, but in their preoccupation the negotiators may have lost sight of them. If the mediator has equipped himself with factual information as to what has happened in similar past circumstances to the same parties or in comparable situations elsewhere, he can do much to emphasize strike costs.

Such efforts can include calculations of the costs of each day of a strike and assessments of possible duration. It is not infrequent for one or both parties to assume a short strike when the realities are quite different.

Recommending a "Package" Settlement

Up to this point, mediator suggestions have been considered solely as ideas for resolution of specific issues. The affirmative function to be considered here is a so-called package recommendation designed to effect total settlement of the case and therefore including all remaining issues in dispute.

The timing of such a recommendation is normally reserved, in the first instance, *to the last few hours before a strike*. The parties face a strike and know it. They have assessed the costs of a strike against the values of the remaining issues. Concessions, if any, have been inadequate to produce a settlement. All procedural proposals to avoid or delay a strike have been considered and rejected.

A second set of circumstances may arise when a strike is in progress, has persisted for some time, and the prospects for early settlement are dim.

Making a package recommendation is not a function that is exercised frequently. The conditions outlined in the preceding paragraphs are substantial limitations. Additional considerations and conditions can be discussed best by attempting to describe five different types of possible recommendations.

A first and best occasion for a package recommendation is in a face-saving situation. For a variety of possible reasons neither party is prepared to make a final proposal that will avoid a strike. However, if the mediator will make a recommendation, it will be accepted by both sides. The content of the package is known to both sides in advance. Both parties have privately committed themselves to acceptance.

A purist might say that if the parties are willing to use this method, they should be able to reach agreement by themselves. This criticism ignores certain bargaining realities. Pride and face are important aspects of human behavior, even in a non-Oriental society. In public or bargaining-table statements, both parties may have gone out on a limb too far to retreat without an assist. The mediator recommendation provides just the necessary element for agreement. Moreover, some parts of the package may be ideas that have been advanced by the mediator.

A second and less desirable occasion for a recommendation is essentially the same as the first, with one significant exception. The mediator knows in advance that the package will have substantial support from negotiators on both sides of the table but that one or both committees will be divided as to its acceptability. Will the fact of a recommendation provide the necessary "handle" for securing strong majority acceptance within each of the bargaining committees? Even if that is likely, will a resulting tentative agreement be ratified by the membership? It is possible that the lack of complete unanimity within the union committee foreshadows membership rejection. These factors will raise serious questions in the mediator's mind as to whether he will make the recommendation. However, when the alternative is a certain and immediate strike or the indefinite continuance of a prolonged strike, the odds will usually favor making the effort.

A third and still less desirable occasion is a situation where the mediator cannot be certain that his recommendation will be accepted by anybody. Circumstances prevent attempts to secure commitments in advance, or attempts have been made and have been unsuccessful. The mediator has only a strong hunch that acceptance will be obtained.

Whether the recommendation will be made under such circumstances depends on several factors. How strong is the hunch? Is the dispute one of great public significance? What are the mediator's best guesses as to strike duration and cost to the public? If the public interest is significantly affected, what are the next probable steps by government? No attempt can be made here to speculate as to how a mediator will answer such questions in hypothetical situations. Nor would it be advisable to illustrate by specific instances of concluded cases. To do so would violate, in almost every instance, the cardinal principle of confidentiality. It suffices to say that in the wide experience of the Federal Mediation and Conciliation Service, a number of hunch recommendations have been made. The success record is by no means perfect, but the batting average has been good.

A fourth possible occasion is where the mediator knows with reasonable certainty that any package that he might propose would not be accepted. However, he is equally certain that a process of recommendation and partial rejection will substantially narrow the issues in dispute. The strike will occur or continue, but the case will be left in better shape for eventual settlement because the issues have been reduced appreciably.

If the mediator makes a recommendation under such circumstances, there is a possibility that his future usefulness in that case will be limited. Since a mediator's basic task is to conduct himself so as to contribute to the earliest possible settlement of a dispute, he may act anyway. It should be clear that he will not act unless he is quite certain that the narrowing of issues will be significant. A rejected recommendation that does not accomplish that result can be worse than futile.

A fifth possible occasion is where the gap between the positions of the parties is so great that no successful recommendation can be made. Moreover, the best speculation is that a recommendation will only muddy the negotiations and probably lengthen the dispute. Discussion of this situation requires few words. No recommendation should be made.

It should be apparent from this outline of five different types of situations that good judgment on the part of the mediator is essential. First, it may be critical to the content of the recommendation. Second, good judgment is required as to timing, method of presentation, and especially whether to act or not to act.

A few more observations about mediator recommendations are necessary. It has been noted already and should be emphasized that they will be made only occasionally. Their use is by no means a standard practice.

Moreover, recommendations will normally not be public recommendations. They will be made privately to the negotiators. Neither the fact of a recommendation nor its content will normally be publicized except with the approval of the parties. And if publicity is desired, the text should be cleared with the negotiators. Public recommendations have been made within the experience of the Federal Mediation and Conciliation Service in recent years. However, the extremely limited number and special circumstances of these public recommendations suggest that private action is much to be preferred. It should also be noted that even the fact of a mediator recommendation was never made public in a majority of all cases known to the author within the experience of the FMCS.

An important third element of the process is preparation of the parties for the recommendation. Normally, even the possibility of such a step will not have been discussed with the parties or even considered by the mediator until quite close to the strike deadline. Unless it is a face-saver, the first warning will not occur until after it is almost certain that a strike will occur. At that point the mediator should sound out the principal negotiators and obtain their reactions to the procedure. The recommendations will ordinarily not be disclosed then. They may not even be fully formulated in the mediator's own mind. If the parties acquiesce or approve, the mediator has a green light to go ahead. If one or both parties protest vehemently against the idea, the mediator will take the reactions into account in determining whether to proceed.

Under no circumstances should the parties be surprised by a

recommendation thrown at them without warning. In no small number of cases, a tentative proposal to make a recommendation has provided the necessary thrust to promote a last-ditch conference and agreement by the parties. Under some circumstances the parties have adjusted their thinking to a certain strike. The threat of a recommendation, if the word "threat" is used in the best sense, may be more potent than a strike threat.

Procedurally, the content of a mediator recommendation is normally made known at a joint meeting of the negotiating committees, though on occasion it may be made to a smaller joint subcommittee. It may either be reduced to writing or made orally. Some time should be provided for each side to caucus and consider its answer to the mediator. Those answers should be given only to the mediator and at substantially identical times.

A final note may be most important. Discussion of the five types of situations should make it obvious that *the mediator must always reserve to himself the decision as to whether or not he will make a recommendation.* If this occasional function should become standard practice, or if to get a recommendation should be construed as a right of either party, the generally adverse results would do more than nullify any accomplishments. There would be an almost certain tendency for some negotiators to key their strategy to a recommendation instead of to normal bargaining. It should be noted in this connection that in several FMCS cases one party pleaded for a recommendation and the mediator steadfastly refused to so act.

CHAPTER VI

MEDIATION:
WHETHER, WHEN, HOW, AND BY WHOM?

What factors determine whether any mediation assistance should be proffered or utilized? At what stage of negotiations should mediation begin? Do any basic policy questions underlie the use or nonuse by a mediator of the various potential functions outlined in Chapter V? Who should mediate? These questions about mediation can be shortened to ask: whether, when, how, and by whom?

WHETHER TO MEDIATE

Direct agreement by the parties without any assistance or intervention should be the desired objective in every contract negotiation. In an ideal industrial relations world, all mediators would be unemployed.

Mediators are not present at about 85 percent of the bargaining tables in the United States. They appear to be needed for the remaining fraction of the new-contract bargaining universe. Several factors influence the use or nonuse of mediation.

Legislative Status of Mediation

At the federal level, the Taft-Hartley Act includes three provisions pertinent to the "whether to mediate" question.

The first is the 30-day-notice provision, found in Section 8 (d)(3) of Title I of the Act. The Federal Mediation and Conciliation Service and any appropriate state mediation agency are to be notified, in writing, of negotiations for renewals of labor agreements in all instances affecting interstate commerce where such negotiations could result in a strike or a lockout. This is a routine, blanket early warning arrangement. The Congress clearly intended that the statutory agencies should know, 30 days in advance of each deadline date, that a crisis could arise.

The second is Section 203(b) of Title II of the Act. It reads:

"The Service may proffer its services in any labor dispute in any industry affecting commerce either *upon its own motion* or *upon request of one or more of the parties* to the dispute, *whenever in its judgment* such dispute threatens to cause a substantial interruption of commerce. The Director and the Service are directed to avoid attempting to mediate disputes which would have only a minor effect on interstate commerce if State or other conciliation services are available to the parties. Whenever the Service does proffer its services in any dispute it shall be the duty of the Service promptly to put itself in communication with the parties and to use its best efforts, by mediation and conciliation, to bring them to agreement." [1]

The third relevant provision is found in Section 204(a) (3), which reads:

"In order to prevent or minimize interruptions of the free flow of commerce growing out of labor disputes, *employers and employees and their representatives,* in any industry affecting commerce, *shall*—
(3) in case such dispute is not settled by conference *participate fully and promptly* in such meetings as may be undertaken by the Service under this Act for the purpose of aiding in the settlement of the dispute." [2]

Provisions of the Railway Labor Act are not the same as in the Taft-Hartley Act. However, it suffices to say at this point that the general import of that statute with respect to mediation by the National Mediation Board is not sufficiently different to warrant special attention here. Similarly, no attempt will be made to review the provisions of the various state laws in those states that have mediation agencies. The laws differ but the variations are primarily of language rather than intent.

In all these statutes, the legislative preference is that the parties reach agreement by direct negotiation. Mediation services are provided at public expense for use when needed. In each actual or threatened dispute, the real question as to whether mediation will be utilized depends primarily on the interplay of agency policy and the attitudes of the parties about mediation.

Positions of the Parties Regarding Mediation

The Taft-Hartley Act provision that both companies and unions "shall" cooperate regarding meetings arranged by the Federal Mediation and Conciliation Service has a compulsory implication. When the word "shall" is used in labor relations circles, it is normally intended to be a strong word.

[1] Italics supplied.
[2] Italics supplied.

However, in reality, there is no compulsion. On infrequent occasions, companies or unions have simply refused to attend scheduled meetings. For two reasons no attempt has ever been made to test the meaning of the Act. The law is silent as to enforcement powers and indicates elsewhere that failure of either party to agree to a procedure suggested by the FMCS is not a violation of obligations imposed by the Act. The more important reason is that legally enforced attendance, even if available, might be counterproductive. A mediator is not likely to be useful if he is not wanted by at least one of the parties, and it is preferable that he be welcomed by both. Thus, even the active entry of a mediator in a case requires the acceptance or at least acquiescence of both parties. This fact emphasizes the voluntary aspect of the process.

A few unions and companies have adopted general policies about mediation. By resolution at conventions or by publicly known executive action, three international unions have adopted a basic policy that no strike will be sanctioned by the international until after the local union has indicated willingness to utilize the services of the FMCS at the bargaining table. These unions are (1) the International Association of Machinists and Aerospace Workers, (2) the Oil, Chemical and Atomic Workers, and (3) the American Federation of Technical Engineers. The Machinists have observed this policy quite consistently, the other two unions somewhat less so. As a practical matter, the effectiveness of such a policy depends on whether the international union has control of strike funds.

The author knows of no international union that maintains a consistent official policy of outright opposition to mediation. However, there are a few international unions which are hostile in some circumstances and would not always welcome a mediator. For example, the former president of the International Typographical Union made public statements a few years ago opposing mediation by the FMCS. However, several local unions of the ITU were requesting FMCS mediation within the time periods covered by those statements.

A union may resist mediation traditionally in certain specific negotiations but generally welcome it in other negotiations. For example, the United Automobile Workers typically resist officially active mediation in the key negotiations with the "Big Three" (General Motors, Ford, and Chrysler). This is so despite occasional public utterances to the contrary. On the other hand, the UAW frequently and even typically welcomes mediation in a very large number of other negotiations.

On the company side, attitudes have about the same range that has been noted for unions. Some few companies, usually small, are so favorably inclined towards mediation that they prefer not to begin contract negotiations until a mediator is at the table. A number of companies resist mediation strongly under almost all circumstances. It is no secret, for example, that UAW resistance to officially active mediation at General Motors is more than matched by company opposition. Since a specific illustration of joint resistance has been cited, it should be observed that both the GM and the UAW opposition is to the normal functioning of a mediator as a participant in and chairman of negotiating sessions. No such resistance has been evident in recent years to certain other types of mediation activity. For example, in 1961 both parties accepted a proposal of the Director of the FMCS, for postponement of a strike and were receptive to certain other mediation activities that year and subsequently. Moreover, General Motors welcomed assistance in the difficult task of avoiding strikes one year at plants where its employees are represented by the International Union of Electrical Workers.

The attitudes of most companies and most unions are reflections of a different form of general policy. It is a pragmatic and hard-headed appraisal on a case-by-case basis. Whether mediation will be welcomed, tolerated, or resisted depends on the status of the particular dispute at the time the question is raised. In other words, attitudes will vary from one dispute to another and from time to time in the same dispute.

This pragmatic approach presents no substantial problems if both parties take similar positions at the same time. If both want to be left alone, the mediator should stay out. If both recognize that assistance is needed, the mediator will be truly welcomed.

The problem arises, of course, when one side seeks mediation assistance—sometimes almost desperately—and the other side resists strongly.

Both union and company reactions to possible mediation intervention are influenced materially by their ideas of the competence, integrity and impartiality of the mediation agency. When the identity of the individual mediator is known or can be determined in advance, impressions of that person as a mediator may also affect attitudes. Companies or unions occasionally "blackball" a mediator, either as a result of past experiences or because of comments made by others. In that event, it may not make much practical difference in a specific case whether adverse reaction is well-founded or in error. Even if it is totally baseless, it can limit the mediator's usefulness in that case unless the parties have reason to change their opinion. More often, parties express preferences for mediators they know and respect.

Mediation agencies usually attempt to give some consideration to reactions of the parties to individual mediators. However, flexibility of assignment is curtailed by the size of the mediation staff at any location and by the extent to which mediators are unavailable because of assignments elsewhere. For these reasons, *the agency necessarily controls and determines the identity of the mediator.*

In areas served both by the Federal Mediation and Conciliation Service and a state agency, individual companies and unions may have strong preferences for one agency or the other.

Thus, support for mediation in the law does not by any means imply complete acceptance of mediation by the parties. The simple but fundamental fact is that mediation must "sell itself" by performance. This is as it should be.

Mediation Agency Policy and Its Effectuation

Should mediators be "hard to get" or should they push hard to effect entrance into a case? Most persons would agree that neither extreme is desirable. If the agency is too reluctant or too slow in providing assistance when it is wanted and needed, the intent of the law and public policy may be frustrated. But, an "eager beaver" attitude may well be an irritant to the parties.

Agencies establish general policy somewhere between the two extremes. In the interest of promoting maximum direct negotiation, policy should be slightly on the hard-to-get side. Statements of agency policy do not disclose very much. This is not because of any desire to conceal; it is because there are inevitable differences among disputes that defy clear distinctions.

Agency policy is effectuated in two steps. The first is the administrative handling of initial requests for assistance or of notices of potential disputes. The second and probably more significant step is the behavior of individual mediators in handling assignments.

Review of the procedures utilized by the Federal Mediation and Conciliation Service will illustrate the basic policy of one agency and how it may be effectuated. Administrative handling of cases begins with the 30-day notices required by the Taft-Hartley Act. These notices are received at the one of seven FMCS regional offices in which the potential dispute may arise. In the case of multiplant companies with a single negotiation embracing more than one region, the notice or notices will be received by or routed to the region in which the negotiations occur.

The 30-day notices do not represent the entire input of potential cases. Since the early 1960s it has been National Labor Relations Board practice to send copies of new certifications to the FMCS regional offices. A new certification occurs when a union wins an election. It is then ready to start bargaining with the employer for an initial agreement. Before that cooperative arrangement was in effect, it was a common occurrence for the FMCS to find out about a newly certified union only after a strike had started. The most important future negotiations in a region, at defense plants in particular, are listed on a calendar in each regional office long before receipt of the 30 day notices.

A principal task of the assistant regional director, one of the two supervisory officials in each regional office, is to screen, consolidate, and assign cases to mediators in the region.

The screening process consists of weeding out those cases in which the need for mediation appears slight. The potential dispute may be too small to be considered under the "substantial interruption of commerce" criterion of the Act. Or, it may be a negotiation in which the parties traditionally and habitually do not require mediation. Or, it may be a negotiation where the parties normally utilize the services of a state mediation agency or should use those services. The assistant regional director is a person who is thoroughly familiar with labor relations in the region. His initial judgment is therefore an informed opinion. The screening process tentatively eliminates a large number of notices.

The next process is called consolidation. Consolidation is a grouping of two or more notices into a single potential mediation assignment in instances of employer association or established coordinated bargaining where it is known that one bargaining table will cover multiple notices.

The potential mediation cases left after screening and consolidation are then assigned to the mediators in the region and become known as "assigned cases." Based on knowledge of past negotiations and the negotiators, reactions of the parties to individual mediators in recent years, respective work loads, and other factors, the objective of the assignment process is to utilize the existing mediation staff at each office with greatest effectiveness.

At any moment in the busy periods of a year, a mediator may have 20 or more assigned cases in his file. The list is changing constantly as settlements are made and new assignments are received. An assigned case becomes the mediator's personal responsibility.

The first mediator activity, known as "initial inquiry," is to check with the principal negotiators on each side in each case, usually by telephone, to ascertain the status of negotiations, to advise the parties of the assignment, and to establish arrangements for further contacts, if any. Most telephone calls, reports and other information received thereafter for each case are routed directly to the assigned mediator.

Subsequently, as the deadline approaches in each assigned case, the mediator will check periodically with the parties to ascertain the status of the negotiations. In important cases, many such checks are made by means of person-to-person conversations, supplemented by telephone conversations.

At some point in this process, direct negotiations may be successful. The mediator receives a brief report of the settlement and files a report to the office, closing the case. Not infrequently a mediator whom the parties know well may perform a meaningful mediation function without even entering the bargaining rooms.

An assigned case becomes an "active case," in FMCS terminology, the moment the mediator sits for the first time at the bargaining table. Normally the case remains active and continues to be the responsibility of the same mediator until it has been settled. Easy active cases may be settled by the parties a few hours after the formal entry of the mediator. Difficult cases, especially those involving long strikes, may remain active for a long period of time.

Only about one half of the cases assigned to FMCS mediators ever become active cases.

Thus, FMCS policy hinges on the administrative thoroughness

or toughness practiced by an assistant regional director in the initial screening process and on the attitudes of the individual mediators as they confer with the parties in the cases that are assigned to them. If a mediator should be overburdened with assignments or be lazy or negligent, he may get into a case actively only when the parties insist vigorously that he enter. In some such instances mediation may be needed and not provided. If the mediator is an "eager beaver," he may enter a few cases in which he is not needed. The assistant regional director tries, with considerable success, to level out the extremes by administrative methods. However, it would not be accurate to say that no inconsistencies exist.

Official policies of the several state agencies vary. A few administrators favor a "hard to get" policy and believe that the state mediators should not enter a dispute until there is evidence of a complete stalemate and a formal or semiformal request has been received. At the other extreme, one state pursued a policy for a period of time of sending letters to the parties, signed by the governor, strongly suggesting state mediation. Those letters were sent routinely upon receipt of every 30-day Taft-Hartley notice. Actual policies of most state agencies do not differ markedly from FMCS policy. As with FMCS procedures, it is probable that policy in any state is influenced materially by the methods of operation of the individual mediators.

It is evident that there is no one clear or consistent answer to the whether-to-mediate question. Varying attitudes of companies and unions, reasonable consistency of basic administrative policies by the agencies, and less consistent practices of individual mediators all interact to produce the total result. Nor is it possible to say that about 85 percent of bargaining without mediation and about 15 percent with mediation was an optimum split for the year 1968.

The two important conclusions that can be reached are (1) that mediation must sell itself by performance and (2) that even the most effective mediation should not be utilized unless it is needed. The first conclusion requires maintenance of the best possible mediation services. The second conclusion requires appraisal of the overall health of collective bargaining at the particular moment. The existing methods of answering the whether-to-mediate question, imperfect as they are, have been time-tested by the industrial relations community and by the agencies. The question is answered realistically and not by any neat, concise formula.

WHEN SHOULD MEDIATION BEGIN?

Once the threshold question of whether a mediator should enter a case has been resolved affirmatively, the next question is the timing of entry.

The "whether" and "when" questions are frequently interrelated closely. In some situations the mediator is wanted just as quickly as possible after the decision to seek mediation assistance has been reached. If his work schedule permits, he may be at his first meeting quickly—like a fire fighter answering an alarm. However, it is more likely that the parties will advise the mediator that he will be needed but that the appropriate time for entry has not yet arrived. A time and date in the near future are agreed upon. Or, the mediator may be requested to keep himself as available as possible but to wait for further advice as to the best time.

As noted earlier, there are a few companies and unions that would like to have a mediator present continuously from the outset of negotiations. Their rationale is that the mediator will contribute something from the beginning, primarily procedurally and to facilitate communications, and thus a possible stalemate may be avoided. Moreover, if a serious deadlock should develop, the mediator will be fully aware of everything that has happened and will be ready immediately to take more affirmative action.

The opposite extreme is a company or union position that the mediator should not intervene until a deadlock appears certain. Since the existence of a stalemate is not always certain until a strike has begun, some companies and unions consider an actual strike to be the appropriate signal for entry. A few bargainers who adhere to this general approach would not even accept the beginning of a strike as the proper time. They hold that the strike should persist for a period of time and that the mediator should not enter the case until it becomes evident that the strike is not performing its function of changing positions.

These extreme positions may be taken by companies and unions in good faith and without firm resistance to the general concept of mediation.

Mediation agencies and individual mediators within each agency may have conceptual notions or policies that differ appreciably. The extremes of position are not likely to be as wide as the company and union positions described above, but the differences can be very real. It is impossible to describe an "ideal" time of entry. However, certain boundaries, substantially narrower than the extremes noted above, can be suggested.

It is not good policy for a mediator to sit at all negotiation sessions. Even if he could be useful in the early stages of negotiations, his assistance would not be of major significance and would be violative of the basic principle that direct negotiation is the desirable objective. Too much and too long familiarity with a case and with the parties has a tendency to lessen the likelihood that the mediator will take aggressive steps if they should be required. Moreover, no mediation agency has a large enough staff to provide this type of service even if it should be desired.

Thus, at one end of the optimum spectrum, it is suggested that the mediator should not enter a case until it becomes reasonably clear to the principal negotiators that the negotiations are "in trouble" or soon will be. This is not an exact definition, but experienced negotiators can usually make reasonably accurate predictions.

At the other extreme, it is seldom desirable to delay the entry of a mediator until a strike has been in effect for some time. It is not even desirable to wait until a deadlock has been demonstrated by the beginning of a strike. Positions tend to become frozen. A strike almost invariably adds new issues. Many of the potential mediation functions discussed in Chapter V cannot even be considered in a strike situation. For these various reasons, the other end of the optimum range is before a strike and hopefully before a deadlock on issues becomes firm.

This narrower optimum time spectrum, beginning after trouble seems certain to the negotiators and ending before a deadlock on issues is firm and certainly before an actual strike starts, normally will represent a span of time. In some cases the certainty of major trouble is known months before the deadline. In other situations there is only a few hours' warning.

In actual practice the time of entry in any case will be influenced by very real problems in definition of an optimum range, by the attitudes of both parties if their concepts are

different, and occasionally by the mediator's work-load problems. If he has two or three assigned cases "peaking" at the
same time, one will have to be given priority. Entry into the
other cases may necessarily be deferred longer than is desirable
unless they can be reassigned to other mediators. These considerations are among the matters that the mediator will be discussing with the parties in the course of securing status reports
on the various assigned cases before they become active cases.

Normally the time of entry is a matter agreed to among the
principal negotiators for each side and the mediator. Occasionally it is an "own motion" decision by the mediator. Timing
usually is worked out by the individual mediators without supervision. In important or difficult situations, the mediator will
consult with his supervisor.

HOW TO USE OR NOT TO USE POTENTIAL
MEDIATION FUNCTIONS

Assuming that the mediator now is at the bargaining table,
what does he do? The obvious first move is to meet all the negotiators. This is accomplished informally as quickly as possible.
The relationship in the next few hours and days will be most
informal. Establishment of a first-name basis at the outset is desirable.

If the parties are not accustomed to mediation, an extremely
brief statement of purpose and function may be necessary. Ver-
bosity or detailed explanation could be fatal.

Within a very short time the parties in joint session should
then review the status of the case with the mediator. Issues in
dispute will be listed, normally with indications of concession,
if any, that have been made by each party on those issues. At
least some mention may be made of issues that have been settled. At this juncture the verbal description of the disputed issues should be brief. This initial meeting serves two purposes.
The primary purpose is to acquaint the mediator with the
overall scope of the dispute. A secondary purpose is to enable
the parties to make sure in each other's presence of the status
of the dispute.

A major purpose of the earlier conversations and informal
status reports that have occurred prior to entry of the mediator
at the bargaining table is to shorten these initial procedures.
Moreover, if the mediator has not been too busy elsewhere,
he will have done some homework prior to entry in order to

acquaint himself as well as possible with the background of the dispute. If the mediator is a resident mediator, as is usually the case, he may be familiar with the parties and with at least some of the problems. Especially is this so if he has participated in earlier recent negotiations. In such instances the preliminary activities will consume very little time.

After the initial joint meeting the mediator will usually meet separately with the parties to obtain more detailed information about their respective positions on the issues.

From this point on there simply are no fixed rules or procedures. The variables are so many that it would be an exercise in futility to attempt to describe either typical or model mediator behavior with respect to sequence, timing, or use and nonuse of the various functions theoretically available. Essentially the mediator's task is to work with the parties by exercising such of those functions described in Chapter V as may be appropriate to that case.

There are a few comments that can be made about the philosophy that should underlie the many judgment decisions that must be made. *One basic principle, designed to promote the maximum of direct negotiation, is that the mediator should do just as little as is required.* If he can confine his activities to appropriate procedural functions, he should do so. If procedural activity is not enough, he may find it necessary to attempt communication functions. If this does not suffice, he may then have to consider using those functions that are more aggressive and hard-hitting.

It cannot be said that the suggested sequence is a nice, orderly one in which the mediator consciously closes one type of activity and begins another. On the contrary, the various functions may overlap. The sequence is suggested primarily to amplify the basic conceptual notion that assistance by the mediator should be proffered only in those areas in which it is needed, and then only to the extent necessary to promote progress by the parties themselves.

If a mediator makes mistakes in judgment as to use or timing of a function or in qualitative performance of a function, as he will, all is not lost. The parties always have the right to reject even a procedural move. Nor are they bashful in exercise of that right. No mediator can afford to be thin-skinned or resentful if people do not agree with him. On the other hand, he must be sufficiently sensitive to know immediately why he is being rebuffed. If an activity or function is unsuccessful, this simply means that that road is probably closed, and it is necessary to try another. The more difficult stalemated disputes may be settled only after a long series of persistent and imaginative approaches have been tried by the parties and the mediator.

In Chapter V the "try on for size" function was described in two different ways. One of the parties may ask the mediator to explore an idea or proposal with the other side. The mediator is then performing a communication function; it is not his idea. The party proposing it wants to get a reaction without making a commitment. In mediation lingo this is an "in the pocket" idea or prospective solution. If it is accepted by the other side, that issue is probably settled and the agreement can be revealed at the appropriate time.

The second aspect of the "try on for size" function is an idea or proposal originated by the mediator. It has no utility whatever unless it is accepted by one or both parties. If it is accepted by one party, it also becomes an "in the pocket" idea or prospective solution.

Mediators are sometimes accused of deception in the way they exercise the "try on for size" function. In the first place, the mediator may not reveal the source of the idea. Did it originate with the other party, or is it the mediator's "trial balloon"? Secondly, if the mediator has one side's acceptance "in the pocket," irrespective of the source of the idea, he may not reveal that fact immediately.

When the "try on for size" exercise is successful, it usually happens that the source of the idea becomes known to the parties at some point of time. In the meantime, absence of full knowledge by the parties of all the circumstances is not deception. It is a necessary aspect of the mediator's confidential relationship. In any event, the idea will usually "sink or float" on its own merits and the source is largely irrelevant.

Another observation can be of importance in some cases. The concentrated stresses of difficult negotiations reveal personality strengths and weaknesses including varying degrees of basic integrity, in ways that are seldom equalled in other activity. A lifetime friendship can be established in two or three days that is based more soundly than one built on two or three years of more normal social or business contact. The reverse is also true. Weaknesses can be so exposed that they are not readily forgotten. The mediator is also subject to such appraisals.

In rare instances, a mediator may be attacked publicly by a negotiator. Regardless of the validity or lack of validity of the attack, a public response in kind by the mediator serves no useful purpose. On other rare occasions, a negotiator will "welsh" on a commitment. Public exposure of such a circumstance by the mediator almost never will settle the dispute. The more likely result is to make it worse.

In short, in addition to the general principle that the mediator should remain in the background as much as possible in publicity releases, any comments that he may properly make should be directed to the issues and not to the personalities.

To close this section on how to mediate, it should be apparent that words are quite inadequate. *Mediation is an art; so is collective bargaining.* Individual mediators are good, bad, or indifferent artists, and most have their good, bad, and indifferent cases. All that has been attempted in this section and in Chapter V is to try to describe the various tools, materials, and techniques that may be used and to make a few pragmatic suggestions as to use or nonuse. Understanding and sensitivity, disciplined by experience and intellect, will determine actual performance. The mediator's role in any one dispute will be little or great, depending on the skill of the principal company and union artisans and his own skill in blending with their performance.

MEDIATION—BY WHOM?

Solo mediation—one mediator in an active capacity, staying with a dispute from start to finish—is the normal variety. It may be modified on occasion by transfer of a case from one mediator to another in midstream due to illness, unexpected peak work-load problems, or for other reasons. This circumstance does not materially alter the dominant solo mediation practice.

Is the mediator a federal mediator, a state mediator, or an individual not employed regularly by a mediation agency? And under what circumstances is there a departure from solo mediation—simultaneous participation by two or more mediators in the same dispute?

Professional v. Amateur

Mediation is not a profession comparable to that of law or medicine. No school or university awards the degree of "Mediator." No professional society of mediators exists. Anybody can claim to be a mediator, but proof of that claim is found only in demonstrated effective performance.

The rough equivalent of professional status is enjoyed by those individuals, in or out of government, who have demonstrated by experience that they are competent and impartial. Competence and impartiality cannot be assessed with complete objectivity. Frequently the judgment is based on an informal, somewhat hit-or-miss, and subjective compendium of information derived from labor, industry, and neutral practitioners in labor relations who have worked with the individual. The totality of opinion permits canceling out the biased or casual extremes of pro or con appraisal. No two lists of professionals would be identical, but most lists would be reasonably consistent.

Who are the amateurs or nonprofessionals? One group consists of those well-intentioned, frequently influential citizens who have concern for the consequences of industrial disorder but who have little or no experience in the highly complicated industrial relations arena. A second group consists of individuals who are experienced industrial relations practitioners but whose experience has been so closely related to one side or the other for so long a period of time that they are widely considered not to be impartial. Many such individuals are badly misjudged. It has been demonstrated that they can be impartial and most effective as mediators.

A third group includes some impartial arbitrators who have extensive industrial relations knowledge, experience, and general know-how. Their experience has been limited almost solely to decision-making. The binding aspect of arbitration does not necessarily subject the arbitrator to the disciplines of acceptability and humility. In fact, some arbitrators are quite sensitive when their decisions are criticized on the merits. When he attempts to act as a mediator, an experienced arbitrator may have great difficulty in avoiding formulation of "his" answers to the issues in dispute, and he may be too ready to suggest those answers. When he is rebuffed, what has been a two-way dispute can degenerate into a three-way dispute.

Another problem encountered by experienced arbitrators is that their work may have been limited solely to grievances. Decisions on grievances are made within the general or quite specific framework of a labor agreement. When it is the provisions of an agreement that are in dispute, there is no comparable framework.

These limitations do not necessarily mean that a labor arbitrator cannot be or cannot become a mediator. In fact, some of the most professional mediators, as defined earlier, are outstanding arbitrators. However, it is a regrettable fact that only a small percentage of professional arbitrators are now also acknowledged in the labor relations community to be professional mediators.

A fourth group consists of a few of the mediators who have been employed by federal or state agencies, sometimes for many years. They have been "too good to be fired" but have not qualified fully in the true professional sense.

For obvious reasons negotiators prefer to work with professional mediators if they have a choice. In fact, some experienced negotiators who would otherwise welcome mediation would prefer to "go it alone" rather than work with an amateur. Despite this general reaction, amateurs may sometimes be successful. Zeal, good intentions, and public influence can offset lack of professional skill under some circumstances.

These observations are not intended to be hypercritical or to glorify the professional traits and qualifications. They are the "facts of life" that will be cited by experienced negotiators when they are in need of assistance.

There is a shortage of professional mediators. The demand exceeds the supply. All available means should be utilized to develop a larger group. Training programs of the established agencies fill only part of the need. They are confined to filling full-time staff vacancies. No fully satisfactory program exists to enlarge the small group of private professional mediators who can be available for part-time or occasional work. There are many amateur mediators in labor arbitration ranks and among past or present labor or management representatives who have the inherent qualifications. More effective mechanisms should be devised to provide mediation training and experience.

Government v. Private Mediation

Why does government overwhelm private mediation quantitatively? The first reason is a simple but important problem of logistics. When a mediator is needed, he may be needed quickly and for an unpredictable time period. The unpredictability of a contract negotiation makes it almost impossible to schedule mediation time accurately in advance. In this respect also, mediation is quite different from arbitration. The relatively few private individuals who merit true professional status as mediators are very busy men. Only an important and major dispute will justify or permit them to give it the necessary priority attention. The administration problems of matching the right man with the required times and places are almost insurmountable except in an emergency. A full-time staff of mediators working for an agency creates the necessary flexibility.

A lesser part of the answer is that mediation by government agencies is free, whereas private mediation must be paid for by the parties, unless the ad hoc mediator is reimbursed by the government. The cost factor would not be major if ad hoc mediation were superior.

Unquestionably, a major reason is the short supply of available professional private mediators. As matters now stand, when parties have the choice of attempting to find a private mediator or turning to an established federal or state agency, few even try to go the private mediator route.

This is not to say that a company and a union cannot overcome these obstacles. They have done so. Certain provisions of the Kaiser-Steelworker Long Range Sharing Plan maintain what amounts to a standing mediation panel of three well-known private mediators (George W. Taylor, David L. Cole, and John T. Dunlop). The Armour Automation Committee likewise utilizes the services of private mediators in a somewhat different manner; Clark Kerr, Robben W. Fleming, and George P. Shultz have all been called upon. For several contracts prior to public ownership, the parties in the transit industry in New York City were assisted in negotiations by a panel of three mediators (George W. Taylor, David L. Cole, and Theodore W. Kheel). Theodore W. Kheel has served extensively as a private mediator in New York City.

There is unlikely to be substantial development of private mediation unless the quality of government mediation should deteriorate and/or the supply of professional private mediators should increase. Either of these eventualities could change the picture.

In a subsequent chapter, these observations will be modified as they apply to mediation and fact-finding in public-sector disputes.

Dual Mediation—Federal and State

One form of departure from solo mediation is so-called dual mediation. Its simplest and most common manifestation is joint participation by a federal and a state mediator throughout the period of active mediation of a case. The two mediators may be cochairmen of the meetings, or one may act as chairman. The lead role in checking prior to the first joint meeting attended by the mediators and the scheduling of meetings may be performed by one of the mediators, or both may participate. The federal agency assumes the dominant role in a majority of disputes, but this is by no means a universal rule. Occasionally one of the mediators will not attend some meetings. Sometimes one of the mediators enters the case after the entry of the other. These variations do not materially alter the basic facts that the two mediators are jointly responsible for the mediation activity and that each man reports back to his own agency.

Dual mediation can exist, of course, only in those states and in the few municipalities that maintain established mediation agencies. The extent of dual mediation varies markedly. In Connecticut, for example, almost all disputes except grievances are dually mediated. At the other extreme, dual mediation is quite uncommon in New Jersey and California. It is the practice on a case-by-case basis in most of the other states.

Dual mediation is only one manifestation of an active or latent jurisdiction problem. Without exception, there is some potential overlapping of jurisdiction when the Taft-Hartley Act is compared with the various state statutes of those states that maintain an active mediation agency.

Only two clear-cut jurisdictional boundaries exist between federal and state agencies. The Railway Labor Act gives exclusive jurisdiction to the National Mediation Board. By indirection, the Taft-Hartley Act preserves exclusive jurisdiction to the states in disputes that are limited to intrastate commerce.

The overlapping jurisdiction that exists with respect to all other disputes is qualified by general but somewhat ambiguous language of the Taft-Hartley Act. The FMCS is directed by the Act to avoid mediation in disputes "which would have only a minor effect on interstate commerce if State or other conciliation services are available." [3] A somewhat similar restriction is implicit in the preceding sentence where the words "a substantial interruption of commerce" are found. However, there is no

---

[3] Section 203 (b) , Title II, Labor Management Relations Act, as amended.

definition of "minor" or "substantial," and the same section of the Act further provides that the FMCS is to exercise its judgment in interpreting these words.

Most state agencies cede jurisdiction to the FMCS in negotiations that involve all plants of multiplant corporations with plants in several states. Likewise, jurisdiction is customarily yielded to the FMCS in important defense-plant disputes. However, there have been numerous exceptions with respect to both types of disputes.

The Taft-Hartley Act also contains restrictions but not prohibitions on the mediation of grievances by the FMCS. Few such restrictions exist in state statutes.

These rather generally accepted restrictions and definitions have the practical effect of giving substantial jurisdiction to the FMCS in the largest disputes and to the state agencies in the smallest disputes. The effects can be observed in those instances where it is possible to compare case statistics that are broken down by numbers of employees involved. But a great deal of caution should be associated with this large v. small line of demarcation. It simply does not hold in many situations.

Over the years, attempts have been made by the FMCS and several state agencies to develop jurisdiction criteria keyed either to size of the bargaining unit involved in the dispute or to size of the establishment. All these attempts have perished for a variety of practical reasons. Analysis suggests that the fault has been primarily due to the method and not to the personalities in the agencies. Understandably the state agencies have not been able to live with any practicable cutoff point on the high side. For equally valid reasons, the FMCS has not been able to adhere strictly to a line of demarcation on the low side. Most state agency administrators and the FMCS have been in agreement in recent years on a negative concept, even if they may have disagreed on other matters. Rigid jurisdictional criteria based solely on size of the dispute are not the answer.

Consequently, FMCS and state agency jurisdiction overlap in probably a majority of disputes in any state that maintains an active mediation agency. In those states where it is the dominant practice, dual mediation provides an easy answer for the agencies. Statutory obligations have been met, or more than met, by both agencies. The state and federal mediators know each other well and, in most instances, work well together. However, there are several objections to the arrangement.

Do the parties really want dual mediation in all instances? A study made by Robert L. Stutz,[4] based on questionnaires sent to labor and industry representatives in Connecticut, concludes that most parties like the dual mediation system. Since Connecticut is the state with the longest consistent practice of dual mediation, it may be presumptuous to question that conclusion. However, the author wonders whether the parties really favor dual mediation to that extent, especially in cases that barely require mediation at all. In a dispute at a small plant with small bargaining committees, two mediators can almost overwhelm the parties.

Another objection is that dual mediation in all cases tends to be wasteful of public funds.

Finally, too consistent reliance on dual mediation has a tendency to divide responsibility unproductively. It can even make mediators lazy or overly timid. There is a tendency for one of the mediators, either state or federal, to "let the other guy do the work." If the "other guy" is competent, the "free rider" can coast and still get credit for handling a case.

For these reasons it appears evident that dual mediation may be a desirable procedure—*but only in selected cases.* The most satisfactory federal-state relationship is one in which the respective supervisory individuals (normally regional director and/or assistant regional director of the FMCS region and the head of the state agency) have a good, pragmatic relationship, including frequent communication about cases. Most dispute cases can be divided up and handled by only one agency after due consideration of all the relevant factors. Known preferences of the parties, size of establishment, type of dispute, defense implications if they exist, ramifications of the dispute inside and outside the state, and other factors are taken into account. Dual mediation will almost always exist under such a relationship, but it will not be the dominant practice.

This type of relationship is by no means easy to maintain. Disputes between agencies and between mediators have developed that have done a disservice to professional mediation. Occasional excesses have occurred on both sides.

Sincere and productive efforts have been made to eliminate

[4] Robert L. Stutz, *Troikas, Duets and Prima Donnas in Labor Mediation,* Department of Industrial Relations, School of Business Administration, University of Connecticut, Storrs, Conn., 1963, Reprint Series (from Octiber, 1962 issue of LABOR LAW JOURNAL) .

unseemly discord. In 1964 a joint committee of the Federal Mediation and Conciliation Service and the Association of Labor Mediation Agencies developed by agreement a "Code of Professional Conduct for Labor Mediators."[5] The Code was approved by the FMCS and ratified by all important state agencies. A grievance procedure has been established under which complaints by either state or federal mediators concerning mediators of other agencies can be considered and appealed to higher levels within each group. A permanent Liaison Committee with members selected by both the FMCS and ALMA meets periodically. It considers matters of mutual concern and is ready to act on grievance problems. It would be foolhardy to suggest that all is sweetness and light in federal-state relationships, but it is a fact that all complaints that have developed since the Code was established have been worked out with reasonable expedition by conference. No dispute has been referred officially to the Liaison Committee.

The goal is to make available to the parties in each dispute requiring assistance the best and most professional mediation possible under the circumstances of that case. Whether this is accomplished best by federal mediation, by state mediation, or by dual mediation is a question that should be decided in each case on the basis of all the relevant facts and circumstances. Jurisdictional or institutional jealousies among the several agencies cannot be eliminated completely. However, they must give way to the need for professional services. If mediators should be unable to resolve differences among themselves, how can they expect to assist others?

ESCALATION OF MEDIATION WITHIN AN AGENCY

The word "escalation" is used here to mean the addition of one or more mediators under the direction of the same agency to an assigned case. Within this usage, the additional persons usually move into active work in the case at some stage without the elimination of the mediators already engaged. Additions occasionally are accompanied by the dropping out of individual mediators who have been active. This occurs when the numbers of mediators involved would otherwise become excessive. Escalation also frequently means that one or more of the additional mediators are at a higher level of the organization structure of the agency.

[5] See Appendix C for full text of the Code.

This section will relate primarily to the Federal Mediation and Conciliation Service. A few of the state agencies have occasionally utilized the escalation idea, modified to suit the smaller size of these agencies.

On the basis of FMCS practice in recent years, an escalation ladder including the following steps can be constructed:

1. Solo mediation
2. Panel of field mediators
3. Panel including regional director
4. Panel including National Representative
5. Panel including Disputes Director, Deputy Director, or Director
6. Panel including private mediator

It should not be presumed that this is a ladder in the sense that all steps will be taken. Steps may be omitted.

Solo Mediation

Solo mediation constitutes the bulk of all work performed. In fiscal year 1968, 93.6 percent of all FMCS actively mediated disputes cases were solo cases. Thus, only 6.4 percent of total cases went up the escalation ladder to any higher step.

Panel of Field Mediators

Normally, the next step beyond solo mediation is to add one field mediator to make a two-man panel. Rarely, two may be added. The additional mediator is a field mediator within the journeyman group and therefore in the same classification as the originally assigned mediator, who continues on the panel. Why would the Service add a second man? A second man occasionally is added either because FMCS supervision or the parties are not satisfied with the performance of the originally assigned mediator. However, this occurs in a very small number of instances. For the most part, the addition of the second man is in no way to be construed as evidence of dissatisfaction with the mediator already on the case.

The other reasons are many and varied. They boil down to recognition of the fact, emphasized already, that mediation is a highly individualistic and creative activity in which important judgments as to use or nonuse of potential functions, formulation of imaginative suggestions, and other determinations must be accomplished frequently and quickly. If a dispute is an especially stubborn one, experience has often demonstrated that two heads are better than one. Mediators can complement each other in personality traits, experiences in collective bargaining, and experiences in prior mediation cases. The competence of field mediators in any one region or at any one office will vary on such technical issues as job evaluation, incentives, pensions, or insurance. If the best available mediation competence is needed on one of these technical issues, it can be provided by means of a panel.

The decision to create a panel within the region is made by the regional director or assistant regional director but is frequently suggested by a field mediator who realizes that he needs help. In a few important cases, active mediation may start with a two-man panel of field mediators.

Dual mediation, discussed earlier, might have the same objectives and results as a panel. Sometimes this is the case. A federal mediator and a state mediator may complement each other. However, when this happens, it may be more by accident than by design. When a regional director selects a second man for a panel, he does not simply add any other mediator. Insofar as he is able to do so, he selects the best available man under all the circumstances of that particular case. By the time the panel is created, the problem areas are usually well known.

The use of a field panel is not a miracle-making procedure. However, its merits, when used sparingly and only for sound reasons, have been demonstrated beyond doubt. If used too frequently, it would tend to lessen the important element of individual personal responsibility that is associated with solo mediation.

Panel Including Regional Director

The regional director and the assistant regional director are the only supervisory employees in each region. By custom and practice they have been promoted from the mediator ranks, in part on the basis of their demonstrated mediation skills.

Because administrative and supervisory responsibilities are constant and extensive, the time that can be devoted to mediation is limited. However, most of the regional directors and some of the assistant regional directors occasionally become active beyond their normal function of keeping in close contact with all important cases by means of mediator reports. Such mediation work, always in close cooperation with the assigned mediator, can include informal participation by telephone or in person, more formal but intermittent participation with the assigned mediator at the site of the negotiations, and formal participation as a member of a panel.

Formal inclusion of the regional director in a panel is the escalation step most directly pertinent to the discussion here. The assistant regional director rarely mediates in this manner. Somebody must "tend the store."

The values of regional director participation in a panel are derived in part from his status and, more important, from the fact that he frequently has special knowledge and skills to contribute. Either because of his prior experience with the same parties as a mediator or because of his indirectly acquired knowledge of prior disputes over a period of years, he may be uniquely qualified to make a contribution to settlement.

Panel Including National Representative

It has been a consistent practice in recent years and a sporadic practice in earlier years for the Service to maintain from three to five National Representatives. These men, better known as "trouble shooters," are stationed officially at the Washington office and report to the Disputes Director in Washington. They have been selected from among the field staff as mediators who have demonstrated skills in the more difficult cases and who are willing to accept a steady diet of tough ones.

National Representatives are added to a field panel, making a total of three mediators, or are added in lieu of a second field mediator by direction of the Washington office. However, this prospective action is frequently suggested by a regional director and is always discussed with him.

Sometimes a decision is also made to request the parties to move the negotiators to Washington when the National Representative enters. Or, that decision may be made at a later date after the trouble shooter has worked with the panel at the normal negotiation site. Even more frequently, the National Representative simply joins the parties and the other mediators at the regular location of negotiations.

What purposes are served by addition of a National Representative to a panel? One purpose is to make available the special skills that these mediators have demonstrated. This is not, however, the only purpose. At all times there have been a substantial number of mediators in the regional and field offices who possess and have demonstrated comparable skills. The status symbol of selection as National Representative may add something in some negotiations. The fact that the case is receiving official "Washington attention" may be important to the intangible elements of mediation.

These reasons take second place to the fact that a National Representative will have fewer inhibitions about performing some of the more aggressive and substantive functions discussed in Chapter V. He does not have to contemplate living with the same parties in the same area for years ahead. If he "breaks his pick," his reputation will not suffer, for his superiors expect that this will happen sometimes. In short, the National Representative is in a better position to take risks. Risk-taking is not always a virtue and can be overdone. However, in the most difficult cases, it often is a necessity.

The Special Assistant to the Director, the Training Officer or the General Counsel, other members of the Washington staff, may also mediate actively on an occasional basis. When they do so they perform the same basic functions as a National Representative.

Appraisal of results suggests that the use of National Representatives has made possible the settlement by the parties of a large number of the most difficult disputes in which the FMCS would otherwise have failed in its efforts. It is equally clear that this procedure should not be overused. It must be reserved for a limited number of cases if it is to retain its effectiveness. Utilization of about 2 percent of a mediation staff as "trouble shooters" is not overemphasis.

Panel Including Disputes Director, Deputy Director, or Director

The Director, Deputy Director, and Disputes Director are the three highest-rated positions in the FMCS. Since these posts are predominantly policy making, administrative, and supervisory jobs in an agency that is "lean" in such positions, the time available for active mediation is severely limited.

Partly for these reasons, the men in these jobs usually mediate actively in only a few cases each year. When they do serve actively on a panel, the reasons are essentially the same as those outlined with respect to regional directors at an earlier step of the escalation ladder.

At a few bargaining tables of obvious national importance that know no realistic regional boundaries, such as those in steel, autos, aerospace, and over-the-road trucking, one of these officials may enter a case as a panel member at the outset or at a very early stage. In other instances, an especially stubborn dispute that may be handled initially by the Service on a regional basis becomes in effect a "Washington case" at a later date with active participation by one of these top officials.

Panel Including a Private Mediator

On occasion, the FMCS has supplemented its own staff by the ad hoc addition to a panel of an outstanding private mediator. Individuals so employed in recent years have included Leo C. Brown, David L. Cole, Donald A. Crawford, John T. Dunlop, James J. Healy, Theodore W. Kheel, and Charles C. Killingsworth.

This type of mediation service by nonstaff members is to be distinguished sharply from the work on special boards (Taft-Hartley Boards of Inquiry, Presidential Boards, Boards appointed by cabinet members, etc.) that will be discussed in a later chapter. In each case of the type being discussed here, the private mediator becomes one member of a panel, all other panel members being FMCS officials or mediators. The panel is administered by and reports solely to the FMCS.

This type of panel represents a favorable blending of several factors. The status, ability, and special talents of the private mediators are made available to the parties and to the other mediators. The provincial or "dog in the manger" attitude of which the FMCS has sometimes been accused is avoided. At the same time, the abilities of FMCS mediators and officials and their acquired knowledge of the case are not lost. An abrupt transition from intensive FMCS mediation to completely independent mediation by others tends to cause a hiatus. The new faces must acquire necessary information about the case, and the parties must become adjusted to the new faces. Addition of one private mediator permits a much smoother transition. Most important, experience has demonstrated that such a team of mediators can work well together and can provide professional mediation in the best sense of the term.

Summary

Having described briefly the various possible steps of the escalation ladder, what are some of the considerations that underlie the decisions that must be made as to whether escalation is desirable?

One obvious point is that escalation must not be automatic. If the parties know in advance that they will or may get the full treatment, there is an inevitable tendency to delay meaningful negotiation until the mediation effort reaches the top step or the step on the ladder at which the case is likely to stop. This problem can also influence mediators. Why should a field mediator knock his brains out on a solo case if he knows that a panel of some sort will be appointed?

To avoid these hazards, the FMCS policy includes several features. If escalation is quite certainly inevitable, the lower steps of the ladder may be skipped entirely. A field mediation panel may be assigned initially. In certain national negotiations, a National Representative, and in rare cases even the Director, may be involved from the beginning.

Escalation does not take place unless it becomes evident that it is necessary. Whenever possible, the mediators involved at any one step agree that escalation is necessary, and usually they suggest it on their own initiative.

Successful application of this policy requires maintenance of an optimum balancing of individual and team morale. Individual pride and sole responsibility are greatly desired—up to a point. A solo mediator has a sort of "property right" to an assigned case. As long as that property right is compatible with the best professional mediation, under the circumstances of that case, nobody wants to inhibit the energy, drive, and motivation that lead to accomplishment. But at some point the property right—and the responsibility—shift to the agency .Team effort becomes necessary in lieu of individual effort. The specific composition of the team will depend on the facts of the case.

To preserve and enhance the team-effort concept, it is especially necessary to avoid "parachuting," which is mediator lingo for a development that is possible in any escalation sequence. Let us suppose that a mediator or a panel has labored long and hard. The parties are almost ready to settle. They may already have agreed informally. The Director of the Service, or some other official, arrives in town and officiates "while the ribbons are being tied." If there is publicity at the signing, it is the official whose face and name appear in the newspapers and on television. Those who really did the work get little or no attention. There is no better way of defeating the values of escalation. The possibility of "parachuting" emphasizes the absolute necessity of confining escalation to instances of real need.

The mediator added to the team must come into the case at a time when he can make a positive contribution to the mediation effort.

On a more positive note, *it is essential for the men working at any step of an escalation ladder to know and feel that they have the full support of those above them in the agency hierarchy.* Most of a mediator's decisions about what to do, what not to do, and how to do it will necessarily be made quickly, based on his intimate knowledge of the case. In some instances he may want to check with a superior and will have time to do so. But this is often not the case even as to moves that entail considerable risk. Monday-morning quarterbacking by others may be advisable for future reference in other cases, but it is seldom useful or desirable for the current case. In short, support by superiors in an agency includes the certainty that mistake will be made. Manager McCarthy did not berate Babe Ruth every time he struck out, even if it was the ninth inning and the winning runs were on base. *Fear of lack of support promotes timidity and ineffective performance.*

ESCALATION OF MEDIATION BEYOND A MEDIATION AGENCY

The statutory mediation agencies provide the only government mediation in most disputes. A few cases, far fewer than is generally believed, receive the attention of government officials outside the mediation agencies. Although these execptions have been limited in number, they have been highly visible controversies. Some of them have been of national importance or have been real national emergencies. They will be discussed in subsequent chapters.

CRISIS BARGAINING

CHAPTER VII

INTERNAL AND EXTERNAL
INFLUENCES ON CRISIS BARGAINING

Issues in dispute are often deeper than their surface indications. Forces—economic, social, and emotional—are sometimes more potent than can be admitted or even recognized by the bargainers. Strongly voiced arguments and contentions may conceal inner uncertainty.

This is not to suggest that collective bargaining is rife with sham and deceit. This is seldom the case despite substantial game-playing aspects of the process. A more accurate statement is that the people on both sides of the bargaining table and those they represent in the shops and in the main offices can be quite individualistic. A collective front may be, in reality, a tenuous compromise of heterogeneous aspirations and objectives or a minority view held strongly by a few dominant individuals.

The conglomerate of individual positions that lies behind a spoken argument is likely to be a mixture of hard-headed realism and wishful thinking or emotion. Even when the controlling factor is economic, it may be extremely difficult to extract the psychological aspects.

What does this have to do with mediation? First, a mediator cannot begin to be useful in a difficult dispute unless he is somehow able to probe beneath the surface. If he does nothing but listen, he may have a very poor understanding of the issues. Second, he may be able, after acquiring understanding, to help strip away the underbrush and assist the parties in getting at the root problems. Or, if the logically extraneous factors are the dominant considerations, as they may be, he may be able to help the parties see that this is so.

The frequent need to explore in depth has numerous manifestations, some of which will be considered in this chapter.

INTERNAL UNION STRESSES

A union represents all its members and those nonmembers, if

137

any, who are in the representation unit. These employees do not all have the same interests and objectives. In formulating its demands, in developing its priorities during negotiations, and in making the hard choices that must be made before a deadline, the union seeks to reconcile these internal differences. There is a significant amount of intra-union bargaining and mediation that precedes or is concurrent with the bargaining across the table with the employer. The task of resolving these intra-union conflicts is not easy.

Composition of the Work Force

One of the more obvious problems within a union stems from the composition of the work force.

Young workers, single or just starting a family, are inclined to stress money in the pay envelope; older workers tend to have a major interest in pension benefits. Long-service employees cherish strong seniority provisions; new employees may wish that seniority could be forgotten entirely. If a plant employs a high proportion of young female employees and the turnover rate is high, starting rates of pay may be more significant than maximum rates. For example, the objectives of operator groups in the telephone industry may be different from those of the predominantly male maintenance and installation groups in which length of average service tends to be much longer .

These are only a few examples of the stresses and strains that can develop out of a wide variety of age and sex groupings within a plant, between plants in the same company and industry, or between different industries.

Skilled v. Semiskilled

In an industrial-type union, skilled workers often believe that their minority voting position has resulted in less relative consideration than is accorded to the semiskilled and the unskilled. This problem was highlighted by the decision of the United Automobile Workers in 1967 to accord separate voting rights and thereby possible veto power to skilled workers. The UAW move was one result of long-standing differences between skilled and semiskilled workers, some of which predate the union itself. Across-the-board wage increases in cents per hour on several occasions amplified these skilled-worker complaints. Elsewhere, similar differences have been accentuated where most semiskilled workers are paid on a piece-rate basis or receive other forms of incentive pay while most skilled workers are not on incentive. The rubber industry is illustrative. Recent outsize wage adjustments in some areas in the construction industry have added new fuel to these differences.

If one or more craft unions represent the skilled workers, the same problems may exist, but they arise at several bargaining tables instead of within one overall agreement. In these instances bargaining may be even more difficult for the employer because no one union is required to reconcile these conflicts within the total work force.

Minority Groups in the Work Force

Increasing demands of black workers for equality, now buttressed by statute, emerge at the bargaining table in a variety of ways. The principal effect is on seniority systems and hiring practices. In a smaller number of situations, discrimination has been reflected in wage rates. Increasingly, efforts are being made for more black representation on bargaining committees and in other official union positions.

These factors are by no means limited to black v. white internal differences. For example, the composition of work forces in the clothing industries—initially Jewish and subsequently Italian —created problems long before American Negroes and Puerto Ricans became significant elements in the same plants. The Chicanos and American Indians, likewise, are properly demanding equal consideration.

Even when there is a sincere desire to correct discriminatory practices, methods of doing so present formidable difficulties. It is not easy to eradicate the effects of years of discrimination without creating new inequities. Those who have benefited by discrimination are not inclined to welcome change. And if the changes should be accompanied by discrimination in reverse, opposition will be formidable.

Strike Experience

Prevalence of labor peace for a number of years coupled with normal labor turnover and substantial expansion of the work force can create differences of attitude within a union about use of the strike weapon. Older workers who have experienced several strikes are usually solid supporters of a strike if they believe that the stakes are high enough to warrant it. But they are not typically "strike happy." Economic action is taken with reluctance. In a sizable number of bargaining relationships, young, new workers who have never experienced a strike may constitute a majority. The main effect of some strikes in recent years has been to acquaint the new work force with the negative aspects of the strike weapon.

Intra-Union Politics

Of necessity, a union is a political organization. Union officials at all levels frequently are elected once and stay in power for an appreciable period of time, but officer turnover has been more common in recent years.

When a close internal political contest is imminent for whatever reason, collective bargaining becomes more difficult. There is a tendency for the "outs" to differ with the "ins" on bargaining issues, irrespective of the merits of the differences. Moreover, the "ins" who are doing the bargaining feel especially hard-pressed to reach a popular total bargain.

A variant of this problem can be illustrated by the 1965 steel industry negotiations. The union election in which I. W. Abel ran against David McDonald, the incumbent president, was held prior to contract negotiations that year. The vote was reasonably close, and McDonald challenged the apparent victory of Abel. The resulting uncertainty of the final outcome and the fact that McDonald's term of office would not expire until after the contract expiration date complicated the negotiations. A probable "lame duck" headed the negotiating team on which Abel was also an important member. The union protagonists collaborated remarkably well in the negotiations, given this set of facts, but there is no doubt that the negotiations were impeded. In addition to internal union problems, the steel companies could not be certain as to who would head the union for the bulk of the new contract term. Under these circumstances, the proposal in mediation of a contract extension proved effective. All parties were agreeable to the idea of a short period of additional time during which the union leadership could be established with certainty. The four-month contract extension that was agreed upon provided enough time for Abel's election to be confirmed and for the new union leadership to take full charge in negotiation of the next contract.

Many union elections have caused major problems that have not been overcome. Hard-pressed to retain office, an incumbent union leadership has often not been able to be realistic enough to negotiate an agreement. Or, a complete change of union negotiating committees has occurred in the middle of the normal bargaining period, leaving insufficient time to complete an acceptable contract. A variety of such circumstances can arise. No small number of strikes have been caused almost solely by internal union political situations.

Nobody desires political impediments to bargaining. Even the "outs" who may benefit politically from obstructive tactics frequently find, if they get elected, that their own actions come back to haunt them. The unfortunate effects of internal political battles are acceptable only in contrast to the alternatives. Dictatorship within unions is even less desirable.

To minimize this problem, many negotiators deliberately attempt to establish contract deadline dates that do not conflict with union election dates. If a contract expiration date is sufficiently ahead of or behind a union election, the democratic process within the union can prevail but its effect on negotiations is not as acute.

Inter-Union Politics and Prestige Factors

Leaders of any organization seek to add to the power and prestige of the organization and to their own stature. Union leadership is by no means immune from this tendency. To outdo a rival organization is an understandable objective. Nor is this sort of competition limited to other unions that pose a direct threat in the sense that there could be a change of union affiliation. Especially during an inflationary period, the desire to produce more than some other union contributes to inflationary pressures.

Inter-union rivalry is mentioned here as an internal influence because it is within the labor movement. The fact that it is external to the specific bargaining unit does not lessen its importance.

The total effect of this tendency is sometimes mitigated by a psychological equivalent. If a union can secure a breakthrough— the negotiation of something new and different—the need for prestige may be satisfied even if the total cost of the settlement is no greater. In fact, some prestigious union victories have been achieved at a lesser total cost to the company because the breakthrough has been visible and popular within the membership.

The Membership Rejection Problem

In 1947, when the Taft-Hartley Act amendments to the Wagner Act were being debated, there existed a widespread notion that was reflected in the congressional action, and, indeed, had appeared even earlier in World War II legislation. It persisted with only slight modification at least through 1959, when the Landrum-Griffin Act was passed.

The basic notion was that union members, permitted to express themselves freely by secret ballot, would be more conservative and responsible than union leadership. A related belief was that union leaders were entering into "sweetheart contracts"— agreements not responsive to the needs of the workers covered by the contracts.

Pointed evidence of this idea that members were more conservative than leaders is found in two places in the Taft-Hartley Act. Under the emergency disputes procedures, a secret ballot on the employer's last offer must be taken 15 days before the expiration of an 80-day injunction unless the dispute has already been settled. The second is a more obscure provision which reads:

> "If the Director [of the Federal Mediation and Conciliation Service] is not able to bring the parties to agreement by conciliation within a reasonable time, he shall seek to induce the parties voluntarily to seek other means of settling the dispute without resort to strike, lockout, or other coercion, *including submission to the employees in the bargaining unit of the employer's last offer of settlement for approval or rejection in a secret ballot....*[1]

This bit of advice to the Director is the one and only congressional admonition as to substantive procedure in nonemergency mediation.

Now, 24 years after passage of the Act, some of the same persons who were the strongest proponents of membership rights are proposing that union members be stripped of their agreement-ratification role by legislative action. It is apparent that some people now believe that union leadership is more conservative and more responsible than the membership. How did this turnabout develop? It has occurred because union members are not voting in the anticipated manner.

Early in the 1960s Federal Mediation and Conciliation Service mediators began to observe an increase in the frequency of membership rejections. These were not rejections of employer last offers. They were membership disapprovals of agreements made in good faith by the union's own negotiators.

A procedure under which all members may vote on a negoti-

[1] Labor Management Relations Act, 1947, Title II, Section 203 (c) (emphasis supplied).

ated settlement is certain to result in a few rejections. However, until about 1960, such rejections were infrequent. The initialing of an agreement by the negotiators or the handshakes at the conclusion of a series of meetings were normally considered to be the successful conclusion. Ratification by the membership was a necessary formality but rarely a problem.

The absence of any factual knowledge of the frequency of the phenomenon caused the FMCS to begin to keep records. In November 1967 a study and paper were completed on the subject.[2] As of that date, union members were rejecting one out of seven agreements that had been negotiated at the bargaining table. The detailed data are shown in updated form in Table 7.

Table 7

MEMBERSHIP REJECTION OF NEGOTIATED AGREEMENTS

Year Ending June 30	Total Agreements	Instances in Which at Least One Membership Rejection Occurred	Rejection Percentage
1964	7,221	629	8.7
1965	7,445	746	10.0
1966	7,836	918	11.7
1967	7,193	1,019	14.2
1968	7,485	893	11.9
1969	8,028	991	12.3

Source: Federal Mediation and Conciliation Service, Annual Reports to Congress.

It should be emphasized that the data in Table 7 relate only to cases in which FMCS mediators were active, which means that these were the more difficult and troublesome negotiations in each year. Undoubtedly, rejection percentages would be lower in the less troublesome negotiations requiring no mediation. Nevertheless, the magnitude and the trend indicate a very real problem. Even the 8.7-percent rejection rate for the 1964 fiscal year was quite certainly higher than during any earlier period in collective bargaining history.

The internal union stresses and strains discussed earlier in this chapter were factors contributing to the rejection problem. The

[2] "Refusals to Ratify Contracts," November 1967. Paper by William E. Simkin for a seminar at the Graduate School of Business, University of Chicago (reproduced with minor modifications in *Industrial and Labor Relations Review*, Volume 21, No. 4, July 1968, New York State School of Industrial Relations, Cornell University, Ithaca, N. Y.)

upswing of cost of living after a period of relative stability undoubtedly influenced the trend. The assassination of President
Kennedy in the fall of 1963, the general trend towards shattered
confidence in established institutions, and some weakening of
power of union leadership as an aftermath of the Landrum-Griffin Act of 1959 all contributed to this development. The small
downturn after July 1967 is a hopeful sign, but there is no sound
reason to believe that there will be an early return to the days
when a negotiated agreement was almost automatically approved
by the membership.

The suggestion, often heard and incorporated in draft bills,
that legislation be passed to make a negotiated agreement binding without membership approval is not the answer.

Some unions have given their negotiators full authority. Where
that is done or can be done voluntarily, it should be encouraged.
It is also a fact that a few unions delegate the ratification authority to a group greater in number than the negotiators but considerably smaller than the total membership. Examples are the Steel-
worker Wage Policy Committees for the principal negotiations in
the basic steel, aluminum, copper, and can industries. Some other
unions confer that authority on the Executive Board. Where
either of these methods is the practice or can be adopted, it is a
form of representative democracy. A good case can be made for
much wider use of such methods. In government, few decisions
are made by direct vote of all the citizens. However, even in government, especially in the smaller jurisdictions, a referendum is
often required on such matters as school bond issues that are vital
to the community and close to the pocketbook.

The principal reasons for opposing a statute that would de-
prive members of a vote on a negotiated agreement can be stated
briefly. Especially now that a majority of agreements are for a
term of three years, stability during the entire term of the agreement is very important. Membership ratification promotes stability. Secondly, if a membership referendum should be made impossible, it is quite certain that some memberships would react
by insisting on "fishbowl" negotiations (extremely large negotiating committees). Since the objective of bargaining is to secure
agreements, any major shift towards fish-bowl negotiations would
complicate negotiations even more than membership rejections
do. Finally, in the absence of membership sanction of agreements,
union leadership would be even more politically hazardous than
it is now. If union members should be required to direct dissatis-

faction with agreements away from the agreement itself and towards the union leadership, union leaders would be less inclined to bargain constructively. In short, as is true of many direct at-tacks on labor relations problems, the legislative remedy would be worse than the disease.

Much can be done voluntarily by unions to eliminate or mini-mize the rejection problem. Procedures at membership meetings and methods of presentation of results of negotiations to the membership can often be improved. A secret ballot, sometimes a mail ballot, is often preferable to a voice or "show of hands" vote. Alarmed by the rejection problem, many unions are reex-amining their internal procedures and taking action to assure membership reaction that is fully representative of all the mem-bers.

In the last analysis, the membership-rejection problem illus-trates a point made at the outset of this chapter. The reconcilia-tion of differing objectives within a union membership may sometimes be as difficult a process as the resolution of conflict be-tween a union and a company.

Nor is a company just an innocent victim; the union members are the company's employees. Even if there were no union to per-form the function of resolving internal employee differences, the company would be faced directly by similar problems of develop-ment of reasonably acceptable wage, benefit, and working condi-tions policies.

Obviously it is to the mutual interest of both union and com-pany negotiators to develop a "package" that will be accepted by the membership. The rejection of a negotiated agreement by the membership is a major problem for the company, and it is a re-pudiation of union leadership. What is to be done? If the parties resume negotiations and "raise the ante" to secure a favorable vote, union leaders are somewhat tarnished by the performance. Most important, a dangerous precedent may have been estab-lished for future negotiations. Employees understandably may get the idea that a way to get more is to reject an initial agreement. On the other hand, if the company stands firm, a strike is quite likely to occur. More than a few strikes have developed in such circumstances.

The rejection problem has created what may be labeled "rejec-tion backlash." Union leadership may be reluctant to agree to any attainable agreement, not wanting to risk repudiation by the membership. Management may be unwilling to make its best offer, deciding to hold something back to "sweeten the pot" after a rejection. In short, the statistics of actual membership rejections do not portray fully the adverse effects on collective bargaining. Strikes can occur primarily because the negotiators fear a membership rejection and believe that ratification is likely only after a strike of long enough duration to "soften" the membership.

Because of the many adverse implications of the rejection problem, a new dimension has been added to contract negotiation and to mediation. The handshake at the bargaining table may not conclude the mediator's job. It may be both necessary and advisable for all parties to discuss and give careful consideration to the methods of presentation to the membership. This is a union function, but management may be helpful indirectly. For example, many companies have cooperated in various ways to permit membership meetings that will assure maximum employee attendance, even to the point of permitting meetings during working hours at company expense. By reason of experiences elsewhere, a mediator is often able to advise the union negotiators about methods and procedures of presentation to the membership that are most likely to result in a carefully considered vote.

INTERNAL EMPLOYER STRESSES

On the employer side, it is sometimes supposed that a company or employer association position in a labor dispute is one of complete unity. This is by no means always the case. Because company structures are less democratic, internal differences are usually well hidden. But they are likely to exist, and occasionally they are exposed. This is especially so when several companies join to bargain through an association.

Some of the causes and effects of these internal differences will be considered next.

Possible Internal Economic Differences

A principal company negotiator wants two results from negotiations. Not only is a strike-free settlement desirable; it will enhance his internal status. A contract that is the best possible agreement for the economic future of the company is even more important. If both are not obtainable, how does he establish the priorities? And who is to determine the limits of an economically acceptable agreement?

The sales department may influence the negotiations. For example, the union committee at a dress plant is pleased if a wage dispute can be brought to a head just a few weeks before the Easter selling season. Sales personnel will scream if production is stopped or even hindered. If a dispute should develop just after Easter, the sales department "couldn't care less."

If a company is about to put a bond issue or a block of stock on the market, a strike may be most unfortunate. The usually conservative financial management heads of the company may be inclined to favor a reasonably liberal negotiation posture. Conversely, if they are very bearish about the economic future, intense internal pressures can be exerted for a cheap settlement.

Production management dislikes strikes. A strike gums up the works, creates havoc with scheduling, and generally upsets the orderly routines of persons who are judged by the efficiency of production methods and performance.

In short, if given full opportunity to express their opinions on some of the difficult company decisions that must be made, and made quickly, as a deadline approaches, the various components of a company hierarchy may very well come up with different answers. This is a major reason why a single top executive or even a board of directors may maintain close touch with company negotiators as the deadline approaches. Somebody has to reconcile internal company differences, and the chief company negotiator is seldom in a power position to make all the requisite decisions entirely on his own.

Most companies present a solid front at the bargaining table irrespective of the internal situation. However, stresses and strains occasionally are fairly obvious. Moreover, intelligent union negotiators know enough about the company's internal structure to permit speculation. If the union speculation is in error, as it sometimes is, the results of inaccurate predictions can be worse than if all the differences were exposed fully.

Intercompany Differences in Association Bargaining

When a number of companies bargain through an employer association, strong differences can exist among the member companies. If the member companies compete with each other in the same product market, as is frequently the case, the weaker companies may believe that the stronger companies have a two-pronged objective—to placate the union and to intensify the competitive problems of the weak. On the other hand, an association position that is dictated by the weakest company in the group will not normally be generous enough to produce a settlement.

Because of differences of equipment, production methods, composition of work forces and other factors, almost any given mix of wage and fringe benefits will not have identical cost implications for all the companies. Each company tends to press for the settlement that will be least costly to it.

Differences may not be confined to economic considerations. Seldom are all members of a group of companies fully in accord on emotional issues, such as union security. Seniority questions may evoke different responses by reason of varied concepts or diverse practical problems of application, or both.

Procedural mechanisms within an employer association may be hard pressed to reconcile these differences. The life of an association negotiator within his own group may be as difficult as that of a union negotiator.

Company Politics

A company or association negotiator is not faced with the necessity of being reelected by a membership vote. But he is always subject to discharge by less democratic methods. It is not unusual for a management negotiator to find himself out of a job after a difficult negotiation if his superiors believe that he has failed. This can happen even if, in reality, he gave a superb performance under all the circumstances.

Intracompany or intra-association political considerations are not always limited to appraisals of negotiating skills. Personality differences within a company hierarchy or between executives of different companies, not related to work performed, may have such adverse effects on a negotiator that he is unable adequately to represent his constituency.

Prestige Factors

Company negotiators are also not immune from appraisal by their peers. In the country club locker room, a management negotiator is just as prone to boast of having made a good deal as a union representative at a convention. Representatives are keenly aware of their reputation and status in the management labor relations community. Their chances of promotion within a company or of securing a better job elsewhere may be determined by the prestige factor.

THE MEDIATOR'S ROLE IN INTERNAL CONFLICT

How is the mediator to react when he knows that substantial

differences exist within each side at the bargaining table as well as across it? He may well have to attempt to assist in resolving the differences. Meaningful collective bargaining may otherwise not occur.

This potential mediation function has obvious dangers. To maintain true impartiality on a three-way basis is not an easy task. There are no blueprints that can be drawn. Such situations have few common specific patterns. However, the mediator who has the respect and confidence of both parties has an asset that is peculiar to his position. Knowing the differences that exist within the groups as well as between them, he is in a position to help develop a settlement area that the parties could not readily reach without assistance. One of the reasons why a "permanent" impartial chairman in the needle trades industries sometimes also acts as a formal or informal mediator in contract disputes is that he acquires a great deal of knowledge of these internal differences. A resident mediator who lives and works in a community for many years obtains similar important background information about many collective bargaining relationships in his area.

EXTERNAL INFLUENCES ON CRISIS BARGAINING

Bargaining is affected not only by internal differences on each side of the table but also by factors external to the bargaining relationship. Powerful pressures over which the bargainers have little or no control may dictate or at least have a significant bearing on the results of a specific negotiation. Some of these pressures are quite impartial in that they bear equally on both parties. Some other factors may have unequal effects.

Inflation, Stability, Deflation

The general economic climate in the nation and in the community has such obvious effects that it would be absurd to labor the point. During a period of relative price stability, as in the first half of the 1960s, cost-of-living changes are small and reasonably predictable. Even when a three-year bargain is being made, this stability minimizes economic uncertainty, which is a major aspect of bargaining at other times.

As an inflationary surge began or seemed to be evident in 1966, bargaining became more difficult. Most companies, including some that had been successful in eliminating them at an earlier time, resisted union demands for cost-of-living escalator clauses.

Even where company objections prevailed, wage settlements were higher, reflecting negotiated estimates of what might happen.

In a deflationary period—not experienced during the last decade—unions struggle to avoid wage cuts and employers seek to impose them in the form of either across-the-board wage reductions or selective cost reductions of various kinds. Those experiences now seem remote, but who can be sure that they will not recur in this decade?

Available labor supply is a well-known potent factor in bargaining. For example, skilled labor shortages have been a major cause of the outsize construction industry settlements of recent years. Since available labor supply is most directly a community or area factor, the national employment statistics are only general guides. Construction industry settlements, just referred to, have varied all the way from some that have been absurdly high to some that have been modest. Interaction of the amounts of local building demand and local labor supply has produced varying results even in an industry renowned for labor mobility.

Foreign Competition

The remarkable postwar foreign industrial recovery, especially in Western Europe and Japan, has made foreign competition a potent factor in bargaining. Its influence has been felt in some industries for many years; textiles, shoe, and watch manufacturing are examples. The direct effect on bargaining in basic steel, electronics, shipbuilding, and man-made textile fibre industries—to name only a few—has been more recent. For example, the steel companies made a major point of foreign imports before and during the long 1959 strike, but the union paid scant heed to this factor. Less than 10 years later, all responsible persons on both sides of the table in that industry acknowledged freely that foreign competition had become a major threat. Even the powerful automobile industry, a prime example of our industrial prowess, can no longer ignore imports from Germany and Japan. Our domestic shipbuilding is so noncompetitive that new construction in the United States survives at a drastically reduced level only under a program of direct government subsidy.

In contrast, those industries that are immune from foreign competition tend to exhibit less wage restraint. Buildings cannot be imported, either from abroad or from outside the community. This is another reason for the excessive cost and price increases in the construction industry in cities that have experienced a building boom.

Although foreign competition is a selective factor, applicable in varying degrees to different industries and to specific products within industries, there can be no doubt but that it is an increasingly important external economic factor.

Domestic Competition

Domestic competition is usually a potent economic factor at the bargaining table. Labor cost differentials, whether on a company, plant, area, or product basis, are important subjects for discussion and consideration.

An often-expressed union objective "to take labor cost out of competition" has been reached in some situations, if wage rate comparisons are the criterion. In basic steel, the CWS (Cooperative Wage Study) job evaluation system has provided substantial identity of basic hourly wage rates, irrespective of geography. Wage rate differences among the "Big 3" in the automobile industry (General Motors, Ford, and Chrysler) are small and are not dependent on plant location. Similar results of collective bargaining can be noted in many other less well-known industries. For example, in 1968, most producers of glass bottles agreed to provisions that will result in substantial nationwide identity of wage rates in the last year of a three-year agreement.

In many other industries, wage rate differentials, if not eliminated, have been narrowed appreciably.

Identity or substantial uniformity of wage rates does not mean identity of unit labor cost. Differences of equipment, methods, scale of production, types of wage payment, and other factors result in different unit labor costs. Thus, domestic competition can be an important influence on a company even when there is identity of wage rates.

The importance of domestic competition is most evident in those industries where there is no pretense that uniform wage rates exist and there is limited adherence to pattern behavior in any one round of bargaining. Comparisons of wage rates, earnings, profits, and predictions for the future are facts with which the parties grapple in arriving at an agreement. Results usually recognize competitive advantages and disadvantages.

Many competitive factors are beyond the control of those at the bargaining table. What is within their control is the adjustment that is to be made to these external facts.

Technological Change

It is unnecessary to attempt to outline the pace and magnitude of technological change. Everyone is aware that changes in equipment, processes, methods, and products have been extensive and rapid and are never-ending. The fact that such changes do not have equal effect in all industries and may occur at an uneven rate means that the parties must recognize the peculiar facts of each relationship.

Bargaining reacts to and anticipates such changes. If a specific new development originates within a particular bargaining relationship, the parties must initiate the necessary labor relations adjustments. If it originates elsewhere, as is often the case, competitive relationships can be altered quickly and decisively. The ability of management to equal or improve on the change made elsewhere may determine the fate of the company or plant. The bargainers, affected indirectly by the external change, will not necessarily ape the bargains made elsewhere. But a realistic bargaining adaptation to the facts will be essential to sound management decisions.

Few people realize the magnitude of the stresses and strains on collective bargaining that are caused by technological change. It is a human characteristic to resist change. Worker reactions at the beginning of the Industrial Revolution in England were not union-inspired; unions were then unknown. In many respects, changes of recent years have been even more far-reaching in their effects, both immediate and long-run.

Examples of sometimes futile and sometimes successful union resistance to change are numerous. Building trades unions have stymied some forms of prefabrication, at least temporarily. Printing trades unions have effectively slowed or prevented introduction of some new processes. A dominant issue in the 1962-1963 strike and lockout of 114 days' duration of the New York newspapers was the desire of the publishers to expand the use of so-called "outside tape."

The long diesel engine dispute involving the firemen and the railroads is a classic example of a major technological change. Complete replacement of steam locomotives by diesel engines eliminated most of the traditional duties of the fireman job. Since many firemen were then in a separate union, a potential additional result was to make transfer to other jobs difficult and to threaten eventual elimination of the union itself. When jobs and union survival are both threatened, bargaining is not a happy prospect. These hard facts were the major explanation for the congressional prescription of compulsory arbitration in 1963. Even that drastic action did not solve the controversy. Aspects of the dispute persisted into 1970, and we may not yet have heard the last of it.

When technological change of major proportions is the dominant issue, bargaining is tested severely. This is especially so when the change is rapid and affects large numbers of bargaining-unit employees.

But observation of the entire collective bargaining spectrum suggests that bargaining in this country has been an efficient and effective method of adaptation to change. In the United States, the typical union approach to technological change is to bargain about the effects but not to challenge management's right to effectuate the change. The occasional serious disruptions are not typical. Most of the necessary adjustments to change have been accomplished quietly and peacefully and in ways that are a tribute to the collective bargaining process.

Labor Cost As Related to Total Cost

Bargainers are necessarily influenced by the relationship between labor cost and total cost of production. For example, wage bargaining is typically not as significant an issue in oil refining as in some metal fabricating industries. A 15-percent wage increase at an oil refinery may add less than $1\frac{1}{2}$ percent to the total cost of the product because labor cost may be less than 10 percent of total cost. A similar 15-percent wage increase at a metal fabricating plant might add 6 percent to the cost of the product if the labor cost percentage is 40 percent. Companies with a high labor cost ratio may be unable to compete successfully for workers in a geographical area that is dominated by industries with a low labor cost ratio.

The Public Interest

The public interest in collective bargaining is or can be an external influence on the bargainers. The problems of a union and a company are their own but they can impinge on the community, on larger segments of the country, and sometimes on the entire nation.

Public opinion can be expressed through nongovernmental channels. It can also be evidenced by legislative or executive action. Either method can have some effect in shaping the behavior of the negotiators.

Whenever a significant labor dispute develops, it becomes a matter of interest to the news media. If it is a controversy of national significance, press, TV, and radio coverage may be extensive. In fact, it is possible for the news media to create a crisis that would otherwise not exist. Smaller disputes may attract the same degree of attention but limited to a community or area.

If one or both of the parties deliberately seek to secure public support for their positions by advertisements, by releases to the press, by TV appearances, by radio, or by "leaks," the dispute tends to leave the bargaining table, at least for a time, and become a struggle for favorable public reaction. Many bargaining deliberations have been sidetracked while attention is diverted or directed to external publicity.

Are negotiations a private matter, or is there a public "right to know"? If there is a public right to know, how is that right to be exercised? Under what circumstances, if any, is public opinion effective in helping to resolve a dispute? What is the public interest in the quality or terms of a settlement, as distinguished from the fact of a settlement?

Discussion of the public right to know is not essentially a matter of theory or philosophy. We begin with the fact that the general public and the news media evince little or no interest in the great bulk of negotiations. Success is not normally news unless it comes after a known threat of a strike or terminates an actual strike. In the absence of a publicized threat of a strike, it may be difficult for the parties to obtain a simple announcement of a settlement, well hidden in the back pages. Except for employees directly affected and a few of their personal friends, even the fact that negotiations are under way may not be known generally.

An actual strike or a credible threat of a strike is newsworthy. There is not much doubt but that public intolerance of strikes is increasing. Public opinion polls, reactions in specific instances, and all other evidence support this conclusion. Public reaction is quite directly proportional to the effect on persons not involved. A strike in a defense plant produces a reaction different from an otherwise comparable strike in a nondefense plant, even during an unpopular war. A real national emergency strike provokes strong reactions. A strike that is not a national emergency but inconveniences many persons may generate as much public opposition as a real emergency. The 1966 airline strike is illustrative.

But growing public intolerance of strikes appears to be a general phenomenon, over and above reactions to specific stoppages. Even during the first half of the 1960s, when statistics show that strikes had substantially less impact than at any time since World War II, public opposition to strikes did not wane.

One major reason is fairly evident. Strikes believed to be caused by struggles to achieve equity by the underprivileged, underpaid, and neglected segments of society command sympathy and support. Most organized workers have progressed both absolutely and relatively to a point where their causes do not often arouse sympathy now. Only migrant workers and a few other groups can elicit such support. Many strikes appear, sometimes quite correctly, to be bare-knuckled power battles between equals. And it is probable that an increasing number of people believe that a union is more equal than an employer.

At least up to a point of probable stalemate, negotiators generally agree that efforts to publicize negotiations should be avoided. Union newspapers and trade journals are frequently exempted, but they reach only those involved and a limited number of outsiders. In short, as long as there is reasonable hope for a peaceful settlement, the parties usually consider their negotiations to be private affairs.

But once a negotiation gets into real difficulty, with or without a strike, the picture may change. Unable to make significant progress at the bargaining table, one or both parties may seek and get publicity. At that point it is not hard to get—trouble is news. News media personnel are then under pressure to produce.

If a strike has not yet occurred but is quite certain, one motive for publicity is to prepare for the worst to avoid surprise. Each side wants to project the best possible public image at the beginning of a strike.

After a strike has started, the union needs to retain the support of its members. The company needs the support of its supervisory and clerical employees and its customers. Support of the general public is sought by both parties.

The obvious major problem is that public statements tend to freeze positions. A firm stand can be taken on an issue in a bargaining meeting and that position can be changed subsequently. Both parties do it, and loss of face is minimal. This is a part of the bargaining process. However, if the same statements appear in print for the outside world to see, the process of mind-changing may be impeded greatly.

Most present-day experienced negotiators are fully aware of the hazards of publicity. The goal of reaching a settlement usually overshadows other motives. Statements that can be attributed are usually confined to matters that will do the least damage when the parties next meet. Hard, inflexible statements about specific issues are avoided.

But what does this do to the notion that the general public should be in a position to appraise the merits and lend weight to the side that merits support? Most difficult disputes are complicated and involved. To provide the public with information on which it can base an intelligent and objective appraisal is no easy task. This is especially so when facts and positions are presented in capsule form, as must usually be the case. Public opinion is likely to be an instinctive reaction. Labor reporters have heavy responsibilities. Their stories should permit the development of an informed public opinion that is as unbiased and objective as possible.

Public interest and public opinion can be significant as a strong pressure for labor peace. In addition, the public is increasingly interested in the quality of the results of collective bargaining. "Peace at any price" is no longer a satisfactory objective.

When public opinion becomes sufficiently aroused about some real or alleged defect in labor-management relations, the legislative process is available to correct the defect. Frequently the process is slow and cumbersome; these aspects are inherent in the democratic process. The important fact is that public opinion can and does find an occasional outlet through legislation. In short, collective bargaining must continue to be politically acceptable if it is to survive. Like all democratic institutions, it is dependent, in the last analysis, on general public support.

The executive branch of government at the federal level is not without substantial power in labor relations matters. Almost all Presidents have had the occasion and have exercised their broad powers in a limited number of labor disputes. Most governors of industrial states or municipal officials have been required to show interest in and sometimes intervene in major disputes important to the state or city. The mood of the public is unquestionably one factor that influences these officials at the time of a major labor dispute.

In all these various ways, the public can voice its opinion about labor disputes. The parties are well aware of this fact. Negotiators "have an ear to windward." In making their private decisions they have concern for the anticipated public reaction. At times it might appear that recognition of public opinion is minimal. However, even in the most extreme situations, an outright "public be damned" attitude rarely exists. Responsible negotiators know that continued public support for collective bargaining is essential to the process and that their own behavior may have an effect on the public's overall appraisal.

THE MEDIATOR'S ROLE AS RESPECTS EXTERNAL INFLUENCES

If a mediator is to be useful, he must acquire some background knowledge of the economic factors that will influence the bargainers. He will not be a professional economist, but he cannot be ignorant of general economic trends. He should know enough about the facts of a given dispute to determine whether foreign competition is a factor. Since the parties will almost certainly differ about the relevance of domestic competition and labor cost ratios, he will not be very helpful unless he is able to form judgments about these elements. His understanding of technological change may be more significant than any other economic factor. This facet of labor disputes is so pervasive that a mediator must obtain a broad background of knowledge of the many ways that companies and unions have adjusted to the effects of change.

In Chapter II, reference was made to the public-interest aspects of the mediator's role. In Chapter V, the necessity for the mediator to maximize the role of the bargainers and minimize his own functions was emphasized, especially with regard to publicity. Those important considerations need not be repeated here. The mediator can also be helpful by encouraging the parties to avoid the negative aspects of publicity. No disputes are settled in the newspapers or on television. They are resolved at the bargaining table.

CHAPTER VIII

CHARACTERISTICS OF CRISIS BARGAINING

A few characteristics of bargaining are almost universal. But the dominant attribute is diversity. It is doubtful whether any other democratic institution exists in as varied forms and shapes. The fact that there are so many mutations is proof of the ability of the process to accommodate itself to the many facets of our industrial scene.

The general environment of a dispute may be as important as the specific issues that are in controversy. The basic climate of contract bargaining and, more particularly, the peculiar surroundings of a specific bargaining relationship, must be understood by a mediator before he can assist in the resolution of differences of opinion within that environment.

Brief review of some of the common elements and some of the diversities will suggest the environmental aspects of collective bargaining to which a mediator may be exposed, to which he must adjust, and concerning which he may exert his influence.

INEVITABILITY OF SETTLEMENT

Collective bargaining is a unique relationship; settlement of a conflict must be reached sometime, somehow.

Most relationships in the business world can be terminated. A buyer can transfer his business elsewhere. A seller can seek other markets. Relationships between nations can be severed short of war and remain without direct diplomatic contact for many years.

A collective bargaining relationship can be nullified under a few conditions. A company can go out of business. A union can be decertified and thereby lose its bargaining rights. A union can be replaced by another union but, in such a circumstance, the employer must still deal with the same union membership. A company can sell its business to another owner, but the new owner usually acquires the same union. These occasional whole or partial exceptions do not negate the general observation that collective bargaining is a continuing relationship.

It may be possible to bypass a conflict situation for a period of time without a strike. However, even when resolution of an issue is deferred, some arrangement must prevail by agreement or by tacit consent until the matter is resolved.

This inevitability-of-settlement characteristic is a potent influence in conflict resolution. At every bargaining table, it underlies action and behavior. The frequent human tendency to avoid hard decisions is overpowered by the fact that a decision can only be deferred, it cannot be avoided. Many decisions cannot even be postponed. The old expression "fish or cut bait" has special significance to collective bargaining.

Even when negotiations are in the doldrums and no progress is being made, everybody is aware that this must be temporary. After an unusually frustrating day, a frequent mediator observation is: "Oh, well, at least we're one day closer to a settlement."

The fact that conflict must be resolved makes it exceedingly difficult to demonstrate the efficacy of mediation assistance. A settlement is not proof that the mediator was helpful. In the last analysis, his role was useful only to the extent that the "sometime, somehow" part of the equation was shortened and was accompanied by less pain and a better quality agreement.

ROLE OF THE STRIKE OR LOCKOUT

A strike or a lockout does not often terminate a company-union relationship. It is a tactical, sometimes painful, interlude. The conflict issues will be settled at the bargaining table. Why, then, do these interruptions of bargaining happen?

1. One (or both) of the parties is unable or unwilling to make decisions required to reach agreement.
2. One (or both) of the parties is unable or unwilling to accept an alternative settlement procedure or a device for postponement of economic action.
3. The issues in conflict are so important to one or both parties that a "test of strength" is needed to change positions.

Many strikes are caused by ineptness. The knowledgeable persons on both sides of the table know about where the settlement area is, with or without a strike. The ultimate agreement probably will be in that area. But the negotiators lack either the authority or the fortitude to make the decisions that would avoid a strike. In such cases, the chances are good that the strike will be of short duration after it has been demonstrated that both sides "mean business" (union's demonstrated willingness to strike and employer's willingness to take a strike). A strike of this nature is an economic loss. It does little except demonstrate firmness. It could have been avoided by more timely decision-making.

Postponement of final decision-making without a strike is often advisable. The parties may have miscalculated the time required for adequate bargaining. The issues may have proved to be too complicated to permit full discussion and to allow creative discovery or viable compromise. There may be no lack of desire to settle the issues. If this type of situation exists, a strike makes little sense.

If adequate time to negotiate is not the problem but the remaining issues are not worth a strike, a mediator's recommendations on the issues or the development of alternative procedures, such as arbitration, may avoid recourse to economic action.

One of the inherent dangers of a strike in the basic situations outlined up to this point is that a strike can change the character of a dispute. If more time is really needed, the negotiators may not find that time until much later. They are too busy in their respective strike and take-a-strike roles. Again, the shock of a strike may harden positions. Emotions may replace reason. Many parties, very close to a settlement just prior to a strike or needing only a little more time for agreement, find that the dispute has been escalated by the strike. New issues appear. Issues that have been resolved reappear. The strike itself creates issues. To avoid these consequences, a major role of a mediator is to assess the realities and take effective steps to forestall a strike.

There remains for discussion the strike that is needed as the final "persuader" or "mind changer." A union negotiator does not always know the real strength of membership opinion and determination. It is one of the brutal facts of collective bargaining that loss of one or more pay checks may be a necessary ingredient of the union's final position. A company negotiator may have misjudged the strength of the union on a strongly contested point. Union solidarity during a strike may be a good convincer. On the other hand, the employer's willingness to take a strike may persuade the union membership of the solidity of a company position. Loss of business and profits may change company attitudes. To permit the interplay of these forces is the legitimate role of a strike in the collective bargaining process. Theoretically, no strike is ever necessary. As a practical matter, some strikes perform an important function in the agreement-making process.

The best negotiators seldom need a strike. On both sides, they are able to predict the likely course of events during a strike. Thus the threat of a strike fulfills the same function as an actual strike without the attendant losses.

A lockout occurs when the employer voluntarily closes the plant gates during a labor dispute and refuses to offer employment when the union has not called a strike. Lockouts seldom occur largely because an employer's willingness to take a strike has an equivalent effect. If an employer persists in a final position at the deadline that is certain to be unacceptable to the union, a self-respecting union may believe that it has no recourse but to strike.

Legal uncertainties about the lockout also have inhibited its use. Why should a company risk an award of back pay in an unfair labor practice case, or incur costs for or unemployment compensation, if a tough position at the bargaining table can force a strike? It is not suggested that this is a common cause of strikes, but it would be naive to assume that it never is.

National Labor Relations Board and court decisions in recent years have provided more legal support for use of the lockout. Whether this is a causal factor is speculative, but it is a fact that the lockout has been used increasingly by employers. Not many years ago, "lockout" was primarily a word in the dictionary or a word used by academicians to show that there was a counterpart to the strike.

In the 1962-1963 New York newspaper strikes, more employees were locked out than were on strike. In several construction industry strikes, one union has gone on strike, sometimes against only a few employers, and the balance of the industry in the local market has engaged in a lockout. During the negotiation of the National Trucking Agreement in 1967, scattered strikes occurred. Trucking Employers, Inc. retaliated with a nationwide lockout of 400,000 employees—undoubtedly the largest lockout on record. Fortunately, the dispute was settled before the full effect of the lockout could be felt. During separate but substantially simultaneous trucking negotiations in Chicago, employers locked out twice. Those lockouts lasted long enough to be felt seriously in Chicago. The dispute between Union Carbide Corporation and several unions in 1966 and 1967, best known for its coordinated-bargaining aspects, began at least technically with a company lockout of employees at the Alloy, W. Va. plant.

There would be little point in speculating about future use of the lockout, but certainly it is now more than an academic term.

One important aspect of the strike should be noted. Real violence is quite rare. In contrast to the bloody conflicts of yester-year, today's strikes seldom are accompanied by loss of life or serious bodily injury. A majority are conducted peacefully with only token picket lines. This does not lessen the potency of the strike or lockout. It does mean that most but not all economic conflicts in the United States conform to the basic notion that the strike is a peaceful withholding of personal services and not a violent or revolutionary device.

A final comment about strikes concerns their statistical significance. The most meaningful statistics are not the raw numbers of strikes or of man-days lost. The relationship of man-days idle because of strikes to total working time is the best measure. To provide a long-run perspective, data are presented in Table 8 for a period of almost 30 years.

Table 8

PERCENTAGE OF MAN-DAYS LOST DUE TO STRIKES
TO TOTAL MAN-DAYS OF WORKING TIME (PRIVATE NONFARM)

Time Period	Percentage*
1941 through 1945	.22%
1946 through 1950	.65
1951 through 1955	.31
1956 through 1960	.29
1961 through 1965	.15
1966	.18
1967	.30
1968	.32
1969	.28
1970	

* The five-year averages are simple arithmetic averages of yearly percentages, computed by the author. Weighted averages might produce figures slightly at variance from those shown.

Source: Bureau of Labor Statistics.

To translate to more readily understood terms, during the best five-year period (1961 through 1965), the 15 hundredths of 1 percent figure means that industrial workers in the United States were on strike for an average of only one day in two and one-half years. Monday morning hangovers probably caused as much loss of work time.

It is recognized, of course, that averages can obscure the very serious effects of some strikes. For example, these statistics were of little solace to copper miners or to the copper companies who endured the nine-month strikes of 1967-1968. But the point is that the strike is not the central feature of collective bargaining. The dominant fact is that most bargains are made without recourse to economic sanctions.

It is also significant that the upturn of strike incidence since 1966 has generated renewed consideration among labor leaders and industrialists of alternatives to strikes and lockouts. Effective mediation is one of the alternatives.

THE YO-YO PRINCIPLE

A characteristic which may be termed "the yo-yo principle" can usually be noted in the observation of a specific bargaining relationship over a period of time. Stated simply, it is the not-very-profound idea that there are ups and downs in the success of peaceful contract bargaining. These variations may be influenced by general economic trends and other external factors. But the notion is that the yo-yo effect may be substantially independent of external forces.

Over a period of about six years concluding in 1954, the National Planning Association sponsored a series of studies entitled "Causes of Industrial Peace." [1] An outstanding committee of management, labor, and public representatives, with Clinton S. Golden as chairman, planned the studies, selected the bargaining relationships to be studied, secured competent persons to make the studies, and offered general comments on the overall project. These research activities grew out of an important observation made by Mr. Golden:

". . . the time has come when, instead of looking into the causes of conflict that we know and read so much about, we ought to try to discover how much peace there is and what makes peace."

The bargaining relationships were selected carefully. Absence of strikes was not the sole criterion; in fact, strikes had occurred in a few of the situations studied. The objective was to portray relationships that had been constructive on an overall basis for extended periods of time in situations of potential conflict that

[1] CAUSES OF INDUSTRIAL PEACE UNDER COLLECTIVE BARGAINING, National Planning Association, Washington, D. C.; 15 case studies published at various dates.

had demanded what has been characterized as "creative discovery" in Chapter I.

Substantial deterioration of the good relationships in most of the cases cited has occurred sometime within the 16 years since the series was published. The decline usually has been only temporary, but it has occurred. Nevertheless, the basic conclusions of the studies are as valid as when published.

Positive change also can occur, as witness the bituminous coal industry. For many years, a coal strike was expected at almost every negotiation. Disputes were major "headaches" for several Presidents. One dispute was the immediate cause of the demise of the National Defense Mediation Board, the predecessor of the National War Labor Board. Another was a principal impetus of the Taft-Hartley Act. However, beginning in 1952 and continuing for about 12 years, there were no strikes of consequence in the industry. Negotiations were conducted so quietly that the general public was not even aware they were in progress. The newspapers carried only modest notice of settlements. More recent indications suggest that the "yo-yo" may be descending and that the absence of strife at the bargaining table was not necessarily accompanied by other aspects of creative stability. In any event, absence of visible trouble for more than a decade was a new feature of coal bargaining.

Reasons for up and down fluctuations are many and varied. No attempt will be made here to list them or to comment on any particular situation. Personnel changes on one or both sides of the table can contribute either to an "up" or a "down" movement. Economic adversity can overwhelm even the best labor-management cooperation. Changes in company or union policy beyond the control of the negotiators can be very important.

To the extent that the yo-yo principle is valid, three concluding observations are pertinent. First, in the worst of relationships, healing factors are present and deserve encouragement. Few persons really want trouble. Chaos can be a stimulant to the development of constructive leadership. Second, the best cooperative effort is not automatically continuous. Vigilance is required to avoid reliance on the past or a tendency to "coast." It may be even more difficult to maintain peace than to secure it after conflict.

Third, a mediator should know whether a relationship in which he is working is at an "up" stage or a "down" stage. Such knowledge may be useful to his performance in a dispute, especially if he can discern the causes. Moreover, if he is a resident mediator and knows the principal negotiators on a continuing basis, there may be things that he can do to minimize or prevent deterioration of a relationship or to stimulate improvements.

DURATION OF CONTRACTS

Labor agreements for a fixed period of time have been the dominant practice in the United States. This is in sharp contrast to the still-prevailing practice in Great Britain and some other democratic countries where agreements are not usually for a fixed term.

A few exceptions in the United States should be noted. Most railroad agreements, some airline agreements, and a few contracts in other industries are "open end." A fixed termination date is replaced by a provision permitting either party to seek changes, with notice, in all or part of the agreement at any time after a stated date. Some agreements are for a fixed term but may be opened at one or more stated dates for negotiation of specified issues. A so-called wage-reopener clause is a common type of re-opener.

A trend towards fixed-term contracts of approximately three years' duration has been pronounced in recent years. Data from negotiations in which Federal Mediation and Conciliation Service mediators have been active, shown in Table 9, reflect this trend.

Table 9

DURATION OF LABOR AGREEMENTS
CONTRACT RENEWALS

Percentages of All Agreements Negotiated in Time Periods Shown
in Which FMCS Mediators Have Been Active

Year Ending June 30	Length of Contract (Months)			
	0-18	19-30	31-42	43 or more
1964	23.4%	40.1%	35.1%	1.4%
1965	19.6	31.8	47.0	1.6
1966	15.0	30.7	51.7	2.6
1967	13.0	32.0	53.5	1.5
1968	9.5	27.8	60.7	2.0
1969	7.4	30.0	61.7	.9
1970	10.1	32.3	56.5	1.1

Source: Federal Mediation and Conciliation Service.

It requires only cursory inspection of the data to note the dramatic increase in agreements of approximately three years' duration. From only about one third of all contract renewals in fiscal year 1964, they increased to about three fifths in a period of five years. The frequencies of agreements running for approximately two years and those for four or more did not change materially. The one-year agreement, once the most common, declined sharply in frequency.

Data for initial labor agreements, not reproduced here, show similar trends. First agreements are typically shorter than contract renewals. However, one-year initial agreements declined from about 60 percent in fiscal year 1964 to about half that figure six years later. The incidence of two-year initial contracts changed little. Three-year initial agreements increased from 16.6 percent to over 40 percent of the total.

Although these data are not all-inclusive, being limited to cases of active mediator involvement, the sample includes between 7,000 and 8,000 negotiations each year in all sizes of bargaining units. There is no reason to believe that it is not representative.

Longer-term agreements tend to complicate contract bargaining. More issues pile up, awaiting disposition. Technological change is so rapid that it is difficult to predict the impact at the work place over a long period. When there is little price stability and employers have resisted automatic cost-of-living wage adjustments, conflict is sharpened since the parties must speculate far into the future. It is especially noteworthy that three-year agreements continued to increase after 1965, even though cost-of-living uncertainties might have motivated a trend toward shorter term contracts. Whether the downturn in fiscal year 1970 foreshadows a change in trend is uncertain.

The trend towards long-term contracts is strong evidence of the great desire of negotiators on both sides of the table for labor peace and collective bargaining stability. A contributing factor is that it may be impossible to accommodate large appetites within a short time span. A cost "package" spread out over three years frequently looks better to employees than a two-year package that is two thirds as large. Sometimes a stalemate on cost items can be broken by alteration of the contract duration that is tied to a company offer or to a union request. When the duration of a new agreement is flexible, the tendency has been to move in the direction of a longer contract.

The trend towards longer-term agreements has special significance to administrators of mediation agencies. Federal Mediation and Conciliation Service data will illustrate. Calculations made from Table 9 will show that the average duration of labor agreements increased from about 2.15 years in fiscal year 1964 to about 2.55 years in fiscal year 1969. Over the same time span, actively mediated disputes increased about 11 percent (7,221 disputes to 8,028), an increase that roughly paralleled a modest enlargement of the FMCS mediation staff. If contract duration had remained static at 2.15 average years, the same negotiations would have "come around" more often. Disputes requiring mediation in fiscal year 1969, calculated hypothetically, could have been about 9,500 disputes. In other words, the trend towards longer term contracts held down the numbers of mediators required. If a sharp reversal of this trend should occur, mediation agencies could be caught shorthanded.

BARGAINING CUSTOMS AND HABITS

Custom and tradition are important elements of bargaining. Companies and unions with a long history of collective bargaining become well acquainted with each other's basic behavior. They will not know the factual content of proposals that will be made until the appropriate time. But they will know about what to expect as to general strategy and methods of bargaining. The advent of a new principal negotiator on either side of the table or a significant change of procedure or tactics by a familiar bargainer can be upsetting until the other party has adjusted to the change.

A mediator must be especially sensitive to the customs, habits, and traditions of each group of negotiators with whom he works. Unless he can quickly make an accurate assessment of the bargaining environment and meld into it, he may do more harm than good.

Custom and tradition can vary almost as much as the 250,000 labor agreements that are in effect. Some new or different "wrinkle" is likely to be encountered in any negotiation. All that can be attempted here is to outline a few of the more significant variables.

Proposal and Counterproposal

The "proposal and counterproposal" method of bargaining is sometimes mistakenly assumed to be the only method. Operating under this concept, the union starts with many proposals or demands and the company has an initial list of offers and its own requests for contract changes. At the outset, the respective positions are usually far apart. Issues are discussed, one at a time or in groups. One party "moves" by officially reducing or modifying its initial list. It is then the turn of the other party. A series of proposals and counterproposals bring the positions closer together until either a company total offer or a union total counterproposal makes an agreement.

In one way or another, this method of bargaining is observed widely. However, the variations may be more important than the prototype. Some are outlined below.

"Whittle Down" v. "Leave on the Table"

Under the "whittle down" method, some issues will be resolved realistically by agreement or by withdrawal of a union or company request. A systematic and positive method of procedure may be observed to record tentative agreements or withdrawals on paper, and these actions may be initialed by the principal negotiators. The issues in dispute are thus gradually reduced until only a few remain. This is a practical equivalent of "proposal and counterproposal."

Frequently, no such formality occurs. Agreement on an issue is only a gentlemen's verbal agreement, sometimes with conditions attached, fortified by notes made by the negotiators and by memories. Technically, the issue is "left on the table." The agreement on the issue will be formalized sometime later if an overall new proposal or counterproposal is drafted and presented at the bargaining table.

Not uncommonly, everything is technically "left on the table" until a final agreement is drafted. The potential problem with this method is that an accumulation of verbal agreements can "come unstuck" when it is time to draft the total agreement. This may happen without any element of bad faith. What appeared to be a verbal agreement was, in fact, incomplete. Or there may be honest differences of opinion as to how the agreement should be reduced to writing.

Listen, Watch, and Wait

In some negotiations there is little or no spoken or written agreement on specific issues until a strike deadline nears. Both parties enter negotiations with "openers"—specific or generalized positions, many of which are understood to be subject to major alteration. As the discussion continues, some demands die a quiet death by inattention or by a firm negative response that is not challenged strongly. Others "shape up" toward agreement without specific accord by a sort of intuitive perception of a settlement area. Certain issues are recognized to be the hard-core items. Quite close to the deadline, one party (usually the company) makes an overall proposal that approximates its final position. If the proposing party has gauged the situation reasonably accurately and believes that a settlement is possible, the negotiations may then move into a proposal-and-counterproposal stage and a settlement. Or, at the least, a drastic narrowing of the differences has occurred before a strike starts.

Under this method of bargaining, it is obvious that the ability of the proposing party to evaluate the opposition position may be crucial. An offer made on an issue that did not require improvement will be difficult to retrieve. Again, a proposal that is wide of the mark may serve only as an irritant.

On occasion, an overall semifinal proposal may be so far from a settlement area that it provokes no counterproposal. The union may merely say "not enough," or the company may reply "preposterous" without offering specifics. In short, a strike may start without clear delineation of the real differences.

Boulwarism

Wide publicity has been given to a company negotiating technique known as Boulwarism because it was developed by Lemuel R. Boulware when he was the principal negotiator for General Electric Company. If a company adopts the concept literally, it makes only one basic proposal. Preparation for negotiations includes extensive economic analysis and a sort of market survey of employee aspirations that is conducted independently of the union. When negotiations begin, the company makes no proposals. It listens carefully to the union negotiators and adds that input to the data already collected. At a point calculated to allow a reasonable amount of discussion before a deadline, but not too much time, the company makes its one proposal. The company will be receptive to union suggestions for minor changes of noneconomic items and for alterations of a money "package" but only if the changes are rearrangements that do not increase the total cost.

As exercised by the General Electric Company with some variations in recent years, this policy is especially disliked by unions. Tabbed with labels such as "Papa knows best," it has been called a form of unilateral determination rather than collective bargaining. Union criticism of the results of the policy is extensive but is overshadowed by frustration. The union's role as the representative of employees is not negated entirely, but it is curtailed sharply.

What is less well known is that Boulwarism is probably practiced more often by unions than by companies, though not under that label. It is seldom seen in major negotiations. However, especially in the construction industry in recent years, local unions frequently have entered negotiations with money demands and simply sat tight until they were granted. In fact, there have been several instances of strikes that were settled at levels above the initial demands.

The mediator's role when Boulwarism is practiced rigidly by either company or union is quite limited. Under unusual circumstances, he might influence the form or content of a proposal to some degree. He might play a part in rearrangement of a package. If there is an overwhelming imbalance of power, he might find it advisable to encourage one party to accept a proposal if he believed the alternatives to be more hazardous. But he has few valid functions unless there is some disposition toward flexibility.

Game-Playing

Another possible form of negotiation has been called "game-playing." The notion in its extreme form could be described as follows: Prior to the official opening of negotiations, one or more secret meetings are held, attended by only one or two persons on each side. A complete agreement is reached on all important issues. Negotiations begin and the same individuals who have "made a deal" put up a vigorous sham battle that may include table-thumping and other histrionics. After everyone on each bargaining committee has been adequately "conditioned," the deal emerges gradually.

Such game-playing has always been infrequent and is becoming more so. Few responsible leaders on either side are in a position to assure delivery on a deal made under such extreme circumstances even if they should desire to participate in the process. The rank-and-file restiveness of recent years has increased the hazards of such a method. Moreover, few true leaders would want to behave in this manner.

Principal negotiators do often sound out each other during or even prior to negotiations. Such contacts may be off the record. More often they take place with the knowledge and consent of all the negotiators. A sense of direction and an assessment of priorities may be critical to success. If a basically good and honest relationship exists, important things can be said in confidence that might ruin the negotiations if disclosed fully too early. No individual is a good negotiator unless he understands the value and necessity of "exploration in confidence" and of timeliness in the development and disclosure of constructive solutions. These legitimate and proper exercises of negotiating skills and sound leadership are by no means the same thing as the improper deals that are sometimes suspected.

Degrees of Sophistication

Negotiators exhibit varying degrees of bargaining sophistication. The differences may be due to experience, personality characteristics, or financial and staff resources.

One aspect of sophistication is the extent of preparation for negotiations. In General Motors-UAW negotiations, for example, almost any fact even remotely relevant to a particular issue is readily available to the negotiators. If it has not been prepared in advance, technical staffs on both sides can secure it promptly. Months of time and effort are expended by both parties before the negotiations begin. The pace is quickened thereafter. This is only one of many such situations, and this type of sophistication is increasing.

At the other extreme, there are some negotiations, even in fairly sizable bargaining relationships, in which reliable relevant information is difficult to obtain. Sometimes it appears that both parties are indifferent to the facts. Lack of adequate information is most common, of course, in the smaller bargaining relationships, where the problem is not one of attitude or intent. The parties simply do not have the financial and staff resources for the kind of preparation job they would like to do.

Of the many aspects of sophistication that might be discussed, only one other will be mentioned here. That is attitude and behavior at the bargaining table.

At one extreme, bargaining can be a brawl. Meetings can be disorderly with little sense of direction or sequence of discussion. Individuals can be profane, vulgar, insulting, incoherent, intoxicated, or some combination of these attributes.

However, such bargaining behavior is quite infrequent. A bargaining session is not a Sunday School class. Discussion can be earthy and pointed, frequently to good purpose. But a typical meeting today is reasonably well organized, and the parties behave toward one another with mutual respect. Having observed collective bargaining proceedings over a period of more than 30 years, one can state positively that there has been much improvement in this aspect of sophistication.

Size of Negotiating Committees

Negotiating Committees, elected or appointed, vary substantially in size. As might be expected, size tends to be proportional to the number of employees covered by the negotiations. However, habit and custom may produce exceptions to this rule.

Bargaining by unusually large committees is sometimes called fish-bowl bargaining. One illustration was the 1964 dispute in the West Coast pulp and paper industry. The Association of Western Pulp and Paper Workers, an independent union, had succeeded two long-established unions. The change of union representation had occurred, in part, because workers believed that earlier negotiations had not been sufficiently democratic. The union negotiated with the Pacific Coast Association of Pulp and Paper Manufacturers, an association of some 18 companies operating 49 different plants with a total of about 20,000 employees. The parties rented the Masonic Hall in Portland, Ore. The union negotiating committee included some 200 members and the association committee consisted of some 150 members. For some time all discussion of issues, presentation of demands, offers and counter offers, and even consideration of procedural matters occurred in that large gathering. It was not until a strike was imminent that agreement could be secured on a subcommittee procedure. Even then, the subcommittee consisted of about 30 members on each side. In the final stages of bargaining during a strike, authorization was secured for subcommittees of 12 members on each side. The negotiating group was never smaller than that.

Bituminous coal negotiations illustrate the other extreme. Most of the direct bargaining has been man-to-man discussion between the president of the United Mine Workers and one man representing the coal operators association. Each consults with a larger group, but there are few if any joint meetings of the larger groups.

Between these fish-bowl and man-to-man extremes, a variety of practices prevail. The majority of negotiations include a combination of joint meetings of all members of both committees and various subcommittee meetings. It is not possible to establish either a typical or an optimum size for a joint committee. In addition to variations due to scope of the employer operations and of the union constituency, the size of manageable meetings will depend on the internal discipline and organization on each side of the table. The only generalization that can be made is that the need to break down into smaller subcommittees at some stage of negotiations is most evident when the committees are large.

Planned Duration of Contract Bargaining

The time required for contract bargaining will depend on the size of the job that lies ahead. If the principal issue will be a general wage increase and it is known that there are few other important items, the time needed may be short. If there are many complicated issues, more time is required. In short, predictions about the probable difficulties of negotiation may be determinative. Typically, company and union officials confer long before the contract expiration date to determine the opening date for the negotiations, the location of the meetings, and all other physical arrangements. In some relationships, arrangements for negotiations conform to well-established practice.

A case in point is a typical negotiation at one of the "Big Five" rubber companies (Firestone, Goodrich, Goodyear, Uniroyal, and General). Company-wide negotiations traditionally begin at least two months prior to the deadlines, largely irrespective of the degree of contemplated difficulty. Moreover, the negotiators plan to work full time for the entire period.

Many other negotiations of comparable size do not begin that early. Negotiations may even be on an off-and-on basis. The parties meet a few days and recess. Continuous or semicontinuous meetings may not begin until a few days before the deadline.

AUTHORITY OF BARGAINERS

On the management side, company bargainers have varying degrees of authority, not always measured accurately by the title of chief negotiator. It is almost always understood tacitly that a chief negotiator's authority is limited to some extent by his president or some other superior or even by the board of directors. The critical questions are the nature of the limitations and how they can be altered.

The chief negotiator may have an overall-cost boundary and possible limitations as to sensitive noneconomic items. Within these broad confines, he and other company negotiators are free to exercise their own discretion. In a few situations the chief negotiator may have to go back to his principals for approval of almost every significant change of company position.

If the authority of the chief company negotiator is severely limited, bargaining is difficult. The real decision-makers must rely on reports that may not transmit the full flavor of the atmosphere at the bargaining table. Moreover, union negotiators are quick to recognize lack of authority. It breeds disrespect for the company negotiator and a desire, sometimes expressed vocally, to "bring the power to the bargaining table." In the tense atmosphere of a strike deadline, inability of management to decide quickly may be the cause of a strike.

These facts of life plus a growing recognition of the importance of labor relations have caused two discernible favorable trends. Not too many years ago it was infrequent to find a chief company negotiator with a position in the management hierarchy as high as vice president. Salaries of labor relations officials were quite low compared to their counterparts in sales, production, or purchasing. The trend now is toward greater recognition and status. There is also a related discernible trend to give the chief company negotiator full authority within broad limits.

Since some limitations are common even with companies that have moved furthest in this respect, it is also quite common for higher company officials to be accessible as the deadline approaches. A company president may be sequestered in the hotel where meetings are being held. Or, if not nearby physically, the key people can be quickly reached by telephone. Many a management-requested caucus, short or long, has been for the purpose of such consultation. Many strikes have been prevented by quick decision. But it must also be stated that unnecessary strikes have occurred because the president or the chairman of the board could not be reached for a timely decision.

These matters of management authority present very sensitive questions to a mediator. Should he seek to induce the real decision-making persons to come to the bargaining table at the critical time? This is a difficult question indeed. If those individuals once participate directly in negotiations, the stature and prestige of the chief negotiator is diminished—possibly for all time. This is especially likely to be the result if the higher company officials personally grant a demand that the chief negotiator has resisted strenuously. Also, it will be difficult for the higher personage to stay away the next time. Moreover, negotiation is a professional job. The chief decision-maker may not be a good negotiator, whatever his merits may be in other capacities. As a general proposition, a mediator does not attempt this step unless the situation is very grave.

An alternative is for the mediator to consult privately with the decision-makers. This procedure provides another line of communication from the bargaining table. Loss of face to the chief negotiator is minimal, especially when he participates in the consultation, as he should. If the company stands firm in such a consultation, the mediator can advise the union of the company's stand. If some concession is secured but the mediator honestly believes that "the well is dry," he can so advise the union.

It must be emphasized that a mediator should not always seek the seat of power. Indeed, the contrary, his dealings should normally be restricted to the persons he finds at the bargaining table.

On the union side, the problem of authority is even more complex. Under most, but not all, union procedures the ultimate "seat of power" resides in the membership. A negotiated agreement can be voted up or down. That problem has been considered in Chapter VII.

Quite aside from membership ratification, the chief union negotiator may not have final authority. This may be so for one or more of three reasons.

The first is the counterpart of the management problem just discussed. One or more higher union officials, not at the bargaining table, may have circumscribed the authority of the negotiator. He can move outside those limitations only with permission. In such instances the mediator may have to make the same sensitive decisions that were discussed earlier. Should he seek to bring the higher ranking union official to the bargaining table? Should he confer with him privately, by telephone or otherwise? The bases for mediator judgement are essentially the same as on the management side.

A union negotiator may sometimes be working under mandates voted by the membership prior to or during negotiations. Union leaders generally seek to avoid this type of limitation for obvious reasons. At the time of crisis, there simply may not be time to call a membership meeting to attempt to lower a union demand. Many a strike, including some that were disastrous to the union, has occurred because the membership restricted the negotiators too severely.

The remaining limitation-of-authority problem stems from the fact that a union is a more democratic organization than a company. The chief union negotiator must obtain a concensus or at least majority approval of the union negotiators on the committee. Especially if he has been working in subcommittee, he must "sell" a tentative proposal to the full committee. It is not at all uncommon for a chief union negotiator to be convinced personally that a specific settlement should be made but be unable to convince the entire committee or even a majority. The mediation role in such a situation may well be to mediate within the committee. There are few logistic impediments. The full committee is normally "on the spot," ready for consultation. The question is whether the mediator can effectively persuade.

WHO IS REPRESENTED AT THE BARGAINING TABLE?

An almost infinite range of representation arrangements can be found at bargaining tables. If only one union represents employees and only one company sits at the table, disparities of size can be enormous. The Pattern Makers League of North America, a union with a nationwide membership of about 13,000, bargains with the giant General Motors Corporation for a few pattern makers. The United Automobile Workers with a membership of more than one million may bargain with an independent parts company employing only 50 workers. Between these extremes, one company, one union combinations could be located at almost any place in a wide spectrum.

Partly because of such disparities, many companies and unions have joined together for purposes of bargaining. They have done so even though the companies may compete with each other in the same product market or the unions may be rivals in seeking to represent workers at unorganized plants. A few examples of bargaining cooperation among companies or unions will be noted.

The Pacific Coast Shipbuilders' Association includes in its membership most of the larger yards in San Francisco, Portland, and Seattle. It negotiates with the Pacific Coast Metal Trades Council, an alliance of some 10 craft unions. In a number of cities, one or more associations of contractors in the construction industry negotiate with a Building Trades Council representing most of the construction unions. These arrangements illustrate situations where there is a coalition for bargaining purposes on both sides of the table.

Numerous examples could be cited of employer associations or informal groupings of employers that bargain jointly with one large union that is dominant in the industry.

Probably the most complex such arrangement is in over-the-road trucking. Virtually all such trucking operations in the United States except in the Chicago area are involved directly or indirectly. Trucking Employers, Inc., is the major employer association, but additional associations have typically been represented or have had a voice within the employer negotiating committees. Other associations and hundreds of individual employers not represented officially are involved indirectly. Officials of the International Brotherhood of Teamsters, Chauffeurs, Warehousemen and Helpers of America at the international level and at conference levels represent some 400,000 employees. A central negotiating committee bargains the principal terms of all agreements; more detailed provisions of a large number of separate contracts are worked out by numerous subcommittees.

Basic steel is another example. Although not formally united as an employer association, a Steel Company's Coordinating Committee has represented 11 major companies in negotiations during the last decade. The Coordinating Committee consults with another group of somewhat smaller basic steel companies, known informally as the Gotham group. On the employer side, actual bargaining of the principal new agreement terms is conducted by a four-man committee selected by the Coordinating Committee. Simultaneous or closely related negotiations on other contract provisions proceed at the company and plant levels. Officials of the United Steelworkers of America represent the many thousands of employees at all these negotiating levels.

Unions long have joined together, formally or informally, to bargain with a single employer. Until recently, the best known joint efforts were by Metal Trades Councils or Building Trades Councils (combinations of craft unions). Also, it is not uncommon for a craft union that represents a minority group in a plant to join informally with a majority industrial union for purposes of bargaining.

Expansion of the union coordination or coalition concept has occurred in recent years, sometimes under the stimulus of the Industrial Union Department of the AFL-CIO and sometimes at the initiative of a dominant industrial union. The primary targets have been large multiplant companies where a variety of industrial and craft unions represent employees in various parts of the United States. Companies affected within the 1966-1970 period include General Electric, Union Carbide, Campbell Soup, and the four major nonferrous metals companies (Anaconda, Kennecott, Phelps Dodge, and American Smelting and Refining).

In most bargaining structures, the existing arrangement has developed over a period of time. Efforts by unions or employers, or both, to "meet power with power" play a significant part in such development. However, convenience and the search for orderly procedures are almost equal factors. In a competitive industry, both companies and unions have often concluded that it is better to have wider representation at the same bargaining table than to attempt to bargain on a fragmented basis.

If a mediator is to work productively in a particular bargaining relationship, he must know the structure of that relationship. It can be more than useful if he also knows some of the history. The sources of the composition of social organisms often explain behavior and attitudes. Moreover, positions on disputed issues can often be understood fully only in the light of the composition of the employer or union group that is supporting those positions.

In most of these multiple company and multiple union bargaining arrangements, the composition of the forces on each side is not in dispute. For whatever reason, each side of the table accepts the representation on the other side. The bargaining of a contract or simultaneous bargaining of several agreements goes directly to the merits of the issues.

Sometimes there is a threshold dispute about the composition of one of the bargaining teams. The coalition or coordinated bargaining aspects of the General Electric, Union Carbide, Campbell Soup, and copper disputes are illustrative. In all these instances, no effective bargaining about contract issues took place for lengthy periods of time. Long and costly strikes occurred in most instances. The companies refused to accept the changes of bargaining structure demanded by the unions. That issue had to be at least partially resolved before either party was willing to come to grips with the usual contractual issues.

Other disputes have illustrated the other side of the same basic problem. The West Coast shipbuilding industry has been noted as an example of coalition on both sides of the table. In 1965 negotiations, three of the 10 unions decided to break away from the

Pacific Coast Metal Trades Council in order to bargain separately with the Pacific Coast Shipbuilders' Association. A relatively short strike by the Machinists and a long strike in 1966 and 1967 by the Electricians brought this situation into public view. The wage disputes in both the Machinist and Electrician strikes were related closely to the fragmentation of the Metal Trades Council. Interestingly enough, the Pacific Coast shipbuilders were trying to bring the unions back together at the same time that General Electric was attempting to avoid joint dealings with unions at its plants.

Other instances could be cited of formal or informal coalitions of unions that have split into smaller groups or have disintegrated completely, often with accompanying bargaining problems of significance. Several have occurred in the construction and newspaper industries.

Bargaining coalitions on the employer side can be altered drastically. The Pacific Coast Pulp and Paper Manufacturers' Association, referred to earlier, disbanded in January 1969, prior to the beginning of negotiations. The result was separate bargaining by the various companies, primarily on a plant-by-plant basis.

This is not the place to discuss the merits or demerits of coordinated bargaining, to explore the details of any of the important disputes that have been noted, or to outline how they were ultimately resolved. They are mentioned here primarily to support a few general observations.

Employer and employee representation arrangements at bargaining tables in the United States are so diverse that they defy description. It cannot be presumed that any existing combination is static or that it will persist indefinitely. Powerful forces at work on the employer or union side may push toward either joint bargaining or separate bargaining. The long-run tendency appears to be in the direction of more and larger groupings. If that trend persists, it may create more public emergency disputes. Bigger bargaining is not necessarily better bargaining.

When a change of composition on one side of the table is resisted by the forces on the other side of the table, contract negotiations can be unusually difficult. The threshold question of who is to bargain and for whom may stymie consideration of the usual contract issues. It follows that mediation is especially difficult during such a transition period. Attempts to assist the parties to resolve the threshold dispute are likely to encounter calculated and emotional responses that are less subject to rational solution than disputes about the content of an agreement.

PATTERN BARGAINING

The words "pattern bargaining" have been used rather loosely to describe a tendency on the part of some negotiators to agree on terms identical to or substantially the same as those negotiated earlier by other bargainers. Pattern bargaining is not the same thing as simple or even highly sophisticated comparison with bargains reached elsewhere. *True pattern bargaining exists only when there is a conscious intent to achieve a result that is substantially identical to some other known "key" bargain.*

If such a conscious intent exists, how is it to be effectuated? Even at those plants, companies, or industries where pattern bargaining is commonly believed to have existed for many years, labor costs rarely are the same. Different units may have started at different levels before pattern bargaining began. Different product mixes, processes, wage classification structures, or age or sex composition of the work forces may produce divergent results even if the starting points were the same. Any method of applying a pattern can have varying effects. For example, the cost of an improvement in pension benefits is quite different in a plant with a work force whose average age is 35 years than in one whose average age is 55 years.

Thus, pattern bargaining is not a simple process even when there is a conscious mutual desire to "follow a leader." The parties must decide how to follow. Quite often the decision to follow a particular pattern is accompanied by insistent demands by the company or the union for realistic modification of the pattern as the different effects of application come to light. Most acknowledged pattern followers on both sides of the table also seek to obtain an "edge" for themselves. A union expression of this desire is "putting frosting on the cake."

Pattern bargaining is a double-edged sword. The key bargain unquestionably narrows the differences for the pattern followers. But it increases the possibility of conflict over what may appear to be small differences. The strike of telephone installation and maintenance workers in Chicago at the time of the 1968 Democratic Convention was a highly visible illustration. Most of the many bargaining components of the telephone industry already had concluded or would ultimately reach agreements at or about the calculated levels of the patterns. That happened in Chicago, too, but only after the strike of almost five months' duration.

In short, even among pattern bargainers the key bargain is only a starting point for intensive negotiations over its application.

A second feature of most pattern bargaining is that the pattern is limited to a few major issues such as wages and significant fringe benefits. Non-pattern bargaining occurs for all other issues. In such cases the public is often misled when it becomes known that a pattern has been established. The tendency is to believe that subsequent negotiations of the pattern followers will be uncomplicated. In addition to the problems of adaptation of a pattern to a specific contractual relationship, the non-pattern issues may be difficult to resolve.

IMBALANCE OF POWER

Power factors on the two sides of the bargaining table are seldom equal. In any event, since there is no common unit of measurement, how is equality to be defined? The financial resources of a corporation can be weighed, but how can one equate those tangible assets against the resources of a union? A union strike fund can be quantified, but it is only the initial weight on the balance scale. The basic resources of a union in a power struggle are the will to resist and the solidarity of its members. Assuming sufficient motivation, union strength has no tangible dimensions.

Moreover, power factors can change drastically from time to time. Fluctuations of the business cycle, of economic factors peculiar to a plant or industry, of unemployment, and of general employee morale can change a union's position from dominant to unfavorable.

Despite these inherent difficulties of appraisal, many collective bargaining relationships can be recognized as embodying reasonable equality. In these situations, bargaining is a civilized method of accommodating the legitimate aspirations of both parties. Rational considerations outweigh the ability to exploit a power position of the moment. Power is exercised with responsibility and with recognition of the strength of a worthy, friendly opponent. An occasional strike may only be evidence of a healthy basic relationship.

Mediation in these relationships can help to preserve civilized behavior and the responsible exercise of power. It can be most useful in the avoidance of needless strikes, in shortening those strikes that do occur, and in facilitating the bargaining process generally. In short, the mediator's function as a catalyst can be of real value to the parties and rewarding to the mediator.

When there is a great imbalance of power, bargaining can also be a valuable and sensible process, provided power is exercised with responsibility. A huge union bargaining with a tiny company is in a power position to put it out of business on short notice. It does not often do so, for there are built-in inhibitions. Jobs are at stake, and no responsible union can ever forget that fact. Moreover, most union leaders want to use their power in such situations wisely and with compassion. Similarly, giant corporations dealing with tiny unions usually evidence a remarkable degree of fairness and equity. Conditions "hammered out" where the power factors are more equal are granted to the weak union even though they could be withheld.

The real collective bargaining trouble spots are situations where there is an appreciable imbalance of power and the dominant party, whether company or union, does not behave responsibly. An out-and-out power struggle under such conditions is not rewarding to a mediator, or to anyone else. The strong party probably does not want a mediator but, if one is present, may attempt to use him as a part of its strategy. The weak party will almost invariably seek mediation assistance, sometimes almost desperately. Help from any source is welcome. But the weak side may be resentful as well as dissatisfied when the mediator is unable to rectify the power imbalance.

It is not suggested that there is any satisfactory way to solve this dilemma. Legal or regulatory remedies are not the answer. The problems of defining power are such that it would be all but impossible to administer such remedies in an effective and fair way.

It is probable that the quiet voice of persuasion, exercised as effectively as possible by a mediator, is a more potent tool than any other known device. In a very real sense, mediation exists as a bulwark to avoid unfortunate legislation that might otherwise emerge if too many illustrations of irresponsible exercise of power should make collective bargaining politically unacceptable. Fortunately, these sore spots in the collective bargaining world are relatively few.

Chapter IX

DOMINANT ISSUES IN CONTRACT DISPUTES

Each contract negotiation has its own peculiar flavor. One issue or a group of related issues is likely to be dominant. Frequently the parties can make accurate predictions, months before discussions begin, as to what will be the central feature. Occasionally the dominant issues emerge only after the negotiations have started. If a strike occurs, the dispute sometimes changes its essential character as a result.

There is no need here to explore issues that have been considered already. Threshold disputes about who is to be represented at the bargaining table, issues arising out of technological change, problems inherent in pattern bargaining, internal differences within a union or within an employer group—any of these can be the most critical aspect of a dispute. There are a number of other issues, however, that merit separate consideration.

WAGES AND BENEFITS

Wage and benefit costs are important factors in virtually all disputes. Some years ago it was common to hear the expression, "Once the general wage increase is agreed to, everything else will fall in line." That analysis is only occasionally valid today.

As fringe benefits (pensions, insurance, vacations, holidays, overtime, special premium payments, etc.) have developed over the last three decades, the word "fringe" is no longer appropriate. Typically, the costs of such benefits are in the neighborhood of 25 percent of total labor costs. The word "fringe" originated when benefits were minor and were sometimes added to a general wage increase as a "sweetener" to conclude an agreement. Years ago, many smaller companies did not even calculate the cost of fringes. It was known that costs were being added, but the amounts were sufficiently small to escape careful attention.

Thus one departure from the "everything else will fall in line" notion is to consider the cost of all direct economic benefits as a "package," and the general wage increase only as the most important item. If the old expression should be changed to read: "Once the cost of the economic package is agreed to, everything else will fall in line," it would apply to a sizable number of present-day disputes.

Most benefit improvements can be translated into a cents-per-hour equivalent. This permits the negotiators to attempt to reach agreement on the total cost of an economic package if they choose that method of bargaining. Once a total sum has been fixed, attention can then be directed to its distribution among wages and the various benefits.

The costing of benefits is not an automatic or simple process. In almost all instances, assumptions have to be made. For example, the cost of almost any pension benefit is dependent on actuarial assumptions, including the interest rate on pension fund investments and the time period over which future benefits are to be funded. Moreover, even the most careful cost calculations are usually at variance with experience during the contract term.

Mediators encounter a wide range of benefit costing situations. In some of the most sophisticated negotiations, the parties have agreed on methods of costing and, in fact, on the costs of all items being considered. In other instances, company and union cost calculations differ significantly, primarily because of different assumptions. In a few cases, cost figures are nothing more than wild guesses. The increasing importance of costing of benefits has made it necessary for mediators to know the basic ingredients of the costing process. Mediators are not pension actuaries. However, no mediator can assist intelligently in a dispute about pensions if he is unaware of the significance of some of the assumptions that cause actuaries to differ. The ability to calculate costs of other benefits, such as vacations and holidays, is now a part of a mediator's job description. When a mediator assumes responsiblity for cost calculations, risk is involved. If he is inaccurate, the parties may blame him for the error or for an injudicious assumption. Such risks are not sufficiently grave, however, to justify the withholding of needed assistance in this aspect of bargaining.

It should not be assumed that all negotiations about economic issues are conducted on a cost basis. Many unions insist on direct discussion of benefits and do not presume to ascribe a specific cost to any one benefit. This does not always avoid cost arguments.

Companies necessarily calculate costs. If a mediator is to be useful in helping to weigh one proposed benefit against another at least an approximation of costs is essential.

Costing introduces another complication, variously characterized as: "override," "creep" or by other names. An increase of basic wage rates may automatically raise the cost of existing fringe benefits such as vacations and holidays and any other benefits that are keyed to wage rates. Because these costs are substantial already, the effect of wage increases on such costs must be determined in order to arrive at true total value of an economic package.

Another aspect of wage and benefit negotiation is becoming increasingly important as the duration of labor agreements increases. In a one-year agreement, most wage and benefit changes are made at the beginning of the new contract. In a three-year agreement, the wage and benefit improvements agreed upon are made effective at various times during the three.year term. The timing of the improvements is of intense interest to both parties. For example, a wage increase of 60 cents per hour may be phased in equally (20 cents, 20 cents, and 20 cents) at the beginning of each agreement year. It may be applied "heavy on the front end" and become 30 cents, 15 cents, and 15 cents, respectively. Or it may be "heavy on the back end" and be 15 cents, 15 cents, and 30 cents, respectively. The same total of 60 cents per hour would cost the company an *average* of 40 cents, 45 cents, or 35 cents per hour under those different methods when the cost is calculated over the three-year period. When a stalemate exists on wage and benefit costs, one method that may be utilized by the parties or by mediators to break the deadlock is to change the timing of wage and benefit improvements.

Juggling effective dates and expertise in costing of benefits may be of great value after the economic gap between the positions of the parties has narrowed to a money difference that is not insurmountable. A strike can occur when the economic difference is not great and would quickly be equalled by strike costs. In short, compromise to avoid a strike can occur in a variety of ways other than by direct retreat from firmly held demands or offers. The addition or subtraction of a benefit or a change in effective dates may be more palatable than retreat from an overall position on a general wage increase.

If the economic gap is substantial and there is no willingness to compromise on the money positions, there may be little merit in attempting to nibble at the problem. One or both sides will have to make basic changes to avoid a strike. A strike over economic matters alone need not be long. Money translates readily into lost business and lost profits on the company side and lost paychecks on the union side. Despite our materialistic society, or possibly because of it, money has limited emotional value. It is when an economic conflict is intermingled with other emotionally charged issues that early compromise or capitulation becomes unlikely.

The long 1959 strike in the basic steel industry is an illustration. If that dispute had been limited to direct money issues, important as they were, there is little doubt but that the strike would have ended sooner. However, the companies' insistence on drastic changes in the "local working conditions" provisions of the agreements (crew size and a multitude of other operating practices) was a highly emotional issue that almost obscured the economic dispute.

HOUSECLEANING ISSUES

An especially virulent type of dispute occasionally arises out of a background that includes all or most of the following elements: Let us assume that a plant has been quite profitable for a period of years. But plant management has permitted gradual development of inefficient and costly work practices. They have escaped attention because of profits and because the more visible hourly wage rate costs are not excessive. Also, provisions conducive to inefficiency may have crept into successive labor agreements until management rights have been substantially eroded. Declining profits or stiff competition has finally alerted the board of directors to the danger. Unit labor costs are too high despite competitive wage rates. Plant management is changed at the top levels, or the existing management is told to "tighten up or else."

When a situation of this type develops, the company may enter the next labor negotiations with a long list of demands for contract changes. It has determined to "clean house." Instead of attempting to correct a few unsatisfactory conditions, the company aims for an "ideal contract" from a management point of view. Every clause in the old contract has been examined with a fine-tooth comb to eliminate plant inefficiencies and to restore management prerogatives. The wage offer probably is quite generous, since wage rates are not considered to be the cause of the problems.

The union's reaction is predictable. No matter how satisfactory the proposed wage increase may be, it will not offset what is often characterized as the company's "take away" program. Employees have not been prepared for the company position. They believe they are working for a sound company and do not visualize the competitive hazards. They do not believe their jobs are at stake. The company that may have been a "soft touch" has suddenly made a complete reversal. Shop stewards who may have been able to secure from foremen almost anything reasonable and some things that were unreasonable see that they will lose status and power if the company proposals are accepted. Employees know they will have to work harder. Despite the proposed wage increase, acceptance of the company's proposals may mean reductions in earnings for some employees. Union leaders may realize that a few corrections must be made, but they also know that acceptance of the complete company proposal would be equivalent to political suicide. The almost certain result is a long strike.

Two cases are illustrative. One involved a Yale and Towne plant in Philadelphia, where a 152-day strike began on August 31, 1961. Wages were not a significant issue. The strike issues were company demands for contract changes, notably in seniority and incentive pay areas. The plant is a large producer of material-handling equipment. Gradual but pervasive product changes had resulted in operations that were almost like those in a job shop. These product changes plus a militant union and a too-acquiescent management had resulted in costly application of seniority and an incentive plan that had "gone sour." Plant practices in both of these areas were much more liberal for employees than were required by a reasonable interpretation of the existing contract. Moreover, certain contract provisions intended to apply to the former production methods had not been rewritten in the light of the changed methods. The plant was becoming financially troubled, and a new management was determined to make wholesale changes. Company proposals for new contract language were far-reaching and restrictive.

It is not essential to the present discussion to develop fully the long story of controversy and settlement. The strike was accompanied by some violence. Emotion frequently exceeded reason—on both sides. Substantial contract changes were made but only to the extent required to preserve the plant's competitive position. Mediation played a significant role in achieving the eventual settlement. A viable relationship was not reestablished solely by a new contract and return to work. The new agreement was in many respects a truce, and much hard work remained to be done to restore sound collective bargaining.

The second illustration is the strike of the Oil, Chemical and Atomic Workers at the Shell Oil refinery and petrochemical plant at Pasadena, Texas. The strike began August 18, 1962, and was not terminated until August 7, 1963, almost a full year later.

Wages were not an important disputed issue at any time. The union struck originally over several lesser issues that became obscured rather quickly by certain company demands. These company demands could have been postponed prior to the strike if the union had agreed to explore the issues after contract signing. The plant was in no immediate danger of becoming noncompetitive. However, faced with a strike in any case, the company made a post-strike decision to press its position on the theory that the issues had to be resolved sometime.

The company demands arose out of a long history of alleged inefficient use of manpower. In an industry in which labor cost is a small percentage of total cost, restrictive work assignment and work performance practices had developed independently of unionization. In the company view, they had become more onerous after union organization and after substantial technological change. The most significant company proposals would have given it an almost unlimited right to change work assignment and work performance practices. Union objections to these management demands were based on fear of loss of jobs and general resistance to change. Of at least equal importance was the union's conviction that it would be converted from a strong, militant union to a weak, ineffective organization.

The dispute was complicated by the fact that the company was able to continue substantially normal operations during the strike. Supervisors, office employees, and research and development personnel, aided by automated equipment, performed the essential tasks of some 2,000 production and maintenance employees without new hires. This was accomplished despite almost complete observance of the strike by union employees.

The strike settlement, aided materially by mediation, resulted in substantial movement toward the company position but with a new set of definitions and criteria to protect union employees against indiscriminate and excessive utilization of restored management rights. Some job losses caused by more efficient utilization of manpower and automation were mitigated by liberalized separation pay and early retirement provisions.

These two cases are outstanding examples of major revisions of day-by-day operating practices of long standing. Not all such strikes are of such long duration. However, it is axiomatic that major surgery of this type is likely to result in a strike and that settlement is extremely difficult. Short of complete capitulation by one side or the other, the development of new, reasonable work rules and practices is a major task even if there is a joint willingness to undertake it. Mediation can be most useful for a simple reason. Once the parties have "locked horns," neither is prepared to initiate viable compromise solutions even though they may become willing to accept proposals made by others.

MARGINAL-PLANT NEGOTIATIONS

A somewhat similar bargaining problem arises when one plant is becoming noncompetitive or claims that it already is noncompetitive in an industry where other plants are prosperous. The management may then enter a negotiation with an ultimatum that it will close the plant permanently unless the union agrees to major contract changes and/or an appreciably lower money settlement than has been made at other generally comparable plants.

In such disputes, an initial question is whether the union and the employees believe the company. Is the threat to shut down a bluff; does the company mean business? Numerous other crucial questions require answers. Assuming that the plant is actually unprofitable, what are the reasons? Are wage rates out of line? Has an incentive plan become nonproductive and unmanageable? If other inefficiencies exist, are they related to costly labor relations practices or contract provisions or to generally poor management? If the union should accede to important company requests, is there a good chance that the plant can be saved, or will it close in the near future anyway? Is the plant located in a small city where it is a major source of employment, or is it in a large city where other employment opportunities exist?

Disputes of this type are quite numerous, even in a period of general prosperity. During a business downturn, the numbers increase markedly. Few such disputes get national publicity, but they may be critical in a smaller community.

If a company position in such a case is "for real," a long strike —sometimes even a short one—may settle the dispute by causing premature plant closure.

Effective, imaginative mediation is especially needed in these disputes and is usually welcomed by both parties. Circumstances are so varied that it would be impossible to outline specific solutions. Some disputes are insoluble. When a mediator is able to assist the parties in a durable resolution, that one accomplishment may justify his salary for many years. Qualitative review of many FMCS achievements in disputes of this type in the period from 1961 through 1968 suggests that a major part of the entire budget of the agency could be supported on this count alone.

DEPRESSED INDUSTRIES

In an affluent society in which most industries have long been at least reasonably profitable, special problems develop for the exceptions. In a depressed industry, most companies and plants are in an adverse economic situation.

A depressed industry can develop because of foreign competition or the nature and structure of domestic competition or because the relentless forces of change make its products relatively unattractive or unnecessary. Examples over the years have been numerous. The advent of automobiles and trucks eliminated or completely transformed a variety of businesses geared to horse-drawn vehicles. Foreign competition has virtually eliminated domestic watch manufacture. Foreign imports and nonunion competitors in the United States have created adverse economic conditions for organized textile, hosiery, cotton garment, and shoe manufacturing firms.

In these and similar industries, the union problem is acute. Wages and benefits comparable to those in the more prosperous industries cannot be paid. Union leaders and members face a continuous problem of accepting less or hastening decline with resultant loss of jobs. Typically, the employer is not financially strong enough to take a strike, and the union is similarly weakened by the economic predicament. Strikes are infrequent in these industries, being luxuries that nobody can afford.

The unionized women's hosiery industry is an extreme example. In the 1920s, hosiery wages were among the highest in the country. The American Federation of Hosiery Workers was a strong, proud union that pioneered in the development of many features of collective bargaining not reached by the large, powerful unions of today until about 30 years later. Economic adversity has reduced that union to a mere shell of an organization—a tiny division within the Textile Workers Union with few members and few labor agreements. Moreover, this happened despite a number of imaginative and courageous attempts by the union to stem the economic tide.

Mediation in a depressed industry situation can be helpful. But when the economic factors are overwhelming, it may sometimes assume aspects of a hand-holding operation.

EXPLOSIVE NONECONOMIC ISSUES

Some of the hardest-fought disputes do not involve money to an appreciable degree. A company and a union hold firmly to differing points of view for reasons of principle.

Union security is a prime example. In one form or another, it has been the major point of controversy in important disputes in the United States for many years. Most unions believe that all employees they represent have an obligation to belong to and support the bargaining agent. The power derived from employee solidarity and the need for financial support are major reasons for this position. In a democratic union, such pragmatic motives are buttressed by a sincere belief that all who have a community of interest should participate in the formulation of union policy as well as pay their proportionate cost of the benefits that are obtained. Many employers object to some forms of union security because they do tend to give the union more power. But many others have fought union security for a different reason. Emphasizing freedom of choice, they have argued that their employees should not be compelled to join or support any organization against their will.

It is not within the scope of this book to attempt to trace all the major steps in the long history of the union security issue or to recite the details of any one dispute. The issue has been of less importance in recent years. But this does not mean that it has disappeared from the labor relations scene. As recently as 1961 and 1962, it was the only residual issue of consequence in several large and important aerospace disputes. In less visible cases it still persists. It was an item of greater or lesser consequence in 1,315 out of 8,028 cases in which FMCS mediators were active in the fiscal year ending June 30, 1969.

Certain other noneconomic issues also can generate strong emotions. Seniority and subcontracting disputes are illustrative of matters often believed to involve issues of principle that are more important to the parties than the practical effects.

BREAKTHROUGH EFFECTS

A somewhat different type of issue that is exceedingly difficult to resolve is a so-called "breakthrough" issue. Unions often place great emphasis on a provision that is something new in collective bargaining—a first in the industry or sometimes a first for all industries.

The Steelworkers' achievement in 1965 basic steel negotiations of pension benefits after 30 years' service regardless of age is an example. Such benefits were virtually nonexistent in any major industry. Unlike union security, this was a direct cost item. Moreover, it was a cost item of uncertain amount. The steel industry resisted it vigorously, and not solely because of cost. The possibility of loss of skilled workers was an important factor in the industry objection. In addition, the regardless-of-age notion was a concept with possible "foot in the door" implications. Once agreement was reached on a 30-year service requirement, future pressures could arise for shorter length-of-service criteria.

In short, breakthrough issues often present more difficult bargaining problems than are apparent in the initial demand. Unions may push hard for two reasons. One is the immediate prestige and publicity value. The other is the foot-in-the-door potential. Companies fear the immediate effects, but they are mindful also of the foot-in-the-door aspect.

UNSATISFACTORY GRIEVANCE HANDLING

A substantial number of difficult contract negotiations and many strikes are traceable to an unsatisfactory grievance procedure.

If the grievance and arbitration procedures work well, the resolution of day-by-day operating problems is reasonably prompt. Contract negotiations can be limited essentially to sought-after changes in the agreement. Such changes may extend to work rules or plant practices, but proposals in this area normally are few in number in any one negotiation if the grievance procedure is adequate. However, if the grievance procedure or the arbitration procedure or both are not functioning well, an accumulation of plant operating problems can pile up to complicate or overwhelm contract negotiations.

The sharp trend toward longer-term agreements has accentuated this problem area. When labor agreements were typically one year's duration, it was possible, though undesirable, to dispose of a backlog of grievance matters in the annual negotiations.

However, if there is a three-year backlog, the potential problem can be more than tripled. The buildup of resentments and frustrations is compounded by time.

Evidence of an unsatisfactory grievance procedure is of three principal types. There may be a mountain of unresolved grievances and union insistence that they can be settled before serious discussion of wages and other critical demands begins. There may be a long "laundry list" of demands for new or changed agreement language that is, in reality, an attempt to settle grievance issues by contract prescription. There may be a union request to eliminate arbitration and restore the right to strike during the life of the argument. These manifestations have appeared in many negotiations in recent years.

Opinion differs as to how much detail should be included in contracts and how much should be handled less formally via the grievance procedure. The underlying conceptual choice is whether to legislate in a massive way or to develop a case-by-case common-law approach. Whichever the approach, the contract negotiation problem arises when the pressures generated by an unsatisfactory grievance procedure cause an eruption at the bargaining table. Subsequent chapters will consider situations of this type in more detail. At this point it suffices to say that this is an increasing problem, that contract negotiation never has been the appropriate time to settle a mass of grievances, and that the obvious need is to restructure or otherwise correct the faulty grievance procedure that produces these results.

REFUSAL TO BARGAIN

The Taft-Hartley Act imposes a statutory obligation on both parties to bargain in good faith once union representation has been established. Regulations and decisions of the National Labor Relations Board and the courts have an important bearing on whether "good faith" exists, under both generalized and specific circumstances. This is not the place to review the legal aspects of good-faith bargaining. Irrespective of the legalities, mediators do encounter situations where for practical purposes, there is a refusal to bargain.

One such circumstance arises often in the negotiation of initial agreements. A union wins representation rights, usually in an NLRB election, perhaps by a close vote. The parties then begin to negotiate a first contract, but the negotiations either are completely fruitless or are so painfully slow that progress is minimal.

In some of these instances, the company has not realistically accepted the union and is quite deliberately seeking to avoid a contractual relationship. This type of case has been aptly labled informally within the FMCS as a "lost ball in the high weeds." It is not suggested that the fault lies entirely on the employer side; a union can negotiate stupidly and without recognizing the realities. Frequently the union does not strike for the simple reason that a strike would be unsuccessful, but at the same time it may hold to unattainable demands.

Elsewhere, a strong union may "play cat and mouse" with a small company, employing a variety of harassing tactics short of calling a strike.

In all of these situations the mediator attempts to cut through the sham and pretense and assist in the consummation of an agreement. The resulting contract will usually reflect the power factors. But the weaker party will normally be better advised to operate under a contract that it considers to be unsatisfactory than to flounder in a long series of fruitless meetings. Sometimes the mediator's efforts will be unavailing, and there may be no alternative but to abandon the effort. However, many such cases are settled by imaginative and resourceful assistance.

A related problem develops in a wider range of disputes when one party (or both) files unfair labor practice charges during negotiations. Often this is a tactical maneuver designed to add fear of legal penalties to the merits of a dispute and to speed the bargaining process, but it may backfire. The existence of charges and the time and energy devoted to processing them can interfere with bargaining or even stop it completely. A mediator will normally exert every effort to avoid this result and to continue the bargaining. If an agreement is reached long before the unfair labor charges have been brought to a conclusion, as is usually the case, a new issue can arise. The party against whom the charges have been filed may insist that they be withdrawn as a condition to agreement. The parties can so stipulate and they usually do so, but this does not necessarily conclude the matter. Once some types of charges have been filed, they cannot be withdrawn without action by the National Labor Relations Board. Normally the NLRB does accede to the wishes of the charging party, and the charges are quashed. To do otherwise might prolong the dispute.

ISSUES DEVELOPING OUT OF A STRIKE

A strike creates issues that did not previously exist. Some of these new issues develop just before the strike starts. Others may arise during the strike and must be resolved before work is resumed.

It requires time to shut down a blast furnace or an open hearth at a steel plant if extensive damage is to be avoided. For many chemical and related operations, a precipitate shutdown might involve great danger to life as well as property. Will the union in the early hours or days of a strike permit its members to handle essential shutdown duties? The answer to this question must be known prior to the critical times for beginning the shutdown of each unit. In some situations the company may plan to continue operations with nonunion personnel or to accomplish the shutdown by using supervisors after a strike begins. Such questions and intentions can seriously complicate negotiations during the hours when bargaining is normally most productive.

After a shutdown has been accomplished and a strike is fully under way, essential maintenance work must be performed to protect plant and equipment and to permit early resumption of work when the strike ends. Who is to do this work, and under what conditions? These are not easy matters to settle, and they also may complicate the final hours of bargaining.

One unfortunate result of discussion of these questions is that necessary attention to such matters may give rise to the belief that a strike is inevitable at a time when cautious optimism is essential to an agreement without a strike.

Even if a strike is completely peaceful, it creates new issues. What is to be done about retroactivity for maintenance employees who may be permitted to work? Are insurance provisions of the expiring contract to be continued in full force and effect during the strike, and, if so, who will pay the premiums? Is strike time to be credited for purposes of pensions and future vacations? If a strike is of long duration, some of these questions involve substantial sums of money.

If any real or alleged violence occurs during a strike and employees are discharged or otherwise disciplined, the issues created can loom as large as the issues that precipitated the strike.

Sometimes court suits or unfair labor practice charges are filed by one or both parties at or after the start of a strike. Disposition of these matters can become exceedingly difficult.

Even if the strike has performed its intended function of changing minds with respect to prestrike issues, the strike-related issues may be charged with emotion. Mediation can be especially helpful in disposing of these issues.

EXTRAORDINARY PROCEDURES

CHAPTER X

MEDIATION IN EMERGENCY DISPUTES

Emergency disputes are defined here as situations **in the private sector of the economy** in which the President concludes, for whatever reason, that a strike or a lockout cannot be tolerated or must be substantially curtailed. The Taft-Hartley Act and the Railway Labor Act contain the existing statutory procedures for handling such disputes. Emphasis here will be on the mediation features of these procedures.

The basic concept underlying emergency dispute procedures in peacetime is that the public interest sometimes supersedes private interests. While strikes and lockouts normally are permissible as persuaders in the reaching of voluntary agreements, in some circumstances the exercise of economic sanctions by the parties can inflict irreparable damage on parties not directly involved. Since collective bargaining is an institutional arrangement within a democratic society, the needs of the total economy sometimes must prevail over the interests of a segment of that economy.

Even in such situations, the existing emergency dispute concept includes the basic premise that agreement should be reached by the parties. At least in theory, the laws defer but do not deny the right of the parties to resort ultimately to economic sanctions. Deferral of that right is accomplished by providing a so-called "cooling-off period." The purpose is to provide time for more negotiation and more time for mediation to assist in reaching agreement. Compulsion enters the picture only if all these extra efforts are unproductive. Even then, compulsion is not spelled out in the laws. It is an ultimate recourse of the public that is not entrusted to the Executive Branch of the Government. Compulsion can be ordered only by the Congress.

The principal purpose of this chapter is to appraise and evaluate these statutory emergency disputes procedures. How well have they served to accomplish the intended objectives?

NATIONAL EMERGENCIES—TAFT-HARTLEY ACT

Sections 206 to 210, inclusive, of Title II of the Taft-Hartley Act contain the relevant legislation. These provisions emerged in 1947 out of (1) a congressional "swing to the right," (2) the postwar wave of strikes in major industries, especially the coal, telephone, and maritime strikes in the first half of that year, (3) the general aversion to compulsory arbitration expressed by both labor and industry, and (4) considerable criticism in some industry circles of nonstatutory fact-finding boards that had functioned in the period immediately following World War II.

The various amendments made in the 1935 Wagner Act by the 1947 statute caused labor to label the results a "slave labor act." It will be recalled that Congress enacted this legislation over President Truman's veto. Although labor objected to other changes, its major opposition was directed to the injunction procedure in the national emergency sections. After certain procedures to be discussed subsequently, a court can issue an injunction ordering the parties not to strike or lock out for 80 days.

Despite this somewhat inauspicious beginning, Sections 206-210 have remained substantially unchanged for 24 years. This has not been due to a lack of proposals for change. Scarcely a year has gone by without the injection into the congressional hopper of a variety of bills by representatives or senators. All have died on the vine. A Committee for Economic Development task force of prominent persons made recommendations. Presidents Kennedy and Johnson made public statements of intent to submit proposals to Congress, but none were submitted. President Nixon made a proposal on February 27, 1970, that will be discussed later.

A major recommendation was a near-unanimous report of President Kennedy's Advisory Committee on Labor-Management Policy. Entitled "Free and Responsible Collective Bargaining and Industrial Peace" and dated May 1, 1962, it includes but is not limited to specific proposals for alteration of national emergency disputes procedures.

The National Labor-Management Panel studied the matter

thoroughly in 1965 and 1966. It pursued this inquiry in accordance with a statutory provision which reads:

"It shall be the duty of the panel, at the request of the Director [of the FMCS], to advise in the avoidance of industrial controversies and the manner in which mediation and voluntary adjustment shall be administered, *particularly with reference to controversies affecting the general welfare of the country.*" [1]

No formal written report was prepared. This was due in part to lack of unanimity among the industry and labor members. However, these 12 knowledgeable men were in complete agreement on many points. Much of the factual data reviewed below dealing with the history and evaluation of Taft-Hartley emergency disputes was prepared by the Federal Mediation and Conciliation Service staff in connection with the deliberations of the Panel.

Frequency of Injunctions

Four Presidents have appointed boards of inquiry in a total of 29 disputes in 24 years, and 25 injunctions have been secured ordering employees not to strike for 80 days.

The year-by-year distribution of the 25 injunctions is as follows:

Number of Injunctions per Year	Years
4	1948 and 1962
2	1959, 1966 and 1967
1	1950, 1951, 1952, 1953, 1954, 1956, 1957, 1961, 1963, 1964 and 1968
none	1947 (after passage of the Act), 1949, 1955, 1958, 1960, 1965, 1969, and 1970, and 1971 (through February)

Boards of inquiry were appointed by Presidents in three additional cases in 1948 (meatpacking, telephone, and coal mining) and one additional case in 1954 (atomic energy), but no injunctions were sought.

It is clear from the record that all Presidents have been reluctant to utilize the national emergency procedures. The average of only slightly more than one Taft-Hartley injunction

[1] Title II, Section 205(b) of the Taft-Hartley Act (emphasis supplied).

per year since the passage of the Act makes it obvious that the injunction powers have not been exercised too extensively, regardless of one's appraisal of any one specific case. The fact that Federal Mediation and Conciliation Service mediators were actively engaged in mediation of from 6,000 to 8,000 disputes in each of these 24 years makes this even more apparent.

Industries Involved

Review of the industries involved in emergency disputes is enlightening. The overall distribution is as follows:

Industry	Number of Times Boards Appointed
Longshore—East and Gulf Coasts	7
Longshore—West Coast	1*
Atomic Energy—Single Plants	5**
Maritime	3*
Aerospace—Single Company	3
Aircraft Engines—Single Plants	3
Coal Mining	3**
Basic Steel	1
Nonferrous Metals	1
Shipbuilding (West Coast)	1
Telephone	1***
Meatpacking	1***
Total	30*

*30 industries and 29 boards of inquiry. A single board was created in 1948 for both West Coast longshore and maritime.
**Injunction not issued in one of these cases.
***No injunction issued.

The first obvious fact is that the East and Gulf Coast longshore industry has been especially subject to the injunction procedure. Only one negotiation since 1947 has been concluded successfully without invocation of the Act.

The second significant observation is that defense needs were the principal cause for many uses of the Act. Atomic energy, aerospace, aircraft engines, and West Coast shipbuilding accounted for a total of 12 boards of inquiry. None of these boards would have been created but for the fact that the facilities covered by the proceedings were engaged primarily in defense work. There were defense implications in some of the other cases.

Presidential Exercise of Criteria

Section 206 limits Presidential exercise of the 80-day injunction in two principal ways.

The first criterion is embodied in the words:

"Whenever . . . , a threatened or actual strike or lock-out *affecting an entire industry or a substantial part thereof. . . .*" [2]

Five of the 29 cases involved injunctions at single plants. The American Locomotive case in 1952 developed out of the fact that the Dunkirk plant of this multiplant company was the sole producer of special materials needed at atomic energy plants. All three aircraft engine cases (General Electric-Evendale and Union Carbide-Kokomo in 1966 and Avco in 1967) involved single plants of multiplant companies producing military aircraft engines or vital parts for such engines. The Republic Aircraft case in 1962 involved a single plant producing one type of military aircraft.

While some question could have been raised about the use of the Act in these five instances under the "substantial part thereof" language, no such contention of significance was made by anybody. Whatever the words of the Act may mean as applied to civilian production, these five precedents make it reasonably clear that an 80-day injunction can be secured on a single-plant basis if that plant produces a military item considered by the President to be essential. Thus, the often discussed partial operation idea has actually been effectuated.

The second major criterion is embodied in the words:

"*. . . imperil the national health or safety. . . .*" [3]

A Presidential determination that a military or defense product is essential has been construed to be a valid "national safety" criterion. The only forceful attempt to challenge such a Presidential determination occurred in the 1959 Steel case. The Supreme Court upheld President Eisenhower's exercise of the Act in that case.

It can be concluded from experience to date that if a President decides to act, court review of his determination is likely to be a formality. Nor is it probable that a future President will be reversed by the courts unless he should elect to use his powers under the Act indiscriminately and frequently.

Have Presidents been consistent? The absence of any major departure from the pattern of about one injunction each year does not answer that question conclusively. Significant year-to-year fluctuations occur in the number of situations that may

[2] Emphasis supplied.
[3] Emphasis supplied.

warrant consideration as national emergencies. More meaningful would be a year-by-year analysis that included "near misses" as well as the cases in which boards of inquiry were officially appointed. Near misses may include cases where a nonstatutory board or panel was appointed in lieu of a board of inquiry, cases where major strikes were allowed to run longer than some critics thought was advisable, and cases that were settled with or without strikes with the assistance of unhampered extraordinary mediation efforts by statutory agencies. In short, any analysis of Presidential consistency must necessarily be somewhat subjective.

The author's answer to the question for the eight years in which he was in a position to make such a subjective judgment would be that consistency did not always obtain. For example, the 1967-1968 copper strikes were allowed to continue for about nine months. Two non-statutory boards were appointed but no board of inquiry. In contrast, it was no great secret that President Johnson was prepared to obtain an injunction almost instantly if the 1965 steel industry negotiations at the White House had failed to avert a strike. However, there are so many factors bearing on a decision as to whether an injunction should be sought that a claim of lack of consistency is difficult to sustain. This is especially true of defense plant strikes. Two cases that are superficially alike may in reality be quite unlike because of differing amounts of product "in the pipeline" or because of immediate or potential needs that cannot be divulged for reasons of security.

In any event, complete consistency may not be desirable. In a potential national emergency dispute, one or both parties frequently include the probability or possibility of an 80-day injunction as a major item in their bargaining strategy. Uncertainty may or may not be essential to real bargaining.

The certainty that the government will not seek an injunction may be vital. In a substantial number of disputes a mediator's reasonably confident assertion that an injunction would not be sought was the key to a settlement. At the other extreme, the consistency of all Presidents in seeking "instant injunctions" in East and Gulf Coast longshore disputes has aggravated those controversies.

Sincere efforts of many knowledgeable people to sharpen the definition of a national emergency for incorporation in revised legislation have always failed. The preceding discussion points up some of the reasons why it is advisable and necessary to give the President considerable flexibility.

Mediation of Emergency Disputes

The language of the Act and some of the discussion in Congress preceding its enactment suggest that there is something magic in an 80-day cooling-off period. The fact that strikes did not occur after the 80-day injunction in 21 of the 29 Taft-Hartley cases to date has also been cited as evidence that the cooling-off process is effective. Incidentally, of the eight post-injunction strikes, six were in East and Gulf Coast longshoring and two in maritime. In only one instance (1948) did an injunction yield a settlement in East and Gulf Coast longshoring. The fact that strikes have not followed injunctions, if these two industries are excluded, is often cited as further evidence of the virtues of cooling off.

In a few cases there was no "cooling off." Intensive negotiation and mediation continued without a break, and a settlement was reached early in the 80-day period. For example, all but one of the several maritime disputes encompassed in the July 3, 1961, temporary restraining order were settled either just prior to the issuance of the injunction or within a week thereafter. The exception was a West Coast Masters, Mates, and Pilots dispute that was not concluded until about two weeks after the injunction had been dissolved.

In the more typical cases, cooling off occurs for a period of time not exceeding the first half of the 80-day period. Thereafter, "heating up" is a more appropriate term.

An injunction creates two new deadlines. The first occurs after 60 days, when the board of inquiry must report again to the President as to status of the dispute; that must be followed by a last-offer ballot if a settlement has not been achieved. The second deadline is the end of the 80-day period, at which time the injunction will be dissolved and a strike can legally begin or be resumed. Partly because of the new double deadline, at least the last half of the 80-day period normally is a period of intensive negotiation and mediation. The fact that the President has already characterized the dispute as a national emergency plus the possibility that he can report to Congress if a settlement is not achieved provides a sense of urgency. In theory and usually in practice, these pressures are stronger than those of the original contract expiration date. Moreover, if a strike did take place prior to the injunction, the union and the employees may be reluctant to resume economic action.

Ordinarily, effective mediation is most needed during the last part of the injunction period. Who provides mediation assistance?

The Act is clear enough on the subject. It says:

" . . . it shall be the duty of the parties to the labor dispute giving rise to such order to make every effort to adjust and settle their differences, *with the assistance of the* [Federal Mediation and Conciliation] *Service* created by this Act. Neither party shall be under any duty to accept, in whole or in part, any proposal of settlement made by the Service."[4]

Elsewhere the duties of the board of inquiry are defined. These duties begin with an initial report to the President, after which an injunction normally is secured. Unless the dispute has been settled, the second task is the submission of a 60-day report to the President. Included in the board's 60-day report is the employer's last offer on which employees will vote. The Act states clearly that the report of the board of inquiry "shall not contain any recommendations."

Thus, a board of inquiry is perhaps best described as a fact-finding body which cannot make recommendations. Mediation is not specifically prohibited but the clear implication is that it is discouraged, especially since the FMCS is charged with the mediation function.

It is of interest to note that the FMCS is not forbidden to make recommendations for settlement. On the contrary, the Act says, in substance, that FMCS mediators can do so if they so choose but the parties are under no complusion to accept. This is in sharp contrast to the restriction on the board of inquiry.

In the first 16 cases under the Act, most mediation during the injunction period was performed by the FMCS. Certain atomic energy cases, in which the Atomic Energy Labor Relations Panel also mediated and made recommendations, were exceptions. In a few instances, the parties would not cooperate fully in FMCS mediation efforts. It is probable that in a few cases members of a board of inquiry performed or attempted to perform some informal mediation activities. If so, those efforts were surreptitious and of unknown utility.

[4] Part of Title II, Section 209 (a) of the Taft-Hartley Act (emphasis supplied).

The 1959 steel case changed this picture. FMCS mediation during the period between July 15, when the strike began, and October 9, the date of appointment of the board of inquiry, had been unsuccessful. Secretary of Labor James P. Mitchell had arranged for a special fact-finding report, which had been issued on August 19 but had not moved the dispute much closer to settlement. In announcing the appointment of the board of inquiry (George W. Taylor, chairman, John A. Perkins, and Paul N. Lehoezky), President Eisenhower authorized the Board to do more than act as transmitter of the evidence submitted by the parties as to the status of the dispute. For the first time, a Board of Inquiry was commissioned to assist in the collective bargaining process. However described, there was Presidential authority for the Board to mediate. Vice President Nixon and Secretary Mitchell also intervened. A settlement between the 11 major producers and the union was announced on January 4, 1960, just prior to the expiration of the injunction. Thus, the Government utilized FMCS mediation, a fact-finding report, mediation by the board of inquiry, and intervention by the Vice President and the Secretary of Labor, successively or concurrently, in this one dispute.

The 12 instances of utilization of the Act since the 1959 steel case have exhibited a variety of mediation procedures. FMCS mediators, sometimes including the Director, Disputes Director, or Deputy Director, were active during the injunction period in all 12 cases. In three cases—Republic (1962), General Electric-Evendale plant (1966), and Union Carbide-Kokomo plant (1966)—the FMCS provided the only mediation assistance both before and after the injunction. In one case, Avco (1967), virtually all of the mediation was under the auspices of the FMCS. Leo C. Brown, S.J., had been employed on an ad hoc basis by the FMCS to work with members of the regular staff in that case. In two other cases, Lockheed (1962) and Boeing (1963), the FMCS provided the only mediation assistance during the injunction period but special Presidential boards (Taylor Board and Wallen Board) had previously been active. The Taylor Board had been able to assist in averting strikes at other companies (North American Aviation, General Dynamics, and Ryan), but Lockheed had refused to agree to that board's union security proposal. The Wallen Board recommendations in the Boeing case had been rejected by the company.

In two cases, maritime (1961) and longshore (1962 and 1963), the boards of inquiry had been authorized and requested by the President to mediate when their appointment was announced. As noted earlier in another connection, the 1961 maritime negotiations in New York were an outstanding illustration of cooperative mediation efforts involving all members of the board of inquiry and various FMCS mediators. The mediation activity of the board of inquiry in the 1962 longshore case was terminated within a month, primarily because board members could not be available consistently on a realistic negotiation schedule. In two other cases, West Coast maritime (1962) and East Coast and Gulf longshore (1968 and 1969), James J. Healy and David L. Cole, the respective chairmen of those boards of inquiry, were individually designated by the President to mediate subsequent to their initial activities as board chairmen. In the 1967 West Coast shipbuilding case, the board of inquiry was not asked to mediate originally. However, by acceptance of an FMCS recommendation, the parties voluntarily converted that board into a mediation board with authority to recommend. Interestingly enough, settlement was achieved without exercise of that authority.

Department of Labor personnel were active in varying degrees in several cases. This was especially so in the 1964 longshore case. As an aftermath of the 1962-1963 dispute, the Department of Labor had conducted an extensive manpower utilization study, and that general issue was the principal problem in the 1964 dispute. Under Secretary James J. Reynolds and David H. Stowe carried the brunt of the mediation effort, assisted in a few ports by FMCS mediators. Secretary Arthur J. Goldberg was active briefly in the 1961 and 1962 maritime cases. Then Under Secretary W. Willard Wirtz was very active in the final West Coast stage of the 1961 maritime case and in the 1962 maritime case. As Secretary, Wirtz was quite active in the 1962-1963 and 1964 longshore cases.

The 1962-1963 and the 1964 longshore cases also required special nonstatutory work by Senator Wayne Morse, James J. Healy, and Theodore W. Kheel.

This review of Taft-Hartley injunction cases, beginning with the 1959 steel case, raises questions since the statutory delegation of mediation responsibility is solely to the FMCS. The basic question is whether the use of mediators other than those under the clear direction of the Federal Mediation and Conciliation Service is contrary to the statute. The statute is quite clear with respect to mediation during the 80-day-injunction period. But no such statutory implication exists when a strike begins or is resumed after the injunction expires. At that point and before the President reports to Congress, the President's broad powers certainly permit him to utilize other resources before throwing the dispute into the lap of Congress. Moreover, as a practical matter, the history of these cases suggests that the President may supplement the FMCS by additional persons of his own choosing even during the injunction period.

The role of the Department of Labor in such disputes is a specialized aspect of the question. If Department of Labor personnel enter the dispute by direction of the President, such action is essentially similar to the President's selection of other persons. Independent intervention by Department of Labor personnel is clearly contrary to the statute in view of the provision of the Taft-Hartley Act that removes mediation authority from the Secretary of Labor and transfers it to the Director of the FMCS.

What about the role of members of boards of inquiry as mediators? If they are mediating by direction of the President, as has always been the situation in the cases cited, this is a result of the President's exercise of his general powers. But there is a complicating factor. Because of the statutory prohibition upon recommendations by boards of inquiry, a board member may not make recommendations. It might be argued that such a board member is wearing two hats—one provided by Congress and the other by the President—and that he could make recommendations while wearing the Presidential hat. But such an argument is too thin. As long as the statute remains unchanged, members of boards of inquiry should not be authorized to mediate unless it is reasonably certain that they will not have to make recommendations. In the cases noted above, the board of inquiry members were such outstanding mediators and the nature of the disputes was such that formal recommendations were not likely to be made during the injunction period in any event.

The real test of whether FMCS efforts should be supplemented during the injunction period is a question of probable success of an overall mediation effort. If the FMCS has or can obtain the requisite mediation capability and has not already "broken its pick," the statutory intent should be observed strictly. However, if the resources of the FMCS need supplementing, the

President has the authority to act and he should do so. In such instances, the Service should cooperate fully with the added personnel.

Cooperation is a two-way street. Quite aside from technical questions about jurisdiction, the total government mediation effort should be a coordinated one. As a practical matter, the Director of the FMCS usually is in the best position to provide such coordination.

Proposed Changes of National Emergency Provisions

No attempt will be made here to analyze or even list the multitude of proposals that have been made to change the national emergency provisions. Assuming no alteration in the existing definition of a national emergency, consideration will be limited to a few proposals that are pertinent to the mediation function and, most important, that are relevant to the central objective of securing a voluntary agreement.

One essentially noncontroversial matter is the vote on the employer's last offer. It is no exaggeration to say that this feature of the Act has proved to be less than worthless. It is an administrative monstrosity. In virtually all cases the issues are so complicated that it is next to impossible for the employer to make a clear total offer. In the absence of union meetings where the offer can be explained, employees seldom know precisely what they are voting on. In any event, the issue on which the employees really vote is whether they have confidence in their negotiators. Since the union negotiators have not accepted the offer, they recommend negatively and employees are practically certain to vote accordingly.

These observations are supported by results. In virtually all cases where the National Labor Relations Board has conducted such a vote (incidentally at considerable expense to the Government) the offer has been rejected. Usually the votes have been overwhelmingly negative.

The effects of last-offer balloting are adverse to collective bargaining and mediation. In the days just prior to the 60-day report when the board of inquiry will receive the last offer, the employer is reluctant to move constructively. Knowing that the vote is likely to be negative, the employer does not want to create a new floor upon which still more improvements may have to be erected. Also, bargaining is inhibited because responsible union officials are put in an almost impossible position. Though they do not want a no-confidence vote, they also are reluctant to have what amounts to a new strong strike vote. A few days later they may have the task of selling a settlement that is not much better than the one that was just voted down decisively.

The only value of the 60-day report and the last-offer ballot is that both parties may be so desirous of avoiding a vote that they will make valiant attempts to settle finally before the board of inquiry is reconvened. Experience has shown that this possible benefit is far outweighed by the adverse factors.

A second matter is the use of the injunction and the normally perfunctory role of boards of inquiry. As noted earlier, the Presidential appointment of a board of inquiry has come to be the real declaration of an emergency. In the early years of the Act, some boards did seek to determine whether a national emergency really existed, and in four instances no injunction was sought by the President. However, the last such case was in 1954. Since then the boards of inquiry (except those instructed to mediate) have simply gone through the motions preparatory to an injunction. As a rule they secure most of their fact-finding information about the dispute from the FMCS mediators who have been active. Often the parties do not even appear at the hearings scheduled by the board; they supply their positions by telegrams. Save for the 1959 steel case, neither side has objected strenuously to an injunction; whatever their real feelings, they normally have considered protest to be futile. In three recent instances the elapsed time between announcement of appointment of a board of inquiry and the actual issuance of an injunction has been approximately 24 hours.

If the President's intention is to avoid a strike, the appointment of a board of inquiry can greatly hinder effective mediation and bargaining. Once it becomes known that a board of inquiry will be appointed, bargaining is likely to stop. Realizing this, the Government tries, not always successfully, to prevent its intentions from becoming known if there are any chances for settlement. The final few hours before the strike deadline are the crucial hours. A leak about Presidential action will destroy the value of those hours. Conversely, in the absence of a leak, FMCS mediators are seriously inhibited and diverted from their essential mediation functions by phone calls from Washington and sometimes by a prematurely designated board of inquiry seeking information for its prospective report.

These considerations argue strongly for elimination of boards of inquiry and of the entire injunction process. The advisory committee on Labor-Management Policy so recommended in its 1962 report.

In most instances both parties will respond affirmatively to a direct request by the President for an 80-day stay of strike or lockout action without any injunction. The Director of the FMCS should be in a better position than a board of inquiry to advise the President as to the positions of the parties and the status of negotiations. If the injunction should be replaced by a Presidential request, the Director or other FMCS mediators could advise the parties of the President's request at the site of negotiations when the official. announcement is made in Washington. The parties' acceptance could be relayed to the White House by the FMCS informally, to be followed by official communications to the President from both parties.

Since it cannot be certain that both parties will always respond affirmatively and to preserve the right of protest of a Presidential action, the existing board-of-inquiry and injunction procedures should be retained as a backstop. They would seldom be needed.

A related matter is the question of who should trigger a Presidential declaration of a national emergency. Existing law is silent on this point. Only the President makes or should make the decision. However, everybody knows that any President will need advisors to assist him in making two appraisals. One concerns the status of negotiations. Obviously there will be no national emergency if a settlement is achieved without a strike. Moreover, there will ordinarily be no real emergency if the prospects for settlement are good after only a short strike.

The second and equally important appraisal concerns the consequences of a strike, including the progressive effects as a strike continues. The President normally will seek information and advice from Cabinet officers (possibly including but not necessarily limited to Defense, Labor, Commerce, and Justice), from the Council of Economic Advisers, and from others. Frequently, in the most important disputes, such matters will be discussed confidentially in advance of a strike deadline.

Information as to the status of negotiations, the best prognosis as to the length of any strike, and the anticipated effects on collective bargaining of a declaration of national emergency can best be secured from the Director of the FMCS. Especially on the last point, the Secretaries of Labor and Commerce may also have pertinent views. Since the status of negotiations is so important a factor in a Presidential declaration of national emergency, it should normally be a report from the Director of the FMCS that triggers the final Presidential decision. The May 1, 1962, recommendations of the Advisory Committee on Labor-Management Policy so provide.

Perhaps the most controversial question concerning the national emergency procedures is whether special mediators should have the authority to make formal recommendations for terms of settlement and, if so, under what conditions. If boards of inquiry should be substantially eliminated as proposed above, this question would be limited to those cases in which the President appoints one or more special mediators to supplement or occasionally supplant mediation under the direct auspices of the FMCS. It is immaterial to the present discussion whether such persons would serve as members of emergency disputes boards or be given some other name.

In the author's opinion, such boards or individuals should have the authority to make recommendations. However, no party to a proceeding should expect recommendations as a matter of right. Individuals should be appointed to such boards primarily for their superior mediation ability. Recommendations should be avoided if possible, and should be made only if it is reasonably clear that they will be useful. The method, timing, and content of recommendations should be within the control of the mediators. They can best appraise these important factors on the basis of their intimate knowledge of the case. In short, recommendations should be made (or not made) in accordance with the criteria developed in Chapter V.

In its 1962 report to the President, the Advisory Committee on Labor-Management Policy proposed that emergency disputes boards be permitted to make formal recommendations only upon specific authorization by the President. Such authority could be conferred by the President at the time of appointment or, more likely, at a later date if the Board should request such authority. The principal objection to such a procedure is a practical one. It should be evident from the discussion about recommendations in Chapter V that there are two problems. One is doubt as to whether recommendations should be made at all. The other is a question of timing. Frequently a mediator is uncertain on both points until the last few hours before a deadline. In the present frame of reference, the deadline is the expiration of the 80-day injunction. If the board had to obtain Presidential approval at a late hour and could not even be sure that it would be granted, the mechanics of obtaining approval and the uncertainty could frustrate its mediation efforts. Conversely, if approval should be sought too far in advance of the deadline, the knowledge that approval had been sought would be almost certain to impede bargaining. Moreover, it would then be difficult for the board to avoid making recommendations. In short, the President should appoint persons on whom he can rely to exercise good judgment in answering these critical questions.

A word should be said about compulsory arbitration in national emergency disputes. Even in such cases it should be avoided. Conceding that compulsory arbitration or its equivalent may be necessary in rare instances, decisions to go that route should be made on a case-by-case basis, and the Congress should approve the action or at least have the opportunity to veto it. Compulsory arbitration is so foreign to our basic concepts of voluntarism that only the Congress should have the power to decide that national interest must override private interests within the context of a specific case.

RAILROAD AND AIRLINE EMERGENCY DISPUTES

Emergency dispute procedures for railroads have remained substantially unchanged since the Railway Labor Act was passed in 1926. Airlines were brought under the Act in 1936. These procedures have some elements in common with the Title II procedures of the Taft-Hartley Act but there are very important differences.

The Railway Labor Act provides for a cooling-off period. Unlike Taft-Hartley, the period is variable. It begins with a formal National Mediation Board declaration of an impasse and unsuccessful mediation, following which the parties maintain the status quo for 30 days. At any time during that 30-day period the NMB can report to the President that, in its opinion, the dispute can become a national emergency. If the NMB does not so report to the President or if the President decides to do nothing after receiving a report, a strike can begin legally at the end of the 30-day period.

At any time after the NMB report but during the first 30-day period, the President may appoint an emergency board. If he does so, the status quo must be maintained for 30 more days, during which the emergency board performs its functions. Not infrequently the parties have voluntarily granted more time to emergency boards, thus further extending this phase of the cooling-off period.

The completion by the emergency board of its report to the President and to the parties signals the beginning of a final 30-day period of status quo. At the end of that time, a strike or lockout is legal.

Thus the total cooling-off period under the Railway Labor Act when an emergency board is appointed can vary from 60 days to 90 days, depending on when the President appoints the emergency board. Any extensions agreed to by the parties and a variety of extraordinary extensions that have been secured in some of the more notorious cases have expanded the 60 to 90 day range.

It is especially important to note that the emergency dispute procedures of the Railway Labor Act do not provide for injunctions. Injunctions that have been issued in a number of instances have not been part of the Presidential emergency procedures of the Act. When Presidents have moved to appoint emergency boards, announced strikes either have not begun or have terminated in almost all instances.

A curious and theoretically absurd provision of the Act and of NMB practice is the use of a proffer of arbitration by the NMB to signal the beginning of the first period of status quo. Voluntary arbitration has been employed more extensively for contract disputes in railroads and airlines than in most other industries. The arbitrators may be selected by the parties or appointed by the NMB. If both parties accept arbitration after unsuccessful mediation, the dispute has been settled. However, if either or both parties reject arbitration, that is the basis for a finding of unsuccessful mediation, an impasse, and an early report to the President (unless the NMB concludes that a strike can be permitted after 30 days and therefore makes no report to the President.) At least in theory, the NMB closes the case upon rejection of its arbitration proposal.

The theoretical absurdity of this arises from the fact that rejection of a mediation suggestion of arbitration has no special significance to most mediators. This is only one of many types of mediation proposals. Rejection of arbitration would never be a reason for closing the case under Taft-Hartley procedures.

In actuality, this NMB formality has some practical value. Most railroad agreements have no fixed terminal date. An NMB mediator can frequently extend the negotiation period by holding back on his proffer of arbitration until the dispute is at a point where he can wait no longer. In short, this device is somewhat like an FMCS mediator's request for an extension of a contract beyond its terminal date. The NMB mediator has much more power in this respect because he controls the timing of the proffer of arbitration. Moreover, while the NMB technically closes the case, it usually does not actually do so. NMB mediators or Board members are frequently active in a dispute long after the case was closed.

The procedure does have a psychological disadvantage. No mediator and no mediation agency wants to admit defeat, and for good reasons other than pride. What amounts to an official statement that NMB mediation has failed tends to limit the usefulness of the NMB thereafter in that case. Also, it has sometimes been alleged that railroad negotiations are prolonged unduly because of the absence of a fixed termination date with the instrument of the arbitration proffer in the hands of the National Mediation Board.

Unlike Taft-Hartley boards of inquiry, emergency boards can mediate if they choose to do so, *and they are expected to make formal public recommendations.*

Having noted the principal ways in which Railway Labor Act dispute procedures differ from Taft-Hartley procedures, let us consider how well the RLA procedures work.

Frequency of Emergency Board Appointments
and Related Matters

The emergency procedures had an auspicious beginning and were outstandingly successful for about 15 years. The favorable beginning is traceable in part to the fact that railroad unions and railroad management really negotiated the procedures and then jointly went to Congress to seek enactment. This contrasts sharply with the "slave labor act" climate in which the Taft-Hartley Act was enacted in 1947.

During the period from 1926 to about 1942, the Act was hailed as a great success by virtually everyone in and out of the industry. Up until June 30, 1942, only 23 emergency boards were appointed, an average of about three boards every two years. All were in railroad cases. Moreover, when emergency boards were required, their recommendations were almost always accepted by both parties with only minor revisions. Effective collective bargaining had almost always preceded the boards' appointment, and the issues had been narrowed to manageable proportions. Strikes were not eliminated entirely but they were minimal in extent and effects.

On May 22, 1942, President Roosevelt issued Executive Order 9172, which created for railroads and airlines a rough counterpart to the National War Labor Board. Known as the National Railway Labor Panel, the nine-member group adopted dispute procedures not unlike those under the Railway Labor Act except for the special wartime urgency and stabilization policies. The panel was discontinued on August 11, 1947.

The period from August 11, 1947, to date is of special interest because it coincides with the period of effectiveness of the emergency provisions of the Taft-Hartley Act. Through June 30, 1969, a period of about 22 years, 126 emergency boards were appointed, 94 for railroad cases and 32 for airline cases. This is an average of between 5 and 6 boards per year. One obvious fact is that this is more than four times the number of boards of inquiry that were established under the Taft-Hartley Act.

These numerical comparisons tell only a small part of the story. Potential Taft-Hartley exposure is many times the railroad and airline exposure. For example, it is a little-known fact that more transportation employees are covered by Taft-Hartley than by the Railway Labor Act. The trucking, intercity bus, local transit, maritime, and longshore industries employ more workers and have more labor agreements than do the railroads and airlines. And, of course, these transportation industries account for only a fraction of Taft-Hartley coverage. It is not feasible to calculate accurately, but rough computations suggest that Taft-Hartley exposure, in terms either of numbers of employees or of numbers of labor agreements within the respective jurisdictions of the two Acts, is at least 30 times Railway Labor Act exposure. Another basis for comparison is numbers of active mediation cases. In 1968, the FMCS was active in 7,587 disputes; the NMB total was 300 cases. This suggests an exposure ratio of about 25 to one.

In summary, the facts suggest that, based on potential exposure, emergency boards are appointed at least 100 times as frequently as boards of inquiry. In other words, if numbers of employees or labor agreements should be the criteria and if national emergencies were to be declared by the President as frequently elsewhere as in railroads and airlines, we would be inundated by boards.

We hasten to add that the statistics present an unfair comparison. All Presidents in this century and earlier have held, in substance, that a national railroad strike cannot be tolerated. There has been no comparable government policy in most industries under Taft-Hartley. A comparison of railroads with East and Gulf Coast Longshoring covers situations where government policies have been similar. On that basis, both records are bad and the railroad record looks relatively good.

Other comparisons are not favorable to railroads and airlines. Over-the-road trucking contracts, now mostly negotiated on a national basis, present a comparable potential national emergency hazard. There never has been a board of inquiry in trucking. In 1967, when the first nationwide lockout occurred in that industry, the government "kept its cool." The termination of the lockout was arranged after about three days, and agreements were concluded soon thereafter. This was accomplished not only without national emergency hysteria but with no government mediation or other intervention except by the Federal Mediation and Conciliation Service. Again in 1970, a crisis was threatened and numerous area strikes of some duration occurred. However, the Government again let bargaining and statutory mediation have a chance. It is not suggested here that the differences in government policy are wholly responsible for the differing experience under the two Acts in these two industries. It is suggested that the parties, government officials, and mediators might well ponder the comparison.

Reasonably valid comparisons can be made between airlines and intercity bus transportation. A number of airline strikes have occurred, with and without national emergency procedures. But 32 airline emergency boards have been appointed since mid-1947, in contrast to no boards of inquiry for intercity buses. During this period a sizable number of difficult disputes and several relatively long strikes have involved Greyhound divisions and other large bus companies. If a case-by-case analysis is made (airlines v. Greyhound, for example), it is difficult to avoid the conclusion that only the less affluent and virtually no government officials ride the buses.

Another important ingredient in the picture is the extremely long delay that too often precedes an eventual railroad or airline settlement. Even the most messy longshore disputes have somehow been resolved not more than five months after the original contract expiration date.

Finally, it cannot be forgotten that the only three peacetime compulsory arbitrations, all ordered by Congress, have occurred in railroad cases.

The lost-time strike record on railroads has been better than in the rest of the economy. This is important, but it has been obtained at a very high price. The adverse effects on collective bargaining will not easily be remedied.

Suggested Changes of Railroad and Airline Emergency Procedures

Numerous suggestions for changes in emergency procedures for railroads and airlines have been made. Complaints about the procedures with no specific proposals for correction have been even more plentiful. Both approaches have been taken by members of the academic community and by some persons who have served on emergency boards. Interestingly enough, the President's Committee in its May 1, 1962, report remained silent as to specifics for railroads and airlines, while making recommendations as to Taft-Hartley. Neither President Kennedy nor President Johnson made specific proposals for change, and most of the intra-administration discussion of new emergency legislation during the 1961-1968 period was directed to the Taft-Hartley Act. Railroad industry spokesmen have been in the forefront of the small group of management representatives favoring compulsory arbitration but have not otherwise proposed significant changes in the Act. Railroad unions have vigorously opposed compulsory arbitration but have been otherwise generally silent about the Act. Airline management representatives have been more divided than their railroad counterparts about compulsory arbitration, and a few have favored putting airline disputes under Taft-Hartley procedures.

On February 27, 1970, President Nixon sent Congress a specific proposal with an accompanying draft bill. Excluding those parts that are not relevant to the present discussion, the proposal would:

1. Transfer railroad and airline mediation to the FMCS.
2. Eliminate the existing arrangements under which the NMB determines the beginning of the first 30-day cooling-off period and replace it with contract termination arrangements similar to those under the Taft-Hartley Act.
3. Offer the President a choice among three statutory options that he might exercise for certain transportation industries if a strike or lockout should begin or be resumed at the end of an 80-day injunction.

4. Otherwise bring railroads and airlines under the existing national emergency provisions of the Taft-Hartley Act.
5. Add maritime, longshoring, and trucking, already under the Taft-Hartley Act, to the transportation industries subject to the proposed options noted in 3. above.

The fate of the Nixon proposal is uncertain at this writing. Comments which follow will be directed to aspects of emergency procedures that are relevant to mediation, including but not limited to existing arrangements and the Nixon proposal.

Transfer of Railroad and Airline Mediation to the FMCS

The Nixon proposal to transfer all mediation of railroad and airline "major disputes" to the Federal Mediation and Conciliation Service has both plus and minus aspects.

On the plus side, one consideration is the efficiency of government operation and improvement in overall mediation administration. The National Mediation Board is too small to maintain the important mediator selection and training programs that the FMCS has been able to develop. Nor has the NMB developed anything like the preventive mediation programs of the FMCS that will be discussed in a subsequent chapter. It should be possible for the FMCS to handle railroad and airline disputes mediation as part of its total mediation workload with somewhat fewer mediators than is the case with two agencies. Finally, the three-man Board structure of the NMB does not produce optimum administration. It may have theoretical advantages, but these are seldom realized in practice, however close the cooperation among the individuals involved.

A potentially more important plus factor probably is the opportunity to inject new ideas and procedures into the railroad mediation bloodstream. A major virtue of the wide industry coverage of FMCS mediation is that mediators work in many diverse collective bargaining situations. Cross-fertilization is often advantageous both to the mediators and to the parties with whom they work. It is no reflection on the competence of the NMB staff to say that concentration on only two industries tends to produce inbreeding. This is especially so in industries where most observers agree that bargaining practices require revision.

The principal disadvantage of the proposal is that many railroad management and union negotiators still take great pride in the fact that the NMB was their own creation. Despite the problems of recent years, the heritage of the 1926-1941 period is very real even today. Moreover, there is understandable fear of the unknown. Since a mediator's usefulness depends so much on the respect and confidence of the persons with whom he works, a change of this sort might not produce the desired results if it should be opposed strongly by the parties affected.

On balance, nevertheless, the transfer proposal has merit.

Semimandatory Recommendations and Decline of Bargaining

The most common criticism of railroad procedures in recent years has been that the strategy of both parties in major railroad disputes is too often keyed to almost certain recommendations by an emergency board. It is claimed that this results in very little bargaining and ineffective mediation, at least until after recommendations have been made. In short, the emergency legislation is such as to induce and encourage an emergency. In this view, the successful negotiations (and there have been more of these than is commonly recognized) occur despite rather than because of the emergency procedures.

This analysis has more than superficial validity. Too often, negotiators have not really "banged heads" at the bargaining table. With an emergency board certain to be around the corner, mediation by the NMB has not succeeded in breaking the lethargy. The dispute is routed to an emergency board, where it is likely to arrive in an almost totally undigested state. Aided (some would say forced) by the traditions of the parties as to methods of case presentation and by the need to produce recommendations within 30 days, the members of an emergency board act like arbitrators and produce a report. Real negotiations then begin if the report is "in the ball park" as to joint acceptability. Mediation by the board or by others may produce a settlement. But if the report is not in the ball park, the one reasonably satisfied party clings to it like grim death. Thereafter, it is an albatross around the neck of the bargainers and any mediators who may work in the case.

In short, the certainty of recommendations and the inability of an emergency board effectively to probe the vital element of acceptability too often results in a procedure that exacerbates the dispute instead of assisting in its resolution.

Not all emergency boards have acted in accordance with this prototype. Some have been able to overcome the roadblocks of traditionally formal procedure and have somehow induced the parties to let them act as real mediators. Settlements have been made without the necessity of any recommendations. In some other cases, successful recommendations have been made.

In one case (Emergency Board No. 167) the board found itself in a position where it could propose nothing specific that had a reasonable chance of success. It had the courage and intelligence to refuse to make specific recommendations. Rather, the recommendations were generalized and directional. They proved to be helpful in resolving the dispute.

Unfortunately, these constructive emergency board actions have generally been ignored or forgotten, as is so often the case when a procedure is under attack.

One result of the Nixon proposal to put railroads and airlines under Taft-Hartley would be to remove the certainty of recommendations. Removal of semimandatory recommendations is long overdue. This aspect of the Nixon proposal is to be applauded.

EMERGENCY DISPUTES PROCEDURES—ALL INDUSTRIES

At the risk of some repetition, a few aspects of emergency dispute procedures already in effect or proposed will be examined futher.

More About Recommendations

The 1962 report of President Kennedy's Committee and numerous other proposals suggest that emergency disputes boards be authorized to make recommendations. The Nixon proposal for railroads and airlines would have the practical effect of curtailing sharply if not eliminating emergency board recommendations. At least superficially, the two proposals point in opposite directions.

Yet the two can be reconciled. Recommendations are not arbitration decisions in disguise. The parties have the right to reject. Recommendations can be useful. But they are a last-resort device to be utilized only after intensive exercise of all other mediation skills. As a preliminary or premature mediation tactic, recommendations can be fatal. Most important, the mediator must reserve to himself and often exercise the option not to make recommendations. Neither party should be certain that this step will ever be taken. It should be taken only when the mediator is reasonably certain that it will truly assist in resolution of the dispute. In short, the discussion in Chapter V about mediation recommendations is as relevant to emergency disputes as to disputes of lesser import.

Government Policy Regarding Toleration
Of an Initial Emergency Strike

It is not just a coincidence that the railroad and the East and Gulf Coast longshore industries have been the principal customers for declarations of national emergencies. These are the only two industries in which Presidents have been consistent in holding that emergency procedures should be initiated either before a strike or almost immediately after a strike begins.

In seven exercises of East and Gulf Coast longshore injunctions, the longest initial strike permitted by the government has been 10 days; the average has been 4½ days. In the last two instances, the procedure for obtaining the injunction was absurdly short and meaningless. The deplorable but hard fact is that the 80-day injunction is no longer a national emergency measure in this section of the industry. The combination of a consistent Presidential "instant injunction" policy and the reaction of the parties to that policy has converted the injunction into little more than an automatic extension of the labor agreements.

In the railroad industry, the same situation exists and is of even older vintage.

Revision of emergency dispute procedures requires careful examination of whether this degree of Presidential consistency is essential or desirable.

In the six instances of East and Gulf Coast longshore injunctions when strikes have occurred after the injunctions have expired, the average strike duration has been about 40 days. Nobody has ever explained why Presidents have always held initially that a longshore strike cannot be tolerated but three or four months later have found that the nation can stand a strike averaging 40 days. With adequate warning to the parties and to shippers of merchandise, some President should at least see what would happen if a longshore strike of some duration should occur before securing an injunction.

The three-day nationwide lockout of 400,000 truck drivers and much longer lockouts in Chicago in 1967 without collapse of the economy suggest the need for a new look at the historical instant reflex action of the Government when a railroad strike is threatened.

Report to Congress and Intermediate Prior Procedures

Both the Railway Labor Act and the Taft-Hartley Act recognize that cooling-off periods and procedures during those periods of time may not be adequate to cope with all national emergencies. Both provide for the possibility of a report to Congress by the President if a strike occurs or is resumed after the statutory procedures have been exhausted. Part of the rationale of that provision is that uncertainty as to what a President will recommend and what a Congress will do furnishes a strong inducement to the parties to settle the controversy. Virtually all proposals for legislative changes retain this last-resort provision.

All Presidents have been reluctant to report to Congress. Under Taft-Hartley, only eight occasions have arisen when a report could have been made (six in East and Gulf Coast longshore and two in maritime). In all eight instances, other measures were taken. A very much larger number of railroad and airline disputes have provided the possibility of a report to Congress. Reports have been made in three instances, resulting in compulsory arbitration, but only after intermediate nonstatutory procedures were tried. In other cases, a variety of nonstatutory procedures have been utilized in lieu of referral of the dispute to the Congress.

Presidential reluctance has not been an abuse of executive power. The Congress has exhibited no eagerness to become involved in labor disputes. On the contrary, the legislative branch hopes that such disputes will somehow go away.

There is an open question of some importance. Should a President be free to improvise by nonstatutory procedures? If so, should the Congress have any veto power over procedures that a President might initiate or propose? In the alternative, should a statute specifically authorize the President to exercise various types of options? The Nixon proposal has the effect of substituting described optional procedures for certain transportation industries for the free-wheeling nonstatutory procedures that have been exercised in the past.

Statutory options may well be advisable. However, there is a serious question as to whether the three options that are spelled out in the Nixon proposal are the only options that should be included. If a President's discretion is to be limited by law, it should not be limited to only some of the potentially legitimate procedures.

An unrelated relatively minor problem could arise if a President must report to Congress on a specific dispute. What if Congress is not in session? It is not a pleasant prospect to contemplate convening a special session of Congress to act on a labor dispute.

Special Procedures for Specific Industries

The Nixon proposal singles out certain transportation industries for prescription of Presidential options. Included would be
the two industries that have been plagued with disputes that
continued after the cooling-off procedures. These, of course, are
railroads and East and Gulf Coast longshoring. It also includes
two lesser culprits, airlines and maritime. But no satisfactory
explanation has been made for inclusion of trucking. Moreover,
West Coast longshoring is included, though no postinjunction
problems have yet developed there.

A decision to draw the boundary lines around the transportation industries might be questioned on the merits, but it would
be understandable. But why then, is the intercity bus industry
not included? It has been more strike-prone than trucking or
West Coast longshoring.

The larger question is whether special legislation should be
directed to specific industries or in a more general way to whatever important bargaining groups present a chronic problem at
a particular time. Although not directly relevant to the postinjunction problem, any discussion of problem industries 20 years
ago would have included coal mining and atomic energy. One
can hope that railroads and longshoring will not present the
same problems 20 years hence that they do today. Legislative
changes are not likely to keep pace with the operation of the
yo-yo principle.

If special procedures are needed to meet a particular type
of problem, as may well be the case, it is suggested that legislation might spell out the general criteria for inclusion or exclu-
sion but that decisions with respect to specific bargaining relationships should be left to the Executive Branch of the Government.

The Nixon Options

The February 1970 Nixon proposal spells out three options
that would be available to the President if a strike should start
or be resumed after 80 days. The President would select one
of the three options but could not use two or more in succes-
sion.

The first option, *a 30-day extension of the injunction,* is a
desirable option but would be unlikely to solve many problems
for the two principal current customers. In the case of railroads,
it is substantially less additional time than has been obtained

under present procedures by a variety of means. It might be advisable to reduce the traditional delays, but if a report to Congress could be anticipated at the end of the 30 days, past experience suggests that railroad management would also anticipate compulsory arbitration and would have little incentive to bargain. With respect to longshore, there is no good reason to believe that the parties would not put 110 days into their strategy calculations instead of 80 days. Moreover, shippers of perishable commodities would find little comfort in having three instead of two potential strike deadlines. These may appear to be cynical observations, but they are not unrealistic. The 30-day-extension option does have potential virtues. Under some circumstances, that much additional time with effective mediation might be sufficient to secure an agreement. Uncertainty as to what a President might propose to Congress and as to how Congress might act plus the certainty that the dispute would go to Congress might provide the stimulus for real bargaining. A second virtue is that the 30 days might be needed to bridge a congressional recess.

The second option, *partial operation* of the facilities involved in the dispute, has considerable merit. As noted earlier, it is already available to some extent under present Taft-Hartley practice. Where defense needs could be demonstrated, we have already witnessed five single-plant injunctions. The longshore and maritime unions have always been willing and ready to move defense cargo during strikes. The railroad and airline unions have indicated willingness to make arrangements for handling essential defense items. The potential merit in the proposal is that under such a statutory provision, the Government might reexamine its heretofore consistent position that a nationwide railroad strike or a longshore strike could not be tolerated. Given 80 days of a full injunction, during which time the very practical problems could be explored, partial operation thereafter has much merit. Partial operation, carefully designed to put adequate economic pressure on both parties and to provide for essential public services, has never had a fair trial.

The third and most intriguing option, *final-offer selection,* should not be cast aside lightly. It is not an entirely new idea. For example, it was discussed along with other proposals by Carl M. Stevens in an article published in 1966.[5] As proposed by President Nixon, this option would require each party to deposit with

---

[5] *Is Compulsory Arbitration Compatible With Bargaining?* Carl M. Stevens, INDUSTRIAL RELATIONS JOURNAL, Feb. 1966, pp. 38-52.

the Secretary of Labor one or two secret proposals for total settlement of the dispute. The Secretary of Labor could then mediate for five days. If the mediation should be unsuccessful, the proposals would be submitted to an arbitration board. The board would be required to adopt one of the proposals without change.

Sponsors of this plan insist that even the threat of such a procedure would produce realistic bargaining. If the threat were to have that result and the positions of the parties moved close enough, it might not even be necessary to continue with the procedure. A settlement might be made prior to the date for submitting offers or during the five days of mediation by the Secretary of Labor. The sponsors go further. If this should not happen, they maintain, at least one of the parties would have submitted at least one proposal that the arbitrators would find to be equitable. Moreover, the device would eliminate the possibility of an arbitration compromise—a result viewed by some persons with disdain.

The problem with this option is that there is no assurance in these very difficult cases that the parties will behave as predicted. Put yourself in the position of the union negotiators. They are asked to make one or two secret proposals to the Secretary of Labor that presumably will be less than any previous proposal. If they do not do so, their proposals will probably be considered unrealistic. Moreover, these lesser proposals will eventually become public knowledge unless a settlement is made in the Secretary of Labor's office. Even then, these lesser proposals may not be adopted by the arbitrators. This is a difficult position indeed for a union official. Experienced negotiators are accustomed to make such proposals confidentially to a mediator, but if they do not produce an agreement, they are never made public. Moreover, a confidential proposal made to a mediator may be an ingredient of a mediation recommendation for which the mediator takes the public responsibility; the union negotiator can accept reluctantly but in good grace. Since union officials are necessarily political creatures, the final-offer-selection device is not likely to stimulate courage.

Management negotiators do not have fully comparable problems. But they too would encounter resistance to the making of secret proposals that will be made public and that are not certain to form an agreement. Moreover, they will know the even greater predicament of the union negotiators and will be gravely tempted to improve prior company offers only superficially—just enough to assert their sincerity to the arbitrators.

There is, of course, the possibility that both sides will feel so strongly about their positions that the secret proposals will be unchanged from previous ones.

In any event, there can be no assurance that the parties will not play Russian roulette with the procedure. An arbitration board might then be forced to decide between two (or four) proposals, no one of which would be remotely acceptable to one of the parties.

It is also highly fanciful to say, as the Administration's explanation does, that:

> ". . . [final offer selection] does not contain those aspects of compulsory arbitration which are inconsistent with free collective bargaining."

This is a form of unvarnished compulsory arbitration that is just as compulsory, if not more so, than the "mediation to finality" euphemism of the Johnson administration. As a last-ditch device, final-offer selection should not be rejected on this account. But it should not be mislabeled.

In short, final-offer selection is a device that merits experimental use under emergency conditions and in circumstances where a President and his advisors may have reason to believe that the hopes of its sponsors will be fulfilled. It is not a procedure that presently merits incorporation into law as one of only three options.

Under the Nixon proposal, there is, in effect, a fourth option. The President could avoid adoption of any one of the three options and let the strike occur or be resumed after the 80-day injunction period.

Other Options

Many other procedural devices have been suggested by various people under what has come to be known as the "arsenal of weapons" concept. At least two of these deserve brief comment.

Plant seizure has considerable collective bargaining history, some of which will be noted in a subsequent chapter on wartime procedures. Certain proposals made by Senator Javits in recent years include plant-seizure procedures that merit careful attention and should be included in an array of options.

What has been called a *statutory strike* also merits consideration under some circumstances as one of several options. Described briefly, it is the continued operation of a plant without strike or lockout but with the deposit of some percentage of employee pay together with payments by the employer in an escrow fund. Negotiations would continue, and if an early settlement were achieved, all money in the fund would be refunded. If negotiations dragged on beyond specified dates, some part of the fund would be contributed to appropriate charities or used for other worthy public purposes. The intent is to provide economic pressures for settlement without loss of production.

Summary Suggestions

At the risk of being presumptuous, the following suggestions are made for revision of the Taft-Hartley Act and the Railway Labor Act. The suggestions are in outline form and will serve to summarize some of the observations made earlier. The public interest occasionally does require emergency procedures that curtail use of the strike or lockout, and these procedures should be designed to maximize the possiblity of voluntary modification of positions sufficient to produce an agreement.

Taft-Hartley Revisions

a. Retain the existing definition and general concept of a national emergency.

b. Eliminate the last-offer-ballot procedure.

c. Substitute a Presidential request for an 80-day stay of a strike or lockout for the existing injunction procedure but retain the present board of inquiry and injunction procedure for use if a Presidential request was not honored or if a party wanted to challenge in the courts the finding of a national emergency.

d. Except as provided in c. above, eliminate boards of inquiry.

e. Rely primarily upon the FMCS for mediation during an 80-day stay but provide for Presidential appointment of emergency disputes boards or special mediators to mediate in cooperation with the FMCS in situations that might require such action.

f. Retain existing provisions giving the Director of the FMCS the major responsibility for the direction of mediation and add provisions authorizing him to coordinate all mediation activity, of whatever variety, during the 80-day stay or any extensions thereof, subject only to the direction of the President.

g. Permit emergency disputes boards and continue to permit FMCS mediators to make recommendations, but not as a matter of necessity or of right of any party to a dispute. Members of emergency disputes boards should be selected on the basis of their mediation skills and should themselves decide whether to make recommendations and, if so, the timing, form, and content of those recommendations. The parties would be under no legal compulsion to accept recommendations.

h. If it should appear that a strike will begin or be resumed at the end of an 80-day stay, the President should announce to the parties:

    (1) that he intends to take no action and that a strike may begin or be resumed in the absence of an agreement at the end of the 80-day period;

    or

    (2) that he is requesting an additional stay of 30 days for the purposes outlined in i. below.

The timing of such Presidential announcement would be at the discretion of the President except that the announcement would be made in sufficient time to permit uninterrupted work if alternative h. (2) is selected.

i. Within 10 days after the end of the 80-day stay, the President, if he has requested an additional 30-day stay, would announce that he is recommending to the Congress one of the following options:

    (1) a further extension of time not to exceed a total of 45 days beyond the original 80-day stay to be utilized for mediation by an emergency disputes board, or by other special mediators and/or the FMCS;

    (2) partial operation of the industry or of the facilities involved;

    (3) final-offer selection;

    (4) plant seizure;

    (5) statutory strike;

    (6) compulsory arbitration;

Prior to the end of the 30-day stay, the Congress would approve the President's recommendation or substitute an option of its own choice.

j. In the event that the option recommended by the President (or a substitute option ordered by Congress) should not result in settlement of the dispute or if the President elected not to exercise any of the options and the strike continued, the President could make a report to Congress with a proposal for congressional action to resolve the dispute.

Railway Labor Act Revisions

a. Transfer all mediation functions in "major disputes" to the FMCS.

b. Apply the revised national emergency provisions of Taft-Hartley to railroads and airlines.

c. As in the Nixon proposal, modify the provisions relating to notice of termination or modification of railroad and airline agreements to conform to those of Section 8(d) of Title I of the Taft-Hartley Act.

Adoption of these suggestions would make it unnecessary to single out any of the transportation industries for special treatment.

It is not claimed that these suggestions represent a panacea for national emergency disputes. There are no foolproof schemes. The outline is presented here for two reasons. It is a partial summary of this chapter, and it may provide food for thought and discussion.

CHAPTER XI

FACT-FINDING AND NONSTATUTORY PANELS

Somewhere between national-emergency-dispute procedures and ordinary mediation, there is a grey area. It includes fact-finding or special mediation by appointment of a government official and personal mediation without formal appointment. In the private sector these activities are sometimes called nonstatutory procedures. On the one hand, they are outside the direction of the established mediation agencies. On the other hand, they are utilized in disputes that have not usually been declared national emergencies.

In the case of public employee disputes, the nonstatutory designation is often inappropriate. Several state laws provide specifically for procedures of the type to be considered here.

The term "fact-finding" came into general use immediately after World War II. National War Labor Board procedures had been terminated and a rash of major disputes and strikes developed. Within a nine-month period (November 27, 1945, to August 7, 1946) a total of 12 boards were appointed. Industries or companies involved were General Motors, U. S. Steel, International Harvester, Greyhound Bus, oil, meatpacking, nonferrous metals, west coast longshore, sugar, Pacific Gas and Electric Co., Western Union, and Milwaukee Gas Light Co. Appointments to these boards were made by the Secretary of Labor except for the General Motors and U. S. Steel boards, which were appointed by the President. Although not all were officially designated as fact-finding boards, most were referred to as such.

In the 14 years immediately following passage of the Taft-Hartley Act, only seven such boards were appointed. They involved Western Union (1947), Kennecott Copper (1949), basic steel (1949), North American Aviation (1952), American Smelting and Refining Co. and Kennecott Copper (1954), Westinghouse (1956), and basic steel (1959).[1] The President appointed both basic steel boards and the North American board; the four others were appointed by the Director of the Federal Mediation and Conciliation Service. The term "fact-finding" was not as generally applied to these boards.

A resurgence in the use of nonstatutory boards began in 1961. During the eight years of the Kennedy and Johnson administrations, a total of 20 boards were appointed in 14 disputes.

In chronological sequence, these disputes involved tugboat workers and captains in the Port of New York (1961),[2] Atlantic, Pacific, and Gulf Coast maritime (1961),[3] West Coast and Hawaii maritime (1962),[4] Canadian vessels and Seafarers (1962), aerospace (1962), Boeing (1962), Ling-Temco-Vought (1962), Atlantic and Gulf Coast longshore (1962 and 1963),[5] Atlantic and Gulf Coast longshore (1964 and 1965),[6] basic steel (1965),[7] General Electric (1966),[8] West Coast shipyards (1967),[9] copper (1968),[10] and Atlantic and Gulf Coast longshore (1968 and 1969).[11]

Appointments to these boards were made by the President in 14 instances, by the Secretary of Labor (sometimes with the Secretary of Commerce) in four instances, and by the Director of the Federal Mediation and Conciliation Service in two instances. None of these boards or panels were popularly known as fact-finding boards.

[1] Basic steel is included because the Taft-Hartley board of inquiry was authorized to mediate at the time of its appointment by the President.

[2] There were two boards with different personnel, one for a crew-size issue and one for job-assignment issues for captains. These employees were not covered by the Railway Labor Act.

[3] This dispute is included because at the time of its appointment by the President the Taft-Hartley board of inquiry was requested to mediate before setting the injunction process in motion.

[4] Special procedures were used in addition to a Taft-Hartley board of inquiry.

[5] The Taft-Hartley board of inquiry was authorized to mediate when appointed. Other special procedures were employed during the strike after the injunction expired, including Presidential appointment of a different special board.

[6] Two special boards were created before and after the Taft-Hartley injunction in connection with manpower-utilization and job-security issues.

[7] A special investigation team (Senator Morse and Under-Secretary of Commerce Collins) was appointed by the President. This was followed by Presidential designation of the Secretary of Labor and Secretary of Commerce to mediate.

[8] The Special board appointed by the President included the Secretaries of Labor, Commerce, and Defense and the Director of the FMCS.

[9] The parties agreed to an FMCS suggestion that the Taft-Hartley board of inquiry be restructured as a nonstatutory mediation panel.

[10] A Special board was appointed by Secretaries of Labor and Commerce. Subsequently the President designated the Secretaries of Labor, Commerce, and Defense to mediate with the special board and FMCS.

[11] The President designated David L. Cole to mediate. He had been chairman of the Taft-Hartley board of inquiry.

This review of experience at the federal level from 1946 through 1968 omits a number of important nonstatutory procedures in railroad and airline cases. This does not reflect an intent to minimize the importance of those cases.

Governors, mayors, and other officials at the state and municipal levels also appointed special boards or panels in specific disputes between 1946 and 1968. These actions will not be reviewed here, although they have contributed to the settlement of disputes in many instances.

It is of interest to note that the term "fact-finding board" reentered the commonly used labor relations vocabulary sometime in the mid-1960s. A large number of fact-finding boards (or individuals charged with fact-finding responsibilities) have been appointed in public employee disputes.

Everyone who is familiar with the functioning of fact-finding boards and other special boards knows that the label is less important than the abilities and proclivities of the individuals named to those boards. Fact-finders may mediate; some who do so find no facts. Persons appointed as mediators frequently do not mediate in a meaningful way but may announce some facts. These differences are not due entirely to the inclinations of the appointees. In many instances the instructions given them are not clear. Reactions of the parties to the process and to the individuals named to work with them may well influence the course of action.

Except where they are pursuant to state statutes, all these special procedures fall in a crack between mediation by or under the direction of statutory agencies and emergency disputes. Is there legitimate basis for these "in-between" activities, of whatever variety?

It is clear from the text of the Taft-Hartley Act and its legislative history that the congressional majority in 1947 did not favor extensive use of such special procedures. The creation of 12 fact-finding boards in nine months had made them unpopular, even though they may properly be regarded as a transition mechanism after the termination of World War II procedures. The principal statutory mediation agency (Federal Mediation and Conciliation Service) was strengthened by making it an independent agency. All mediation authority was removed from the Department of Labor. National emergency procedures—applied for the first time to a peacetime economy—were intended to apply to the most important disputes as a last resort.

The fact that there were only seven special boards in the next

14 years indicates that the Presidents during that period and other federal officials were generally in accord with—or at least observed—the intent of Congress. This conclusion is reinforced by the fact that four of the seven boards were appointed by the Director of the FMCS. The Taft-Hartley Act gives the Director almost unlimited authority to appoint mediators. A board designated by him reports directly to him and is an aspect of FMCS mediation.

What changed the picture? The first significant event occurred in 1959 when President Eisenhower authorized mediation by a Taft-Hartley board of inquiry in the basic steel case. It is apparent that the President decided that mediation beyond the expertise of the FMCS was required in that situation. Even more important was the bypassing of the board of inquiry's mediation effort in the same case by special mediation activities of Vice President Nixon and Secretary of Labor Mitchell.

This breach in the dike of congressional intent by a Republican administration was enlarged substantially by the activist Kennedy Administration and especially Secretary of Labor Goldberg. As attorney for the Steelworkers, Goldberg had fought vigorously in the courts in 1959 to preserve the union's right to strike indefinitely. It should be noted, however, that attorney Goldberg in 1959 would have welcomed more aggressive mediation than had been performed in the steel case by the Federal Mediation and Conciliation Service and that his efforts in court could in no way be construed as an attack on effective mediation.

By the time of President Kennedy's assassination, special boards had been created in eight disputes, and in addition special procedures had been utilized in certain airline and railroad cases. There was no effective opposition to these actions.

During the Johnson Administration, the use of special procedures declined materially even though there were more virulent disputes. However, occasional use continued. It was a Johnson innovation to name Cabinet members as officially appointed members of special boards.

Most public utterances and actions of the Nixon Administration suggest reversion to 1947 congressional intent. However, Department of Labor officials have been active in several railroad and public employee disputes, and firm predictions as to the future policy and practice of this administration cannot be made.

This chronology does not answer the question posed earlier. Legitimacy of a course of action is not proved by the fact that there are precedents. But executive precedents in government can have significance comparable to that of a statute. This is especially so in the absence of effective opposition.

The real problem is that there is a grey area between mediation by the statutory agencies and invocation of national-emergency-dispute procedures. The President may conclude that a statutory agency (Federal Mediation and Conciliation Service or National Mediation Board) is unable to cope with a specific important dispute, that a dispute has political implications that might jeopardize the important nonpolitical aspect of all FMCS endeavors, or that the statutory agency has had adequate opportunity to settle a dispute and has failed. On the other hand, he may be reluctant to order a cooling-off period, especially since the Taft-Hartley Act makes no provision for special procedures during the injunction period. If a nonstatutory board may be required later, why not try it earlier and perhaps avoid the distasteful injunction process?

It is probable that the absence of strong opposition to special procedures during the period from 1947 to date is due in large part to their infrequent use in industries covered by the Taft-Hartley Act. The use of nonstatutory procedures in 21 disputes in 23 years can scarcely be called extreme, and the average during the 1960s was only a little over two disputes per year. The subject is worth further consideration because most of those disputes were important ones.

As for railroads and airlines, the recent operation of emergency board procedures has been so unsatisfactory that special procedures have often been utilized in an attempt to avoid the necessity of requesting congressional action.

If the Taft-Hartley Act and the Railway Labor Act should be revised along the lines suggested in Chapter X, there is good reason to believe that this grey area could be narrowed substantially. Without changing the existing concept of what constitutes a national emergency, some of the disputes in the private sector that have been the occasion for special nonstatutory procedures could properly have been considered national emergencies. Substantial elimination of the distasteful injunction procedure and greater flexibility in the discretionary use of recommendations would permit statutory handling of certain important disputes that have been given nonstatutory treatment. At the other end of the grey area, modest expansion of use of the higher steps of the FMCS escalation ladder, discussed in Chapter VI, would provide an effective means of handling disputes not properly characterized as national emergencies. In retrospect, the author is convinced that several disputes in the 1961-1968 period would have been better handled by an FMCS panel including one outstanding outside mediator than by a special nonstatutory board.

It is unlikely that nonstatutory procedures will ever be eliminated entirely. This probability, together with the great uncertainty as to whether, when, and how legislative changes will be made in the Taft-Hartley and Railway Labor Acts, justifies further consideration of the three principal types of nonstatutory procedures in private-sector disputes— (1) fact-finding, (2) special mediation boards or panels, and (3) personal mediation by government officials not formally assigned to the dispute in question.

In all instances it will be assumed that the parties have engaged in a reasonable amount of direct negotiation and have failed to agree. It will also be assumed that a statutory mediation agency has already attempted mediation, that the dispute is still unresolved, and that public opinion or national defense needs exert pressures on the Executive Branch of the Government to "do something different."

FACT-FINDING

Fact-finding will be defined for present purposes as a semijudicial process in which major reliance is placed on the facts of a dispute and the fact-finding board attempts to exercise few mediation principles or tactics. It is recognized that fact-finders do not always conform to this definition. Many do, however, and the fact-finding process, unadulterated by mediation, deserves separate discussion.

The rather obvious implication of fact-finding is that somebody has not known the facts of a dispute and that the establishment and proclamation of the facts will somehow assist in settlement. Who is that somebody who is unaware of the facts? In a labor dispute, what are facts? How will facts, once discovered and proclaimed, assist in settlement?

There are at least four types of fact-finding. The differences among them are significant.

Fact-Finding Without Recommendations After a Stalemate Develops

The notion that facts alone will help settle a dispute is best exemplified by fact-finding procedures in which the fact-finders are not authorized to make recommendations. Since the discussion here assumes a labor dispute in which an impasse has developed, it is advisable to examine the events that may have preceded the advent of the fact-finder.

There is great variance in the degree to which demands or requests made by bargainers at the outset of negotiations are based on facts. At one extreme, the union may say, in effect, "We want it and who cares about the facts?" Raw power is the only fact of significance. At the other extreme, one or both parties may do a tremendous amount of prenegotiation research. Positions on each issue are supported by an elaborate array of real or alleged facts considered to be pertinent to that issue. In most negotiations, initial factual material falls somewhere between these extremes.

As negotiations proceed, certain facts are agreed to explicitly or tacitly, some are soft-pedaled or withdrawn, some are quietly ignored, some are irrelevant, and some remain in dispute.

If an issue is settled, factual differences about it are not consequential. But if negotiations on an issue become stalemated, a fact-finder will explore and evaluate the areas of factual difference. In the absence of intent or authority to make specific recommendations for settlement, that is all he can do.

Is any good purpose served by this type of factual analysis? Most reasonably sophisticated negotiators will not be surprised by the results of such fact-finding. Even if one party has not faced up to unpleasant facts, the issue is not the facts but whether they are decisive or should be given little or no weight. In other words, it is the significance of the facts, not the facts themselves, that is the core of the dispute on the issues. Moreover, if the previous mediation by the statutory agency has been adequate, the negotiators already will have been subjected to "deflation" tactics by a mediator's use of such facts.

What about the value of publicizing the facts? In a few situations, publicizing the facts may bring pressure on the negotiators from their constituencies. For example, facts damaging to a union that are published during a prolonged strike may result in greater willingness on the part of members to compromise demands. Facts detrimental to a company position may bring pressure from the board of directors. However, such results are uncommon; most labor disputes are so complicated that a mere portrayal of facts does not provide a "handle" for action or even point the way to a settlement area.

For the same reasons, the relevance of facts to the disputed issues usually is not sufficiently clear to generate useful public pressures. A published fact-finding report may enable editorial writers and columnists to make fewer misstatements of fact, but it seldom changes any preconceived notions they may have had.

Fact-finders not empowered to make recommendations on the issue occasionally have assessed blame on one of the parties. This device seldom settles a dispute; it is much more likely to exacerbate it. For example, two members of a special Board of Accountability in the 1962-1963 New York newspaper strike-and-lockout dispute issued a report on January 11, 1963, placing the major blame on union leadership. That report did not facilitate settlement.

In short, fact-finding without recommendations after a stalemate has been reached *in a private-sector dispute* is almost certain to be an exercise in futility. If it is successful it will be because the fact-finders are skilled mediators and act as such. In that event the process should be called mediation, not fact-finding.

Fact-Finding Without Recommendations in Preparation for Negotiations

There is one type of fact-finding without recommendations that is not even included in most conceptions of fact-finding. This is the occasional situation where an impartial person or agency is retained or appointed well in advance of negotiations to develop factual background for future use by the bargainers. Some companies and unions have retained impartial actuaries or insurance experts to provide them with a single set of facts about the costs of a variety of hypothetical pension and insurance benefits. Some years ago the parties in the West Coast longshore industry retained Max Kossoris, on leave from the Bureau of Labor Statistics, to develop factual data preliminary to negotiation of the Mechanization and Modernization Agreement noted earlier. The U.S. Department of Labor conducted an extensive study of East and Gulf Coast manpower utilization practices as factual background for 1964-1965 negotiations. The impartial members and staff of the Armour Automation Committee have performed a similar function.

Companies and unions normally develop their own factual material in preparation for negotiations. However, as the scope of bargaining has expanded to include more complicated and technical matters, there is an increasing potential need for negotiators to retain competent experts in whom both sides have confidence. Such technical assistance can be utilized in two ways.

The parties can jointly select the individual or organization to work with them and develop the facts from scratch. Or, if a factual difference develops out of separate analyses, an acknowledged expert can be brought in not to mediate a settlement but to reconcile the facts.

This type of fact-finding was recommended by President Kennedy's Advisory Committee on Labor-Management Policy in its May 1, 1962, report. It is a procedure of substantial merit. Normally it will precede a stalemate and hopefully will help avoid one.

Fact-Finding Without Recommendations on the Issues but With Procedural or Directional Recommendations

A type of proceeding that can properly be considered within the scope of fact-finding is one in which facts are supplemented by directional recommendations but without specific findings on the contractual issues. An illustration is the work of the Taylor-Higgins-Reedy Board in the 1967-1968 nonferrous disputes. The parties were stalemated on the demand of the unions for coordinated bargaining and had not been able to bargain conclusively on other issues even after strikes of six months' duration. The Board, created early in 1968, did not attempt to examine the specific economic and noneconomic issues. It properly concerned itself first with the history of the bargaining structure in the industry and at each major company. It then proceeded to recommend a revised structure for bargaining within the companies in the light of the facts and the current positions of the companies and unions. Although the unions initially rejected those recommendations, the work of the Board did provide the base on which settlements were made subsequently.

An outside party may be able to recommend criteria or a procedural device to get the parties around a roadblock to bargaining. This type of fact-finding has not had enough use. It is more than a compromise or way station between recommendations and no recommendations. Where the circumstances warrant its use, it is a practical application of the basic principle that the maximum amount of direct bargaining should be preserved.

Fact-Finding With Recommendations

When fact-finders are given the responsibility to make specific recommendations on the disputed issues after finding the facts, their assignment departs from the fact-finding principle. Recommendations are not facts. Nor are they deduced from facts except by the exercise of value judgments.

Some may question these assertions. It may be claimed that recommendations can be based solidly on facts with minimal value judgments. It is undoubtedly true that the extent of such judgments varies with the issue, but it is difficult to find any issue on which a recommendation is wholly devoid of the judgment factor.

Let us assume that a union in a manufacturing plant is requesting full pension rights after 20 years of service regardless of age. It is reasonably certain that the company could show beyond doubt that such a benefit is virtually nonexistent in manufacturing. That is an important fact, but it does not dispose of the issue. Collective bargaining is an innovative process. Practices that are now commonplace had to start somewhere. If the fact-finder recommends against the union, as he probably will, other considerations are involved. He may conclude that the benefit is not advisable on its merits, that the cost would be excessive, or that the request should not be given priority over other requests. These and similar reasons involve value judgments. If he should conclude that so obvious an innovation should not be obtained through a third party, that is itself a value judgment.

Another illustration may be given. During the wage-price guidepost period, it was an announced executive policy of the Council of Economic Advisers, supported by the President, that labor-cost increases under new agreements should be held to an average of 3.2 percent per year. In the absence of statutory authority for that policy, it was a value judgment if a fact-finder decided to apply it in his recommendations in a specific case. In view of the large number of departures, plus and minus, from that policy even when it was most acceptable, no fact-finder could take automatic refuge in it. Moreover, even if he did apply the policy as an exercise of judgment, its application never was a matter of precise arithmetic. Some benefits could not be accurately costed. Certain exceptions were stated in the policy. Did the facts of a specific case qualify for an exception, and, if so, to what degree? How should costs be distributed over the term of a multi-year agreement? In short, even the application of a mathematical formula required value judgments and not just arithmetic.

When noneconomic but emotional issues are also involved, when there is an imbalance of power, or when serious personality conflicts exist at the bargaining table—all too frequent ingredients in collective bargaining—who can say honestly that recommendations can be based solely on facts?

The procedural aspects of fact-finding with recommendations, as commonly practiced require comment. One writer has characterized the process as "compulsory arbitration's cousin."[12] With or without genealogical comparison, the procedural aspects are superficially similar to those of arbitration. Hearings tend to be formal. The fact-finder may even believe that it is improper for him to confer with one party in the absence of a representative of the other party. Having secured the facts (evidence and testimony), the fact-finder withdraws to his sanctuary and prepares his recommendations. In short, he acts like an arbitrator. If this is the procedure, as it usually is, it is equivalent to arbitration, though with a major difference. In arbitration there is an advance commitment to accept the award as final and binding. Recommendations, on the other hand, are not binding; both parties see and study the terms before deciding to reject or accept.

The need for acceptance cannot be overemphasized. If the procedure has been as described above, the fact-finder has no good clues as to the reactions of the parties. He finds out only after the recommendations have been issued.

Another aspect of the process almost always assures a quasi-arbitration procedure. The parties know in advance that recommendations will be made. From the outset each side is devoting its full effort to convince the fact-finder and to secure the best possible set of recommendations. Bargaining is almost certain to be suspended, at least until after the recommendations have been issued.

Given all these features of the process, it is not surprising that it sometimes fails. Indeed, it is remarkable that it succeeds as often as it does. It is a "one-play ball game" with the odds heavily weighted against success.

NONSTATUTORY MEDIATION PANELS

Many of the special boards or panels and some of the boards improperly called fact-finding boards that were created during the period from 1945 through 1968 were intended to be special forms of mediation. Mediation by the statutory agencies had not in-

---

[12] Robert G. Howlett, *Arbitration In the Public Sector*, PROCEEDINGS OF THE 15TH ANNUAL INSTITUTE ON LABOR LAW, p. 249.

duced the parties to settle. A President or a Secretary of Labor had decided to enlist the services of other persons.

The 1962 report of President Kennedy's Advisory Committee on Labor-Management Policy includes two paragraphs pertinent to this subject:

"In all but a relatively few exceptional cases the Federal, State, and local mediation services provide the only appropriate form of government service. At the national level the National Mediation Board renders these services in the railroad and air transportation industries, and the Federal Mediation and Conciliation Service in other industries. Local service and intrastate industries are in many instances serviced by State or city agencies." [13]

"In the case of *major industries, involving whole or important segments of critical industries,* extraordinary measures may be found necessary. Normal mediation may prove unequal to the task of removing a strike threat or ending an actual strike." [14]

The italicized words are less restrictive than the "national health or safety" criteria of the Taft-Hartley Act. Moreover, the Committee proceeded to recommend that the statute be amended to provide specifically for the possible creation by the President of emergency dispute boards in situations that would qualify under the broadened language even if such a dispute did not justify an 80-day cooling-off period. This recommendation was opposed by only one member [15] of the 19-member group (Secretary of Labor, Secretary of Commerce, five public members, six industry members, and six union members). Committee members were among the most distinguished persons in their respective fields. All were knowledgeable in the practical aspects of collective bargaining.

At an earlier date, the Committee for Economic Development had published a report with similar recommendations.

Both the President's Committee and the CED recommended strengthening the effectiveness of the Federal Mediation and Conciliation Service and the National Mediation Board. The President's Committee envisioned a harder-hitting type of mediation than had been apparent in some periods of time after 1947.

Thus it is clear that these two prestigious groups favored special procedures, to be used sparingly, to fill a gap between "normal mediation" and "national health and safety" situations. By

[13] FREE AND RESPONSIBLE BARGAINING AND INDUSTRIAL PEACE, Report to the President From Advisory Committee on Labor-Management Policy, May 1, 1962, Part III, D, p. 4 (U.S. Government Printing Office).
[14] *Id.,* Part IV, p. 4 (emphasis supplied).
[15] Henry Ford II.

so recommending, they went beyond the 1947 intent of the Congress. It is equally clear that neither the President's Committee nor the CED were thinking of fact-finding of the prototype discussed earlier. They had in mind a "beefed-up" type of mediation, using persons of stature and prestige greater than that customarily enjoyed by representatives of the statutory agencies.

Neither President Kennedy nor President Johnson saw fit to implement the 1962 report of the President's Committee by a specific proposal to Congress. Instead, they proceeded to appoint nonstatutory boards in a few instances. Thus, as of this writing, the type of action under consideration here continues to lack statutory authority.

As a coopted participant in the deliberations of the President's Committee in 1961 and 1962, the author supported the May 1, 1962, report, including the recommendation for legislation authorizing creation by the President of emergency disputes boards in cases that might not qualify as emergency disputes under the existing Act. As a result of experience and reflection during the subsequent eight years, he now disagrees with that part of the Committee's recommendations. Some of the reasons are implicit in the text of Chapter X and earlier portions of this chapter. Those opinions need not be repeated here, but a few additional reasons will be noted.

The first reason is that statutory support for emergency disputes boards in this grey area would be almost certain to lead to expanded use. Expectations would be created, especially in the mind of the weaker party. Although the terms "major industries" and "critical industries," as used by the Committee, are intended to be restrictive, few people like to believe that their industry is not "major" or "critical." If a strong hope or belief exists that a higher level of mediation may be available than is provided by an established agency, agency mediation could be considered as only a way station on the road to a higher step. It is recognized that this problem exists with respect to escalated mediation steps within an agency. However, the problem would assume different psychological proportions if the law made provision for a special Presidential emergency disputes board. In short, any President and his advisors would have to be extremely vigilant to prevent use of such boards in "all but a few exceptional cases" in order to effectuate the Committee's intent. As matters now stand, the simple fact that any special procedures are nonstatutory tends to limit the number of such cases.

Secondly, the number of available persons who would be certain to exercise superior mediation skills is not large. Unless members of emergency disputes boards are better mediators than can be made available by the established agency, there is little purpose in the creation of such a board. The status afforded by a Presidential designation has some influence at the bargaining table, but there is an adverse reflection on the President and on the process if the anticipated skills are not exhibited.

Review of the 12 nonstatutory boards created since May 1, 1962, suggests the very limited need for special mediation devices in the grey area. Although the Committee's report never became law, it gave a degree of moral sanction to Presidential action. In two cases (Temco (1962) and West Coast shipyards (1967)) the special procedures were initiated and carried out under the direction of the FMCS, so they were not really nonstatutory. Four cases (West Coast and Hawaii maritime (1962) and three Atlantic and Gulf Coast longshore (1962 and 1963, 1964 and 1965, and 1968 and 1969)) involved procedures during or after Taft-Hartley injunctions and therefore would be included in revised national emergency procedures, as discussed in Chapter X. Thus, only six nonstatutory procedures in 6½ years would have been sanctified by law if the President's Committee report had been enacted into legislation immediately.

Beyond question a sizable number of other disputes within the same time period that were mediated solely by the FMCS would have been emergency disputes board cases if the law had been revised. There is no good reason to believe that such treatment would have been any more effective.

Revision of legislation should be limited to the suggestions made at the end of Chapter X. Resort to special mediation procedures in the grey area just short of national emergency cases should be expected, but continue to be nonstatutory and infrequent.

Even though special mediation boards may be few in number, the relationships between such boards and the statutory mediation agencies are of sufficient importance to justify comment. In its recommendations regarding emergency disputes boards, the President's Committee said: "The board should work closely with the Federal Mediation and Conciliation Service." Similar language and intent have appeared in announcements of the appointment of most of the special boards that have been created.

The basic purpose of such instructions is twofold. Mediators of the statutory agency will have acquired extensive knowledge of the dispute, and their mediation skills may continue to be utilized. Secondly, the statutory agency has been superseded. Subsequent participation by persons from the statutory agency with the new board can lessen the inevitable loss of prestige to the statutory agency. In other words, the objectives of cooperation are both pragmatic and psychological.

To what extent can these objectives be realized? The answer to that question requires examination of several factors, including among others (1) reactions and attitudes of the statutory agency, (2) reactions and attitudes of the members of the new board, (3) attitudes of the parties, (4) the realities of the specific case, and (5) pragmatic possibilities and limitations of cooperation.

One possible attitude of a statutory agency is to take a "dog-in-the manger" position toward the appointment of any special boards. An agency could maintain that special boards are never justified. And if one is created anyway, the agency could wash its hands of responsibility and fail to cooperate. Such a reaction is irresponsible and self-defeating. The agency should realize that a few special boards are inevitable. In situations that require it, the agency head should take the initiative and recommend the procedure. If the agency head believes such action to be ill-advised, he should say so in no uncertain terms and give his reasons—within the confines of executive discussion. If he is overruled, as he may be, the agency should accept that decision and cooperate fully.

Attitudes and behavior of members of a newly appointed board can be quite variable. At one extreme the board can assume that the statutory agency has failed completely, that those mediators previously associated with the case have nothing to contribute, and that it must start from scratch. If this is the approach, the board may tolerate, even welcome, a short preliminary briefing by the mediators of the statutory agency. But thereafter the agency personnel are effectively out of the picture. At the other extreme, cooperation is real indeed. Within the practical limitations of the operation, the potential of the statutory agency for assistance is utilized fully.

Attitudes of the parties are important. In the crisis atmosphere usually associated with special board operation, there is an understandable tendency for the parties to write off agency personnel.

The power resides in the new board. Why bother with the individuals who have been benched, irrespective of their capability? The reverse situation also can exist. If the parties are not in sympathy with the special procedure that has been thrust upon them, the negotiators may make this evident to the agency personnel and seek to undermine the work of the new board. The reactions of the parties will be influenced heavily by their perception of the degree of cooperation between the board and the agency mediators. If they are given reason to believe that a high degree of cooperation exists, they too will utilize fully all the assistance that is available.

The realities of the specific case also are important. At one extreme, the statutory agency has, in fact, struck out. It has had ample opportunity to do everything within its capability. The mediators have "broken their picks." Their usefulness is limited primarily to acquainting the new board with the factual background and the efforts that have failed. This can be an important contribution, but only the board can provide new approaches. At the other extreme, the statutory mediators may have been instrumental in the exploration of solutions that are close to fruition. The creation of the new board may have been a mistake or a response solely to public pressures. In such a situation, to push the statutory mediators into the background or to eliminate them will almost surely prolong the dispute.

Aside from motive and intent, there are practical problems of cooperation between an agency and a special board. In the few cases that do go the special-board route, the statutory agency may have had as many as three mediators active in the case. A typical special board has three members. Six or more mediators will overwhelm the parties if they all insist on equal participation. Practicable cooperation means almost automatically that the agency mediators will play a secondary role.

Railroad and airline dispute procedures beyond the emergency board procedures of the Railway Labor Act have seen limited participation by National Mediation Board members in special mediation activity. The NMB has been relegated to a back seat with little opportunity for cooperation in many instances.

Recognizing that logistic problems involved cannot be surmounted entirely, it is nevertheless clear that maximum cooperation between special boards and the statutory agencies is desirable.

NONSTATUTORY PERSONAL MEDIATION

Government officials who are not representatives of statutory mediation agencies have sometimes become involved in mediation. For the most part, Presidential involvement has been limited to public or private admonitions to the parties. On rare occasions, negotiations have been moved to the White House, primarily for the symbolic effect of Presidential concern. Only under most unusual circumstances has a President attempted to mediate as to the specifics of a dispute. The potency of Presidential pressure is obvious, and the right of the President to intervene is not open to question. Most observers believe, however, that personal intervention in the specifics of a dispute is undesirable. President Roosevelt's grant of more favorable terms to a railroad union than had been recommended by an emergency board sometimes has been characterized as the beginning of the end of successful emergency board procedures. The procedures would have broken down in any event. Nevertheless, the stigma remains. President Truman was criticized severely, with or without reason, for his actions in certain cases. On the other hand, President Eisenhower was sometimes criticized for inaction. President Kennedy and President Johnson were praised by some and blamed by others for certain actions in connection with the wage-price guidepost policy that had both direct and indirect impact on specific disputes. Probably the low point of all time was President Johnson's indirect participation in the 1966 dispute between the airlines and the International Association of Machinists. That was a notable event not because the White House became involved but because its efforts were unsuccessful. No President can escape criticism; and it was inevitable that someday there would be a failure. Considering all the burdens that a President must carry, it is probably correct to conclude that few if any labor disputes are of sufficient importance to warrant the President's direct and public involvement.

Vice President Nixon's involvement in the 1959 basic steel dispute with Secretary Mitchell has been noted earlier. It is about the only Vice Presidential excursion of consequence into labor disputes. It was successful, but it left scars that have not healed completely.

Senators and members of the House of Representatives have often expressed concern about labor disputes in their areas. On several occasions they have proposed procedural devices. For example, Senators Mansfield and Metcalf made procedural proposals in the copper strikes of 1967-1968. However, few congressmen have engaged in personal mediation of a dispute. A principal exception was Senator Wayne Morse, who was drafted for service in longshore and railroad disputes. His situation was unusual because of his arbitration and National War Labor Board experience prior to his service in the Congress. A member of the Congress can bring more mediation clout to an emergency dispute than most persons, partly because he will have substantial influence if the dispute ultimately winds up in the Congress. This fact contributed to the success of the Morse Board in the 1962-1963 longshore dispute. There were indications that the Senator's activity in the 1966 Machinist dispute contributed to his defeat in the 1968 election. If so, this is a tribute to his courage, but it is not likely to stimulate congressional zeal for personal mediation.

The relatively recent history of personal mediation involvement by Secretaries of Labor is of interest. During the long tenure of Secretary Frances Perkins, she assiduously avoided direct personal involvement. The United States Conciliation Service was then an integral part of the Department of Labor. It would have been a likely sequence for parties to seek the assistance of the Secretary when the activities of the subsidiary agency proved to be unsuccessful. The fact that this did not happen is probably due to two factors. First and foremost, it was her firm personal policy not to become involved. Secondly, the National War Labor Board was functioning during part of her tenure, and all disputes that were likely to escalate were referred to it.

Lewis B. Schwellenbach, who succeeded Secretary Perkins, did attempt some mediation. He inherited a rash of disputes after the completion of the War Labor Board period. However, he had little personal liking for mediation and had no notable successes.

As has been observed earlier, the Taft-Hartley Act in 1947 converted the United States Conciliation Service to the Federal Mediation and Conciliation Service, an independent agency. Moreover, the Act dealt decisively and even brutally with the matter of mediation by the Department of Labor. The pertinent part of Title II, Section 202 (d), of the Act reads:

> "All mediation and conciliation functions of the Secretary of Labor or the United States Conciliation Service . . . are hereby transferred to the Federal Mediation and Conciliation Service. . . . The Director and the Service shall not be subject in any way to

the jurisdiction or authority of the Secretary of Labor or any official or division of the Department of Labor."

For practical purposes the intent of that provision was observed until sometime after the appointment of Secretary of Labor James P. Mitchell in 1952. Mitchell was a popular and able Secretary who had had extensive labor-management experience prior to his appointment. He had the confidence of President Eisenhower, and it was natural and inevitable for the Department of Labor to play a more active role in the settlement of disputes. The Nixon-Mitchell role in the 1959 basic steel strike highlighted this fact.

When President Kennedy selected Arthur J. Goldberg as his Secretary of Labor, it was obvious that he would not revert to an inactive role. Goldberg was known as a hard-driving, highly knowledgeable, idealistic activist with policy-making and negotiating experience far greater than that of the average labor lawyer. He was held in the highest esteem by the new President and was given broad authority in labor matters. No White House assistant was an intermediary between the President and the Secretary.

Secretary Goldberg set the tone for his personal involvement in disputes at a very early date. That story is well known and need not be repeated here. What is not so well known is the fact that the Secretary's involvement was limited to a very few disputes and that he supported completely the development of a more effective mediation service. He would not have welcomed a labor-relations intermediary at the White House, cherishing his direct access to the President. But he made no attempt to intervene or interfere in the internal affairs of the FMCS. He was fully aware of the content of the law. What actually occurred was that the President gave the Secretary personal responsibility in a few labor disputes and general responsibilities as his primary labor-relations advisor over and above the official duties of a Secretary of Labor.

During the tenure of Secretary W. Willard Wirtz, a similar relationship existed, modified by the Secretary's lesser personal liking for mediation. Secretary Wirtz' years in office were also somewhat different as a result of the emergence of Joseph Califano as a White House intermediary and the increasing activity of Under Secretary Reynolds as a trouble-shooting mediator.

A statement that no friction ever existed existed between the Federal Mediation and Conciliation Service and the Department of Labor would be less than candid. In a few instances there were strong differences of opinion about policy in the mediation of a specific case after joint or separate efforts had begun. However, there was neither major nor continuing friction. Relationships for the most part were cordial and cooperative.

The simple fact is that any President who is fortunate enough to have a Secretary of Labor or an Under Secretary who is a talented mediator will want to utilize him occasionally in that capacity. Statutory agencies should cooperate fully as long as his activity is infrequent. Aside from understandable differences of opinion that may now and then arise between strong-minded friends who respect each other, no major problem will develop as long as there is no move to develop parallel and competing agencies, which there has not been. Nor is there evidence to support a charge that Secretaries of Labor have interfered with the internal operation of the FMCS, whose independence it is important to preserve.

A different form of mediation involvement by Cabinet members was initiated by President Johnson. This was the appointment of such persons by the President to special mediation boards. The first instance was in 1965 in a longshore dispute, where the Secretaries of Labor and Commerce served with Senator Morse. Subsequently, both the Secretaries of Labor and Commerce were designated officially to mediate in the 1965 basic steel case, the 1966 General Electric case and the 1967-1968 nonferrous cases. In the two latter instances, the Secretary of Defense was also named by the President.

Cabinet members have public stature. In some instances, those involved also have been skilled mediators and for that reason have been accorded status in the labor-management community. But in almost no instance has a Cabinet member been able to give undivided attention to the dispute. Is the stature of such persons so much greater than that of other potential appointees that it is worthwhile to jeopardize their performance of other duties? As a general proposition, this innovation by President Johnson should not be perpetuated except under the most unusual circumstances.

Governors, mayors, and other officials of political subdivisions have sometimes attempted to mediate personally in disputes in their geographical area that were important to the state or community. In a limited number of instances judges have attempted to mediate the issues in dispute when a case has come to court on other grounds, such as violence on the picket line. In almost all these cases a statutory agency (frequently the FMCS) is already active in the dispute. Most such efforts are well-intentioned and are not premised on possible political gain. Sometimes, the statu· tory agency supports or even solicits such assistance, and the mediation effort then is usually a cooperative and joint endeavor. The local official has a legitimate interest in the dispute and may be of great value. On the other hand, such intervention is sometimes undertaken without warning to the mediators involved, is ill-timed or badly handled, and serves only to prolong the dispute. In most states and cities the FMCS attempts to maintain a cordial working relationship with local officials to assure maximum cooperation and a mediation effort that is most likely to be helpful to the parties.

In addition to personal mediation efforts by government officials at various levels, public-minded citizens or ad hoc committees of various types occasionally intervene. If the individuals so motivated have sufficient public stature, their efforts can be helpful. Unfortunately, probably a majority of such activities, however well-intentioned, are either ineffective or may actually prolong the dispute.

In closing this chapter, it is important not to leave an an erroneous impression. The great majority of disputes requiring mediation assistance are mediated by the statutory agencies. Activity by others is limited to a small fraction of all disputes. The statutory agencies do not and should not have a monopoly on a procedure that is voluntary. Both the statutory agencies and any others who may seek to intervene have a major responsibility that transcends any parochial tendencies that may exist. It is to provide the most effective total mediation effort that is consistent with the needs of each specific case.

CHAPTER XII

MEDIATION ASPECTS OF WARTIME AND OTHER SPECIAL DISPUTE PROCEDURES

Emergency dispute procedures of the Taft-Hartley and Railway Labor Acts were designed for peacetime. Both Acts were passed not long after major wars and were expected to apply to peacetime conditions. As has been noted in Chapter X, the passage of time and defense requirements have resulted in the use of those procedures for other than peacetime purposes. However, war and preparation for war have also required special dispute-settlement procedures. One of the many unfortunate aspects of war is that the normal voluntarisms of a free society are modified in order to meet military objectives.

Yet even in wartime, it has been our national objective to preserve voluntarism in labor relations as much as possible. Mediation, not compulsion, has been the dominant feature of government involvement in labor disputes even in such extreme circumstances. Examination of wartime labor disputes procedures and of special arrangements restricted to limited segments of defense production supports these assertions.

WARTIME AGENCIES

Although a War Labor Board existed in World War I, its history will be ignored in keeping with the previously noted intention to restrict this book to more recent periods of time. Consideration will be limited to World War II, the Korean War, and the war in Vietnam.

National Defense Mediation Board

Rearmament in the United States, the very real probability of our early involvement in World War II, and an upsurge of strikes in the late fall and winter of 1940-1941 led to the establishment of the National Defense Mediation Board by Presidential Executive Order 8716, dated March 19, 1941.[1] The NDMB was a tripartite agency. Its membership included three public members, four labor representatives, and four management representatives. Alternate members and a relatively small staff assisted in the handling of a total of 118 cases over which the Board assumed jurisdiction during its life of approximately 10 months.

It is apparent that President Roosevelt concluded that the United States Conciliation Service, then an agency within the Department of Labor, was inadequate to handle all mediation responsibilities with a war around the corner. In the approaching war crisis, it was known that aggressive mediation by the Government would be required. Rather than attempt to make fundamental changes within the existing agency, the decision was made to expand the USCS mediation staff and hope for as many settlements as possible but at the same time to superimpose a new agency for the more difficult cases. It would have been difficult if not impossible to develop within the USCS structure the type of tripartite mediation that war needed for some disputes.

The NMBD assumed jurisdiction only in cases that were referred to it by the Secretary of Labor after conciliators had not been able to secure settlements. All NDMB cases were disputes in plants involving military production. In more than half the cases (64 out of 118), strikes were in progress when the disputes were certified by the Secretary of Labor.

The Executive Order contained no ban on strikes or lockouts, and no general no-strike, no-lockout pledge had been secured from labor and management. An early major policy of the NDMB was to decide that it could function effectively and accomplish its intended purposes only if strikes were not in progress while it was active in a case. Accordingly, it required a commitment not to strike during mediation, or the suspension of any strike already in progress, before it would begin to mediate. As a part of this process, the Board developed a practice of securing from the employer a voluntary commitment to make wage increases retroactive, thereby assuring employees that the delay in settlement would not be at their expense. This retroactive-pay policy could only have been effectuated under near-war conditions and in disputes affecting war production.

---

[1] GOVERNMENT REGULATION OF INDUSTRIAL DISPUTES, by George W. Taylor, Prentice-Hall, 1948, has been relied on heavily in connection with discussion of the National Defense Mediation Board and the National War Labor Board.

Initially the NDMB had no sanctions other than public opinion. It usually made recommendations which were released to the public and were accepted by both parties. In some instances it was not even necessary to make public recommendations. However, the Board came to grief over union security issues.

In a case involving the Federal Shipbuilding and Drydock Corporation and the Industrial Union of Marine and Shipbuilding Workers (CIO), the Board recommended a maintenance-of-membership clause. The company rejected that recommendation, and the union called a strike on August 6, 1941. This was the first instance of a strike directly attributable to rejection of a Board recommendation. On August 23, 1941, the Secretary of the Navy seized the shipyard under a directive issued by the President. Employees returned to work, but the union security controversy was not resolved and became an early legacy to the National War Labor Board.

Thus, even though it was seldom used, plant seizure [2] of a war production facility became recognized as a potential backstop to NDMB recommendations. The obvious conclusion is that the Government decided it could not then afford the luxury of rejection of a mediation recommendation at a vital war production facility. Mediation with the potential sanction of plant seizure clearly is different from the mediation discussed heretofore in this book. It was acceptable only because of the special prewar circumstances.

The second major union security issue arose soon thereafter in a captive-mine case, when the steel companies owning the mines refused to grant the union shop in response to a demand by the United Mine Workers. A strike started but was terminated when the NDMB assumed jurisdiction. A panel of the Board then recommended arbitration. The union rejected the Board's recommendation and again went on strike. The President intervened, the second strike was terminated, and the parties agreed to submit the issue to the full NDMB for a recommendation on the merits. By a vote of 9-2, with CIO members dissenting, the Board recommended against the union shop. Thereupon a strike began

[2] There were two other plant seizures in NDMB cases not related to union security. The first occurred on June 9, 1941, after workers at the Inglewood plant of North American Aviation Company engaged in a strike during mediation activity despite assurance to the contrary from union representatives. The second started on October 30, 1941, when a company (Air Associates, Inc., at a plant at Bendix, N.J.) refused to accept a Board formula for termination of a work stoppage.

for the third time. The CIO members resigned from the Board and requested that action be discontinued on all other pending cases involving CIO unions.

Although the NDMB continued in existence until January 12, 1942, and acted on a number of non-CIO cases, it was apparent that the withdrawal of the CIO had all but ended its usefulness, at least temporarily. Pearl Harbor and the active entry of the United States into the war created a more urgent situation. Whether the CIO would have returned to the NDMB and thus enabled it to survive is a question that will never be answered. The National War Labor Board emerged as the successor agency.

The demise of the NDMB tended to obscure its many achievements. As noted earlier, the Board developed procedures that were almost universally accepted to forestall strikes or to secure resumption of work while mediation was in process. Plant seizure had occurred in three cases, thus providing a "mediation with a club" atmosphere in plants vital to military production. But this atmosphere was the exception, not the rule. In the great majority of cases, the mediated results were accepted with good grace by both parties. Even on the most controversial issue, union security, the Board's maintenance-of-membership recommendations started a process of exploration of solutions that assisted the successor agency in its subsequent deliberations.

Perhaps the greatest achievement of NDMB was its experimentation with tripartite mediation. Labor and industry representatives had learned to work together and with public representatives to solve many extremely difficult problems in a near-war atmosphere.

National War Labor Board

National War Labor Board procedures [3] have too often been referred to as a form of compulsory arbitration. Memories fade. Some critics sought to emphasize compulsion even while the Board was active. The fact is that NWLB procedures were dominated by mediation and voluntary arbitration.[4] Only for certain

---

[3] The Termination Report, National War Labor Board, Volumes I, II and III, prepared under the auspices of the United States Department of Labor, U.S. Government Printing Office, contains a wealth of information concerning the National War Labor Board and its subsidiary agencies.

[4] *Wartime Handling of Labor Disputes,* by Edwin E. Witte, Harvard Business Review, Vol. 25, No. 1 (Autumn 1946), pp. 169–189, is an excellent article on this matter and on other aspects of the National War Labor Board.

companies and a few unions was the voluntary aspect of the process more theoretical than real.

The essentially noncoercive character of the National War Labor Board was established prior to its formal existence. The Wartime Labor-Industry Conference that preceded it set the tone for the next four years.

With the National Defense Mediation Board in disarray, the December 7, 1941 attack on Pearl Harbor and the almost immediate declaration of war dictated that something be done about labor disputes—and quickly. Fortunately and wisely, President Roosevelt decided to convene a group of high industry and labor officials. Based on recommendations as to personnel made by the National Association of Manufacturers, the U.S. Chamber of Commerce, the American Federation of Labor, and the Congress of Industrial Organizations, 12 industry and 12 labor representatives met in Washington from December 17 to December 23, 1941. William H. Davis, chairman of the NDMB, was Moderator and Senator Elbert D. Thomas was Associate Moderator.

The basic report to the President was simple. Its conclusions were:

1. There shall be no strikes or lockouts.
2. All disputes shall be settled by peaceful means.
3. The President shall set up a War Labor Board to handle these disputes.

The conferees reached complete agreement at a fairly early stage of their deliberations on all but one issue. The union security issue that had plagued the NDMB persisted in conference. Management representatives insisted that union security be excluded from "all disputes," and union representatives insisted that it be included. Upon receiving this report, the President advised the conference that:"The three points agreed upon cover of necessity all disputes that may arise between labor and management." The employer representatives accepted this judgment with some reluctance, and the Conference was adjourned.

Thus the War Labor Board to be named by the President was based on a no-strike, no-lockout agreement among representatives selected by the most prominent management and labor organizations. In substance, the new Board was created as a voluntary mediation and arbitration agency. Critics have challenged the word "voluntary" on the ground that no 24 men had the authority to bind thousands of companies and the many union officials not present at the Conference. The absence of legal authority to bind companies and unions not represented directly did not detract from the moral and psychological effect of the Conference decision. The prestigious character of the 24 men and the widespread support for the war created an atmosphere in which open approval of the agreement was voiced promptly by many companies, employer groups, and unions. The wounds caused by the CIO defection from the NDMB had been healed. Most groups and organizations that did not officially approve the agreement accepted it tacitly.

Moving with necessary speed, President Roosevelt issued Executive Order 9017 on January 12, 1942, creating the National War Labor Board and transferring to it the staff and unfinished business of the National Defense Mediation Board. The NWLB included 12 regular members (four public, four industry, and four labor). Alternate industry and labor members were named at the outset. The public members originally had no alternates, but several Associate Public Members soon were named who acted principally as mediators. The President designated William H. Davis as Chairman and George W. Taylor as Vice Chairman.

The Executive Order spelled out the basic procedural guides. It provided, first, that agreements should be reached by direct negotiations. Failing that, the next step was to call in conciliators from the United States Conciliation Service. If conciliation failed, the Secretary of Labor would certify the case to the NWLB. Unlike prior NDMB procedures, the NWLB could also intervene on its own motion after consulting with the Secretary of Labor. Having taken jurisdiction, according to the Executive Order, "the Board shall finally determine the dispute, and for this purpose may use mediation, voluntary arbitration, or arbitration under rules established by the Board."

Especially during the first year of Board operation, a substantial proportion of cases were settled by mediation without the necessity of official Board action. Mediation continued as the primary objective of the Board throughout its life, but the percentage of cases so settled diminished considerably as time went on. In the more important cases, regular Board members frequently acted as the mediators. In a larger number of cases, Associate Public Members and sometimes staff members worked with alternate or substitute industry members. Except for the occasional use of single Hearing Officers, most mediation was performed by a tripartite team (one public, one industry, and one labor member).

The "voluntary arbitration" provision of the Executive Order was effectuated occasionally in new-contract disputes by persuading the disputants to agree to arbitration. The arbitrator was selected directly by the parties or was appointed by the Board. However, the principal development of voluntary arbitration occurred in grievance disputes. In that era grievance arbitration was practiced in a few industries (notably apparel and printing) but was not widely used in the newly organized mass production industries. A major achievement of the NWLB was its promotion of grievance arbitration. This developed in large part out of public members' belief in the process and gradual industry and labor acceptance of the concept. Pragmatically, it was furthered by early acquisition by the Board of a heavy workload of contract disputes. It was necessary to find other means of handling the large number of grievance disputes, some of which tended to erupt in the form of strikes or threatened strikes.

The final means of settlement, "arbitration under rules established by the Board," was formal recommendations by the Board itself in the form of "Directive Orders." If a Board panel or one of its mediation panels failed to achieve a complete settlement by mediation, a recommendation on all remaining disputed issues was made to the Board. The Board considered the recommendations, adopted or modified them, and issued a Directive Order.

During the early months, the Board was concerned almost solely with the settlement of disputes and avoidance of strikes. However, inflationary trends soon became evident, and in April 1942 the President publicly called for wage and price restraint. On July 16, 1942, the Board announced what became known as the Little Steel Formula. Developed specifically for a dispute case involving four steel companies, it established a pattern for decisions on general wage increase issues. On October 2, 1942, the Congress amended the Emergency Price Control Act, and on the following day the President issued Executive Order 9250, delegating wage stabilization authority to the NWLB.

Thereafter the Board functioned in two capacities. It retained its responsibility to resolve all disputes. It acquired the responsibility to approve, disapprove, or modify all wage increases, including those agreed to voluntarily by the parties. To accomplish this dual purpose, the Board revamped its structure and procedures. A Disputes Division and a Stabilization Division were created. However, the full Board retained control and supervision over both disputes and wage stabilization.

The tremendous increase in work load caused by wage stabilization and an accelerating volume of disputes required decentralization. The Washington, D. C., offices simply could not handle the load. Moreover, the Board favored decentralization in order to keep the decision-making process as close as possible to the parties. Accordingly, 12 Regional War Labor Boards and a Board for Hawaii were established to decide most cases on a regional basis. It also developed that some industries could be handled best by industry commissions or panels. Beginning in September 1942 and at various times thereafter until the end of 1944, a total of 17 commissions or panels were created.

All regional boards, the commissions, and the panels were tripartite (public, industry, and labor) and functioned in essentially the same manner as the National Board. They were delegated authority to issue Directive Orders, except that some of the panels were limited to making recommendations to the National Board. Directive Orders of Board agencies could be appealed, thereby reserving final authority to the National Board. While the National Board retained original jurisdiction in a few major disputes, its work load increasingly became that of a policy-making agency, including action on appeals.

The NWLB and its subsidiary agencies decided 17,650 disputes during the period from January 12, 1942, to August 18, 1945. A substantial number of dispute cases were closed between then and December 31, 1945, when the Board was terminated. The four-year total was about 20,000 cases.

Since emphasis here is on the mediation aspects of Board operations, no attempt will be made to set forth the many policies that were developed or to discuss the great variety of important disputes that were decided. Such information can be found elsewhere.[5] Strikes were not avoided entirely. In fact, during the four-year period from 1942 through 1945, strikes averaged 4,106 per year, a figure almost as high as for any other consecutive four-year period from 1927 through 1965. However, few large strikes occurred, and strike duration was much shorter than in other periods of time. Strike time lost as a percentage of total working time averaged 0.1 percent during the first three years of the Board's existence (1942 through 1944). Lower strike incidence has been recorded by the Bureau of Labor Statistics only in

[5] Notes 1 and 3 above.

the three-year period at the beginning of the Great Depression (1929 through 1931). Strike-time losses were higher in 1945, in part because, after the termination of the shooting war, the Board began a process of orderly liquidation in August. The no-strike pledge then lost much of its effectiveness.

With wage increases severely restrained and a very tight labor market, the Board made a remarkable record in keeping war production relatively unhindered by strikes. The record of acceptance of Directive Orders was good. In approximately 95 percent of all the Directive Order cases, both parties accepted immediately and with no appreciable repercussions. The bulk of the remaining 5 percent of cases were situations where a company or a union (usually a local union) delayed for a short time before accepting. Sometimes strikes occurred in these cases. The Board used a variety of means to secure compliance, the most effective one being the work and attitude of Board members. Regardless of how the industry and labor members had voted in a particular case, they always were unanimous in insisting on compliance. Personal efforts of industry members with noncomplying companies and of labor members with noncomplying unions usually were successful. Public members of the Board, staff members of the Disputes Division, and a small number of compliance officers also worked on these cases. In important situations, the National Board and the regional boards sometimes held "show cause" hearings. By this informal and essentially case-by-case approach, the hard core of noncompliance cases was reduced to a minimum.

Forty-six noncompliance cases were considered to be of sufficient importance to justify a report to the President, either directly or through the Director of Economic Stabilization. A telegraphic request by the President secured early compliance in five of these cases. A sixth case, involving the American Federation of Musicians, was not pursued beyond an unsuccessful request because the war effort was not threatened. Seizure was resorted to by the Government in the remaining 40 cases. It will be recalled that plant seizure had been utilized in three NDMB cases. As in those instances, the early NWLB case seizures were based on the authority of the President as Commander-in-Chief. On June 25, 1943, the Congress passed the War Labor Disputes Act. Among other things, that Act affirmed the President's seizure powers.

The merits and demerits of seizure as a compliance mechanism

---

[6] EMERGENCY DISPUTES AND NATIONAL POLICY, by Archibald Cox, Harper and Bros., 1955, includes an excellent section, *Seizure In Emergency Disputes*, pp. 224–242.

have been analyzed elsewhere.[6] Seizure is noted here because it is evident that compulsion was involved in these 40 cases (also in four additional cases where the Director of Economic Stabilization applied economic sanctions). These 44 cases were about equally divided between employer and union noncompliance.

The Board itself had no direct enforcement powers other than persuasion. On wage matters, the October, 1942, Act of Congress did include a potent sanction: Unapproved wage increases could be disallowed as wage costs for income-tax purposes. The use of plant seizure in a few cases and the knowledge that seizure could be employed undoubtedly created a certain aura of compulsion, but this is the only ground for calling Board procedures compulsory arbitration. In general, it is fair to say that mediation and voluntary arbitration were the dominant features of NWLB procedures. This assertion is buttressed by the fact that an additional substantial number of Directive orders were not complied with fully by companies or unions despite the exercise of persuasion. No compulsion was attempted in those cases, and the disputed issues were not resolved.

How did the Board and its agencies mediate? It should be recognized at the outset that this was mediation with reserve powers not normally available in peacetime mediation. The reserve power held by a tripartite mediation panel was the certainty of recommendations to the National Board or to a regional board and a subsequent Directive Order if the parties did not agree. Undoubtedly this had some influence on the parties. The most realistic negotiators preferred to settle to avoid delays. However, if the power factors were quite unequal, the weaker party was inclined to wait for a recommendation, hoping for a better deal than could otherwise be obtained. It was common practice for the tripartite mediation panel to disclose to the parties its tentative recommenadations to the Board. Many settlements were agreed to when the recommendations became known informally, often with minor revisions to make the agreement more palatable to one side or the other.

The tripartite composition of the mediation panels was a valuable asset. The industry member normally had the confidence of the company negotiators and spent much time with them. The labor member was similarly regarded by the union negotiators. The public member talked to both sides, jointly and separately, but performed his most important mediation functions in executive sessions of the tripartite panel. Thus, the mediation sessions were a combination of (1) direct negotiation between the parties in the presence of the full panel, (2) sessions of the mediators with the parties separately and (3) mediation within the panel.

Recommendations made to the Board often were unanimous. Even more often, probably, panel members were in complete agreement but one or more thought it necessary to "dissent for the record."

With the advent of wage stabilization, the character of the mediation was altered. On the almost always crucial issue of general wage increases, the panel's mediation function became largely a matter of advising the parties as to the amount of wage increase, if any, that was permissible under stabilization policies. More meaningful mediation was possible with respect to noneconomic issues, fringe benefits, inequity adjustments, and the like. However, as time went on and stabilization lines became more sharp, Board policies governed many of the issues. The development of a Board policy as to union security almost removed that issue from effective mediation in specific cases. In short, the elbow room normally available to the parties and to a mediator gradually diminished, though it was never eliminated entirely. Even in 1945, many issues in a typical dispute were susceptible to true mediation. However, Board panels increasingly became conduits for the adaptation and application of established Board policy to the facts of a specific case.

With the advent of the War Labor Board, conciliators in the United States Conciliation Service faced a difficult role. The existence of the Board was both a challenge and a menace to a proud and able conciliator. The challenge was to assist in securing a settlement before it became necessary to certify the dispute to the Board. The menace was the probability that one or both of the parties would not give the conciliator a chance but would seek to use him as a certifying agent to get the dispute before the Board as quickly as possible. Many competent and conscientious conciliators were frustrated and hamstrung by this situation. If they refused to recommend certification, a union could force the issue by calling a strike. In any event, the denial of full cooperation to the conciliator virtually doomed his efforts. The less able and less insistent conciliators often gave up the battle and did not really try to mediate; they washed their hands of the case by immediate certification. The supervisory staff of he USCS attempted to meet this problem by establishing ratings. A sort of batting-average system was established based on percentage of cases settled without certification. This provided an imperfect measure of conciliator effectiveness, but as can be imagined, it also amplified some problems.

In an effort to meet these problems, the Board and the USCS developed a liaison arrangement. Moreover, conciliators were kept advised of NWLB policy decisions. As these policies developed, an able conciliator could perform as competent a job of helping the parties adapt to these policies as a Board mediation panel. Despite the fact that the NWLB case load increased steadily throughout its existence, it is quite certain that this was due primarily to factors other than lack of competence of conciliators. The number of situations in which conciliators were involved increased even more rapidly than the NWLB case load.

Mediation by the NWLB did not stop at the tripartite panel stage. If the case was not settled and recommendations were made to the Board, a great deal of additional mediation occurred frequently before a Directive Order was issued. Mediation occurred in executive sessions of the National Board or in comparable meetings of the regional boards and commissions. It was common practice for representatives of both parties to be present in Washington or at other headquarters cities while their case was being considered. Industry, labor, or public members discussed the cases informally with these representatives, and every attempt was made to develop Directive Orders that were as acceptable as possible. Alternative decisions were "tried on for size" before a Directive Order was finally formulated. This was not a secretive, surreptitious process. It was deliberately encouraged.

A final feature of mediation existed by reason of the always tenuous tripartite Board structure. It will be recalled that the National Defense Mediation Board had all but collapsed when the CIO members resigned. In every hotly disputed NWLB case, it was possible that a Directive Order too obnoxious to industry or to labor would result in a similar disastrous consequence. This was a threat that was seldom voiced; the relationships within the Board were too good to permit that. But all Board members were realists, and this latent possibility provided an effective check against total unacceptability. Some critics have challenged the tripartite structure on this account. The argument is that this feature promotes compromise rather than objective decision-making. Those of us who have participated in the process feel strongly that the merits greatly outweigh any disadvantages. Bureaucracy needs effective checks and balances. Among a group of dedicated and public-spirited men (and the War Labor Board and its agencies were that), the tripartite structure provided the essential ballast to keep the ship steady.

Perhaps the best illustration of the Board's mediation function was its handling of the emotional union security issue. From the very beginning of NWLB operations, it was known that an acceptable union security formula must be developed. The NDMB had almost succeeded by using varieties of maintenance of membership but had run afoul of the Federal Shipbuilding and Drydock Corporation and the United Mine Workers in two different cases on opposite sides of the ledger. The conference preceding the establishment of NWLB had almost foundered on this issue, and industry had accepted President Roosevelt's inclusion of it within NWLB jurisdiction with great reluctance. Painfully but surely, the internal mediation processes within the Board developed maintenance of membership with an escape clause. This formula effectively disposed of the issue for the duration of the Board's existence. Industry members almost invariably dissented, but the heat was gone.

In a variety of other difficult matters, including stabilization policies, it was the Board's ability to develop generally acceptable solutions internally that permitted the peaceful settlement of wartime disputes.

The NWLB engaged in a rather special variety of mediation. The first mediation was normally performed by a tripartite panel. It was mediation with the power in reserve to make recommendations and cause the issuance of a Board Directive Order. The second mediation step was mediation within the tripartite panel if recommendations became necessary. The third mediation step was mediation within the tripartite Board after receipt of recommendations in difficult cases. Board members were usually in close contact with representatives of the parties at this step.

Throughout these steps, the tripartite composition of the Board and its agencies was a vital element working towards acceptance by the parties. Acceptance was sometimes reluctant but was achievable within the context of a nation at war. The ever-present possibility that the tripartite structure might collapse was an effective deterrent to bureaucratic arrogance.

Directive Orders were somewhat comparable to voluntary arbitration decisions, but they were decisions arrived at after intensive mediation. Some ingredients of Directive Orders were often disliked by one or both parties to the dispute. That is a not infrequent result of direct bargaining. The process was essentially voluntary in the great majority of cases. It was compulsory arbitration only in those cases that were accompanied by executive seizure and in some few additional instances where the threat of seizure was very real.

Wage Stabilization Board [7]

President Truman's decision to send troops to Korea in mid-1950 was the beginning of the next war emergency. A threat of inflation caused the Congress to pass the Defense Production Act in September of that year.

On September 9, 1950, the President issued Executive Order No. 10161 establishing an Economic Stabilization Agency, within which was created the Wage Stabilization Board. The WSB was a tripartite agency (three public, three industry, and three labor). The agency was given no power or authority with respect to labor disputes; it was only a stabilization agency. It will be noted that this was the opposite of the World War II sequence. The National Defense Mediation Board and the National War Labor Board operated for more than a year as disputes agencies before the NWLB was given important stabilization responsibilities.

This first Wage Stabilization Board, like the first World War II agency, collapsed on February 15, 1951, when all labor members withdrew. The immediate occasion for defection was the issuance of General Wage Regulation No. 6, a cost-of-living general wage increase adjustment formula from which the labor members dissented. A major contributing factor was the absence of any disputes function in the Board's jurisdiction. On February 28, 1951, labor members also withdrew from all other participation in the Economic Stabilization Agency.

The President then created a National Advisory Board, on which labor representatives agreed to serve. It was a 17-man tripartite group with Charles E. Wilson as chairman. The Advisory Board's report to the President proposed the reconstitution of the Wage Stabilization Board with labor dispute responsibilities of a much more limited character than had been the case with the NWLB. A no-strike, no-lockout pledge was not obtained, and the Board was given responsibility for disputes in only two situations. One was where both parties requested the Board to issue non-binding recommendations or a binding arbitration award, accord-

---

[7] Wage Determination Under National Boards, by Abraham L. Gitlow, Prentice-Hall, Inc., 1953, Ch. 9 and 10, pp. 180–220, provide a summary of Wage Stabilization Board history and policies.

ing to their choice. The second was certification where a dispute was certified to the Board by the President in situations considered by him to be sufficiently critical to the Korean war effort. In the latter case the Board was to make recommendations to the parties and to the President. On April 21, 1951, the President issued Executive Order 10233 establishing a reconstituted Wage Stabilization Board of 18 members (six public, six labor, and six industry). Its authority was as recommended by the Advisory Board.

The Wage Stabilization Board utilized regional boards and a few other subordinate agencies. However, these were concerned almost solely with stabilization. The limited disputes functions were handled by the 18-member Board in Washington.

In its first year of operation (April 21, 1951, to May 7, 1952), the reconstituted WSB was asked to take jurisdiction in 34 disputes cases. Voluntary submissions, usually for recommendations only, occurred in 22 instances. However, the Board refused to accept six voluntary submissions, and an additional seven cases could not be handled because of subsequent developments. The President certified 12 cases.

On March 20, 1952, the WSB issued recommendations in a hotly disputed steel industry case. Those recommendations, affecting wages, other cost items, and the perennial union security issue, had significant repercussions. Among other things, a congressional investigation by the House Committee on Education and Labor [8] began on May 6, 1952, and lasted more or less continuously through the month of May.

Soon after the House Committee's 1952 hearings were completed, the Congress amended the Defense Production Act to strip the WSB of any effective disputes jurisdiction. Moreover, the Board was required again to be reconstituted, this time with Senate confirmation of the members of a new 18-member tripartite Board. The third WSB was short-lived. In the late fall of 1952 it modified downward a wage increase that had been negotiated by the coal operators and John L. Lewis. The miners went on strike. During his "lame duck" period in office, President Truman overruled the Board and, on December 3, 1952, approved the full amount that had been negotiated. Thereupon, Chairman Archibald Cox and all the industry members resigned. Soon after

[8] 82nd Congress, 2nd Session, INVESTIGATION OF THE WAGE STABILIZATION BOARD BY HOUSE COMMITTEE ON EDUCATION AND LABOR, U.S. Government Printing Office, 1952.

assuming office, President Eisenhower issued an Executive Order terminating all activities of the Board.

This somewhat unhappy history of the WSB, at least so far as its disputes functions were concerned, is in sharp contrast to the record of the NWLB. What were the reasons? One was the difference in the public's attitude toward the two wars and the effects on the economy. World War II was a more popular war, supported almost unanimously by the people. Moreover, it required a much more drastic diversion of manpower and money to the war effort. Under World War II circumstances, all segments of the economy were more willing to subordinate personal and group interests to the overriding need to prosecute the war.

No general no-strike, no-lockout agreement was obtained during the Korean War. The absence of this vital ingredient limited WSB effectiveness.

At least a subsidiary reason was that the Taft-Hartley Act had been passed in 1947. The emergency disputes sections of that Act had made provision for certain types of emergencies. It appears that many members of Congress questioned the need for WSB disputes procedures on the ground that the Taft-Hartley Act was adequate. Moreover, an independent Federal Mediation and Conciliation Service was in a better position to meet the mediation needs than the United States Conciliation Service had been in 1941.

For these and perhaps other reasons, the Wage Stabilization Board does not occupy a high niche in the annals of emergency disputes procedures.

The War in Vietnam

The Vietnam war was the next occasion for testing the efficacy of collective bargaining when a substantial proportion of the nation's resources and manpower are diverted to military action. A little-noticed feature of the Vietnam war has been the absence of any special wartime labor disputes procedure. No War Labor Board or its equivalent has been created. Several Taft-Hartley injunctions have been due directly to defense preparation or participation in the war. Similarly, activity by some nonstatutory boards has been traceable to the war. However, resort to such measures has not been appreciably more frequent than during the period prior to Vietnam. How is this to be explained?

One reason is that the Kennedy, Johnson, and (through January 1971), Nixon administrations have made a conscious decision to avoid mandatory wage and price controls. Controls would necessarily have resulted in a wage stabilization agency, and that step would have had a tendency to expand into a special labor disputes procedure. The voluntary restraint program of the guideposts (1962 to 1966) complicated mediation, as recounted previously, but as long as the program was voluntary, no new bureaucracy was needed.

It is outside the scope of this book to explore the question as to whether the government's "guns and butter" approach was a wise one or whether it can be continued. In any event, the decision to avoid mandatory wage controls is not a complete answer. In World War II, disputes machinery preceded controls by at least a year.

A major reason why a War Labor Board was not proposed was a firm policy decision at the highest levels of government and within civilian leadership at the Pentagon. Briefly stated, it was to give collective bargaining every possible opportunity to work. Direct and frequent liaison between the Defense Department and the Federal Mediation and Conciliation Service resulted in frank and candid appraisal of maximum strike time that could be accommodated by military needs on the one hand and the best prognosis as to whether a strike would occur and, if so, its expected duration on the other hand. Time and again, initial gloomy Pentagon estimates as to criticality were softened after more thorough checking. In short, the Defense Department did not push the panic button in its final informal reports to the FMCS unless there was a real and pressing urgency. Effective civilian control at the Pentagon tempered the normal military reaction to labor disputes in wartime. At most war production plants the FMCS was thereby able to utilize the full collective bargaining pressures of a contract deadline and a possible strike threat. And even if a strike started, the absence of official hysteria permitted hard-hitting mediation in lieu of government decision-making.

The keen appreciation of the importance and the needs of collective bargaining that was evidenced by Defense Secretary Robert S. McNamara and numerous others on his top staff was a principal reason for the absence of a War Labor Board during his tenure. His successor, Clark Clifford, continued the same basic policy, and it would appear that Melvin Laird has followed the same course.

The FMCS sought to gear its mediation policies and performance to meet the specific needs of each important defense production dispute. Defense cases generally were given priority, and, where necessary, more aggressive mediation tactics were used than in otherwise comparable nondefense disputes. The FMCS was not always successful, as evidenced by the few Taft-Hartley injunctions and nonstatutory boards reviewed elsewhere. But in many instances settlements were achieved by collective bargaining, assisted by intensive mediation, that would unquestionably have gone the War Labor Board route if such a board had been in existence. Many disputes that can be characterized as "near misses" were settled when the alternative was a Taft-Hartley injunction.

With few exceptions the parties responded to defense necessities by engaging in real collective bargaining. In case after case, negotiators on both sides of the table subordinated some of their institutional objectives to the war situation. This cooperation was aided in no small measure by the fact that negotiators came to believe that they were getting honest and candid information as to the criticalness of their dispute. Moreover, the most thoughtful and farsighted negotiators were always conscious of the fact that if collective bargaining failed too many times in a war situation, decision-making would be removed from the bargaining table.

The strike record in the 1960s compared with World War II and the Korean war is shown in table 10.

It will be noted that the strike record during the Vietnam war has not been as good as during the National War Labor Board's three most active years. However, the absence of a no-strike, no-lockout pledge and the fact that the Vietnam war was never accorded the same popular support as World War II suggests that the record of the 1960s has been remarkably good. If the comparison of Vietnam is with the Korean war period, the evidence is even stronger. Korea was more palatable to the American public than Vietnam, but the strike record during the Korean war was not as good.

As an exercise of "Monday-morning quarterbacking," there is an additional consideration supporting the absence of a counterpart of the War Labor Board during the Vietnam war. Despite the many problem areas of collective bargaining, labor and industry are generally united in an intense desire to retain the process. Even during wartime, the record reviewed in this chapter shows that decision-making away from the bargaining table was successful only during the National War Labor Board period. On all other occasions the mechanisms failed after limited periods of

Table 10

STRIKE INCIDENCE—
WORLD WAR II, KOREAN WAR, AND VIETNAM WAR

War Period	Year	Strike Time Lost as Percentage of Estimated Total Working Time (Private Nonfarm)
World War II	1941	0.32%
	1942	.05
	1943	.15
	1944	.09
	1945	.47
Korean War	1950	0.40%
	1951	.21
	1952	.57
	1953	.26
Vietnam	1961	0.12%
	1962	.16
	1963	.13
	1964	·18
	1965	.18
	1966	.18
	1967	.30
	1968	.32
	1969	.28

Source: Bureau of Labor Statistics.

successful operation. Just prior to V-J Day, there were even indications that the NWLB was operating on borrowed time. In other words, decision-making under government auspices is likely to be successful only for a limited period of time. The duration will depend on the totality of the circumstances, but only the length of time is in doubt. Any War Labor Board disputes procedure that might have been attempted during the Vietnam war probably would have been short-lived. Collapse would have left wartime labor relations in a worse condition than before.

SPECIAL PURPOSE AGENCIES

In addition to wartime labor-dispute agencies with potential jurisdiction over any enterprise essential to the prosecution of a war, we have had limited experience with special-purpose dispute procedures.

Atomic Energy Labor-Management Relations Panel [9]

Most atomic energy installations are government-owned but privately operated facilities. During both the construction and operating stages of these facilities, the contracting companies have employed many thousands of civilian workers. The extreme secrecy surrounding the beginnings of atomic energy production, when it was known as the Manhattan Engineering District, appeared to government officials to preclude union organizing activity at the research and production facilities. Top officials of the AFL and the CIO agreed to refrain from such activity. However, by March 1946 this ban was lifted, and the Secretary of War officially notified the National Labor Relations Board that it might certify bargaining units at Oak Ridge, Tenn. Union organizational efforts since that date have resulted in substantial union representation, first at Oak Ridge and subsequently at other places.

The period from March 1946 to April 26, 1949, witnessed an effort by the Atomic Energy Commission, others in government, and the unions to determine the best way to handle labor relations in atomic energy. Labor disputes did occur at Oak Ridge. In fact, the first Taft-Hartley injunction was secured on March 8, 1948, in a contract dispute at that site. In September 1948 President Truman appointed a special commission headed by William H. Davis, former chairman of the National War Labor Board, to make recommendations regarding labor relations policy and procedure at atomic energy installations. The commission examined the matter thoroughly, visiting the sites and having discussions with many responsible interested persons. The commission's report was dated April 18, 1949.

On the commission's recommendation, the President on April 26, 1949, established the Atomic Energy Labor Relations Panel. The first Panel comprised the same three men who had been named to the Special commission (William H. Davis, chairman, Aaron Horvitz, and Edwin E. Witte). The Davis Panel, augmented subsequently by additional members, served until February 27, 1953. For house-keeping purposes, the Panel was under Atomic Energy Commission jurisdiction, but it was not answerable to the AEC on policy matters or the handling of specific disputes.

[9] LABOR DISPUTES IN ATOMIC ENERGY CO..MISSION EXPERIENCE, New York University Fourth Annual Conference on Labor, by Donald Straus, Matthew Bender and Company, 1951, pp. 233–259, is a short but good report of the origins of the Panel and its first two years of operation.

On March 24, 1953, shortly after taking office, President Eisenhower announced that a new panel, renamed the Atomic Energy Labor-Management Relations Panel, would be designated to be housed administratively within the Federal Mediation and Conciliation Service. Shortly thereafter he named Cyrus S. Ching as chairman. It was known thereafter as the Ching Panel.

On July 1, 1956, President Eisenhower returned the Ching Panel to the Atomic Energy Commission but otherwise made no significant changes. Except for some additions and resignations of Panel personnel, the Ching Panel served continuously until Mr. Ching's death in 1967. Shortly thereafter, Leo C. Brown, S.J., was named chairman and continues to serve in that capacity.

In 1956 Secretary of Labor Mitchell appointed a Committee on Labor-Management Relations in Atomic Energy Installations to make recommendations as to the future handling of disputes in this industry. The five-man Committee, chaired by David L. Cole, submitted a written report on January 31, 1957.[10] Some features of that report will be referred to hereafter.

At least superficially, the basic procedures of the Panel have not been altered in major ways since 1949. It was empowered at that time to take jurisdiction, at the request of one or both of the parties *or* at the request of the AEC, in a dispute "which collective bargaining and the normal processes of conciliation have failed to resolve and which threatens to interfere with an essential part of the atomic energy program." To fulfill the first requirement the Panel normally assures itself that the parties have bargained to or nearly to an impasse. The FMCS has been active in mediation of the dispute. There is no formal certification by the FMCS to the Panel. This transfer-of-jurisdiction problem was a major reason for the Eisenhower decision in March 1953 to move the Panel from the AEC to the FMCS. The FMCS had complained that the Panel was too quick to assume jurisdiction. Though the FMCS "won that round," only three years later the AEC and the Panel "won the second round" before the same President, when the Panel was moved back to the AEC.

It can be stated unequivocally that no important problems of this kind existed in the 1960s. In every instance of possible or actual assumption of jurisdiction by the Panel, the move was discussed in an informal but searching manner by Chairman Ching and the Director or Disputes Director of the FMCS. Invariably

10 REPORT OF THE SECRETARY OF LABOR'S ADVISORY COMMITTEE ON LABOR-MANAGEMENT RELATIONS IN ATOMIC ENERGY INSTALLATIONS, JANUARY 31, 1957, U.S. Government Printing Office, 1957.

the decision was a mutual one. Moreover, to achieve a fully cooperative working relationship and to maintain close communication, the Executive Secretary of the Panel, a part-time assignment, was also the General Counsel of the FMCS. This liaison device had been suggested by Chairman Ching.

The second requirement for Panel assumption of jurisdiction underwent substantial changes over a 20-year period. An important original reason for the Panel's creation was the reluctant decision by the Davis Commission in 1946 that strikes could not be tolerated in bargaining units at virtually all atomic energy installations. There were two basic reasons for this position. One was the inherent hazard of any shutdown, given the production processes then in use. The second was the fact that there was no stockpile of atomic energy products. What was then considered to be an adequate defense supply was just beginning to be acquired.

By January 1957, when the Cole Committee reported, these two reasons had largely disappeared. New and improved production methods had removed most of the hazards posed by a strike. Moreover, the stockpile of atomic products was substantial. Except for a few of the most sophisticated new products, confined to a small number of locations, the change had become even more pronounced by the mid-1960s. In fact, at almost any time during the Vietnam war, atomic energy plants would have been well down any priority listing of defense production facilities.

Thus, criticalness has assumed a new and different meaning. Strikes of some duration at atomic energy installations have occurred. Unions, workers, and management have been surprised when no special action was taken by the Government. This has been good for collective bargaining. However, candor requires an additional comment. Even in recent years the Panel has taken jurisdiction of disputes that would not have received government attention beyond FMCS mediation if they had occurred in any other industry. Stated simply, the ready availability of a special disputes mechanism makes it easy to use it. This is especially so when it is a competent instrument, as the Panel has been.

Once the Panel takes jurisdiction, the procedures are somewhat like those of the Railway Labor Act, with important exceptions. The parties agree to continue operations and otherwise maintain the status quo while the Panel is active in the case. Moreover, if the Panel makes recommendations, the parties agree not to strike or lock out for at least 30 days while the recommendations are being considered.

The exceptions may be more significant than the similarities. While the Panel is active in the case it almost always attempts mediation, sometimes successfully. If mediation does not result in agreement, the Panel may make recommendations but is not required to do so. The theory and the general practice has been that the Panel should be flexible in its case-handling, varying the procedures according to the nature of the case. It has a much better record in this respect than emergency boards in railroad cases. This success has been due in large part to the fact that the Panel members become very familiar with the special aspects of the industry and with its personalities.

A second difference is that the Panel procedure is not based on statute. Originally President Truman did not even dignify the Panel procedure with an Executive Order. He issued a press release, and subsequent minor changes have been handled in a like manner. This provides an element of voluntarism that is beneficial. It may also give some parties an "out." At certain installations for varying periods of time, one or both of the parties have rejected the Panel even when the AEC has desired intervention. In such instances the FMCS provides the only mediation, and the dispute is handled in the same manner as any other dispute.

A final difference concerns the procedure if Panel recommendations are not accepted by the parties, as has happened in a number of instances. Occasionally the same Panel members go back to clarify their recommendations and possibly for further mediation. The more common course of events is for the FMCS to resume jurisdiction of the case. This is in sharp contrast to railroad procedure. A number of settlements with FMCS mediation assistance have occurred after Panel recommendations have been rejected. How can the FMCS be successful when it presumably failed only a couple of months earlier, prior to the Panel's intervention? Part of the answer is that the dispute is usually in a different posture after recommendations. Another important element is that strikes have been permitted in this industry in recent years—just often enough to make the parties realize that a strike can occur.

In any event, no Taft-Hartley injunction has been needed at atomic energy installations since May 1957. The combination of FMCS and Atomic Energy Labor-Management Relations Panel cooperation and generally good bargaining has kept strikes at a very low level.

When the Cole Committee reported in January 1957, its basic

recommendation was that the Panel should be discontinued at the earliest feasible time and that labor-management relations at atomic energy installations should be handled by the Government essentially as in other important industries. The primary basis for this recommendation was the Committee's fear that collective bargaining would wither away and that undue and unnecessary reliance would be placed on the Panel by the parties. For whatever reasons, 13 years have passed and the recommendations have not been effectuated.

At least since 1957 the Atomic Energy Labor-Management Relations Panel, though not an essential arm of government, has been a very useful device. Fears that collective bargaining would atrophy have not materialized. The fact that the government has "kept its cool" and permitted a few strikes has enhanced bargaining.

Whatever may have been the situation years ago, excellent cooperation has existed between the FMCS and the Panel for at least 10 years. The Panel includes within its membership a number of very competent, devoted, and conscientious men who have accumulated vast knowledge of labor relations policies and practices in the industry as well as technical knowledge. That asset should not be discarded lightly. Despite some defections, most of the companies and unions in the industry still have confidence in the Panel.

Equally important, the Panel has no statutory authority and even has nebulous executive authority. Except for its origin and the fact that the Atomic Energy Commission foots the modest bill for its part-time members, the Panel is not now significantly different from a private disputes mechanism. The odds favor its continuation as long as the conditions noted above persist.

Missile Sites Labor Commission [11]

Early in 1961, soon after the Kennedy Administration began, major labor relations problems developed at missile sites. Public knowledge of these problems was confined primarily to Cape Canaveral (subsequently renamed Cape Kennedy) in Florida. In the Senate, hearings conducted by the McClellan Committee highlighted strikes and alleged uneconomical labor practices at the missile test facilities there. It was also apparent that construction of ICBM launching bases at various geographical locations

[11] THE MISSILE SITES LABOR COMMISSION—1961 THRU 1967, by Wayne E. Howard, U.S. Government Printing Office, 1969, is an excellent study of the Commission's history and activities.

was being accompanied by numerous labor difficulties. This construction program was gigantic. Without doubt it was the largest coordinated construction program ever attempted.

There were several ingredients of the labor problem. Many of the sites, including Cape Kennedy, were in generally remote areas which lacked an adequate labor force. Many of these areas were essentially nonunion localities, but nonunion employees with the requisite skills could not be obtained in sufficient numbers. Such situations were not without precedent. Thus, large dams and power plants had previously been built in remote locations. It had been customary in such instances for one or a small number of contractors to assume complete responsibility for all major segments of the job. Such a method of operation normally results in a job that is all union or all nonunion. However, in the case of the missile sites, the Government's method of letting contracts was designed to provide as much opportunity as possible for local contractors to bid. The result was a sizable number of contractors on the same site, some union and some nonunion. Many employees were "boomers"—nonresidents of the area who were attracted to the sites or referred by the skilled trades unions in response to urgent appeals for competent manpower. To anyone familiar with traditions of the building trades, the difficulties involved in side-by-side union and nonunion operations require no elaboration.

The second major problem was that recognized craft jurisdictional lines were of limited value. The technology of missile site construction was so different from anything ever attempted before that a host of unprecedented jurisdictional issues arose.

A third problem developed out of the need for "concurrency." The missiles themselves and much of the related launching equipment and hardware were built by aerospace, electronic, and other manufacturers away from the sites, but these firms had the responsibility for installation and testing. On conventional construction jobs, the building is substantially completed before outside firms move in for installation. In the case of the missile sites, the Defense Department concluded that it could not afford the time lag. Construction and installation occurred concurrently. Employees of the manufacturing firms were predominantly union employees, but the unions were industrial and not building trades unions. Moreover, there were real problems in determining just where construction stopped and installation began, creating new types of jurisdictional arguments.

The Kennedy Administration did not want to create a special dispute mechanism of broad scope. Although there also were labor problems elsewhere, there was no apparent need or justification for an overall War Labor Board type of organization. It was equally clear that the missile sites problems demanded attention. Unless these trouble spots could be handled, there was some possibility that public opinion might generate demand for more sweeping action than was needed. The Administration therefore decided to create a special-purpose device. It was to be limited strictly to operations at missile and space sites. The space program, then in its infancy, was expected to encounter comparable problems.

In planning a procedure to attempt to meet these site problems, two basic planks were derived from National War Labor Board experience. One was the advisability of securing a no-strike, no-lockout pledge. Conferences with the unions and with many of the principal contractors were successful in this respect. It should be noted that the pledges were secured insofar as was possible directly from the companies and unions that would be involved.

The second objective, requisite to attainment of the first, was the creation of a tripartite agency with dispute-settlement authority. Each one of the three legs of the triangle was designed to represent appropriate interests. For example, one public member was John T. Dunlop, closely identified with the settlement of building trades jurisdictional disputes. The second was David H. Stowe, somewhat similarly identified with interunion disputes among the former CIO unions. The third was David L. Cole, the principal arbitrator selected by the AFL-CIO under the jurisdictional pact created as an outgrowth of the merger of the AFL and the CIO.

Unlike the NWLB, representation was not equal as among the public, industry, and labor members. The MSLC was a 5-3-3 arrangement. In addition to the three public members mentioned above, the Secretary of Labor was designated as chairman and the Director of the Federal Mediation and Conciliation Service as vice-chairman. With Secretary Goldberg as the chief spokesman, these two had been the principal designers of the Commission format.

Especially in view of the nature of the anticipated problem areas, it was obvious that a Washington-based agency would be unsuccessful if it had to decide many cases. Disputes of the types noted earlier cannot readily be resolved at long distance. Nor could the delay that had characterized NWLB procedures be tolerated for these problems. They were more akin to multiheaded grievances than to disputes at contract expiration time. Some mechanism had to be developed for quick on-the-site solutions.

To meet these requirements, Missile Site Labor Relations Committees were established at each missile base. Beyond the general principle that the committees should include appropriate representation of labor, management, and government procurement agencies actually working at the site, the Commission deliberately avoided predetermination of any specific committee format. The committees varied widely as to both size and method of operation.

At each location an FMCS mediator, stationed as near as possible to the site, was designated as chairman of the site committee. He was assigned the principal responsibility for initial organization and continued operation of the committee. No decision-making powers were delegated to the committees, but a few of them assumed limited authority in some circumstances by local agreement. The FMCS mediator was a combination committee chairman, promoter, advisor, Commission agent, and mediator of specific disputes. Important matters that could not be resolved were referred to the Commission in Washington. A major objective of the committees was to anticipate troublesome issues and resolve them rather than to wait for disputes to assume crisis proportions.

Executive Order 10946, issued by President Kennedy on May 26, 1961, spelled out the basic procedural arrangements, such as the composition of the Commission, the role of the Missile Site Labor Relations Committees (referred to above), and the authority of the Commission. If a dispute was not settled at the committee level, the Executive Order provided for the establishment of special Commission panels with authority to act. The full Commission also could act. In either event, the authority given the Commission by the President in the Executive Order was defined as follows:

". . . to make findings of fact, to make recommendations for the settlement of such disputes, to obtain agreement for final and binding arbitration of such disputes, to mediate such disputes, to issue such directives and to take such other action as the Commission may direct."

In actual practice, most of the disputes work of the Commission was performed by two panels. A Construction Panel composed of John T. Dunlop, C. J. Haggerty (president, Building and Construction Trades Department), and James D. Marshall or subsequently William E. Dunn (successive executive directors, Associated General Contractors) handled most disputes involving construction unions and contractors. An Industrial Panel composed of David H. Stowe, Nicholas A. Zonarich (alternate to Walter P. Reuther) and Douglas V. Dorman (vice-president, The Martin-Marietta Co.) handled most disputes involving missile manufacturers and their employees. The panels took final action in some instances and reported to the Commission with recommendations in others.

One unusual feature of the Executive Order was suggested by the possibility of disputes between building trades unions and industrial unions. As noted earlier, three of the public members were chosen with their special experience in mind. In addition, the three industry and three labor members were similarly chosen. George Meany, president of the AFL-CIO, and Edgar F. Kaiser, president of Kaiser Industries Corp., were appointed partly because of their relationship to or dealings with both building trades and industrial unions, thus providing a "swing man" on each side of the table. Moreover, the Executive Order provided that if votes should be required in such a case, only the five public members would vote. These rather elaborate precautions had been suggested by the fact that in a limited number of instances, the National War Labor Board had been stalemated by reason of a division between labor members then affiliated with the AFL or the CIO. It is of more then academic interest that only one dispute between building trades and industrial unions ever reached significant proportions. All others were settled amicably by conference and mediation.

The basic aim of settling most controversies at the sites was achieved. As might be expected, the site-committee performances were not equal, and the inherent problems were much greater at some sites than at others. The Commission as a whole took formal action in only 32 disputes in its six-year history. In a larger number of instances, Commission members or Panels informally assisted in settlements that were formalized at the site level, thereby avoiding official Commission action. However, the fact remains that the site committees and the FMCS mediator chairmen performed their work in an exemplary fashion.

The strike record also was good. A total of 485 strikes occurred during the six-year period, but most of these were of very short duration. Over 70 percent lasted less than two working days, and almost half of these were terminated within the first day. Only 10 percent of the strikes lasted five days or longer. The key figure of strike time lost averaged 0.27 percent of time worked for the six years. This was somewhat higher than the corresponding BLS figure for the entire economy but about half the figure for the construction industry. Moreover, the six-year average was only about one fourth the comparable figure at missile sites prior to establishment of the Commission. Striketime losses increased in the latter years of the life of the Commission. For the first three years, lost time was at the remarkably low figure of 0.08 percent of time worked.

In addition to its action in specific disputes, usually after recommendations from one of the Panels, the Commission acted as a policy-making body. Six formal policy statements were issued. Their importance, both as to the amount of work involved in their formulation and their effect on labor relations at the sites, was far greater than their small number might imply.

An unprecedented aspect of the Commission's work was its rulings on uneconomic practices. Baldly stated, this sometimes involved the actual cutback of fringe pay provisions of existing labor contracts or of established practices, and it almost always involved the establishment of guide limits beyond which approval would not be granted. The technical form of such actions, which numbered 32, was official notice to the procurement agencies that reimbursement by the Government to contractors need not be allowed beyond the limits established by the Commission. No such actions occurred on Commission initiative; the procurement agencies initiated questions, on which the Commission then ruled. In practical terms, these rulings usually resulted in corrective action at the work place. The total direct effect of these Commission rulings may not have been great, but the indirect effects were substantial, especially since no statutory stabilization policy existed and the Executive Order was the only authority given the Commission to act on such matters. Moreover, even under statutory stabilization during World War II, the National War Labor Board never sought to cut back any properly established contractual pay practice.

The general approach of the Commission was to utilize fully the mediation methods available in a tripartite structure. These have been set forth in the section above on the National War Labor Board and need not be repeated here.

If the Missile Sites Labor Commission was so generally success-ful and useful an agency, why did President Johnson issue Execu-tive Order 11374 on October 11, 1967, terminating the Commis-sion and transferring its remaining functions to the Federal Mediation and Conciliation Service? A major part of the answer to that question lies in the nature of the no-strike, no-lockout pledges secured early in 1961. Those pledges had been obtained because of the criticalness of the missile program. By late 1964 or early 1965, the scheduled missile-site construction program had been substantially completed. The NASA space program had a later and different time cycle. Space construction was at about its peak during the declining months of missile-base activation. It did not fall off until late 1965 or early 1966, and appreciable remnants remained as late as 1967. Yet the space program never possessed the same aura of criticalness in labor ranks that the mis-sile program did. In short, the psychological base for the no-strike pledge tended to disappear as missile-site construction neared completion.

The declining effectiveness of the no-strike pledge was evi-denced by increases in relative strike incidence. Numbers of strikes decreased, but time worked declined at an even faster pace. In some respects the developments were somewhat compara-ble to the history of the Atomic Energy Labor-Management Rela-tions Panel. The major original reasons for creation of a special disputes mechanism had ceased to exist.

But why terminate the MSLC after about six years in contrast to continuation of the Atomic Energy Labor-Management Rela-tions Panel after 21 years? In some respects, the factors noted at the end of the Atomic Energy Panel section chapter would sug-gest continuation. For example, within the Commission there was accumulated knowledge of missile and space labor relations that might be lost. However, there were important differences. The Atomic Energy Panel program had always been concerned princi-pally with operations, which continue. The main concern of the missile sites program had always been with construction, not op-eration. Manning of both missile bases and NASA space sites after completion of construction has been predominantly by mili-tary or NASA personnel rather than by contractors. Moreover, the Atomic Energy Commission has consistently favored contin-uation of the Panel, whereas, as early as 1964, the Defense De-partment began to urge discontinuance of the MSLC and NASA did likewise late in 1966. Again, as noted earlier, the Panel has become almost like a private mechanism with no statutory base and a limited executive base. It has not had a full-time staff for many years, and the Panel members serve only when and as needed. The MSLC was similar in that Commission members were always part-time, but it did have an official status by Executive Order and a small full-time staff. In summary, the odds favored discontinuance of the MSLC. No adverse repercussions have occurred as a result.

Life span is not a gauge of the value of a special-purpose labor relations device. The Missile Sites Labor Commission ranks high in the annals of labor relations agencies. In large part, it accomplished the purposes for which it was created.

Construction Industry Collective Bargaining Commission

On September 22, 1969, President Nixon established the Construction Industry Collective Bargaining Commission by issuance of Executive Order 11482. It is a 12-member tripartite body. Three of the public members are government officials (Secretary of Labor, Secretary of Housing and Urban Development, and Director of the Federal Mediation and Conciliation Service). John T. Dunlop is the fourth public member. The four industry and four labor members represent construction contractor organizations and the building trades unions.

Unlike the two other special-purpose agencies discussed above, the settlement of specific labor disputes is not the major function of this group. Nor does the Commission have wage stabilization functions as such. A no-strike, no-lockout pledge was not sought or secured. The FMCS is expected to provide most of the mediation assistance in specific labor disputes, and the Commission has not yet developed a formalized mechanism for Commission disputes action. However, the Commission has provided informal mediation assistance and has established close liaison with the FMCS. One of the important features has been the development of a comprehensive "early warning" system under which both the Commission and the FMCS will be fully aware, well in advance, not only of labor contract expiration dates but of the probable important trouble areas in pending disputes.

Other and perhaps even more important objectives of the Commission are to develop policies and programs for assistance in (1) various aspects of employment opportunities for minority groups, (2) reduction of seasonal fluctuations of employment in construction, (3) improvement of labor mobility in the industry, (4) improvement of productivity and managerial skills, (5) special arrangements for low-cost housing, and (6) promotion of better safety standards and procedures. Most of these are long-range objectives on which tangible progress has been made already. It is hoped and expected that the Commission structure will provide a better basis for promotion and development of these needed programs than has existed heretofore. To the extent that the Commission's goals are achieved, the favorable effects on collective bargaining could well be even more significant than those exerted by a commission devoted almost solely to dispute settlement.

President Nixon issued an Executive Order on March 29, 1971, creating a type of construction industry wage stabilization program. It is not now possible to predict just what effect this action will have on the prior program of the Commission.

ADDITIONAL COMMENTS ON TRIPARTITE MEDIATION

All wartime and other special-purpose agencies discussed in this chapter have been tripartite organizations, except for the Atomic Energy Labor-Management Relations Panel. Throughout, the values of tripartitism have been noted, especially for mediatory techniques and procedures.

In contrast, tripartite structure or tripartite mediation of specific disputes has been almost nonexistent in the two federal mediation agencies (Federal Mediation and Conciliation Service and National Mediation Board). The National Labor Management Panel, bipartite in composition, does advise the Director of the FMCS as to policy and procedure. Quite informally, it has been of assistance in a few specific disputes, but its members have never been utilized officially in that capacity.

At the state and local levels there are a few tripartite structures. Thus, the Connecticut State Board of Mediation and Arbitration, the Office of Collective Bargaining in New York City, the Toledo (Ohio) Labor-Management Citizens Committee, and the Louisville (Kentucky) Labor Management Committee are tripartite. However, these are the exceptions that almost prove the rule. The great bulk of mediation in the absence of a shooting war is performed by mediators with no direct labor or management assistance.

This practice has also characterized the work of almost all statutory and nonstatutory boards and panels. Under both the Taft-Hartley Act and the Railway Labor Act, no direct provision is made for tripartite Boards, and none have been utilized. Only two tripartite boards or panels have been named in nonstatutory proceedings—the Greyhound Fact-Finding Panel appointed by the Secretary of Labor in 1945 and the Temco Aerosystems Panel appointed by the Director of the FMCS in 1962.

If tripartitism is so valuable, how is this situation to be explained? One reason is that labor and industry members flanking an impartial mediator are presumed not to be impartial, but they are most useful when they can properly assume at least a semiobjective posture, especially with the impartial mediator and to some extent with the parties. This posture is most readily attainable in a shooting war or in a real emergency. It is less likely in most peacetime disputes.

A second reason, closely related to the first, is that, in the case of the National War Labor Board, labor and industry members or alternates had a status by virtue of their appointments that was not related to any specific case. Industry and labor representatives are less likely to tolerate being "put on the spot" in a dispute that is not a part of a total assignment. Moreover, except in wartime or in a real emergency, the most competent labor and industry representatives are less likely to be available, when and as needed. They are busy men and would find it difficult to adjust their regular work to accommodate to the unpredictable needs of a particular dispute. This is also true, of course, of public members, but it may be an even greater problem for labor and industry representatives.

Another important reason is that single mediators normally function in a manner that is in a sense tripartite. In almost all difficult situations, a formal or informal tripartite subcommittee meets when and as required. The labor and industry members, of course, are the principal negotiators for the parties, rather than representatives with no direct interest in the result. This has advantages and disadvantages. The disadvantages are related to the fact that the principal negotiators are likely to be less objective than persons not involved in the immediate dispute.

Finally, custom and practice play a part. Since it has been normal to utilize only public members for mediation, officials responsible for making or recommending appointments are inclined to overlook the concept of tripartitism. If they do think about it under the time pressures that usually exist, they are unwilling or unable to make the extra effort required for selection of labor and industry members.

Tripartite mediation should not be employed universally. On the contrary, it should be reserved for disputes that are especially well suited to that method of mediation. It is too valuable as a problem-solving mechanism, however, to be restricted to war-crisis use.

OTHER MEDIATION FORUMS

CHAPTER XIII

MEDIATION OF GRIEVANCES

Mediation of grievance disputes occupies a relatively small niche in the totality of conventional mediation activity. Most of the vast number of grievances in the United States are resolved by the parties without the need for any outside assistance. When assistance is required, it is usually in the form of arbitration.

However, there are a number of situations in which a mediator or mediation tactics may play a part in grievance settlement. They are as follows:

1. when a backlog of accumulated unresolved grievances is added to other issues at the time of negotiation or renegotiation of the labor agreement;
2. when the labor agreement contains no provision for arbitration;
3. when the labor agreement contains an arbitration clause but specific issues are excluded from arbitration;
4. when the contract contains an arbitration clause but the parties elect to mediate one or more grievances in lieu of arbitration;
5. when the grievance procedure of the labor agreement includes mediation as a formal step prior to arbitration;
6. when a wildcat strike occurs despite an agreement provision to arbitrate.

The possibilities, special problems, and hazards of mediation in these various situations justify some explanation.

POTENTIAL MEDIATION SITUATIONS

Grievance Backlog in Contract Negotiations

When a grievance procedure works well, the parties enter contract negotiations with no appreciable backlog of grievances. The objective of both parties to meet the day-by-day problems of plant operation on a timely basis has been achieved. A few grievances in process may be delayed a bit by preoccupation with the more important negotiations, but both sides are content to let this happen. A little delay for all but the most urgent cases, such as discharges, will be understood. The parties thereby can concentrate on proposed changes in the new agreement.

However, a quite different situation can exist. Because the grievance procedure is not adequate, a large backlog of unresolved matters may have accumulated. Not infrequently, the grievance arbitration arrangement or the arbitrator, or both, have been considered unsatisfactory for one reason or another. As a practical matter, an effective boycott of arbitration may have existed for months. Occasionally a union will cause this to happen in the belief that it will achieve a better resolution of these grievances under the pressures of a strike threat at contract expiration.

For a variety of such reasons a small mountain of unresolved grievances may be dumped on the bargaining table in addition to all the usual requests for modification of the agreement. Although statistical data are not available to support the assertion, appraisal of mediators' reports in recent years suggests that this unhappy situation has been becoming more frequent.

What can be done by the parties, with or without mediation assistance, in such a situation? The obvious basic need is to correct the defects in the grievance and arbitration procedures. If this can be done during the negotiations in a manner that is satisfactory to both parties, it is often possible to obtain agreement to lay aside the specific grievances for subsequent handling.

If the grievance procedure has become so sour that it cannot be corrected by changes in contract language, a special plan may be required. Its effectuation as well as the resolution of specific grievances can then be deferred until after the new contract becomes effective. But there must be reasonable assurance that something constructive will happen. This will be discussed later as one aspect of noncrisis dialogue.

Sometimes there is no alternative that is acceptable to the union but to slog through the accumulation of grievances in negotiations and grind out some answers. Under the time pressures that usually exist, it is not feasible to give each grievance the attention it may deserve. The normal consultation with foremen, stewards, and employees may be difficult to arrange. A frequent expedient is to settle the grievances somehow—by "trade-offs" and no-precedent answers. If the company concedes too much, it is encouraging a repetition of the same situation at the end of the next contract. If it yields too little, it may have a strike on its hands. Union officials are similarly disadvantaged. If they make poor grievance settlements, they may face a membership rebellion and a rejection of an otherwise good contract. If they win too much, they too have built trouble for the future. Such situations often have produced strikes. Disposition of the grievances can consume so much time that the basic issues in the contract negotiations are neglected. Again, if the grievance-settlement job is not done well enough, a strike may occur for that reason alone.

In short, contract negotiations under strike deadline pressures cannot be a satisfactory avenue for settling a large number of grievances. A mediator will seek to help the parties avoid these pitfalls and find more orderly and sensible solutions.

A variant of this type of situation is less undesirable. If handled properly, it may even be helpful. A union may throw on the bargaining table only a few selected pending grievances that are directly related to specific union demands for contract changes. These can give credence to the demands and provide more potent support than hours of generalization or table thumping. However, if the union confuses the issue by adding extraneous grievances, the beneficial effect will be lost.

Mediator participation and assistance in "clearing the decks" for the main purposes of contract negotiations by whatever means, is incidental to the negotiation of an agreement and is not included in any statistical data that will be noted subsequently. It may well consume more total mediation time than mediation of grievances outside times of crisis.

Absence of Grievance Arbitration

A few international unions and a somewhat larger number of local unions will not agree to grievance arbitration. There are ominous indications that many local unions with grievance arbitration experience are becoming disenchanted. The numbers of union requests to eliminate arbitration and the no-strike clause from the agreement have been increasing in recent years. Not long ago it was most unusual to find a union opposing arbitration. Most such requests have not been successful, though some have led to changes in arbitration provisions. However, the trend has significance. Recent public expressions of dissatisfaction with arbitration of grievances, as at the September 1970 convention of the Steelworkers, suggest that one cannot assume automatic continued general acceptance of grievance arbitration.

A decreasing yet sizable number of companies will not agree to grievance arbitration. This is not particularly surprising in view of widespread employer opposition less than 30 years ago.

The result of these minority union and company positions is that approximately 5 percent of the labor agreements in the United States have neither an arbitration clause nor a no-strike clause. An unresolved grievance can cause a strike at any time.

In such situations, both state and federal mediation agencies frequently receive requests for mediation assistance. These requests usually come after a strike starts or when there is a serious strike threat.

When a mediator enters such a grievance dispute, he is out of his normal mediation habitat. The issue typically involves interpretation or application of a clause of the labor agreement. However, most mediators have grievance experience in their employment backgrounds and are well aware of the basic differences between grievance handling and contract negotiation.

If a strike is in progress, a mediator will usually attempt first to get the strike terminated. He may try to persuade the parties to arbitrate the issue in question even though they have not agreed to arbitrate all issues. He may attempt to persuade the union to terminate the strike while he mediates—may, indeed, make that a condition of his continuing on the case.

If the issue involved in the grievance is a "yes" or "no" question of contract violation or compliance, the mediator would be gravely in error if he attempted to obtain a compromise in the absence of willingness of both parties to do so. In such a case the mediator can only seek to persuade one party that it is wrong. No mediator should seek to change a clear and explicit provision of an agreement unless both parties want to change it.

As will be developed in more detail in a subsequent section, many grievances are not "yes" or "no" contract violation or compliance cases. In such situations, the mediator is in a better position to facilitate a realistic disposition of the issue consistent with the contract.

Sometimes the parties will agree that the mediator should make a recommendation, and they will also agree in advance to accept his recommendation. Such a proposal is a technical release of the mediator from his agency's prohibition, if any, upon decision-making. A commitment in advance to accept an unknown recommendation is the practical equivalent of arbitration. In any event, this happens occasionally, and most agency officials shut their eyes and ears.

A mediator's functioning in a grievance case is not radically different from that of an arbitrator, with two significant exceptions. Few mediators would tolerate the elaborate case presentation that occurs too often in arbitration. More meaningful is the fact that the parties have given him no decision-making authority in advance. Even if they suggest the recommendation gambit noted earlier, they do not normally do so until he has worked with them in the case. Sometimes they may know what the recommendation will be before they make the commitment to accept. The voluntary commitment is then not drastically different from some uses of the recommendation procedure in new-contract disputes.

Limited Arbitration

Many labor agreements contain limited-scope arbitration clauses. For example, the General Motors— UAW contract specifically precludes arbitration of production-standards disputes. The General Electric—IUE agreement contains even more limited arbitration provisions. In both of these illustrations, the no-strike clause covers only those matters that are subject to arbitration. A legal strike can occur over matters that are not arbitrable after certain procedural steps have been followed.

In some other agreements, the scope of arbitration is limited in various ways but the no-strike clause is all inclusive.

On rare occasions the parties will welcome a mediator in such disputes. They have agreed not to make themselves subject to a decision. But if the dispute is serious enough, they may agree to mediation primarily because the mediator has no authority to decide. Having exhausted each other's proposals without success, they may be willing to listen to new proposals.

Mediation in Lieu of Arbitration

There are a number of situations in which the parties will agree to mediate a grievance even though their contract contains an arbitration provision. Sometimes the cost of arbitration is an effective deterrent to its use. Free mediation may be preferred. A second cause may be uncertainty about arbitration jurisdiction. The labor agreement may be silent on the grievance issue, or one party may express serious preliminary doubt for other reasons about an arbitrator's authority to issue a binding decision. In some situations, the arbitration clause may be ambiguous. Rather than argue such questions before an arbitrator, the parties may elect to mediate. Each side thereby preserves its right of effective dissent on the merits of the issue.

A final and rather rare type of circumstance is where the contract is clear enough, but neither party wants it to be applied to the case at hand. Instead, they may seek mediation.

Mediation Prior to Arbitration

Grievance procedures in a small number of contracts provide for a specific mediation step between the last bipartite stage and submission to arbitration. In essence, it is a formal screening step, designed to reduce the number of cases that must be arbitrated.

One variety of this procedure calls for the use of a professional mediator, who meets informally with representatives of both parties to review briefly all grievances pending arbitration. The mediator is free to meet separately with the parties and usually does so. However, relatively more time usually is spent in joint sessions than is characteristic of contract mediation. The mediator makes informal suggestions and sometimes specific recommendations. The union withdraws some cases, the company makes acceptable settlement offers on some, and the remainder are submitted to arbitration. As a rule the representatives of both parties are free to tell their colleagues and the grievants that they acted, in part, at the suggestion of the mediator. But in all instances the decision to settle is made by the parties. The mediator has no decision-making authority.

A variant of this arrangement, considered heretical by some persons, is use of the permanent arbitrator for the same purpose. The process is not essentially different except that the arbitrator proceeds at a subsequent date to hear and decide grievances not settled at the mediation step. David L. Cole pioneered in this procedure at Inland Steel and elsewhere. A thorny dispute about grievance procedure in the 1967 Goodrich-URW negotiations was settled by agreement of the parties to this type of procedure. At last report, it was working to the satisfaction of both parties.

The discussion to this point has been concerned with a regularized, continuing procedure. Another exercise of the same idea, utilizing either a mediator or the permanent arbitrator, has been a "one time" procedure to clean up accumulated grievance backlogs. In such situations the parties have not wanted to make a commitment that this procedure will become established but have agreed to try it once. It has been used predominantly either just before contract negotiations begin or just after a new contract has been signed. Occasionally it has coincided with contract negotiations but with a different group of union and company representatives and with a mediator or arbitrator not active in the negotiations. In all these circumstances the purpose is to avoid most of the unfortunate effects on contract bargaining of a grievance backlog that were noted earlier.

An illustration can be cited. In the mid-1960s at a sizable military aircraft servicing and repair company in a southern city, a joint request was received by the FMCS for three mediators for a month's time to help resolve a backlog of more than 150 important grievances. Many cases had been arbitrated in the months prior to the request, but the backlog had enlarged instead of diminishing. Contract negotiations were about six months distant, and both parties were afraid that the grievance backlog would be the cause of a strike. Three mediators could not be spared; the FMCS could assign only one mediator for no longer than two weeks. All grievances were resolved well within the allotted time except for one that was arbitrated. Of greater significance is the fact that no backlog accumulated during the next three years, and only a few grievances were arbitrated. The "one shot" approach thus cleaned up the backlog and also, somehow corrected the basic faults of the grievance procedure without further mediation assistance.

Wildcat Strikes

Wildcat strikes sometimes occur over grievance issues even though the contract contains arbitration and no-strike clauses. More often than not union officials do not want a strike but are powerless to prevent it. On occasion some of them encourage the wildcat, openly or surreptitiously. Typically the strike occurs over an arbitrable issue that has not yet been submitted to arbitration.

In such cases, most companies adopt the sound policy of refusing to discuss the issues until the wildcat has been terminated. Any other course of action may invite more illegal stoppages. However, a company may seek the assistance of a mediator to help effect a return to work. The attitude of union officials about mediation in such cases will normally be dependent on their position on the strike itself. If they oppose it, they may be just as eager as the company for mediation assistance. If they approve of the strike, openly or secretly, any support of mediation is likely to be merely lip service.

In these circumstances the mediator has a limited objective—to help get the employees back on the job. If union officials are really supporting the wildcat, the mediator will have to fight off union insistence that he mediate the issues underlying the strike. Since the mediator's only valid objective is to assist in terminating the strike, he has little to work with. However, if the company stands firm, such strikes tend to be short-lived. The mediator can help make arrangements for prompt arbitration once the strike has been terminated. He can help see to it that the company does not "go overboard" in disciplining strikers and can assist in mediating the back-to-work terms. Perhaps most important, a mediator's strong recommendation to return to work may provide an "out" for the strikers when they realize that the action was ill-considered.

A much more difficult type of wildcat is one that occurs after grievance arbitration and in protest of a decision. If the mediator urges revision of the arbitration decision, he will be likely to undermine the arbitration process, a much more serious matter than the merits of almost any grievance. If he believes that the decision was correct, he can do much to help sell it. And at the appropriate time, his recommendation to terminate the stoppage may be effective. Even if he believes that the arbitrator was wrong, he must do what he can to support the arbitration principle, but this will be a tough task.

In a long, persistent wildcat either before or after arbitration, a mediator may be confronted with a most difficult decision. Both parties may quietly tell him that they want him to mediate the grievance issue while the strike continues. Both may be aware of the dangerous precedent, but they may be sufficiently desperate to insist on that course of action. There are few, if any, inflexible rules about mediation, and there are none in this type of situation. As a general proposition, the first requirement is to secure a resumption of work. Mediation of any arbitrable grievance issue while a strike is in progress can create a bad precedent that may haunt both parties for years.

WHO MEDIATES GRIEVANCES?

Grievance mediation may be performed by federal mediators, by state or local mediators, by mediators selected privately by the parties, or by arbitrators.

Federal Mediation and Conciliation Service

During calendar year 1968, FMCS mediators were involved actively in a total of 283 grievance assignments.[1] This was an average of only slightly more than one case per mediator per year. As a percentage of total active mediation cases of all varieties, grievances constituted only 3.1 percent.

Section 203 (d) of the Taft-Hartley Act reads:

"Final adjustment by a method agreed upon by the parties is hereby declared to be the desirable method for settlement of grievance disputes arising over the application or interpretation of an existing collective-bargaining agreement. The Service is directed to make its conciliation and mediation services available in the settlement of such grievance disputes *only as a last resort and in exceptional cases.*"[2]

One result of this congressional mandate was the immediate elimination of so-called free arbitration that had been provided by the United States Conciliation Service. The small staff of former USCS arbitrators was dismantled. A few left government service and went into the private practice of arbitration. The others became mediators. Thereafter, other mediators who had sometimes acted as free arbitrators along with their normal mediation work were instructed to discontinue the practice. As has been noted earlier, this instruction is occasionally "fudged" by the parties agreeing while the mediator is on the job to accept a recommendation before its contents are known. However, this is not a frequent occurrence.

Prior to 1947 it had been an occasional practice for a federal mediator to arbitrate in a private capacity during his vacation period or by taking time off without pay. The most newsworthy illustration was in November and December 1941, when John R. Steelman, then Director of the United States Conciliation Service, went off the government payroll and acted as the chairman of an arbitration board in the captive mines union security dispute. Ever since the passage of the Taft-Hartley Act, FMCS mediators have been instructed that it is inconsistent with the official duties to arbitrate in a private capacity at any time.

It may be noted that a few state and local agencies do not observe one or both of these limitations. Few state statutes prohibit arbitration by mediators. A few state agencies provide free arbitration, either by mediators or by agency employees who devote most of their time to arbitration. Some permit mediators to arbitrate

---

[1] Source: FMCS reply to questionnaire.
[2] Emphasis supplied.

in a private capacity during their off-duty time, but often it is required that the work be done outside the territory in which they work as mediators.

To implement further the first sentence of the congressional mandate, FMCS mediators use their best efforts to encourage the inclusion of grievance arbitration provisions in labor agreements. They also encourage broadening of the scope of restricted arbitration clauses.

If a labor agreement provides for an intermediate mediation step prior to arbitration, FMCS mediators do not urge elimination of that step, but they do attempt to persuade the parties to provide for mediation other than by federal mediators. If this attempt is unsuccessful, the parties have been advised that FMCS mediators can be made available only on a contingent basis. Contract disputes have first claim on mediators' time, with preventive mediation activity a close second.

FMCS grievance mediation is further minimized by the application of the "last resort and exceptional cases" criteria. "Last resort" is normally interpreted to mean a strike or a real threat of a strike. "Exceptional" is a handy but not very definitive adjective. These criteria may be applied tightly or loosely, depending on two other considerations. If a dispute is important, and especially if it is at a defense plant, a liberal application is likely. How the criteria will be applied also depends to some extent on how busy the mediators at that location happen to be at the time.

In any event, the incidence of FMCS mediator activity in grievances is so low that the basic intent of the law is being observed. There is no appreciable cost to the taxpayers because most grievance work is done when mediators would otherwise not be active in other disputes.

National Mediation Board and National Railroad Adjustment Board

The distinction between contract negotiations and grievances is made in the Railway Labor Act by means of the words "major disputes" and "minor disputes." These words are, in part, a matter of tradition. They are also a result of the fact that most railroad agreements do not have fixed termination dates. The distinction between "major" and "minor" is not clear-cut. However, for present purposes, it is reasonably accurate to conclude that, since 1934, "minor disputes" are roughly comparable to grievances elsewhere. Within this context, National Mediation Board media-tors perform no mediation of grievances. Nor do they arbitrate.

However, the National Railroad Adjustment Board, created as a semi-independent agency in 1934, does provide for arbitration of grievances at government expense. The considerable dissatisfaction with NRAB arbitration is not relevant to this discussion of media-tion.

State and Local Agencies

State and local agencies reported mediation of 1164 grievance cases in calendar year 1968.[3] This was 18 percent of their total mediation case load. Thus, the state and local agencies combined mediated four times as many grievances as the FMCS, and their percentage of mediation case load was almost six times as great (18 percent as against 3.1 percent).

Great variation exists among the state and local agencies. Some mediate more grievance disputes than new-contract disputes. Others, even those with a sizable total work load, mediate almost no grievance disputes. These variations in practice appear not to stem from differences in state statutes. Despite the absence of a detailed survey of state laws it can be said that there are few, if any restrictions on grievance mediation like the one in the Taft-Hartley Act. It is probable that differences among the states are due primarily to varying agency policies.

The principal explanation for the higher incidence of grievance mediation at the state level than at the federal level probably is the size of the establishments where mediation is performed. State and local agencies typically mediate at smaller establishments. Collec-tive bargaining agreements at these smaller units are less likely to contain arbitration clauses. If they do, cost considerations may en-courage mediation in lieu of arbitration.

Undoubtedly the statutory restrictions on grievance arbitration by the FMCS encourage some parties to seek the assistance of state or local agencies for grievance mediation. This may be so even if the FMCS is utilized, with or without state-agency cooperation, in new-contract disputes. In the occasional jurisdictional disputes that have existed between the FMCS and state agencies, certain overzealous FMCS mediators have suggested that the Taft-Hartley restriction on grievance mediation be relaxed. It has been main-tained that freedom to mediate grievances gives the state agencies

---

[3] Source: Replies to questionnaires by state and local mediation agencies.

a statistical case load advantage and may also encourage some parties to use the state agency in contract disputes.

Any easing of the Taft-Hartley Act restriction should be based solely on a belief that constructive grievance mediation has not yet been explored adequately. There is much merit in the idea of an intermediate step between bipartite grievance processing and arbitration. As long as the mediation is effective, it matters not whether it is performed by a state or a federal mediator. Many grievance arbitration cases would be screened out by any good intermediate mediation device. A grievance mediation step may be one of the productive arrangements that can be encouraged to minimize growing dissatisfaction with grievance arbitration.

Private Mediators

On rare occasions the parties may select an impartial person not employed regularly by a mediation agency to mediate one or more grievances. As noted earlier, this can happen (1) in cleaning up an accumulated backlog, (2) as a regular or occasional screening step prior to arbitration, or (3) in a variety of situations where arbitration is not called for in the contract or arbitrability is in dispute. In all instances the common factor is that the parties agree to mediation in lieu of arbitration and it is clearly understood that the mediator has no decision-making power.

To secure some idea of the extent of this type of mediation, a question concerning it was included in the questionnaires answered by arbitrators. Arbitrators are not the only persons who could be utilized in such a capacity. However, there are few private mediators who have not had some arbitration experience, and it is probable that the arbitrators who answered the questionnaires performed most of the work being considered here.

The answers can be summarized briefly. A total of 44 arbitrators reported some experience with grievance mediation in their entire labor relations lifetime. This is only about 10 percent of those who responded to the questionnaire. The 44 individuals reported a total of 786 cases. Sixteen of the arbitrators had had only one such case, and seven others had had from two to five cases. This leaves only 21 arbitrators who had had six or more grievance mediation cases.

In calendar year 1968, 15 arbitrators mediated a total of 72 grievances. This compares with 1164 such cases handled by state and local agencies and 283 cases by the FMCS.

Mediation by the Arbitrator?

We turn now to a final type of grievance mediation, namely by the arbitrator who has been selected by the parties and has been given decision-making powers for the same case or cases. The question is popularly phrased: "Should an arbitrator mediate?"

Beginning soon after World War II and continuing spasmodically to date, this question has consumed much time—in arbitration hearings, at conferences or seminars, and at annual meetings of the National Academy of Arbitrators. Among many others, the author participated in the exchanges by writing a monograph in 1952 entitled *Acceptability as a Factor in Arbitration Under an Existing Agreement.*[4]

The most specific stimulus to intelligent discussion of a possible mediator-arbitrator role was an address delivered by Dr. George W. Taylor on January 14, 1949, before the National Academy of Arbitrators.[5] Dr. Taylor's theme was that the grievance procedure, including arbitration, usually includes certain agreement-making aspects. Since this is so, he stated a preference for a type of arbitration that permits the maximum of acceptability of the results by the parties. The impartial-chairman concept, he suggested, has been chosen by some bargainers who deliberately want their arbitrator to mediate as well as to decide grievance issues. Contrasting with this is the umpire concept, which involves little or no mediation but emphasizes decision-making. Because of these conceptual differences and the fact that the title given the arbitrator does not always accurately reflect his function, Dr. Taylor stressed the need for a meeting of minds on the type of arbitration that is desired.

A different position on these issues was taken by Francis A. O'Connell, Jr., before the National Academy of Arbitrators in January 1965. The title of his address was *The Labor Arbitrator: Judge or Legislator?*[6] It was an exposition of the so-called "management's reserved rights" concept, and the notion that collective bargaining is limited to the writing of an agreement. Under this concept, the grievance procedure and grievance arbitration are confined to the literal application of the contract. Using sub-

[4] One of nine monographs in: LABOR ARBITRATION SERIES, George W. Taylor, editor, University of Pennsylvania Press, 1952.

[5] *Effectuating the Labor Contract Through Arbitration,* in THE PROFESSION OF LABOR ARBITRATION, Selected Papers from the First Seven Annual Meetings of the National Academy of Arbitrators, 1948-1954, pp. 20-41, The Bureau of National Affairs, Inc., 1957.

[6] PROCEEDINGS OF THE EIGHTEENTH ANNUAL MEETING OF THE NATIONAL ACADEMY OF ARBITRATORS, pp. 102-139, BNA, 1965.

contracting as the major example, Mr. O'Connell argued that too many arbitrators decide grievances on their merits when they have no authority to do so. However, he also jumped to the conclusion that the fault with many arbitrators is that they are mediators at heart and improperly practice mediation instead of arbitration.

The O'Connell paper highlights the frequent confusion of two quite different and only indirectly related controversial aspects of grievance arbitration. One is the scope of decision-making authority conferred on the arbitrator. To what extent, if any, is an arbitrator permitted or required to go beyond the bare language of the agreement in order to decide an issue that is properly before him? That question must be answered in innumerable cases without regard to questions about mediatory tactics.

The mediation controversy concerns procedure after the initial hurdle has been cleared. If a decision is permitted or required and the language of the agreement is insufficient to provide a complete answer, should the parties and the arbitrator create or find some mechanism for three-way participation in its formulation? Or should the arbitrator decide the case and legislate indirectly without benefit of any contact with the parties apart from the formal argument presented at the hearing? Appraisal of this concern about any possible mediation role by the arbitrator requires examination of the various types of grievances that may go to arbitration.

Grievance arbitration cases fall, with some inevitable fuzzy edges, into one of five categories:

a. "yes" or "no" cases;
b. cases involving inadvertent or deliberate ambiguity of contract language;
c. cases involving contract language that was intended to be general and effectuated through the grievance procedure;
d. cases involving issues on which the labor agreement is silent;
e. cases involving issues as to which the contract is embarrassingly explicit.

The "yes" or "no" cases constitute a sizable fraction of the work load of most arbitrators. The award is "grievance granted" or "grievance dismissed." It is this type of grievance that gave rise, historically, to the "umpire" title in grievance arbitration. In baseball, there is no compromise between a ball and a strike or between safe and out. The umpire "calls 'em as he sees 'em," including the close ones. For this type of case, an arbitrator may be accused of bad eyesight, but neither he nor the parties try to invent some new prescription for "the one that just grazes the corner."

The extreme management's-reserved-rights advocate would like to believe that there are no other valid types of grievances. In rare circumstances, a contract is so written that that is its clear intent. There is then no need to look further. The arbitrator is a "balls and strikes" man, and that is it. But so restricted a contract is almost nonexistent in the real collective bargaining world.

In any event, the "yes" or "no" type or grievance is not a case for mediation. No arbitrator in his right mind will seek to change a clear and explicit provision of a labor agreement, unless it is very evident that both parties want to alter the agreement.

The second type of case, less frequently seen, has two manifestations. In one of these, a contract provision is written with a reasonably clear mutual understanding as to its meaning and application. Subsequently, a new and perhaps unpredictable situation arises. The words and the intent of the negotiators provide no clear answer. Something more is involved than whether the ball "cuts the corner." With no lack of intent, the parties simply did not define the strike zone.

Deliberate ambiguity arises in a different manner. At 11:40 p.m., with a midnight strike deadline, somebody has put new words on the bargaining table. Both parties look at the words and take some comfort in them, but they also know that if the intent is explored, even briefly, there will be no agreement. To avoid a strike they accept the language, but they also know that the first grievance case may well produce serious disagreement, more bargaining, and possible arbitration.

In either of these situations mediatory tactics may or may not be advisable or possible.

In the third type of case, the company and the union agree upon a general principle. They know that it will be applied in so many varying circumstances that it is either impossible or inadvisable to attempt to spell them out in the contract. They believe that the grievance procedure and possibly even supplemental agreements will be required to implement the clause. They also know that future disputes about effectuation will be arbitrable.

Illustrations of this type of contract language are many. Two will be cited. In many labor agreements the only substantive reference to discipline is a few words such as these:

> "The Company shall have the exclusive right to discipline, suspend, or discharge employees for *just cause*." [7]

A basic seniority principle for application in some situations reads as follows:

> "Skill and ability and length of service shall be the determining factors. Where *skill and ability are approximately equal*, length of service shall govern." [8]

What is "just cause"? When are skill and ability "approximately equal"? These words must be applied to fact situations, and the agreement provides for arbitration of disputed cases. Again, mediation may or may not be possible or desirable.

A fourth type of case is the grievance about which the contract is silent. More grievances than most people care to admit fall in this category. The "Christmas turkey" case is an illustration. For as many years as anybody can remember, the Company has given a turkey at Christmas time to all regular employees. One Christmas the Company decides not to give the turkeys. The contract says nothing that could reasonably be construed to apply to turkeys, but a grievance is filed and submitted to an arbitrator. A similar situation may occur when a practice of allowing wash-up time on certain jobs once or twice a shift has been in effect for many years and is then discontinued. Significant cases of this general type also develop out of rapidly changing technology or corporate business decisions made with little or no warning. Some of these cases are subject to mediatory techniques; some are not.

A final type of situation is where the contract is embarrassingly explicit. An illustration may help make the point. Many years ago, a union official visited the author's office to arrange for a hearing under a contract in which I was named as the impartial chairman. In the informal atmosphere that was characteristic of that relationship, he outlined the case in a straightforward manner and then added the enlightening comment: "We're worried about the financial condition of this company. On request, our accountant has examined the books, and the company is in bad shape." I took a quick look at the applicable clause. It was one of the first guaranteed annual wage plans ever negotiated anywhere. Business conditions had suddenly deteriorated soon after it had been negotiated. After a moment, I said: "Do you want an arbitration? We will almost surely put this company out of business and a lot of jobs will be lost. Let me suggest that if I

[7] Emphasis supplied.
[8] Emphasis supplied.

get into this case at all, it should be as a mediator rather than as arbitrator." The union official accepted the suggestion readily, and the company officials too were glad to agree. With the full approval of the employees, meetings were arranged as mediation sessions. The contract was altered by mutual agreement to adjust to the changed business climate but without elimination of its basic intent. The company stayed in business.

The comment may properly be made that if the parties want to change their own contract, they should do so of their own volition. Usually this is what does happen. In some circumstances, however, there is a mutual desire to amend the contract but the parties have an honest disagreement as to just what should be done. If an arbitrator participates in such a proceeding at all, his role must be essentially that of a mediator rather than an arbitrator.

Review of these five types of grievances shows that the pure umpire concept as the caller of "balls and strikes" is not applicable to all grievances. Many grievances of the second, third and fourth types cannot be resolved by applying specific contract language, yet must be handled in a manner that is consistent with the agreement. The arbitrator's authority to decide such cases may flow from the fact that arbitration is the contractual substitute for a strike.

It is not suggested that the arbitrator has the authority to decide all of the last four types of grievances. Under some contracts he does. A few give him no authority at all. Usually his delegated power is somewhere between these two extremes. In some instances a threshold question of importance is whether he does or does not have authority.

The point that is pertinent here is that the arbitrator's decision as to whether to accept jurisdiction and decide the grievance issue is not ordinarily dependent on whether he likes to mediate or whether the parties want him to mediate. The question is whether the grievance must be answered on its merits, with or without mediatory techniques. Regardless of his persuasion, an arbitrator cannot avoid an answer to that queston when it is a part of the dispute. In some cases the threshold question is not even raised; the parties already have agreed to submit the issue for an answer on the merits.

How may an arbitrator mediate or use mediatory tactics once he has the issue and must make an answer on the merits? Some have the notion that the arbitrator who has a proclivity to mediate will interrupt at some time during the hearing and say: "Come now. Let us mediate." Thereupon he casts aside his quasi-judicial robes and starts to mediate—if the parties will let him proceed. If any arbitrator did this, he probably did it only once. This is a caricature.

The extent to which mediatory tactics are used overtly is determined by the parties. Mechanics for mediation must be created by agreement. What are the available devices? In general, they are

    (a) a tripartite arbitration board;

    (b) a practical equivalent of a tripartite board;

    (c) the impartial chairman concept; and

    (d) techniques used by the arbitrator at the hearing.

Tripartite Arbitration Boards [9]

The typical tripartite board consists of one person named by the company, one by the union, and an impartial member. The company and union members may be from outside the ranks of the company and union involved, but usually they are not. They may even have been the principal spokesmen at the hearing. Obviously they are partisan. They are not expected to cast aside their direct interest in the decision.

Representation by the parties on such boards serves many purposes other than possible mediation. The partisans are technical advisors. They serve as "sounding boards" against which the chairman can test his tentative conclusions in the "yes" or "no" contract violation cases. They can prevent the chairman from writing something inadvertently in the opinion that may create more trouble than the issue that is being decided. This may well be the extent of the partisan members' functions.

In the best tripartite arrangements, however, the company and the union expect their representatives to participate in a mediation function. They may be able to "let down their hair" and give the impartial chairman a much truer picture of the real positions of the parties than was presented at the hearing. More often, their principal and exceedingly important function is to work closely with the chairman in the process of "trying on for size" possible alternate answers that are consistent both with the agreement and with conditions in the plant.

[9] For an analysis of tripartite grievance arbitration boards emphasizing the negative aspects of such boards, see: *Uses and Misuses of Tri-Partite Boards in Arbitration,* by Harold W. Davey, in DEVELOPMENTS IN AMERICAN AND FOREIGN ARBITRATION, Proceedings of the Twenty-First Annual Meeting, National Academy of Arbitrators, pp. 152-179, BNA, 1968.

The functioning of the partisan members of such boards is determined largely by the policies of their principals. However, the role of the impartial member may be crucial. If he considers them unnecessary and cumbersome adjuncts to his dominant role of decision-making, the conditions that give rise to criticism of such boards are likely to be present. But if the chairman believes in the values of tripartitism, the results are reasonably certain to be more satisfactory than decisions of an arbitrator arrived at in solitary splendor. Since at least some awards effectuating an agreement will necessarily verge on the legislative area, who is to say that the parties who must live with the decisions should not have maximum participation in making them?

Some tripartite boards act by majority vote. This feature is sometimes considered objectionable. Arbitrators tend to disfavor it even more than the parties. A cynical rejoinder is that if the impartial arbitrator can't get anybody to agree with him, he needs to reexamine his position. More seriously, there are a variety of ways to secure a majority vote even in the most difficult cases. For what it may be worth, the author's fairly extensive experience with tripartite boards over a period of 23 years of full-time arbitration includes only two instances of major difficulty with the majority-vote problem. A decision was reached in those two cases, but additional time was required. In retrospect, the extra time was justified. The ultimate decisions were better suited to the cases than if I had had the authority to issue earlier decisions without concurrence.

The rather frequent unanimous decisions of tripartite boards prove the values of the procedure. Signatures of the union and company representatives add materially to acceptability. It is also no secret that some dissents are "for the record." Both board members may in reality agree with the decision. In a real sense, the operation of a tripartite arbitration board at its best is a form of three-party bargaining.

A tripartite board in which the partisan members serve in the same manner in all other respects but have no voting rights appears to be gaining favor. For example, the board of arbitration under the U.S. Steel Corporation—United Steelworkers of America agreement has operated with distinction in this manner for many years after an early short period of operation under the majority-vote principle.

The reader will quickly recognize the similarities between satisfactory operation of tripartite grievance arbitration boards and the tripartite aspect of the National War Labor Board. Handling of grievances instead of contract disputes does not obscure the values of active participation by representatives of the parties at the decision-making level.

Tripartite boards may have greater opportunities for successful operation in so-called permanent arbitration arrangements than in ad hoc arbitration. The board members know each other better. In some respects, however, the potential value is even greater in ad hoc cases. The chances of truly bad decisions due to lack of knowledge are minimized.

Practical Equivalents of Tripartite Boards

In some grievance arbitration arrangements no formal tripartite board exists but the company and the union create the practical equivalent. It is clearly understood that the arbitrator is expected to consult with selected representaives of the parties after the hearing but before issuing his final decision, at least in the more difficult cases. Such consultation may be limited strictly to conferences in which both parties are represented. It would be considered highly improper for the arbitrator to consult separately with one side or the other.

On the other hand, there are some arrangements under which it is just as clearly understood that the arbitrator has complete freedom to consult with one side at a time, separately and privately, or with both together. Full-fashioned hosiery grievance arbitration operated in this manner over a period of almost 40 years. The parties once discharged an arbitrator after less than a year's service primarily because he would not observe this tradition. In such arrangements, a primary reason for separate consultation is to prepare the losing side for an adverse decision. Face-to-face discussion with the loser, including detailed explanation of the reasons, can be much more productive than the coldness of a decision that arrives in the mails.

Such activities are considered highly irregular and improper by many companies and unions. When that is the case, it would be unethical for an arbitrator to engage in them. In short, there must be a clear understanding as to procedure among the principal representatives of the parties and the arbitrator.

Most such arrangements are confined primarily to so-called permanent-arbitrator systems. If the same arbitrator is selected repeatedly, however, an ad hoc system may be tantamount to a permanent arbitrator system. In such a case, it is not infrequent for the parties to want to have the advantages of consultation.

The Impartial Chairman Concept

The true impartial chairman concept includes aspects of the case-handling methods discussed in the last two sections. Usually it is an informal consultative arrangement rather than a formal tripartite board. It may also include two additional features.

The first is outright grievance mediation. Even though there is consultation after an arbitration hearing, the parties may not want even the appearance of an adversary proceeding that exists at the hearing table. Consequently, they come privately to the impartial chairman for assistance in the resolution of a grievance issue. There is no record of the conference. Sometimes the impartial chairman is not notified until later as to precisely what has been agreed upon.

A similar arrangement may prevail with respect to disputed issues when the labor agreement is being negotiated. It is clearly a direct form of mediation.

A case in point is the men's clothing industry in Philadelphia, where for almost 40 years an impartial chairman has performed these functions. No strikes have occurred during that period over contract negotiations. Wildcat stoppages have been virtually unknown. Most of the difficult problems—and there have been some —have been resolved by direct negotiation. A sizable number of such problems have been settled after utilization of the mediation-consultation relationship with the impartial chairman. Some grievances have been decided by written decisions issued by the impartial chairman after hearings. For the most part, these decisions have involved issues of lesser significance. The major reliance is on negotiation and mediation.

The Arbitration Hearing

We turn now to the arbitration hearing, which can be conducted by the arbitrator so as to include mediation techniques. This can be so even if there are no posthearing arrangements of the types noted in the preceding three sections.

To begin with, the simple fact of an arbitration hearing has cathartic effects. A grievant has his "day in court." Complaints are exposed instead of festering with no outlet. Sometimes the exposure is more important than the decision.

In order for this feature of the process to be most productive, everybody at the hearing table should somehow leave the room with the feeling that the arbitrator understands the problem. This is not accomplished readily. Certainly it is not achieved if the arbitrator sits like a sphinx and utters not a word. Normally the arbitrator should keep quiet until the case has been outlined by both parties and some of the argument is in the record. Thereafter, he should become an active but not obnoxious participant. A summation of the issue, verbal indication that he understands the major arguments of the parties, a few questions on points not clear to him, and an occasional additional question or comment may accomplish the desired result. When both parties feel that the issue is understood, they are usually inclined to quit talking. They are satisfied that that part of the process has been completed. In many situations a visit by the arbitrator to the work place will help achieve this objective as well as enlighten the arbitrator.

A much more hazardous exercise is for the arbitrator to reveal his reactions. How can this be done? His summation of the issue and of the major opposing arguments may be suggestive. If one of the parties has belabored an argument and the arbitrator omits it entirely from his summary or gives it little importance, any intelligent person at the table can draw the correct inference. In response to a query, the arbitrator may give his reasons. This serves two purposes. If the arbitrator is in error, there is opportunity for correction. If not, he has accomplished the mediation function of "deflating an extreme position." Again, the arbitrator may ask a question about a particular point in a way that implies but does not fully reveal his reaction.

Admittedly, such behavior entails risk. However, much has been gained if the parties can leave the hearing room with an educated guess as to what the decision will be. Experienced arbitrators frame a general area of decision in perhaps 75 percent of grievance cases by the time the hearing has been completed. Seldom has the arbitrator irretrievably tipped his hand. But he has said enough to leave inference in the minds of the parties. When this is added to the parties' own prehearing appraisals of the case, there is little room for surprise when the decision is received. And both parties have had an opportunity to correct an error before it is too late.

Quite obviously, some of the hearing tactics noted in the last two paragraphs cannot and should not be used in cases that are extremely difficult and concerning which no general area of decision is in the arbitrator's mind at the close of the hearing.

An amusing exercise of the "penetrating question" procedure may be recounted. A well-known arbitrator was conducting the hearing. The parties were represented by able but vociferous and theatrical lawyers. Argument had been loud and strenuous with some table-thumping. The arbitrator interrupted, made a brief comment and asked one short, searching question. Faces around the table reflected amazement and horror. Both sides asked for a recess. After the recess, the hearing resumed with similar fireworks, but both sides had completely reversed their positions. A single question had opened up vistas that the parties had not thought about.

A perplexing question is whether an arbitrator should indirectly assist one party at the hearing whose case has much merit but is being poorly presented. No definitive answer is suggested, but another illustration may serve to show that it is sometimes both necessary and advisable.

The union had an extremely weak case but was doing a superb job of making the best of it. The principal company spokesman, who was an able production superintendent but a neophyte in arbitration, had a strong case but was doing almost everything possible to botch it. The arbitrator asked several questions and made a few oblique comments. As the hearing closed, everybody in the room except one man knew that the union would lose the decision. The company spokesman came up to the arbitrator, pumped his hand vigorously and said: "Well, no hard feelings. No hard feelings. You have your job to do."

CONCLUSIONS

A principal purpose of the chapter has been to suggest the wide variety of mediation procedures and techniques that are available to the parties if they should choose by agreement to make grievance resolution most responsive to collective bargaining needs.

The mediation procedures that are available provide the opportunity for more participation by the parties in the decision-making process. Less emphasis on the arbitrator as a judge and more reliance on him as a problem-solver in a sort of three-party process can give appropriate emphasis to participation and preserve the great values of the no-strike clause.

Another aspect of grievance procedure and grievance arbitration is often overlooked. A grievance decision arrived at by the parties or by arbitration is not necessarily a permanent answer. At each contract negotiation, either the union or the company has the opportunity to change a grievance answer that has been found to be unacceptable. Such changes usually require new or amended contract language. This is but one of the many ways by which the underlying mutual-agreement aspect of collective bargaining can be effectuated. In other words, the grievance process is adopted by mutual agreement in the first instance, and the parties also have the occasion periodically to alter specific results of the process. The objective of the grievance procedure, of course, should be to provide answers that continue to be acceptable and need not be changed, except as the result of a change in underlying circumstances. If too many changes are needed or sought for other reasons, the process itself requires reexamination.

Chapter XIV

NONCRISIS DIALOGUE AND PREVENTIVE MEDIATION

The labor mediator's traditional role—as a firefighter in crisis bargaining—has been examined in some detail. His limited functions in grievance settlement also have been considered. The third collective bargaining forum mentioned briefly in Chapter I, noncrisis dialogue, remains to be considered.

The various forms of noncrisis dialogue have several common characteristics that may be summarized as follows:

1. Any such program must be entirely voluntary.

2. It will be utilized to consider one or more mutually recognized important problem areas, limited to and probably peculiar to the parties to the arrangement. It is possible that two different programs might have the same general objectives. It is not likely that the factual background, the collective bargaining climate, or the specifics of any one program will be the same as these aspects of any other.

3. The problem on the agenda is one that cannot or is not likely to be dealt with adequately within the time limits normally available in crisis bargaining at contract expiration time. To illustrate by a negative, general wage adjustments would not often be discussed since wage negotiation often requires deadline pressures. Moreover, the problem is one that the parties believe cannot be handled adequately in the grievance procedure.

4. The "rules of the game" normally provide for freedom to discuss or suggest without commitment, for no interim publicity or even ultimate disclosure as to specific content of discussion, and for other internal procedures designed to stimulate inventive dialogue.

5. As a rule, the mutual agreements that may be arrived at under such a program are limited to recommendations only, requiring approval at other bargaining levels.

The collective bargaining sophisticate will note immediately that there is nothing inherently new in these characteristics. For as long as mature bargaining has existed in the United States, discussion of this general type has taken place among the principal leaders in some bargaining relationships. For example, in a number of situations within the apparel, printing, and construction industries, informal procedures meeting these specifications were in effect long before World War II. However, they were seldom formalized,[1] were sometimes sporadic, and occasionally were quite secretive.

In the late 1950s and early 1960s, the noncrisis forum attained considerable public exposure. It was then frequently labeled "continuous bargaining." "Noncrisis dialogue" is preferred here because it emphasizes that it is removed in time from contract negotiations and because such discourse is seldom continuous in a literal sense. The Kaiser Long Range Plan, the Armour Automation Committee, the Human Relations Research Committee in basic steel (later renamed Human Relations Committee), the American Motors Progress Sharing Plan, the "New Look" at International Harvester, and others emerged as formal programs or procedures. The Presidential Railroad Commission had similar objectives but differed from the others by reason of government sponsorship.

Many of these arrangements were tripartite. In varying numerical combinations and with somewhat different functions, impartial members were utilized. This, of course, had been a part of the impartial-chairman role in some instances years earlier.

These developments served to stimulate wide-ranging editorial predictions about a new era in collective bargaining, cautious interest on the part of many companies and unions, and substantial enthusiasm among the ranks of neutrals. Grievance arbitration had become well established. Still growing quantitatively, it had passed through its principal pioneering stages. This seeming new field for endeavor was of understandable interest. Proceedings of the Annual Meetings of National Academy of Arbitrators in 1961 and 1962 [2] record discussions of the subject. A rereading of these

---

[1] Frontiers of Collective Bargaining, Dunlop and Chamberlain, editors, Harper and Row, 1967, Chapter 9, *Special Study Committees*, by William Gomberg, pp. 235-251, contains a good analytical review of five experiments prior to the great depression.

[2] Arbitration and Public Policy, Chapter V. *Use of Neutrals in Collective Bargaining*, pp. 135-167, BNA, 1961 and Collective Bargaining and the Arbitrator's Role, Chapter IV, *Neutral Consultants in Collective Bargaining*, pp. 83-116, BNA, 1962.

presentations underscores the breadth and intellectually penetrating analyses made by the two principal speakers as to the need for and potential values of noncrisis dialogue. It is also evident that only those discussers who had had practical experience in this field were aware of important limitations.

Some 10 years later, what is the status of the noncrisis-dialogue idea? Was it a "flash in the pan" or is it an enduring element in collective bargaining? What predictions, if any, can be made for the future? The optimistic predictions of 1961 and 1962 have not yet been fulfilled. However, the basic idea is very much alive. *The modest growth of noncrisis dialogue is the most encouraging single feature of collective bargaining of the last decade.*

QUALITATIVE APPRAISAL OF NONCRISIS DIALOGUE [3]

Not unexpectedly, the special values of this type of bargaining contain the seeds of failure.

The peculiarity of the principal agenda item or items and the special-purpose objectives of most such programs mean that there are few guidelines or precedents on which to build. Innovation is attractive, but if the parties involved do not have sufficient drive and imagination, the process can founder. A nonstandardized procedure in an uncharted area is not likely to expand at a rapid rate, and many failures will occur.

"sweep issues under the rug." This may not be the intent. The requisite pressures to get the job done have not been present even though few of the issues that merit noncrisis dialogue will remain hidden for very long.

The absence of a strike deadline is normally a necessary feature. The principals in these projects are usually busy men. The lack of time pressure has a tendency to put the program in a low-priority position. In fact, study committees and dialogue under different names have often degenerated into mechanisms to

The need for frank and candid discussion, for keeping conversation and proposed ideas confidential, and related attributes of the process create suspicions in the minds of the nonparticipants. It is easy for others in both the management and union hierarchies to get the opinion that the relationship is "too cozy." In short,

---

[3] CREATIVE COLLECTIVE BARGAINING, by James A. Henderson, Edward R. Hintz, Jr., Jerry V. Jarrett, Robert G. Marbut, and William J. White, edited by James J. Healy, Prentice-Hall, Inc., 1965. Chapters Five through Nine, pp. 106-288, contain a detailed description and evaluation of a number of examples of noncrisis dialogue.

the nonadversary characteristics may be misunderstood as improper collusion.

If the process works well, there is some tendency for the participants to become incautious. Adequate reporting to their constituencies of the results of discussion (in contrast to how those results were achieved), securing ratification and approval where required, and obtaining necessary approval for additional areas of exploration may be neglected. Success on one subject may encourage the participants to rush into another without consolidating their accomplishments.

In view of these various hazards, it is not at all surprising that the well-publicized programs of the early 1960s have not all been outstanding success stories. The mere fact of survival may be a good index of achievement.

What has happened to some of these widely heralded devices? The Railroad Commission did not achieve many of its anticipated objectives. Most of the work-rules controversies of that industry persist. But in view of the magnitude of the problem areas explored, it would have been foolhardy to predict many instant or even early solutions. The loudest critics of the Commission would probably concede that its deliberations have been of value in subsequent disputes.

The Kaiser Long Range Plan is still very much alive after 10 years. It has made significant contributions to the resolution of difficult individual or group incentive pay problems but, as might be expected, has not solved all of them. The "fruits-sharing" aspect of the plan must be judged to have contributed to industrial peace and efficiency as well as to the pockets of employees. Faulty grievance procedures have been vastly improved. Perhaps most significantly, this company and the Steelworkers have been spared the crisis aspects that marked 1965 and 1968 contract negotiations elsewhere in basic steel.

The Armour Automation Committee also is still active. Its achievements with respect to the humane handling of plant closings and other consequences of the technological revolution in that industry have been significant, even if they have not fulfilled all the hopes. In 1967 the Committee became the major vehicle for an early contract settlement, an objective not even remotely contemplated when the project began.

The Human Relations Committee in basic steel has popularly been termed a casualty. Technically this is correct, since it went out of business officially in 1965. Staff employees of the union assumed too much direct control, and elected members of the union hierarchy at intermediate levels resented the relative diminution of their power. The Committee's excursion into the negotiation of most of the major contract renewal provisions, including wages, is not likely to be repeated. However, it is no secret that the same essential process has been utilized subsequently in more limited ways. For example, perennial problems relating to incentive pay built up enough pressure by 1968 to create a strike issue on both sides of the table. Something had to be done. A strike was averted by agreement to establish the basic steel Incentive Study Committee.

The "New Look" at International Harvester has resulted in major improvement of the grievance procedure. Some of the innovations of that program have been adopted elsewhere.

The American Motors Progress Sharing Plan was a casualty of economic forces. With little or no progress to share, a basically sound idea did not have a fair test.

Some other study committees have had limited or indifferent success. General Electric-IUE committees foundered in 1966, ostensibly because of the company's unwillingness to agree to the confidentiality that marked the work of most such groups and the union's unwillingness to proceed on any other basis. Attempts to utilize this device in the New York newspaper industry have not had significant success, although Theodore Kheel has maintained a frequent consultative role in that industry in addition to and in support of his mediation work in contract disputes.

In 1963 the Labor Management Institute, a subagency of the American Arbitration Association, started a program of sponsoring noncrisis dialogue. The initial objectives included promotion, education, and action in the selection of neutrals in a fashion similar to the AAA's role in the appointment of labor arbitrators. The Institute's work over a period of three or four years was productive from an educational standpoint. A series of conferences resulted in a thoughtful book on several aspects of bargaining.[4] The promotional endeavors had limited success. The appointment-of-neutrals function did not materialize. These AAA efforts have been rechanneled into the National Center For Dispute Settlement.

Again on the more positive side, Chrysler-UAW prenegotiation study committees undoubtedly contributed in a major way

---

[4] Frontiers of Collective Bargaining, Dunlop and Chamberlain, editors, Harper and Row, 1967.

to successful 1964 contract negotiations between these parties. More limited successful work has been done elsewhere in the automobile industry. As noted earlier, this general type of procedure was a major factor in the negotiation of the M & M program in West Coast longshoring. A massive study by the Department of Labor was rather less helpful in East Coast and Gulf Longshore, but there is doubt whether any agreement on the manning issue would have been made without it. A substantial number of unheralded but very successful programs have been developed by parties with no outside assistance. For example, the Lithographers and Photoengravers International Union, AFL-CIO, has developed an outstandingly successful arrangement with a national association of book and periodical publishers. To these should be added the preventive mediation program of the Federal Mediation and Conciliation Service, about which more will be said later.

No informed critic can write off noncrisis dialogue. The 1960s were a testing period for new forms of an old device. The successes outweighed the failures. Even the failures contributed to the future. Despite the essentially no-precedent characteristic of the idea, some lessons have been learned about what to do and what not to do. As collective bargaining becomes increasingly complex, the old notion that it can be confined to a few days or weeks every two or three years, with routine handling of a few grievances in the meantime, becomes progressively less realistic.

ROLE OF MEDIATION IN NONCRISIS DIALOGUE

There is little or no controversy about the basic role of neutrals in noncrisis dialogue. If neutrals are utilized in any capacity, their function is normally restricted to various forms of mediation. Moreover, in most instances the mediation techniques stop short of formal recommendations and do not include the more aggressive functions sometimes exercised in crisis bargaining. This is a semi-obvious statement. If the discussion is free-wheeling and the partisan members take few formal positions, it would not be expected that the neutral should act in the same way as at a time of crisis. Suggestions are a different matter. Suggestion making is the essence of noncrisis dialogue, and the neutral is expected to contribute.

The impartial members are often utilized for a function that is of less significance in contract bargaining. Factual studies may play an important part in noncrisis dialogue. The neutrals may be selected because of their proved research ability, and the parties may desire that any independent study that is undertaken be done by them or under their supervision. For example, a number of factual surveys were conducted by the Armour Automation Committee under the supervision of its neutral members. In such activity, the research is not of a theoretical nature. It is a practical study designed for and keyed to a specific problem area.

The principal purpose of the impartial member or members, however, is to function in the best mediator tradition—to assist the parties in developing their own proposed solutions.

A few exceptions to these generalizations may be noted. The Kaiser Long Range Plan provides that the three impartial members may make formal recommendations on some subjects. It is a tribute to the competence of the men selected (David L. Cole, John T. Dunlop, and George W. Taylor) that they have seldom had to exercise that authority.

A more extreme exception is seen where the neutrals are selected in advance with specific authority to arbitrate if a mutually satisfactory result is not achieved. That was the arrangement provided in the basic steel Incentive Study Committee established by 1968 negotiations. It was a nine-member tripartite body with the three public members to act as an arbitration board if resolution was not reached within one year. As the Committee actually operated, the partisan members declined to allow the public members to act as mediators throughout the year. For reasons extraneous to this discussion, the partisan members accomplished little in their private discussions. At the end of the year, the entire problem was dumped in the lap of the arbitration board almost as if the Committee had been a bipartite committee.

It may be noted that the same parties did not function in this manner on an earlier occasion. The Steel Commission established on March 30, 1945, had a somewhat similar composition and purpose except that it was an agency created by the National War Labor Board. The Commission had authority to decide, but that authority was exercised seldom and primarily only on procedural and lesser issues. With the Commission as only a backdrop, the parties accomplished one of the most extensive and constructive collective bargaining achievements of all time—the CWS job evaluation program.

The principal controversy about noncrisis dialogue is whether impartial persons should be used at all. Some parties do and some don't, which is as it should be. As is the case with so many other collective bargaining matters, variety is more than the spice of life. It enables companies and unions to tailor a procedure specifically to their own problems and their own desires.

Mediators are sharply divided about noncrisis dialogue. At the risk of oversimplification, some mediators believe that they can be useful only in the traditional impasse or strike situation. A cogent spokesman for this position has been Allan Weisenfeld, former Executive Secretary of the New Jersey State Board of Mediation. Perhaps his best exposition of this position was in a paper entitled "Mediation or Meddling?" presented in January 1954 at a meeting of the Industrial Relations Research Association.[5] Although it was directed to the earlier rather than the more recent preventive mediation program of the Federal Mediation and Conciliation Service, it expresses a common belief that mediation should be restricted to fire-fighting activities. It asserts emphatically that the utilization of neutrals in noncrisis dialogue is no panacea. On that point I can agree readily, even though I disagree with many other aspects of the Weisenfeld thesis.

Participation by Private Neutrals

Answers to questionnaires [6] returned by 423 arbitrators show only 16 individuals who have ever had experience in noncrisis dialogue. This probably understates the true situation because the questionnaire did not include a pointed reference to noncrisis dialogue. Moreover, a few other persons have had related experience in a true impartial chairmanship.

It is clear that the expectations of arbitrators in 1960, 1961, and 1962 have not been fulfilled. The parties who have employed this type of procedure have not used private neutrals or they have not selected arbitrators or they have selected those few individuals among the arbitrators who are known to be experienced in this aspect of bargaining. This is a somewhat surprising finding, but there it is.

Participation by State and Local Mediators

Only four state and local mediation agencies reported participation by agency mediators in noncrisis dialogue in the year 1968.[7] A total of 49 cases were reported by these four agencies.

[5] *Industrial and Labor Relations Review,* Vol. 7, No. 2, January 1954, pp. 288-293.
[6] Questionnaires answered by arbitrators.
[7] Questionnaires answered by state mediation agencies.

This is a larger showing than for private neutrals. At least super-ficially, the one-year total is larger than the lifetime total for arbi-trators. However, it is certain that no state agency case compares qualitatively or in terms of time requirements with the better known programs such as the Kaiser Long Range Plan or the Ar-mour Automation Committee that utilize private neutrals.

These 49 state and local cases compare with 4,326 reported pri-vate contract-disputes cases, 1,164 grievance-mediation cases, and 976 public employee disputes. In short, noncrisis dialogue cases at the state and local mediation agency level in 1968 represented only about three quarters of 1 percent of the total case load.

In at least some of the agencies not reporting any such cases, one may suspect that a few mediators did some work that would qualify. If so, such instances were not included in the answers to the questionnaire because the agency had no such reporting cate-gory or a negative administrative policy existed on this subject. In any event, it is evident that state and local mediation agencies are not now an important source of supply of neutrals for work in noncrisis dialogue. Nor is there evidence that the state agen-cies are encouraging or promoting the concept.

The National Mediation Board

The National Mediation Board reports that it has no program or announced intention of engaging in noncrisis dialogue.

Department of Labor

The U.S. Department of Labor has done some work in this area. Not long after entering office in 1961, Secretary Goldberg obtained from the Congress a line in the departmental budget that became known as "climate money." The term was derived from the expressed intention to provide services to improve the climate of collective bargaining in a variety of ways.

DOL personnel undertook an extensive study of work-assign-ment and manpower-utilization practices in the East and Gulf Coast longshore industry. A few lesser studies have been made in other industries. The Department has performed an extensive amount of practical research in railroad disputes that have reached or passed the emergency-board stage. Some work has been done on a so-called "early warning" system and on other special studies, but these have been primarily for the Secretary's informa-tion.

Only a small percentage of the "climate money" has been used for noncrisis dialogue as these words are used here. The longshore study was a monumental exception.

Preventive Mediation by FMCS

The preventive mediation program of the Federal Mediation and Conciliation Service goes back to the Taft-Hartley Act. During the 1947 discussion in Congress, in committee and to a lesser extent on the floor, a number of congressmen expressed the general opinion that the Government should do something about the root causes of strikes and that the new independent agency should not act solely as a firefighter.

As Section 203 (a) emerged in the Act, the principal functions of the Service were defined as follows:

"It shall be the duty of the Service, in order to *prevent* or minimize interruptions of the free flow of commerce growing out of labor disputes, to assist parties to labor disputes in industries affecting commerce to settle such disputes through conciliation and mediation."[8]

The words "preventive mediation" were coined by the Service to include in a general way those activities of mediators not related to contract deadlines, to mediation of specific grievances, or to public relations. The origin of these words is evident. Preventive maintenance and preventive medicine were newer concepts then than now. There are parallels in the objectives of the two concepts.

As the program developed in the early years, it was directed primarily to small or medium size plants where the labor relations climate was known to be bad. A common symptom then, as now, was a faulty grievance procedure. When a mediator could secure the cooperation of a company and a union, meetings of stewards and foremen, separately or jointly, would be arranged. The mediator would chair an informal discussion, avoiding specific pending grievances wherever possible, and directing his attention to more orderly and effective contract administration through the grievance procedure as well as the general development of better day-by-day relationships in the plant.

Some mediators found this activity rewarding even though it was likely to cut into their free evenings. However, they also en-

---

8 Emphasis supplied.

countered impediments in getting the points across solely by verbal discussion. A small, dedicated, and imaginative group at one location spent their own time and money to develop a few slide sequences. Each of these sequences portrayed a hypothetical gripe in a plant that was handled badly by a steward or foreman, or both. These slide sequences served to stimulate discussion, to deter discussion of specific pending grievances, and otherwise to assist in an educational program. The FMCS secured money for projection equipment and for copies of the slides. Thus, the audio-visual program was born as the major direct element in a preventive mediation program.

Throughout the latter part of the 1950s, the audio-visual program was improved in a number of respects. Additional sequences were developed. Slides were replaced by film strips and slide projectors by film projectors. In addition, labor relations conferences were presented in conjunction with a number of universities and colleges in areas where such meetings had been unknown. Some mediators developed a continuing consultative relationship with company and union officials at various plants.

Beginning in the early 1960s, the preventive mediation program assumed new proportions. Some stimulation occurred because of the well-publicized private developments discussed earlier. An even greater stimulus was provided by a group of mediators who were dissatisfied with the limitations of the audio-visual program but who had acquired a keen appreciation for the potentials of noncrisis mediation.

The National Labor-Management Panel, reactivated by President Kennedy on May 26, 1963, made a careful study of preventive mediation and related matters as one of its first undertakings. Its enthusiastic support of an expanded and revitalized FMCS program was evidenced by issuance of a unanimous public report on December 30, 1964.[9]

The site-committee activities of 40 field mediators, noted earlier in connection with the work of the Missile Sites Labor Commission, provided still another stimulus. These actvities were a concrete form of preventive mediation in a coordinated effort. Their general success and the experience gained through them helped persuade the bulk of the staff of the merits of the program.

[9] Second Report by the National Labor-Management Panel, December 30, 1964, reproduced as Appendix D.

The preventive mediation program needed these injections of vitality and enlarged purpose. A faithful band of mediators had been continuing to use the audio-visual sequences productively. However, they were a distinct minority. Audio-visual was retained and improved in several ways, but it became only one of many aspects of a program that enjoyed the active support of virtually the entire staff. By mid-1968, all experienced mediators had participated actively in some phase of preventive mediation.

The statistical record of the preventive mediation efforts of FMCS after it was revitalized in the early 1960s is depicted in Figure 2. For purposes of clarity, the statistical record is exclusive of missile sites work and therefore understates the total program.

Defining a mediation case of any variety is not a simple matter. An assignment is counted as a case only when the mediator actually meets physically with company or union representatives or both. The 1,321 cases in fiscal year 1969 involved a total of 7,748 separate or joint meetings. Almost all FMCS mediators were involved in at least one case. On the average, each mediator handled five such active cases in 1969. The average preventive mediation case required at least as much time as the average active contract-disputes case.

Noncrisis dialogue assumes many forms. The major types of mediator activity are described below:

Prenegotiation committees are joint committees that meet long in advance of a strike deadline to discuss, study, and make recommendations on one or more specific issues that are judged to be otherwise certain to become most troublesome in the upcoming negotiations. The issues selected are those that require more time and study than is typically available in negotiations. Examples are significant seniority plan revisions, proposals for improvements of insurance or pension plans, and broad revisions of incentive plans.

Postnegotiation committees are essentially the same except as to timing. It has not been possible to resolve an entire new-contract dispute. However, the bargainers have been willing to conclude a contract on all other issues before or after a strike and to agree to defer one or more issues for resolution by a postnegotiation committee. Frequently the contract bargainers have established criteria within which the committee works. Most of the types of disputes noted as illustrative subject matters for a prenegotiation committee can also be handled by a postnegotiation committee.

Figure 2

FMCS Preventive Mediation Cases by Fiscal Year, 1962-1969

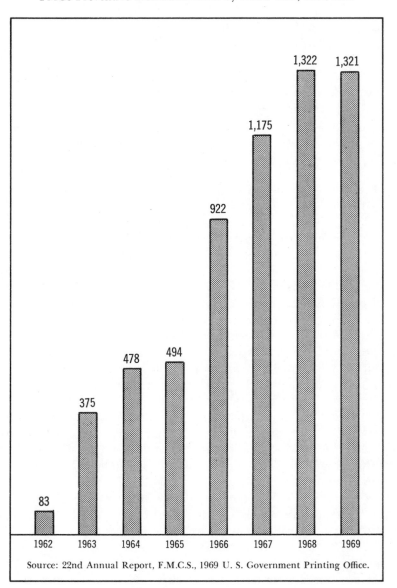

Source: 22nd Annual Report, F.M.C.S., 1969 U. S. Government Printing Office.

Grievance-procedure-correction committees are established for the express purpose of attempting to do whatever may be necessary to revitalize a grievance and arbitration procedure that is not accomplishing its intended purpose. Such programs often include extensive steward and foreman training programs.

The special-purpose objectives of the three types of preventive work noted thus far mean that such activities usually have a reasonably definitive beginning and end. The time span will depend on the circumstances. The mediator's role may include some or all of the following functions: (1) stimulation of the idea, (2) assistance in the formative stages, and (3) active participation in the work of a formal or informal committee. The mediator's general objective is to participate actively for as short a time as possible. In many circumstances, he meets with a committee to help get it started and later only if roadblocks develop. Steward and foreman training is done frequently by union, management, or nearby college or university personnel if available. In a number of instances, the mediators have participated in a leadership capacity throughout the training period.

Consultation covers a wide variety of trouble-shooting or advisory services performed during the life of a labor agreement. Both parties know the mediator. He probably has worked with them in earlier contract negotiation disputes and knows many of the problem areas. He is called in by the parties for informal advice and assistance about matters not within the normal scope of the grievance procedure. Frequently the issues in question almost surely would cause serious trouble in the negotiations that lie ahead, and the parties want to lay the groundwork for resolution but do not wish to establish a formal prenegotiation committee. In many instances such quiet preliminary work by a mediator has eliminated the necessity for his presence when the negotiations occurred some time later. This type of mediator activity may be especially appropriate at medium-size owner-operated plants in smaller cities where the management does not retain outside consultants and the local union officials are somewhat remote from the international union.

Continuing labor-management committees are normally created at the company or plant level. Frequently the membership includes higher-level company and union personnel who do not normally participate in contract bargaining or in routine grievance procedure. A committee usually meets at regular intervals throughout the contract and is expected to do so during subsequent agreements. Unlike prenegotiation and postnegotiation committees, such a group does not have a precise single-purpose objective. Nor is it an appeal body from the grievance committee. Commonly there is a rigid rule excluding specific pending grievances from the agenda. Likewise, it is a frequently specified that the agenda may not include items normally discussed in contract bargaining. What then can the members talk about?

There are many subjects that lie between or beyond grievances and contract bargaining issues but that are of general interest to management and employees. The business outlook, company plans for expansion or contraction, technological changes that lie ahead, and similar matters can be explored informally by management with a select union group. Intra-union and interunion problems and union aspirations can be explored with management. Effective ways for both parties to meet their responsibilities as to equal employment opportunity and community needs can be explored beyond the specific applications of those subjects to the labor agreement.

Many managements and unions are reluctant even to open the door to such possibilities. In such cases the idea of a continuing committee may be rejected entirely. Or, if it is accepted, the agenda will be limited to quite inoccuous matters. After a few meetings, enjoyable and worthwhile in that new people on each side of the table to get to know each other as persons, the committee begins to "die on the vine." However, some managements and some unions have decided that the potential values exceed the hazards. Beginning hesitantly as to subject matter, serious joint discussion and exploration are attempted. If the results are mutually satisfactory, new ventures can be undertaken.

An illustration may suggest the potentials of such committees. The company, here unnamed, was preparing to bid on an important long-term contract involving one of its principal products. The labor agreement had eight months to run. A major problem was uncertainty as to future labor costs. The company decided to explore the matter candidly and fully at the labor-management committee meetings. After discussion, the union representatives offered to recommend to the members that the agreement be renegotiated early. The members agreed, and the negotiations were successful. What is sometimes characterized as an "early bird" agreement was reached. The labor-management committee did not negotiate the agreement. That was done by the usual negotiating methods. It was not a cheap contract, but the company could predict its labor costs with certainty before the bid was made. and it did secure the contract. Employees benefited by expanded work opportunity, good contract terms, and a strike-free renewal of the agreement. This illustration is intended only to indicate that there are possibilities in the labor-management committee that can lift it well above an innocuous social mechanism. Absent the continuing committee, the idea of an early-bird agreement idea never would have surfaced.

. Mediators can assist in the organization of such a committee, and in some instances the parties will want them to continue to participate beyond the formative stages. It is the general policy of the FMCS to encourage mediators to withdraw from active participation after a committee becomes well established. Or, if the idea does not "jell" and committee members lose interest, it may well be that strenuous efforts to revive it are not justified. In short, the casualty rate will be fairly high, but those committees that do develop in a satisfactory manner more than repay the effort.

Area-wide labor-management committees have some similarities to the company or plant groups just discussed. A major difference is that several companies and several unions in the same geographical area are represented. Such committees were established more than a decade ago in the South Bend—Mishawaka area in Indiana and at Chattanooga, Tenn. They have been active continuously. In both instances FMCS mediators were active with management and union representatives in the formation of the committees, and they have continued to be influential. The major purpose was and is to create and maintain a good labor-management climate in the area. Mediators and some committee members in these areas have been able to work together informally in disputes situations. To a limited degree the tripartite National War Labor Board procedures have been applied.

A variant of such a committee can be found in the more recent establishment of a Western New York (Buffalo) Chapter of the Industrial Relations Research Association. Most IRRA chapters have been established with primary sponsorship and initiative from members of the academic community. This was not the case in Buffalo. Recognizing the absence of any meeting place for labor and industry in that region except at individual bargaining tables, two FMCS mediators spearheaded a movement by labor and industry to create a chapter. It includes the academic community but is clearly dominated by the industry and labor mem-

bers. Its vigorous program of meetings and conferences is designed to improve industrial relations in the area.

It is not suggested here that an average FMCS preventive
mediation case is equivalent to the Kaiser Long Range Plan or to
the Armour Automation Committee. However, a substantial
number have been as successful, perhaps even more so, if establishment size is taken into account. It should not be assumed that
the FMCS program is limited to small plants, for it is not. Sizable
plants and big-name companies frequently have been involved.

Why is it that the FMCS preventive mediation program has
grown so dramatically during a period when there has been no
appreciable growth in the utilization of private neutrals and
when other mediation agencies have not chosen to develop such
activity? The answer is not to be found in a publicity campaign.
Publicity has been muted. Moreover, mediators have been instructed not to engage in "door-bell ringing."

One important reason is that the crisis disputes mediator is in
an especially favorable position. He works with and lives with the
parties at a time of stress when the weak points in their bargaining relationship become all too apparent to all three participants
(labor, management, and the mediator). Most negotiators desire
to correct such weaknesses. If the mediator has earned the respect
and confidence of the parties, a hint by him may inspire a desire
to experiment. Not infrequently the hints come the other way.
The parties ask the mediator to assist in formulating a program
designed to improve the weak spots peculiar to their relationship.

Evidence that this is so is found in the statistics. In the first
half of the 1960s, well over 90 percent of all new preventive mediation cases developed directly out of crisis disputes that usually
were marked by strikes. The mediator who started the preventive
case was the same one who had mediated the dispute, and the
preventive work began within a reasonable time after the contract issues had been settled.

But a new factor entered the picture in the latter half of the
1960s. The 90-percent-plus figure dropped to 57.2 percent in
fiscal year 1969. Most of the remaining 42.8 percent of cases in
1968 and 1969 resulted from direct requests by parties who had
not been involved in recent disputes cases with FMCS mediators.
Inquiry shows that the bulk of these requests were due to word-
of-mouth recommendations of management and union associates
who themselves had experimented with noncrisis dialogue. Thus
the preventive mediation objectives are being realized increas-

ingly by the very best type of promotion—quiet favorable comment by parties who have found noncrisis dialogue to be truly productive.

Chapter XV

MEDIATION AND IMPASSE PROCEDURES
IN PUBLIC EMPLOYEE DISPUTES

Strikes by public employees continue to be illegal in almost all jurisdictions in the United States. But they have happened in the recent past, and it must be expected that some will occur in the future. The incidence of such strikes is much lower than in the private sector of the economy, but this fact does not diminish the news value of those that do arise. Two reasons underlie the developments of recent years.

One is the rapid spread of union organization. Teachers, garbage collectors, welfare workers, nurses, clerks, and many other groups of public workers—once citadels of nonunion behavior—are now swelling the ranks of unions. Membership growth rates are far in excess of the modest expansion in the private economy.

Unions are not new in government. Postal workers and skilled workers at Navy shipyards have been organized for many years. At the TVA and the Government Printing Office, most employees long have been represented by unions. In a few major cities such as New York and Philadelphia, unions of municipal workers have existed for 20 years or more. Firemen and policemen in many cities have been organized for a considerable time. These established unions have enlarged recently, but it is the new crop in the hitherto unorganized areas that is mainly responsible for the membership surge.

The second reason is the militancy that has been exhibited lately by both the old and the new public employee unions. Only a few years ago, strikes by public employee unions were virtually unknown. Surface peace created a public illusion that obscured the fact of the considerable amount of organization that did exist. A few strikes in New York City were a sign of militancy but could be passed off on the premise that "New York is different." But when teachers in widely scattered places and finally the

postal workers struck, the new potency of public worker organizations became apparent nationally. The tragedy of Dr. Martin Lu-
ther King's assassination in Memphis highlighted the fact that
public worker aspirations are not limited to white employees.

A temptation to explore the causes of growth of public employee organization, to outline the increases to date, to indicate
the unions involved, and otherwise to develop the historical background will be resisted. The information presently available
would in any case be outdated by the time this book is published.
Similarly, no attempt will be made here to consider in any detail very important subjects such as (1) the present status of state
laws and municipal ordinances, (2) the extent of legal rights of
public employees to organize, (3) procedures for determining the
composition of bargaining units and for union recognition, (4)
grievance procedures, or (5) the permissible content and scope of
labor agreements. These matters have been clarified in some jurisdictions, but most states and cities have not yet faced up to the
onrushing problems.[1]

This discussion will be concerned almost solely with mediation
and other impasse procedures. It will be assumed that a union
has been recognized somehow—by legal procedures, by voluntary
recognition, or by a strike or threat of a strike. A government
agency has agreed to negotiate an agreement with the union. Direct negotiation has not been successful. This is the traditional
circumstance under which a mediator functions in the private
sector.

Neutrals become involved in public employee disputes as mediators, fact-finders, members of impasse panels or special boards,
or as arbitrators. All these forms except arbitration come within
the scope of this book because mandatory decision-making is not
involved.

MEDIATION AND IMPASSE RESOLUTION

State and local mediation agencies, private individuals not regularly employed by government, and federal agencies have been

---

[1] PICKETS AT CITY HALL, The Twentieth Century Fund, New York, 1970, is a
report by a task force that includes an analysis and recommendations on many of
these matters.

The Changing of the Establishment, an address by Arvid Anderson at the U. S.
Conference of Mayors, Denver, Colo., June 14, 1970, includes an excellent summary.

COLLECTIVE NEGOTIATION FOR PUBLIC AND PROFESSIONAL EMPLOYEES, edited by
Robert T. Woodworth and Richard B. Peterson, Scott, Foresman and Company,
1969, is a collection of many articles directly relevant to this chapter.

utilized in public employee disputes. Questionnaires answered for the most part in mid-1969 provide comparative data.[2]

State and Local Mediation Agencies

For calendar year 1968, agencies in only 18 states reported mediation of any public employee disputes. The states and reported numbers of cases are as follows:

Handling of Public Employee Mediation or Fact-Finding Cases
by State and Local Agencies, 1968

State	Number of Cases
New York	332
Michigan	250
Minnesota	80
Connecticut	70
Wisconsin	63
New Jersey	37
Washington	32
Massachusetts	31
Rhode Island	25
Pennsylvania	21
Oregon	10
Ohio (Toledo LMCC)	8
Illinois	6
North Carolina	5
Kansas	3
Arkansas	2
Wyoming	1
California	*
U. S. Total (excluding California)	976

* Public disputes mediated but no separate statistics for private and public.

No known state or local mediation agency was omitted from the survey. Eight states did not anwer the questionnaire. However, these eight states (Colorado, Louisiana, Mississippi, Missouri, New Mexico, South Dakota, Texas, and West Virginia) are known to exercise no mediation assistance of material consequence even in the private sector. It can be assumed that the total of all public employee disputes mediated by or under the direction of state and local mediation agencies in the United States in 1968 was about 1000 cases.

[2] Questionnaires answered by governmental agencies and individuals.

The first obvious conclusion is that 32 states either had no mediation facilities for public employee disputes or did not use the facilities that were available. Of these, 22 are without known mediation agencies within their borders. The remaining 10 states have agencies that mediated at least some private disputes but no public employee disputes.

The 28 states with mediation services and Puerto Rico reported a total of 6,515 mediated cases of all varieties. Thus, on an overall basis, public employee disputes mediated in the United States in 1968 were about 15 percent of state and local agency case loads. In New York and Michigan, the leading states in public employee mediation, the percentages were higher (35 percent and 20 percent, respectively).

Two states (New York and New Jersey) have created separate agencies for public employee disputes. The Public Employee Relations Board in New York (PERB) and the Public Employee Relations Commission in New Jersey (PERC) operate independently of the long-established state agencies for private disputes. PERC was in business for only a short time in 1968. The New Jersey statistics for 1968 therefore include public employee mediation by the New Jersey State Mediation Board in that year. The New York total includes the office of Collective Bargaining in New York City and a local agency in Suffolk County.

PERB, PERC, and the Office of Collective Bargaining have very small full-time mediator staffs. Therefore, mediation, fact-finding, and similar activities are performed mostly by private individuals assigned on an ad hoc basis. Michigan attempts to separate mediation and fact-finding. In that state most mediation is performed by staff mediators, but when a case is considered to have reached a fact-finding stage, private individuals are usually utilized. Only four other agencies reporting public employee disputes mediation indicated any use of part-time mediators or fact-finders. In the remaining 12 states, all mediation of public employee disputes in which there was state-agency involvement was performed by staff mediators.

If later information were available, the totals would certainly be somewhat higher. Some state agencies with no public employee mediation in 1968 have had at least a few cases recently. A few of the 32 no-public-mediation states in 1968 have enacted legislation since 1968 or are considering such action seriously. However, the 1968 data are generally indicative of the national picture.

Does the absence of state or local public disputes mediation in 32 states mean that there are no serious controversies in those states or that public employees are not even organizing? Organization is spotty geographically. In a number of the 32 states there are few public employee unions today, and those which do exist are concentrated in a few of the larger cities. However, it would be foolhardy to believe that organization will stop at its present boundaries. Teachers are becoming more union-minded almost everywhere. Firefighters are extending their organizational efforts dramatically. Strikes of public employees in Tennessee (Memphis), Louisiana (New Orleans), and Florida, three of the no-mediation states, have attracted national attention. The Toledo Labor-Management Citizens' Committee is the only mediation agency in Ohio. Public employee disputes elsewhere in that state have required the attention of the Federal Mediation and Conciliation Service recently, and it is apparent that organization in Ohio is spreading rapidly.

The question is not whether public employees in these states will organize. It is how fast it will occur. When organization does develop, mediation and related services will be essential. If these states maintain a head-in-the-sand attitude for too long, they will be ill prepared when crises do develop.

Private Mediators and Fact-Finders

Data on public employee disputes were secured by questionnaires answered by 423 individuals who are not full-time employees of any local, state, or Federal Government units.

Of these persons, 133 reported having mediated or acted in a fact-finding capacity in at least one public employee dispute at some time during their labor relations lifetime. The lifetime number of cases was 839. The frequency distribution is shown on the next page.

It should be emphasized that no cases are included in this survey where the individual had authority to issue a final and binding decision. In other words, the survey covers arbitrators but not for those cases where they had the authority that is characteristic of arbitration.

The same 423 individuals also reported on their 1968 experience. A total of 318 public disputes cases were handled in 1968 by 77 different individuals. The frequency distribution, not shown here, again indicates considerable variation. Of the 77 arbitrators, 22 had only one case each in 1968.

Public Employee Disputes
Mediation and Fact-Finding
by Arbitrators
(labor relations lifetime)

Number of Cases	Number of Individuals
1	33
2-5	47
6-10	28
11-20	17
21 or more	8
Total cases—839	Total individuals—133

If the 318 individual case total is compared with the approximate 1,000 agency case total for 1968, it would appear superficially that ad hoc mediation and fact-finding was only about one third of the agency mediation case load. Two factors make this direct comparison invalid. The first is that there is substantial overlap. In Michigan, for example, the same case may be mediated by a state mediator and a fact-finder may function subsequently. PERB and OCB cases in New York are somewhat different. These agencies count a case when there has been no staff mediation. The ad hoc mediator or fact-finder appointed by PERB or OCB also reported the same case. The other major factor is that the individual questionnaire data do not include all ad hoc mediation and fact-finding. Despite almost complete returns from members of the National Academy of Arbitrators and data from an additional 100 individuals, it is apparent that much ad hoc mediation and fact-finding was performed in 1968 by persons who received no questionnaires and by the few who did not complete the questionnaires that were sent.

It is possible to estimate the number of ad hoc cases missed. This has been done by comparison of the agency reports of ad hoc cases with the totals of the individual reports of cases handled for those same agencies. That calculation plus a small estimate for cases not handled through any agency suggests that the reported ad hoc total for 1968, 318 cases, should be increased about 50 percent, to 477 cases.

By somewhat similar methods, it is estimated that the overlap of agency-reported cases and individually reported cases amounts to about 370 cases.

It is estimated that about 1,100 public employee disputes were subject to mediation or fact-finding by state and local agencies and by individuals in 1968. This estimate is derived as follows:

Reported by state and local agencies	1,000
Reported by 423 individuals	318
Estimated for individual cases not reported	159
Total	1,477

Less:	
Estimated overlap (same dispute reported by agencies and by individuals)	370
Net	1,107

Work for experienced arbitrators as mediators and fact-finders in the public sector has already far surpassed the amount of work that has been made available to them as neutrals in private sector noncrisis dialogue. Another fact is of interest. The lifetime total of 839 public disputes cases reported by 423 arbitrators can be compared directly with the 318 total for the one year of 1968. The 839 figure includes the 318 cases in 1968, additional cases for about the first half of 1969 at an apparently accelerated rate, and all cases prior to 1968. The evidence is quite clear that ad hoc mediation and fact-finding of public disputes in 1968 was in greater volume quantitatively than the cumulative total of all such work done in all years prior to 1968.

Will ad hoc mediation and fact-finding continue to expand? Any answer to that question would be speculative. When and as the 1969 and 1970 data become available, there is every reason to believe that the totals will be progressively higher.

Federal Mediation and Conciliation Service

In 1968, only 20 public employee disputes were mediated by the Federal Mediation and Conciliation Service. The main reason probably is that most public sector disputes up to the end of 1968 had developed in state and local government.

Another reason is found in FMCS policies. The Service has refused to take jurisdiction in nonfederal disputes where a state or local agency is available. In the states and areas where no mediation agency exists, fewer disputes subject to mediation have developed. The Service has not automatically refused to take jurisdiction in such instances. However, until recently the Service has insisted on a joint request for mediation. There were several reasons for this. Staff and budget restrictions prevented the assumption of much additional work. Too, the impact of some of these disputes on interstate commerce character was doubtful. The FMCS also preferred to utilize its limited staff resources in cases where the chances of success were best. Finally, and of greatest significance, the Service had serious doubts about the wisdom of direct federal intervention in disputes involving agencies of state and local government.

As for disputes at the federal level, the volume of crisis disputes has not yet been great despite the high visibility of the postal strike. Until the issuance of Executive Order 11491 on October 29, 1969, the FMCS had no delegated authority to mediate even in the federal sector. Jurisdiction of some disputes involving federal agencies was accepted. A very much larger number could have been mediated were it not for the fact that the mutual-request requirement was also applied to the federal sector. The reasons for that roadblock were essentially the same as those stated in the preceding paragraph.

Executive Order 11491 changed the situation substantially. Section 16 of the Order reads:

"The Federal Mediation and Conciliation Service shall provide services and assistance to Federal agencies and labor organizations in the resolution of negotiation disputes. The Service shall determine under what circumstances and in what manner it shall proffer its services."

Acting under the last sentence of Section 16, the FMCS has issued rules for mediating negotiation disputes. For all practical purposes these rules are similar to those applicable to the private sector. The mutual-request requirement has been eliminated. Moreover, preventive mediation may be exercised under appropriate circumstances. The Congress has also appropriated limited additional funds for this new responsibility, permitting modest staff expansion.

The volume of increased work and the rate of growth are somewhat speculative. There is little doubt as to the need. Long before October 1969 pressures for additional mediation services at the federal level were increasing. A good record of success in the limited number of cases handled experimentally was adding to the pressures. The elimination of the mutual-request requirement and the delegation of specific authority are certain to result in increased volume. During the fiscal year ending June 30, 1970, the FMCS total of public employee disputes mediated increased to 68. Most of these were federal employee cases. Early activity in fiscal year 1971 indicates a rapid expansion of work load.

It is of special interest that the FMCS preventive mediation case load in the public sector, primarily a form of educational program for collective bargaining in the federal sector, was 101 cases in fiscal year 1970. The fact that the preventive mediation case load was heavier than the disputes case load suggests that preventive mediation for some years to come will be even more important in the public sector than in the private sector.

Federal Labor Relations Council and Federal Services Impasse Panel

Executive Order 11491 also created a Federal Labor Relations Council and a Federal Services Impasses Panel. The Federal Labor Relations Council is essentially a top policy-making body. The chairman is the Chairman of the Civil Service Commission. The other members are the Secretary of Labor, an official of the Executive Office of the President, and such other members of the Executive Branch as the President may designate.

The Federal Services Impasses Panel, an agency of the Council, is given quite broad powers in impasse disputes. In July 1970 President Nixon named the first chairman (Jacob Seidenberg) and six other members. It appears that present plans call for all members to serve part-time. A full-time executive director was named in June 1970, and a small staff has been acquired.

The functions and policies of the Impasses Panel will undoubtedly develop gradually as specific cases are handled. Subject only to the policies of the Federal Labor Relations Council, the Panel is an agency of last resort in federal employee disputes.

Federal Reserve System Labor Relations Panel

Not subject to Executive Order 11491 or its predecessor (Executive Order 10988), the Board of Governors of the Federal Reserve System issued a Policy Statement on labor relations on May 9, 1969. It bears some similarity to Executive Order 10988 but also incorporates a few of the features that emerged later in Executive Order 11491. It was deliberately designed to fill a need for a Federal Reserve labor policy and to adopt the general governmental arrangements to Federal Reserve functions and structure.

Administration of all aspects of the Policy Statement, including representation questions, unfair labor practices and disputes settlement, are to be handled by a three-man Federal Reserve System Labor Relations Panel. Two members of the Board of Governors and one outside person make up the membership. The first Panel was named on January 21, 1970.

SPECIAL MEDIATION PROBLEMS IN THE PUBLIC SECTOR

Most mediation principles, policies, and techniques applicable to private disputes are transferable to public employee disputes. The ever-present need to adapt to different situations makes it possible for an experienced mediator to be useful in the public sector almost immediately. But it would be quite in error to suggest that there are no differences in public sector mediation. Some of these are characteristics of bargaining seldom encountered before; others are differences of form and degree rather than totally new problems.

Scope of Bargaining—Limitations By Law

The potential scope of bargaining in the private sector is almost unlimited. With few exceptions the bargainers are at liberty to agree or to refuse to agree on contract provisions covering almost any subject directly or indirectly related to wages and working conditions.

Public sector bargaining is much more limited. The Congress, state legislatures, and municipal governing bodies have created a vast network of laws or ordinances dealing with compensation, fringe benefits, and personnel policies. Where public employees have been given the right to bargain, these preexisting laws have not often been repealed or amended. On the contrary, most enabling legislation or executive actions to permit or encourage bargaining have provided that such bargaining is to be within the statutory limitations.

The problem can be illustrated by the limitations placed on wage bargaining. Wages of Federal Government employees covered by the Classification Act are fixed periodically by Congress. Therefore wage rates are eliminated as a subject for collective bargaining. This is the most typical federal agency situation. In many other Federal Government installations, wages are determined by special wage boards, normally on the basis of comparability with wage rates for like jobs in the private sector of the economy. If a union secures bargaining rights for some employees at one of these installations, it does not have any right to bargain directly about wages. In recent years, union representatives have been admitted to membership of many of the wage boards. Unions may thus acquire a voice, but it is an indirect one. Until recently, the maximum form of Federal Government bargaining on wages existed at the Tennessee Valley Authority. By law, TVA wages are governed by the comparability principal. This, of course, is a limitation that can apply in the private sector only by agreement, but the TVA and the unions with bargaining rights do bargain directly to determine how the comparability principle shall be applied. Recent legislation will permit postal wage bargaining of a wider scope than the TVA.

Examples can be found in state and local government of most types of limitations on wage bargaining noted above for the Federal Government. However, particularly at the local government level, there are many actual or potential collective bargaining situations where direct wage bargaining is permissible. The limitations in such instances are not legislative. They are budgetary restrictions, a subject to be discussed later.

Wages are by no means the only subject matter as to which collective bargaining in the public sector may be either eliminated or restricted severely. Retirement plans, health and accident insurance, sick leave, vacations, veterans' rights, and many other matters may be fixed by law, in whole or in part. On some of these subjects limited bargaining may be possible. For example, if basic vacation rights and benefits are determined by legislation, bargaining could occur on the selection of preferred vacation times.

Rules and Regulations

Personnel policies of most government agencies have been administered under a massive proliferation of rules and regulations that implement the statutes and also cover may subjects on which the laws may be silent. Almost inevitably, these rules and regulations have increased in quantity and specificity over the years. In some agencies they are so voluminous that only a few individuals in the agency profess to know what they mean. The matter is complicated further by rules and regulations issued by other agencies, such as the Civil Service Commission. Assistant Secretaries for Administration, Directors of Administrative Management, and their immediate staffs are typically the custodians of these rules and regulations, and they have substantial power in the administration of personnel policy.

The relevance of this to the matter at hand is that some bargaining in the public sector may be limited by agency rules and regulations as well as by law. Extreme application of this limitation could mean that there was almost nothing to bargain about. In some government agencies the combination of legal limitations and the rules-and-regulations limitations have so frustrated the union that it has been almost impossible to negotiate a contract.

The mediator's role in such a situation is onerous indeed. Somehow the parties must reach a fundamental distinction on many disputed issues. Is the scope of bargaining really limited by law and by obviously necessary and proper interpretations of law? If so, what is the extent of that limitation? Or is a rule or regulation being cited by agency management simply as an excuse for not doing something it doesn't choose to do? The mediator cannot be a decision-maker on such matters, but he must help the parties thread their way through the maze.

This process will be employed extensively in public sector bargaining in the future. In many public jurisdictions, the scope of bargaining will remain more limited than in the private sector because of laws and their necessary and proper interpretation. But if bargaining is to be meaningful, many other rules and regulations will have to be thrown into the collective bargaining hopper for decision by the bargainers on the merits.

Authority of the Bargainers

In the private sector, union negotiators usually bargain with considerable authority, but frequently the resulting agreement must be ratified by the membership. On the management side, the negotiators' authority may be more limited, but they can usually get approval or disapproval quickly from the president or the board of directors for modification of those limitations. The authority of private sector management negotiators becomes a serious problem only when the negotiators are little more than messenger boys.

Union negotiators in the public sector are often new at the game, and this presents temporary problems. One is the occasional instance where the union negotiators come in with "non-negotiable demands." These may not be limited to the high-priority type of demand that a private sector union negotiating team may adhere to even to the point of striking. There is a tendency for new union negotiators to believe that formulated union demands, possibly approved by the membership, simply are not subject to change. These and similar problems mostly will disappear with experience. Many of the public employee unions have imported into their ranks individuals who have had extensive experience in private bargaining, or they have sought ad hoc assistance from experienced bargainers.

Public management bargainers have exhibited some of the same tendencies attributable to inexperience. Moreover, there has been less use of experienced management bargainers as permanent staff members or as ad hoc advisors. The agency side has often exhibited too much of the "messenger boy" attitude and management versions of "nonnegotiable demands." These, too, will disappear as more experience is obtained.

The much more difficult additional problem is that agency negotiators may really have sharply limited authority and no avenue for quick approval. This is especially so where wages are negotiable but the source of higher wages is the legislative authority to levy taxes. A business corporation may hold out indefinitely against a wage increase above a certain level. But the same people who make the decision do so for what they consider to be sound business reasons also have the authority to increase prices if they care to do so.

One response to the problem of separate negotiating and taxing authorities is to complete negotiations before budget-making and budget-allocation time. The practical effect of this is to develop a type of management referendum somewhat comparable to union-member ratification. The negotiated settlement becomes a joint recommendation to the legislature or other tax-levying authority. Obviously this method presents major problems when the tax authority refuses to approve the negotiated results, just as union members' refusal to ratify an agreement creates problems.

When uncertainties are created on both sides of the table about the finality of a negotiated settlement, the effect on bargaining is not good. If the tax authority can be brought into the bargaining process, the uncertainty on the management side can be minimized. However, this is not accomplished readily.

Much the same situation can exist on matters other than wages. A law may stand in the way of an otherwise possible settlement, and the only avenue of release is to change the law. That takes time, and the results are unpredictable.

Should Public Employee Strikes Be Made Legal?

Probably the greatest single difference between private and public bargaining, at least in theory, is that strikes in the private sector ordinarily are legal, whereas strikes in the public sector are almost universally illegal.

There can be no denying the fact that the strike, or much more often the threat of one, is a major inducement to settlement of contract disputes in the private sector. Time and again a dispute is resolved at the eleventh hour almost solely because the costs of a strike to one side, or to both, would be greater than the values of the last-minute gap between the positions of the parties. For this reason many persons believe that the way to develop sound collective bargaining in the public sector is to legalize the strike for public employees, subject only to procedures generally comparable to private sector emergencies. It can be pointed out that there is little difference between public and private procedures in Great Britain, that a limited right to strike exists in Canada, and that two states (Hawaii and Pennsylvania) have recently enacted legislation providing a limited right to strike. In both Great Britain and Canada, public sector bargaining has a much longer history than in the United States.

It is often argued, too, that it is unwise to have laws on the books that have been repeatedly flouted. In Michigan, for example, a substantial number of illegal teacher strikes have been permitted to go unpunished. The postal strike, almost nationwide, was illegal and the first massive violation of a once-sacred principle that no federal employee could strike against the Government. No violators have yet been punished. It is sometimes maintained that such violations of or indifference to the law are worse than no law at all.

There are several arguments for retention of legal prohibitions upon public employee strikes. One is the practical consideration that few legislative bodies in the United States would be prepared now to legalize public employee strikes. Recent congressional postal legislation does not legalize strikes even though it does create a semiprivate agency in lieu of a department of government. There have been no indications that the Congress would vote favorably to legalize strikes elsewhere in the Federal

Government. When many states do not even accord public employee unions legal rights to organize and to be recognized, it is almost inconceivable that many legislative bodies will sanction strikes of any kind at an early date. The new Hawaiian and Pennsylvania laws are not likely to start a significant trend.

A second argument, old-fashioned but still not invalid, is that a segment of the public should not be permitted to strike against the public at large simply because members of that segment are in an employee relationship. In an indirect sense, a public employee on strike is striking against himself. It is essential to preserve the basic concepts of representative government.

A related argument is that wages and other money benefits are paid out of tax revenue rather than from the proceeds of sales of a product or services by a private employer. If employee wages and costs in the private sector are increased too much, the customers can and sometimes do refuse to buy. Some firms go out of business. But most governmental services are essential, or in any event a government unit seldom ceases to function. The market restraints in the private economy are not likely to be matched by similar restraints in public services. The only final restraint in the public sector is a taxpayer revolt. Such a revolt would normally express itself by political action. The restraints in the private sector are primarily economic; in the public sector they are political.

The argument that strikes should be legalized to preserve respect for law is not very compelling. Laws are not repealed simply because there are a few violations. Experience has demonstrated that laws providing excessively severe punishment, such as the former Condon-Waldin Act in New York State, cannot be enforced. But to raise serious questions about the equity or practicality of particular forms of penalties for violation of a law is not the same thing as to suggest that there be no legal restrictions.

The final, and probably the strongest, argument against legalization of strikes is pragmatic. Even those who hold most vigorously that public strikes should be legal concede that severe restraints are necessary for the most essential services. For example, most agree that police strikes should not be permitted. To give the right to strike only to the less essential public employees might be of little practical value to them. This would be especially so if public employers were free to resort to the tactics sometimes utilized by strong private employers (discharge, replacement of strikers, lockout, subcontracting of work, etc.).

On balance, the proposition that an answer to public employee bargaining problems is to make nonessential strikes legal is questionable. The tough problem is to find satisfactory alternatives to the strike for employees who perform essential services. If that problem were solved, there would be little difficulty with respect to nonessential services.

Public employee strikes have served the useful function of jolting the public and many agency officials from their lethargy. If the lesson has not been learned, it does not make much practical difference whether strikes are illegal or legal; they will happen anyway. If they occur in too many places over too long a time, the development of sane and orderly procedures for public disputes will become increasingly difficult. The present imperative is to develop adequate alternatives to the strike. Debate about strike legality or illegality tends to divert energy and attention from this critical need.

Alternatives to Public Employee Strikes

Alternatives to the public employee strike most commonly voiced are (1) improved direct negotiation, (2) mediation, (3) fact-finding with recommendations, (4) voluntary arbitration, and (5) compulsory arbitration. Noncrisis dialogue should be added to that list.

The only fully satisfactory alternative is *improved direct negotiation*. There is too much emphasis now on various forms of intervention. Unless the basic objective of all parties, including the neutrals, is to increase the number of settlements made without any outside assistance, no procedures will suffice.

An obvious part of the present situation is inexperience on both sides of the table. Public sector bargaining is in the "growing pains" period, somewhat comparable to the late 1930s and early 1940s in mass production industries. There is no fully satisfactory substitute for the acquisition of bargaining capability by experience—learning the hard way. As bargaining relationships mature, improved performance at the bargaining table should be expected. But the "trial and error" method can be supplemented.

Public employee unions are doing much, though not enough, by providing special training programs for new negotiators. As noted earlier, many of these unions have strengthened their staffs by importing experienced bargainers from other unions.

Agency officials have as much to learn about bargaining as the union representatives, and perhaps more. Steeped as they have been for years in the implementation of unilateral rules and regulations, they first must accept the fact of a union and the necessity to deal with a union constructively. Once over that big hurdle, training for bargaining is needed. The formation of a Labor Management Relations Service by the U.S. Conference of Mayors, the National League of Cities, and the National Association of Counties is a most constructive move in this direction.

Noncrisis dialogue is especially important in the public sector. Since the scope of bargaining is more limited than in private industry, there is much more room for constructive consultation. Matters now excluded from incorporation in labor agreements simply will not remain excluded by the expedient of refusing to talk about them. If discussion is deliberately kept separate from contract negotiations, the two-way educational experience can do much to relieve tension. If an agency has a specific nonnegotiable matter that cannot survive the light of open discussion, it should be reexamined. If it is a sound policy, suspicions and rumors can be allayed. Improper encroachment on agency prerogatives can best be avoided by extensive noncrisis dialogue. Mediators can assist in the establishment of this type of program.

Mediation is typically underrated. Many of the reasons have been noted earlier, but there are additional factors in the public employee area. Inexperienced bargainers may be ignorant of the mediation process, and may not know how to work with a mediator. They may be suspicious of him and therefore unwilling or unable to deal with him in the confidential manner that is essential. This is more likely to be true of agency negotiators than of union negotiators. Again both sides may expect more of the mediator than he can deliver. Not uncommonly, the two reactions are found together. Thus the mediator's principal initial task may be to explain the mediation function. Only then can mediation of the issues be productive. On the other hand, the education and mediation functions can not be separated completely; vital issues of the case may be the media by which the educational process can be accomplished.

Negotiations in the public sector can be too time-consuming. In the absence of a strike or a real strike threat, it is not uncommon for a mediator to find that direct bargaining, or what has been called bargaining, has been going on for months. If the mediator should accept the slow pace, the dispute could drag on interminably. His usefulness may then be limited, and his time is being wasted. In short, the mediator must find some way to step up the pace. In addition to the unchartable ways by which a mediator can accomplish that purpose while on the job, two procedural suggestions can be made.

The first is that the mediator must retain control of his own time. He should be free to remove himself from the bargaining table temporarily whenever he believes that progress is not being made or that the parties should meet alone for a period of time. A related arrangement may be necessary or desirable. When it accepts a case, the mediation agency can indicate the approximate maximum amount of mediator time that can be made available. This can be an imperfect equivalent of the pressures of a strike deadline. In several instances the Federal Mediation and Conciliation Service has utilized this device with surprising success.

Because strike-deadline pressures normally are absent, a mediator may have to exercise more of the aggressive functions noted in Chapter V. Suggestions on specific issues will be required more often than in private cases, partly because the bargainers are relatively unsophisticated. Moreover, package recommendations may be needed more often. Since the use of recommendations by mediators can be unproductive if utilized too frequently, it is probable that steps beyond mediation will be required in public sector disputes more often than in private sector disputes.

Fact-finding with recommendations has been discussed in Chapter XI. It is unnecessary to restate the author's dim view of this procedure in the private sector unless it is, in reality, an advanced stage of mediation. In the public sector at the present stage of development, the use of fact-finding is more constructive and legitimate for those cases that do not yield to aggressive mediation. Inexperience in bargaining means that the parties are not as knowledgeable about relevant facts and are not as sophisticated in the use of facts to deflate each other's extreme positions. Thus, resourceful marshalling of the facts and effective presentation of them can be of important assistance to the bargainers.

A fact-finding report can be an important method of presentation to a tax-levying authority, since an independent appraisal of the facts may be helpful or even necessary. Moreover, the essentially political rather than economic restraint on bargaining in the public sector makes it especially important in a disputed situation for the general public to have the opportunity to appraise the facts. Only a small fraction of the public in a political entity will take the time and trouble to digest facts and to avoid primarily emotional reactions. However, those who will do so may be influential. They have a more direct interest as taxpayers than as consumers of a product of a privately owned business. Moreover, even the consumer interest may be much more direct. For example, parents have an intense and legitimate interest in the quality of education in addition to their desire to avoid teacher strikes.

A mediator's use of facts in the private sector usually is restricted to direct discussions with the negotiators. The special features of public employee negotiations may require him to utilize facts outside as well as inside the bargaining rooms. In some circumstances, however, external use of a formal report and recommendations should not be attempted; for excessive use of public recommendations might represent too great a departure from the agency's normal policies.

It does not follow that fact-finding as a step beyond mediation should be a formal procedure or that recommendations should be made without regard to their acceptability. That approach is not likely to be successful even though some public employee disputes have been resolved by such methods. Successes of this method to date have come about because the fact-finders have had a wide target area. In many jurisdictions, public employee wages and some working conditions have lagged so far behind comparable private wages and practices that a report acceptable to employees has been likely. As public employees close the gap, it will be increasingly difficult to develop recommendations that are acceptable to both sides. In other words, fact-finding will continue to be important in the public sector as a reluctant step beyond mediation, but mutual acceptability will be increasingly hard to obtain.

Impasse panel, a term now used increasingly in lieu of fact-finding panel or fact-finding board, is much more descriptive of the real function that must be performed if initial mediation steps should be unsuccessful.

Arbitration is reasonably certain to be utilized more frequently for contract disputes in public employment than in the private sector. Although arbitration of contract disputes in the private sector is widely frowned upon by both companies and unions, it has had considerable acceptance in industries most closely associated with public service. Local transit and public utilities have frequently utilized contract arbitration even where no legal impediments to the strike have existed. It is highly significant that the AFL-CIO did not oppose provisions of the recent postal legislation that bar strikes and provide for the equivalent of arbitration of new-contract disputes.

In summary, resourceful use of alternatives can keep public sector bargaining essentially strike free. The obvious danger is excessive use of arbitration or impasse-panel procedures. The only way to avoid that unhappy result is to develop maximum agreement by direct negotiation. To the extent that the assistance of neutrals may be required, effective mediation is the best form of intervention. As we proceed in this new area of collective bargaining, mediation agencies carry a heavy burden. Unless imaginative, resourceful mediation is the principal form of intervention, collective bargaining in the public sector could too easily travel the path that has bedeviled the railroad industry.

OTHER POLICY QUESTIONS

The wide variety of types of mediation agencies, mediation practices, and other impasse settlement procedures is a healthy condition. No single procedure or practice could fit the many different situations both within and between the federal, state, and local government jurisdictions. There are a few policy questions, however, that deserve comment.

Separate Mediation Agency?

At the state level, it has been noted that PERB and OCB in New York and PERC in New Jersey have been established separate and apart from the mediation agencies for private disputes. In most other states, public disputes are handled by the same agency that mediates private disputes. In the Federal Government, consideration was given to establishment of a separate federal disputes mediation agency, but Executive Order 11491 reflects a decision to assign this work to the agency that handles private disputes (the FMCS). What are the pros and cons of these two courses of action?

There are major advantages to the single-agency approach. Economy of operation is one that is almost self-evident. Even the largest mediation agencies are small. Administrative costs of two separate agencies would be greater, and a single agency is likely to attract more competent leadership than two smaller ones. Moreover, mediators usually function best when they are stationed near the source of a dispute, and a larger agency can maintain offices in more cities. There is more flexibility of case assignment in each area and to adjacent areas if there is more than one mediator at a regular station.

It might be argued that the differences between public sector and private sector mediation demand specialization and therefore separate agencies. Granted that differences exist, the similarities are even more pronounced. Required mediation skills are essentially the same. It is much easier and quicker to acquaint a skilled mediator with the peculiar features of public disputes than to make a competent mediator out of an individual who happens to have knowledge of the special features of government employment but lacks mediation experience. A larger agency can do a much better job than a small one in training new mediators and in the continuous process of keeping experienced mediators up to date on changes in collective bargaining practices.

It might also be argued that mediators who work in the private sector will seek to transplant unwanted private practices and contract clauses into government agency contracts. Admittedly this is a danger. However, it is equally clear that there are some advantages to cross-fertilization. Moreover, the dangers will not be eliminated by having two separate mediation staffs. The unions (and agency management less frequently) will attempt to inject private sector experience in any case whenever it is to their advantage. The mediator who knows both the advantages and disadvantages of private sector practice is best able to know whether it should be transplanted, modified, or disregarded in a public sector dispute.

On balance, the advantages of a single agency for mediation of public and private disputes are overwhelming—if the agency restricts itself primarily to mediation.

Full-Time Government Mediators or Part-Time Private Mediators?

PERB, OCB, and PERC do not attempt to maintain a full-time mediation staff of any size. Most of the mediation is performed on an ad hoc basis by private individuals. Most of the other agencies use staff mediators primarily, resorting occasionally to outside mediation assistance and the use of ad hoc fact-finders. It is too early to reach firm conclusions about these two approaches. However, some speculation may be hazarded.

If experience in private sector mediation is any guide, the odds are on the side of full-time government mediators. It has been shown that ad hoc mediation of private disputes has never attained significant proportions for two reasons. First, too few persons have the demonstrated mediation skills, experience, or inclination to mediate. The potential supply may be enormous, but it is extremely difficult to find the right people. It is much easier to find people who are willing to make decisions for others. Second, even when competent private mediators can be found, the logistics problems are great. To match up available men with the times and places required in a dispute is an enormous problem.

It is probable that the policies adopted to date by PERB, OCB, and PERC have been pursued primarily because there is a substantial supply of men in the northeastern section of the United States who arbitrate but who have also demonstrated mediation competence.

A significant part of the answer to future courses of action lies in the willingness of private individuals to devote the thought, time, and energy that is essential to the acquisition of mediation skills. Arbitrators will have to do more than take an occasional public mediation case when they have spare time. Nonarbitrators who have potential ability may be required to make difficult adjustments of other business activity. The National Academy of Arbitrators is embarking on a program to train arbitrators for mediation. Will the arbitrators give the time and energy to make that program successful, and will a "new crop" of competent public sector mediators emerge? If the answer to this question is affirmative, there is every reason to believe that ad hoc mediation of public disputes will increase. If the answer is negative, the agencies will have no alternative but to enlarge their staffs of full-time mediators and lessen the number of ad hoc assignments.

One possible result of a policy of not employing full-time mediators could be to emphasize fact-finding and deemphasize mediation. If mediation should be short-changed for this reason, public sector bargaining would suffer greatly.

Other Agency Functions

Another policy question is whether a public disputes mediation agency should also have such functions as unfair labor practice determination, bargaining unit determination, and conduct of representation elections. It appears that the decision to have such a structure in New York was a major reason for the creation of PERB and OCB as separate agencies. A variety of ways of handling this policy question may now be observed.

As additional states establish procedures for public sector disputes it probably will be almost necessary to combine these functions in a single agency. In most of the states where the total volume of work will be smaller than in New York, the practical considerations will result in acquisition of all public disputes functions by the same agency that mediates private disputes.

Federal v. State and Local

Logical considerations suggest that each state and many of the larger cities should establish mediation agencies for public employee disputes. The most compelling reason is that even a non-political federal agency like the FMCS should not become involved in disputes that may be intimately tied in with tax decisions of a state or a local community.

The other side of the picture is that the states and major cities are not moving fast enough. Disputes arise, and mediation is needed. Occasionally private citizens can be obtained for ad hoc service. But with increasing frequency insistent demands are made for FMCS assistance. In many areas where there are no state or local mediation agencies, federal mediators are well known, and they are the only mediators around. Hence the FMCS must fill the vacuum to the extent that its budget and manpower will permit.

The obvious danger is *de facto* acquisition of jurisdiction by the FMCS that might be difficult to undo.

Is the Public Sector an Artificial Concept?

Throughout this book, as in most labor relations discussions, the private sector and the public sector have been treated as two quite different worlds of collective bargaining. The technical distinction is reasonably clear. The public sector includes governmental agencies (federal, state, or local) and authorities established by those political units. Almost everything else is in the private sector. The private sector definition usually implies a profit-making motive. Hospitals and a variety of other nonprofit establishments not publicly owned are thus in a sort of no-man's land.

The technical distinction tends to obscure a number of realities. Type of product is not a controlling distinction. Electric light and power is predominantly privately owned and operated, but rates are regulated by agencies of government; the TVA is a governmental authority; a few cities own and operate power plants directly. The product is the same in all three circumstances, but one is considered to be in the private sector and the two others in the public sector. A number of local transit systems, once privately operated, have been acquired by municipal operating authorities. Unions are shifted overnight from private sector bargaining to public sector bargaining with no real difference in the work of the employees they represent. Retail liquor stores in Pennsylvania and certain other states are a state monopoly, owned and operated by the state. Elsewhere they are private businesses. One city collects garbage with its own equipment and employees; that is public sector. A neighboring city contracts for garbage collection, and that is private sector.

Ownership of the property is not controlling. Some munitions plants, atomic energy installations, and other defense establishments are owned by the Federal Government down to the pencils in the offices. The entire output is for the Government. But if they are operated by a private contractor, they are considered to be in the private sector. Only if employees are government employees, as in a Navy shipyard, is the operation considered to be a part of the public sector. At other defense plants, some of the buildings and part of the equipment are owned by the Government; other facilities are owned privately. Output of the establishment may be sold both to the Government and to private customers. This is private sector.

The most critical interest of the public in the bargaining process is not whether it is in the public sector or in the private sector. In a labor dispute, the question is: "How essential to the public is the product or service?" Public tolerance or intolerance of strikes does not depend on whether the operations are labeled "public" or "private." The public sector is generally considered more essential than the private sector because more of the services and products are essential.

Now that collective bargaining has arrived in the public sector, there are obvious dangers and challenges. One danger is that we will attempt to meet the problems with a proliferation of procedural devices in lieu of bargaining. If we do that, it may reasonably be predicted that bargaining will break down or never really develop. Nor would it ease the problem to make public employee strikes legal. To do so might well hasten the breakdown.

There are no easy answers—perhaps there are none at all—but the challenge is evident. It is somehow to develop viable collective bargaining in the public sector while it is in the formative stages so that it will function without excessive governmental intervention or multiplicities of procedural escapes from bargaining. It will be difficult but necessary to avoid hitting the panic button when an occasional strike occurs.

Mediation in all its manifestations is the one form of government intervention that has the potential to accomplish the desired objective. It is the only form of third-party activity that emphasizes the need to assist the parties in arriving at their own settlement.

Chapter XVI

CONCLUSIONS

Conflict can be devastating; it can also be creative. Out of cauldrons of conflict have been distilled many of the institutions and forms of behavior that we characterize as achievement and progress.

Here in Lexington, Mass., there are reminders of the fact that the shots on Lexington green and at Concord bridge contributed to the birth of a new nation almost two centuries ago. But even here it requires conscious effort to make the connection between those historic events and a primary election or the next meeting of the Town Selectmen to consider matters of importance to the citizens of this overgrown village.

Terms and conditions of employment at the workplace—one of the oldest and most persistent sources of conflict—are now usually worked out at the bargaining table by institutional methods that we call collective bargaining. In its several forums—negotiation, grievance procedure, and noncrisis dialogue—solutions are devised for the multitude of problems that arise. It is a never-ending process. A viable solution now may require revision later. New issues develop as old contentions are resolved. But the process continues, and all participants know that each issue must be resolved sometime, somehow. This inevitability is a potent influence, stimulating agreement; it is also a factor sometimes promoting a show of force intended to hasten the time of agreement.

Like all human institutions, collective bargaining is an imperfect instrument. When it works well, achievements tend to be taken for granted. Those not participating or directly affected do not even know what has happened. This is the subsurface part of the collective bargaining iceberg. But when it works poorly or when the issues are especially thorny, the conflict aspect of the process shows itself in the form of strikes or threats of strikes. This is the visible part of the iceberg.

The greatest values of collective bargaining are not the specific achievements or the details of agreements, however important these may be to the bargainers. The overriding feature of the process is that it is a mechanism for participation in decision-making. The dignity of work is enhanced when workers or their representatives join with employer representatives to determine the terms of employment. Although they may not realize it, employers are also liberated from the degrading effects of dictatorship, however benevolent.

Bargainers do not operate in a vacuum. There is a legitimate public interest in the process, especially when the conflict factors appear to be dominant. The public interest can express itself in different ways. It can attempt to repress, to prohibit, or to limit the external eruptions of conflict. It can attempt to remove the decision-making process from the bargainers and impose terms and conditions of employment from without. Or it can attempt to assist the parties in reaching their own solutions.

Mediation is the public or private exercise of the last alternative. It is not repression. It is not dictation or decision-making for others. It is third-party participation in the bargaining process to minimize the external manifestations of conflict and to maximize the chances of agreement. It is intended to hasten agreement in the least offensive way. A mediator's lack of the customary forms of power is his greatest asset. The power of persuasion can be more potent than the powers of compulsion or suppression.

Labor mediation has a longer history and a greater degree of acceptance than mediation in other conflict situations. In this age of strife in so many other areas—nation against nation, minority groups striving for dignity and economic equality, alienation of parent and child, student upheavals in schools and colleges, and sharply increasing violence in the streets—do the principles and practices of labor mediation offer any solutions?

One of the few books that has been written about mediation [1] is directed to that question with special emphasis on the similarities and differences of mediation in international disputes and labor disputes. The National Center for Disputes Settlement [2] and the more recently established Board of Mediation for Community Disputes [3] are seeking to utilize basic mediation principles in various conflict situations. These activities are in conflict areas such as (1) claims of job discrimination, (2) landlord—tenant

---

[1] MEETING OF MINDS, by Elmore Jackson, McGraw-Hill, 1952.

[2] The National Center For Dispute Settlement with headquarters in Washington, D. C., is affiliated with the American Arbitration Association and is supported, in part, by grants from the Ford Foundation. It was established early in 1968.

[3] The Board of Mediation for Community Disputes in New York City is affiliated with Automation House. It also is supported, in part, by a Ford Foundation grant. It began operations early in 1970.

disputes, (3) consumer—retailer disputes, (4) student—faculty —administration disputes in schools and colleges, and (5) public employee disputes in areas not served by established mediation agencies.

It is not suggested that labor mediation techniques can be transferred without modification and inventiveness. But the basic principles are not dissimilar. Moreover, as experience is gained in mediation in these other areas, labor mediation can benefit by the infusion of new ideas and methods developed elsewhere.

If there is an aura of evangelism about mediation in this book, it is intentional. Of all forms of intervention, it more than any other is dedicated to *nonrepressive assistance in problem-solving —by and not for the individuals or groups involved in a conflict situation.*

APPENDIX A

MEDIATION AGENCY DATA AND MEDIATION AND RELATED EXPERIENCE OF ARBITRATORS

PURPOSE AND METHODOLOGY OF STUDY

No comprehensive data are available about the extent of mediation and related activity in the United States. The principal federal agencies (Federal Mediation and Conciliation Service and National Mediation Board) and some state agencies publish annual reports. Other state and local agencies have no regular public reporting systems. Federal and state agencies that do issue annual reports employ quite different record-keeping and reporting arrangements.

A first purpose of this study was to attempt to secure both comprehensive and comparable data from all federal, state, and local mediation agencies. To accomplish this result, a questionnaire (Exhibit A-1) was mailed to all known agencies in June 1969. The same questionnaire plus requests for supplemental data were submitted to the FMCS and to the NMB. In some instances, information from these various inquiries has been augmented by personal conversations.

As will be noted by reference to Exhibit A-1, basic agency information requested was limited to calendar year 1968. The FMCS, the NMB, and some state agencies have reported on that basis. Some state-agency reports are for fiscal years extending into 1969 or 1967. However, all the reports are for one full year of mediation activity and can be considered as representative of calendar year 1968. Historical trends would be of interest but are beyond the scope of this study. In any event, the 1968 data are quite representative of all years in the last half of the 1960's with one exception. Public employee disputes, while important, had not attained the heights that probably were reached in 1969 and can be expected in the 1970s.

The second major purpose of the study was to try to obtain comprehensive information about ad hoc mediation and related activity by individuals not employed full time by any mediation agency. No information of consequence is presently available on this subject. Some agencies occasionally employ ad hoc private mediators, but agency reports do not fully reflect the extent or absence of this practice. Officials at the federal and state levels sometimes appoint ad

hoc mediators or fact-finders, but no single source of information provides adequate data about such work. Companies and unions may employ private mediators, but only the parties involved may be aware of
it. The result is that notions exist that have little factual basis. At
one extreme, there are some who believe that George Taylor, Ted
Kheel, Dave Cole, or a handful of other well-known persons mediate
virtually all disputes of any importance; the work of many others and
of the agencies is unknown. At the other extreme, there is an understandable tendency for agency mediators and officials to think that
their own agency performs most of the important mediation functions. Statistics can never portray fully the significance of any segment
of activity, but it is believed that a useful purpose will be achieved in
presentation of facts.

The task of acquiring adequate and accurate information is a formidable one. The approach here was to assume that the bulk of the
labor mediation and related ad hoc work is being performed by persons who also do arbitration work. With numerous qualifications and
exceptions, this is a valid assumption. Accordingly, Exhibit A-2 is a
questionnaire that was mailed early in June 1969 to all members of
the National Academy of Arbitrators and to a selected list of arbitrators who are not members. The NAA is the only professional organization of labor arbitrators. It includes within its membership most of
the better known arbitrators in the United States. The nonmember
arbitrators were selected from a list of some 500 additional arbitrators
on the roster maintained by the Federal Mediation and Conciliation
Service and from lists secured from state agencies. The selection was
by the author on a basis of relative amounts of arbitration and fact-
finding work performed, as known by the FMCS, and somewhat hap-
hazard guesses and occasional information about work by these and
other individuals outside the grievance arbitration area.

It is recognized that the 473 questionnaires mailed do not "cover
the waterfront." Mediation and fact-finding work is not confined
solely to arbitrators. Even among arbitrators, men who received no
questionnaires may have been quite active. However, a method of
cross-checking is available in this overall study. By comparing the
agency reports against the totals of the individual reports, it is possible to obtain a good estimate of the ad hoc work that has been
missed.

By combining the agency and individual reports for calendar year
1968, it is possible to obtain a reasonably accurate picture as to who
performed mediation and fact-finding during that year and in what
volume.

Another purpose of the questionnaire sent to individuals was to obtain a sort of lifetime profile of mediation and related work. To what
extent have the arbitrators performed labor relations functions that
have not included decision-making authority? Answers to this ques-

tion are of some interest and may cast light on experience qualifications for mediation.

Response to Questionnaires

At the federal level, the Federal Mediation and Conciliation Service and the National Mediation Board have cooperated fully. Forty-three states and Puerto Rico answered the questionnaire. In three of these states two state mediation agencies exist, and complete coverage was obtained. In New York, the New York State Board of Mediation works in the private area and the Public Employee Relations Board (PERB) in the public sector. In New Jersey, a similar division of responsibility exists between the New Jersey State Board of Mediation and the Public Employee Relations Commission (PERC). PERC was not established until late in 1968, but some public sector disputes prior to that time were handled by the mediation board. The New Jersey data are complete for the year. In Maine, no full-time state mediators are employed; a report from the Department of Labor and Industry covers a small amount of mediation work performed by administrative employees of the Department, and another report from an ad-hoc Panel of Mediators covers the additional mediation activity.

No answers were received from Colorado, Louisiana, Mississippi, Missouri, South Dakota, Texas, or West Virginia. However, six of these states perform no mediation functions, and mediation activity in Missouri is confined primarily to a very small number of public utility disputes. Thus, the state coverage can be considered to be virtually complete.

Five local agencies are known to exist, and all five answered the questionnaire. They are the Office of Collective Bargaining in New York City, the Louisville (Kentucky) Labor-Management Committee, the Toledo (Ohio) Labor-Management Citizen's Committee, the Suffolk County (New York) Department of Labor, and the Citizen's Committee of Greater Wilkes-Barre (Pennsylvania). A few other local mediation committees have been created from time to time, but these five are the only ones known to the author that have had substantial continuity and were active in 1968. So-called mini-PERB's (local agencies in New York) are included in the PERB data.

The response to the individual questionnaires sent to arbitrators was amazingly complete. Replies were received from 323 of the 346 United States members of the National Academy of Arbitrators to whom questionnaires were sent. This is a better than 93-percent response. Moreover, examination of the list of names of the 23 who did not respond would suggest that more than half of them probably did no mediation or related work in 1968. None of the Academy members generally known to have performed any substantial amount of ad hoc mediation or fact-finding work failed to reply.

The response by nonmembers of the Academy was not quite so good. One hundred of 127 questionnaires were returned, a 79-percent response.

On an overall basis, the 423 replies to 473 inquiries (a response rate of about 90 percent) can be said to be more than satisfactory.

Problems of Definition

Since a primary purpose is to depict comparable data for the year 1968, the first questions are what data to present and how to secure it. Two measures are obtainable. One is mediation time; the other is numbers of cases handled. Both present some problems. A preliminary question of importance is how to draw a line between mediation and arbitration.

LINE BETWEEN MEDIATION AND ARBITRATION

For purposes of this study, all reported activities of third parties in disputes settlement or prevention of disputes were considered as forms of mediation if the individual had no decision-making authority. What is normally called mediation or concilation was counted up to and including the use of mediator package recommendations. Fact-finding was included provided that the parties were not bound to accept recommendations. Special boards or panels were included, again provided that any recommendations could be rejected. Arbitration in any form was not included. Moreover, a case was not counted if the arbitrator had the power to decide even though the issues might have been settled by mediatory tactics. This division is consistent with the introductory comments in Chapter II.

MEDIATION TIME

The basic time measure utilized here is the mediator-year. It has been customary to classify mediation agencies by size of the full-time nonsupervisory mediation work force. This measure requires adjustment. Mediators employed by some agencies perform certain functions not considered here as mediation. A few agencies provide free arbitration by mediators. Several agencies conduct representation elections and otherwise assist in determination of representation rights. In a few instances, mediators may perform factory safety inspections under state laws. Information was sought (see Question 9 (b) of Exhibit A-1) to permit a downward adjustment of full-time mediators to reflect the net time devoted to mediation.

Upward adjustment has been made to reflect a different circumstance. Administrative or supervisory employees, frequently going as high as the head of the agency, often devote some time to active mediation. Answers to Question 3 of Exhibit A-1 permit the addition of such mediation time.

In short, for all mediation agencies, net mediator-years have been obtained by (1) starting with the full-time non-supervisory mediation staff, (2) adding mediator-years, if any, attributable to active mediation by supervisors and administrators, and (3) subtracting mediator-years, if any, attributable to activities not considered mediation.

For the arbitrators (Exhibit A-2), information was requested as to total days of work in 1968 on the ad hoc cases reported. These days have been totaled for each category. Assuming a five-day work week and allowing for vacations, holidays, and illness, about 200 reported days could be considered as one mediator-year. However, a lower figure will be used to assure full equivalency with agency mediation. Agency mediators necessarily spend considerable time on the telephone and in personal conversations with the parties on cases that are assigned to them for checking and investigation but never become "active cases." That time is part of a mediator-year for an agency mediator. No counterpart of that time has been allowed for by the arbitrators who have reported only days spent on active cases. As an admittedly rough measure, but appropriate to this study, 150 days spent on ad hoc cases will be considered a mediator-year.

ACTIVE CASES

An alternative measure is number of cases. All agencies and individuals have reported case figures.

It should be recognized at the outset that number of cases is an imperfect measure. At one extreme, the parties may settle a relatively simple dispute a few hours after the mediator first enters the room. At the other end of the spectrum, a single important case may require two or three months of mediation time. An average active case, in recent FMCS experience, requires approximately four days of a mediator's time with the parties plus additional time away from the bargaining rooms. Available evidence indicates somewhat less time for state and local agency disputes in the private sector. Disputes in the public sector appear to average more than four days of mediator or fact-finder time.

Despite these imperfections, case figures are of importance. As indicated elsewhere, they provide a measure of the extent to which bargainers utilize mediation. Moreover, within the context of a comprehensive analysis of mediation, they provide a basis for comparison of the several types of mediation.

But the word "case" requires further definition. The problem may be illustrated by the two types of cases now used in FMCS reports. An "assigned case" is a potential dispute referred to a mediator for checking and follow-up until it is settled. An "active case" is one of these assigned cases that does develop into a dispute *and* that requires the actual presence of the mediator in the bargaining room for varying periods of time. In the most recent reporting year, only about 43 percent of assigned cases developed into active cases. For purposes of this study, only the active cases were counted.

State agencies have various methods of record keeping and case definition. A comparative study would be of limited value if case definitions varied widely. The author has analyzed the data from all the state agencies in a variety of ways and has concluded that almost all of the states have used a reasonable approximation of the same "active case" definition in responding to the questionnaires. In two states that shall be unnamed here, the case data are out of line on the high side, and in one of these notably so. The state agency in question insists that its data are accurate and in accordance with the definition. Accordingly, I have used the doubted figures without change. In any event, the questionable data do not affect the totals significantly.

In order not to identify by indirection the two states noted above and, more importantly, because some minor differences in definition may exist elsewhere, the data shown in tables that follow group the states in the following categories:

1. States reporting 10 or more mediator-years:
   New York (State Board and PERB)
   Michigan
   California
   Pennsylvania

2. States (and Puerto Rico) reporting five or more but less than 10 mediator-years:
   Minnesota
   Massachusetts
   Puerto Rico
   New Jersey (State Board and PERC)
   Wisconsin
   Illinois

3. States reporting one or more but less than five mediator-years:
   Connecticut
   Alabama
   Indiana
   South Carolina
   Rhode Island
   North Carolina
   Oregon
   Washington
   Arkansas

4. States employing no full-time mediators but reporting one or more cases mediated by administrative or supervisory personnel in state labor department:

    Maine (Panel of Mediators and Department Personnel)

    Alaska

    Idaho

    Maryland

    Kansas

    Wyoming

    Vermont

    Delaware

5. States with no mediators and no cases reported: 24 states (all those not listed above)

Within each grouping, the states are listed in descending order of the best available measures of size of the mediation operations in the state.

MEDIATOR MAN-YEARS AND CASES REPORTED

Federal

Utilizing the definitions and distinctions noted above, Table A-1 shows the mediator man-years and case-load data for the Federal Mediation and Conciliation Service and for the National Mediation Board.

State and Local

Table A-2 summarizes the data for all state and local mediation agencies.

Private Mediators

Table A-3 summarizes the information received from 423 arbitrators. Since these 423 arbitrators did not perform all the ad hoc work, I have examined in detail the various state agency and individual reports, the evidence as to work obtained directly from the parties, and other available evidence to permit reasonably reliable estimates of the ad hoc work that was missed by the individual-questionnaire method. Table A-4 shows the allowances made.

Totals for All Mediation and Fact-Finding in 1968

Table A-5 combines the data in Tables A-1, A-2, A-3, and A-4. This total information is also the basis for the chart that appears in Chapter III.

As indicated by footnotes to Table A-5, the total number of reported cases is somewhat greater than the total number of disputes. A principal cause of this is mediation of the same dispute by a federal and a state mediator. By separate calculations, not shown in detail but based on the estimated extent of dual mediation in the various states, I estimate that about 1,000 disputes were mediated on a dual basis in 1968. Some duplication also exists by reason of the fact that some of the state and local agencies (notably PERB and OCB) reported cases that were also reported by individual arbitrators. Practically all of this duplication occurs in public employee disputes. In a very few instances, two or three individuals who served as a panel of mediators or fact-finders may have reported the same case, again resulting in somewhat more reported cases than actual disputes.

The mediator man-year grand total also includes a small amount of duplication by reason of state agency and individual reporting of the same time. Dual mediation does not have any effect on total mediator man-days because both mediators were active in the same case.

Table A-1

Mediation Man-Years and Cases Reported
Federal Mediation and Conciliation Service
and National Mediation Board, 1968

Mediator Man-Years	FMCS	NMB
Full-time mediators	271.0	20.0
Plus: administrative and supervisory		
mediation time	3.0	2.4
Ad hoc mediators	0.2	
Less: Work on representation cases		4.0
Totals	274.2	18.4
Types of Cases (active only)		
Contract—private sector	7587	300
Grievance	283	
Public sector	20	
Preventive mediation	1322	
Totals	9212	300

Table A-2

Mediator Man-Years and Case Load
State and Local Mediation Agencies, 1968

Type of Agency and Size (Mediator Man-Years)	Mediator Man-Years				Case Load (Active Cases)				
	Full-Time Mediators	Adminis-trative & Super-visory	Outside Ex-perts[7] (Ad hoc)	Total	Contract Private Sector	Griev-ance	Public Sector	Preven-tive Media-tion	Total
State									
10 or more [1]	50.1	10.4	8.8	69.3	1919	326	563		2808
5-10 [2]	34.9	2.2	0.1	37.2	1584	565	217	28	2394
1-5 [3]	19.0	3.1	0.5	22.6	642	105	144	6	897
No full-time media-tors[4]		1.3	0.6	1.9	73	49	4		126
No full-time media-tors[5]		0.3		0.3					
Local[6]		3.7	1.5	5.2	108	119	48	15	290
Totals	104.0	21.0	11.5	136.5	4326	1164	976	49	6515

Note: Where states are listed below, they are in descending order by size of agency.

[1] 10 or more mediator man-years—4 states: New York (State Board and PERB), Michigan, California, and Pennsylvania.

[2] 5-10 mediator man-years—5 states and Puerto Rico: Minnesota, Massachusetts, Puerto Rico, New Jersey, Wisconsin, and Illinois.

[3] 1-5 mediator man-years—9 states: Connecticut, Alabama, Indiana, South Carolina, Rhode Island, North Carolina, Oregon, Washington, and Arkansas.

[4] No full-time mediators; one or more cases mediated by administrative or super-visory personnel—8 states: Maine, Alaska, Idaho, Maryland, Kansas, Wyoming, Vermont, and Delaware.

[5] No full-time mediators; no cases reported—24 states: all states not listed above.

[6] Local agencies; no full-time mediators but cases reported—5 agencies: Office of Collective Bargaining (New York City), Louisville Labor-Management Committee, Toledo Labor-Management Citizens Committee, Suffolk County (N.Y.) Depart-ment of Labor, and Citizens Committee of Greater Wilkes-Barre (Pa.).

[7] Includes fact-finding.

Table A-3

Mediation and Fact-Finding by 423 Arbitrators[1]

Ad Hoc Appointments, 1968

Sources of Appointments and Types of Cases	Members—NAA			Nonmembers of NAA			Totals		
	Arb.	Cases[2]	Days	Arb.	Cases[2]	Days	Arb.	Cases[2]	Days
Source of Appointment									
Federal									
President	3	3	98	1	1	50	4	4	148
Secretary of Labor	2	3	23	1	1	2	3	4	25
FMCS	1	1	8				1	1	8
National Mediation Board	1	1	3				1	1	3
Atomic Energy L-M Panel	2	5	25				2	5	25
Other	2	2	32				2	2	32
Federal subtotal	9[3]	15	189	2	2	52	11[3]	17	241
State and local									
State or local agency	51	197	820	17	87	374	68	284	1194
Governor	4	5	16	1	1	10	5	6	26
Other (mayors, etc.)	15	33	217	4	20	38	19	53	255
State and local subtotal	55[3]	235	1053	21[3]	108	422	76[3]	343	1475
Nongovernmental agency (AAA)	12	19	96	2	2	10	14	21	106
Parties direct	17	76	225	5	12	79	23	88	304
Totals	68[3]	345	1563	24[3]	124	563	92[3]	469	2126
No experience in 1968	255			76			331		
Percent with appointments in 1968	21%			24%			22%		
Type of Case									
Contract—private sector	25	72	469	3	7	59	28	79	528
Grievance	10	53	66	5	19	85	15	72	151
Public sector	58	220	1028	19	98	419	77	318	1447
Totals	68[3]	345	1563	24[3]	124	563	92[3]	469	2126[4]

[1] 323 members of National Academy of Arbitrators and 100 nonmember arbitrators.
[2] Cases are as reported by arbitrators. Therefore, if three arbitrators were on the same panel, case totals would show three cases.
[3] Totals less than sums because some individuals reported more than one source of appointment or more than one type of case.
[4] 150 days being an approximate mediator-year for active cases, total is 14.2 man-years.

Table A-4

Ad Hoc Mediation and Fact-Finding by Private Individuals
Allowances for Work Missed by Questionnaires, 1968

	Reported by 423 Arbitrators (Table A-3)		Estimated Additions for Work Missed	Totals		
	Cases	Days	%	Cases	Days	Mediator Man-Years
Contract—private sector	79	528	20%	95	634	4.2
Grievance	72	151	20%	86	181	1.2
Public sector	318	1447	50%	477	2170	14.5
Noncrisis dialogue						1.0[1]
Totals	469	2126		658	2985	21.0

[1] Total estimate for year.

Table A-5

Mediation and Fact Finding 1968

	Cases						Mediator Man-Years	
	Contract Private Sector	Griev- ances	Public Sector	Non- crisis Dia- logue	Totals	Percent of Total Cases	Man-Yrs.	Percent of Total Man-Yrs.
Federal								
FMCS	7587	283	20	1322	9212	55.2%	274.2	60.9%
NMB	300				300	1.8	18.4	4.1
Federal-total	7887	283	20	1322	9512	57.0	292.6[3]	65.0
State and local agencies	4326	1164	976	49	6515	39.0	136.5	30.3
Ad hoc work by individuals	95	86	477		658	4.0	21.0	4.7
	12308[1]	1533	1473[2]	1371	16685	100 %	450.1	100 %
Percent of total cases	73.8%	9.2%	8.8%	8.2%	100%			

[1] This total includes approximately 1,000 cases dually mediated by federal and state mediators. Therefore, the total of private sector contract disputes mediated in 1968 was about 11,300 disputes.

[2] This total includes approximately 370 cases reported both by a state agency and an individual. Therefore, the total number of public sector disputes in 1968 that required mediation and/or fact-finding was about 1,100 disputes.

[3] This total does not include approximately one (1) mediator-year by Department of Labor personnel in 1968.

MEDIATION AND RELATED EXPERIENCE OF ARBITRATORS—LABOR RELATIONS LIFETIME

The labor relations lifetime experience of the 423 arbitrators has been secured in two segments.

Full-Time or Part-Time With Continuing Appointment

Table A-6 gives information about those arbitrators who were full-time employees of an agency for a period of time in mediation or related disputes work or who worked part-time but with sufficient continuity of appointment to be significant.

Less than 30 percent of the arbitrators had had experience with any of the agencies listed.

It will be noted that 14.9 percent of the total had experience with the National War Labor Board and that 16.1 percent had some period of full-time employment by a federal or state mediation agency. Interestingly enough, the National Academy of Arbitrators, sometimes facetiously referred to as the National War Labor Board Alumni Association, now includes only 17.3 percent of members who had NWLB experience. Moreover the number of members who have had full-time mediation agency experience is now almost as great (15.5 percent).

Ad Hoc Appointments

Table A-7 shows the ad hoc appointments reported by the same 423 arbitrators in two ways: (1) source of the appointments and (2) type of cases.

Only 47 percent of all the arbitrators reporting had received any ad hoc appointments from any source other than their regular grievance arbitration work during their entire labor relations lifetimes. Appointments by state and local agencies, primarily as fact-finders, account for about one half of the total appointments.

The breakdown between private sector contract cases, grievances, and public sector disputes shows reasonably equal numbers of cases in all three categories. However, the growing importance of public sector disputes is highlighted by reference to Table A-3. Of the lifetime total of 839 such disputes which runs up to mid-1969, 318 were secured in the one year of 1968. In 1968, public sector cases represented 68 percent of all ad hoc cases.

Table A-6

Mediation and Related Experience by 423 Arbitrators[1]
Full-Time Work Experience or Part-Time With Continuing Appointment,
Labor Relations Lifetime

Agency	Members—NAA		Nonmembers of NAA		Totals	
	Arb.	Percent Reporting	Arb.	Percent Reporting	Arb.	Percent Reporting
Experience Background[2]						
National War Labor Board	56	17.3	7	7.0	63	14.9
Wage Stabilization Board	16	5.0	2	2.0	18	4.3
Atomic Energy L-M Panel	6	1.9	2	2.0	8	1.9
Missile Sites Labor Comm.	4	1.2	1	1.0	5	1.2
Full-time mediators (Federal or state agency)	50	15.5	18	18.0	68	16.1
Total	98[3]	30.3%	25[3]	25.0%	123[3]	29.1%
No Experience of Types Noted Above	225	69.7%	75	75.0%	300	70.9%

[1] 323 members of National Academy of Arbitrators and 100 nonmember selected arbitrators.

[2] Arbitrators included only if they reported full-time experience for a period of time or continuing part-time assignment to an agency.

[3] Totals less than sums because some individuals reported work for more than one agency.

Table A-7
Mediation and Related Experience of 423 Arbitrators[1]
Ad Hoc Appointments, Labor Relations Lifetime

Source of Appointment and	Members—NAA		Nonmembers of NAA		Totals	
Type of Case	Arb.	Cases[2]	Arb.	Cases[2]	Arb.	Cases[2]
Source of Appointment						
Federal						
President	44	154	4	9	48	163
Secretary of Labor	19	40	2	3	21	43
FMCS	16	44	2	2	18	46
NMB	13	34			13	34
Other	14	14	3	3	17	17
Federal Subtotals	65[3]	286	8[3]	17	73[3]	303
State and Local						
State or local agency	70	659	24	359	94	1018
Governor	25	57	5	8	30	65
Other (Mayors, etc.)	37	161	9	35	46	196
State and local Subtotals	102[3]	877	36[3]	402	138[3]	1279
Nongovernmental agency (AAA)	23	78	3	15	26	93
Parties direct	58	575	14	307	72	882
Totals	155[3]	1816	45[3]	741	200[3]	2557
No ad hoc experience	168		55		223	
Percent with ad hoc appointment in lifetime	48%		45%		47%	
Type of Case						
Contract—private sector	84	654	15	278	99	932
Grievance	34	536	10	250	44	786
Public sector	102	626	31	213	133	839
Totals	155[3]	1816	45[3]	741	200[3]	2557

[1] 323 members of National Academy of Arbitrators and 100 nonmember selected arbitrators.

[2] Cases are as reported by arbitrators. Therefore, if three arbitrators were on the same panel, case totals would show three cases.

[3] Totals less than sums because some individuals reported more than one source of appointment or more than one type of case.

Exhibit A-1

STATE OR CITY LABOR AGENCY
MEDIATION QUESTIONNAIRE

Date_____

1. Name of Agency _____

   Address _____

   _____

   _____

   Person answering
   this questionnaire _____
                                 Name and Title

   _____
                              Telephone Number

2. Please check appropriate box below:

   a. This agency has statutory or delegated authority to mediate labor disputes. In addition to supervisory and administrative personnel, it employs on a *full-time basis* persons whose primary function is to mediate and who *have no supervisory responsibilities for other mediators.*   ☐ [1]

   b. This agency has statutory or delegated authority to mediate labor disputes. It employs no full-time mediators, but mediation work is performed by supervisory or administrative personnel or by other employees who do a substantial amount of other work or by nongovernmental labor relations experts appointed by the agency.   ☐ [2]

   c. This agency has no statutory or delegated authority to mediate labor disputes and:

      (1) Such work is performed in this (State, City) by: ☐ [3]

   _____
                          State or City Agency
                          or Title of Official

----

[1] If box 2a is checked, please answer all questions in this questionnaire.
[2] If box 2b is checked, please answer questions 3, 4, 5, 6, and 7 and ignore the subsequent questions.

_____

_____

Address

(2) This (State, City) performs no labor media-
    tion work.   ☐ ³

3. What administrative or supervisory officials or other personnel in the
   agency (other than non-supervisory mediators) performed actual mediation work during calendar year 1968 and what approximate percentage
   of a full-time mediation year was performed in 1968 by each such
   person?

                                                        Approximate
                                                        Percentage of
                                                          full-time
                                                       mediation year

Head of Agency:

_____   _____

              Name

_____

              Title

Other Agency Personnel:

_____   _____   _____

        Name   Title

_____   _____   _____

        Name   Title

_____   _____   _____

        Name   Title

_____   _____   _____

        Name   Title

_____   _____

        Name   Title

                                                       Yes   No
4. (a) Did the agency employ part-time outside ex-
       perts as mediators during calendar year 1968?   ☐   ☐

   (b) If the answer is yes:
       (1) How many such persons were employed
           in 1968?   _____
       (2) Approximately how many total days did
           all such persons devote to mediation for
           your agency in 1968?   _____

_____

³ If box 2c (1) or 2c (2) is checked, no additional questions need be answered.

5. During calendar year 1968, how many active mediation cases [1] were completed [2] by your agency?   _____ cases

6. If a breakdown of the cases included in question 5 is available, please indicate the breakdown as follows. If precise breakdowns are not available, your estimates will be quite acceptable but label them as estimates.

   Labor contract renewals or initial
   contract negotiations in the private sector   _____ cases

   Grievance cases   _____ cases

   Cases involving employees of a governmental
   agency or non-profit organization   _____ cases

   Preventive mediation cases [3]   _____ cases

   Other _____   _____ cases

                        Total   _____ cases

7. Does your agency have a yearly or other periodic printed report?

   Yes   No
   ☐   ☐

   If so, please send copy of latest report.

8. How many full-time persons whose primary function was labor mediation and who had no supervisory responsibilities for other mediators were employed by your agency as of January 1, 1969?
                                                         _____ [4]
                                                         Number

---

[1] An "active mediation case" is defined as a case in which the mediator actually participated with the parties at the bargaining table. If your agency statistics do not disclose such data readily or a good approximation on this basis cannot be made, please submit what data are available with a brief explanation of the criteria used.

[2] Since some cases are usually in process both at the beginning and at the end of a period of time, cases actually completed will normally be representative. If a substantial difference existed between the "in process" cases at the beginning and at the end of the period—enough to make the closed cases not representative—please explain. If data for the January 1, 1968, to December 31, 1968, period are not readily available, the closest possible one-year period will suffice but please note the time period used.

[3] A preventive mediation case is defined as a situation involving parties to a specific bargaining relationship in which the mediator actually participated actively with the parties in a labor-management committee, study committee or other similar activity where no strike existed or was threatened by a contractual or announced deadline or by a strikeable grievance. It does not include attendance at conferences or seminars or other public labor relations functions, with or without responsibilities for the program.

[4] If the number employed as of January 1, 1969, was abnormal for any reason, complete the answer as of January 1, 1969, but explain the abnormality in a separate statement.

9. (a) Did any or all of these full-time
mediators or their predecessors
perform any significant functions
other than labor mediation during   Yes   No
calendar year 1968?   ☐   ☐

   (b) If the answer is yes, indicate the
approximate percentage of total time
devoted to these other activities as follows:

Approximate Percentage[1]
of total time in calendar
year 1968

Arbitration   _____

Representation Matters   _____
Factory safety inspection,
     wage and hour regulations, etc.   _____
Teaching[2]   _____
Other (specify)   _____

10. How are new mediators selected by your agency?
    (a) By Agency Head from Civil Service Roster   ☐

    (b) By Agency Head but not from Civil Service Roster ☐

    (c) By other method   ☐
        Specify _____
                _____
                _____

11. Does your agency have minimum requirements for
    new mediator employment?
                                            Yes   No
    (a) Experience   ☐   ☐
        If so, explain briefly _____
        _____
        _____

                                            Yes   No
    (b) Education   ☐   ☐
        If so, explain briefly _____
        _____

---

[1] An analysis for each mediator is not required. Use your best approximation of a weighted average percentage for all the mediators noted in question 8.
[2] Teaching should not be noted here if it occurred outside normal working hours and did not interfere with a normal full-time mediation work load.

12. (a) Do full-time mediators employed by   Yes   No
     your agency have civil service tenure rights?   ☐   ☐

    (b) If civil service tenure rights are not
     applicable, what other tenure rights, if
     any, are applicable? Explain briefly _____

_____

_____

13. Explain briefly here or on a separate page, the new mediator
training procedures of your agency _____

_____

_____

14. Does your agency have an established salary range   Yes   No
for full-time non-supervisory mediators?   ☐   ☐

If so, please indicate the range applicable
as of January 1, 1969, for each
classification of nonsupervisory
mediators:

Classification	Range	
	Minimum	Maximum
____	__	__
____	__	__
____	__	__

15. Are increases certain or expected   Yes   No
during calendar year 1969?   ☐   ☐

If so, please indicate extent of
known or probable increases:

Exhibit A-2

INDIVIDUAL LABOR MEDIATION QUESTIONNAIRE

Name _____ Date_____

Address _____

_____

1. Have you ever acted as a mediator
   in a labor dispute (See letter   Yes   No
   before answering this question.)   ☐   ☐

   If the answer to question 1 is yes,
   please complete the following questions:

2. What over-all span of time covers
   your experience in labor mediation?   _____ to _____
                                        year   year

3. Were you ever employed full-time by
   an identifiable labor mediation   Yes   No
   agency as a labor mediator?   ☐   ☐
   (Exclude National War Labor Board,
   and Disputes Boards during Korean
   War in answering this question.)

   If the answer is yes, indicate the
   agency and approximate time period:

   _____   _____
               Agency   Time period

   _____   _____
               Agency   Time period

   Please *exclude* experience covered
   by this question 3 when answering
   all following questions.

4. What was the source of your selection
   or appointment as a labor mediator
   and how many cases or time periods   Approximate Number of
   were involved?   Cases or Time Periods

   (a) Federal Appointment by:
         President
                                         _____
                                            Cases

         Secretary of Labor
                                           _____
                                            Cases

Federal Mediation and
Conciliation Service
(not arbitration)

_____
Cases

National Mediation Board
(not Adjustment Board)

_____
Cases

Atomic Energy Labor
Relations Panel

_____
Time period

Missile Sites Labor
Commission (disputes only)

_____
Time Period

Taft-Hartley Board
(only if given
authority to mediate)

_____
Time Period

National War Labor Board
(disputes only—do not
count stabilization functions)

_____
Time Period

Disputes Board During Korean
War (disputes only—do not
count stabilization functions)

_____
Time Period

Other _____

       (specify)

_____
Cases or
Time Period

(b) Appointment by State or
local government agency:

State Mediation Agency:

_____

       (specify)

_____
Cases

Governor:

_____

       (specify State)

_____
Cases

Other:

_____

       (specify)

_____
Cases

(c) Appointment by Non-
governmental association:

_____

       (specify)

_____
Cases

_____

       (specify)

_____
Cases

(d) Direct selection by disputing
parties:

_____ (specify)	_____ Cases
_____ (specify)	_____ Cases

5. In your total labor mediation experience
covered by question 4 above, approximately
how many cases were involved?
Grievances Only

_____ Cases

Disputes involving employees
of governmental units (Federal,
State or local) or non-profit-
making organizations

_____ Cases

6. Did you actually serve as a labor
mediator during calendar year 1968?

Yes ☐ No ☐

If the answer is yes, complete the following:

	Number of Cases	Approximate Number of Days of Service
(a) Federal Appointment by:		
President	_____	_____
Secretary of Labor	_____	_____
Federal Mediation and Conciliation Service	_____	_____
National Mediation Board (not Adjustment Board)	_____	_____
Atomic Energy Labor Relations Panel	_____	_____
Taft-Hartley Board (only if given authority to mediate)	_____	_____
Other _____ (specify)	_____	_____
(b) Appointment by State or local governmental agency:		
State Mediation Agency:	_____	_____
_____ (specify)		
Governor:	_____	_____
_____ (specify)		

Other: ———— ————

_____
(specify)

(c) Appointment by non-
governmental association: ———— ————

_____
(specify)

(d) Direct selection by
disputing parties: ———— ————

_____
(specify)

TOTAL 1968 ACTIVITY AS
A LABOR MEDIATOR ———— ————

Included in this total,
the following were:

Grievances only ———— ————

Disputes involving
employees of govern-
mental units or non-
profitmaking organiza-
tions ———— ————

MEDIATOR SELECTION PROCEDURE

(Federal Mediation and Conciliation Service, 1961-1969)

The details of the FMCS mediator selection process during the 1961-1969 period are outlined below.

No formal recruiting program existed. Many applicants were labor or management representatives who had worked with FMCS mediators in disputes and who became interested by reason of this type of personal exposure. FMCS mediators were advised to encourage and even seek out management and union representatives who might be promising candidates. However, they were also advised that no commitments of any sort could be made. In other words, an informal but no-commitment sponsorship arrangement accounted for many applications. Teachers of labor relations at the graduate level at a number of universities were encouraged to advise their more mature students and ex-students about mediation. A very large number of applications and inquiries were received, the source of stimulation being unknown.

All applicants filed the standard Federal Government application forms. These applications were analyzed in the Washington office. Many applicants clearly not qualifying either for mediator or mediator-trainee positions were rejected, and the applicants were so notified promptly.

At this first screening step at the Washington office, applications were examined first in the light of the normal FMCS qualification standards, which are summarized as follows:

1. Length of Qualifying Experience

   Minimum of seven years of satisfactory qualifying experience for GS-12 hiring rate (six years for GS-11).

2. Education

   No minimum education requirement but two years' credit for bachelor's degree and three years' credit for advanced degree (master's or better).

   These education credits can be applied to reduce the total of normally required years of satisfactory qualifying experience.

3. Satisfactory Qualifying Experience Other Than Education

   a. Management Background

      (1) Negotiation and preparation for contract bargaining in a responsible capacity.

      (2) Grievance procedure and/or arbitration presentation in a responsible capacity.

      (3) Personnel administration, but only if very closely related to negotiation and grievance procedure.

   b. Labor Union Background

      (1) Negotiation and preparation for contract bargaining in a responsible capacity.

      (2) Grievance procedure and/or arbitration presentation in a responsible capacity.

   c. Other Experience

   Mediation, teaching, arbitration, National Labor Relations Board experience, or other work in a neutral capacity closely related to labor relations.

It will be noted that actual experience at the bargaining table is the prime requirement, only partially offset by education.

Applicants not meeting these normal standards were not rejected automatically. The screening committee, including the Deputy Director, who was an experienced mediator, held open all otherwise promising applications that did not technically meet the criteria. A careful appraisal of possible candidates for mediator-trainee positions was also a part of the screening process.

Applications of all persons who seemed to possess the requisite qualifications "on paper" or were otherwise interesting passed this first screening process.

The second screening step was made by the regional director in the area in which the applicant happened to reside. The first actions of the regional director were to conduct personally or supervise two lines of informal *confidential* inquiry. All mediators in the region who might know the applicant were asked for their opinions. The regional director also made informal confidential inquiry in labor and management ranks of persons of integrity who might know the applicant. Such inquiry was not limited to the persons listed on the application as references. Because of the recognized importance of good mediator selection, there exists in all areas of the country a very sizable number of management and union leaders who know the work of the Service and who are willing to give candid confidential opinions. This is especially important as respects advice from persons on the other side of the labor-management fence from the applicant.

If these confidential inquiries of mediators and labor and manage‐ ment representatives were generally favorable, the regional director arranged a personal interview with the applicant.

Upon completion of the regional director's screening procedures, a personal recommendation was made to the Washington office with reasons. Some recommendations were favorable. Some were unfavorable in varying degrees. Some were noncommital with a suggestion that a National Office interview might well be worthwhile.

Upon receipt of the regional director reports, the screening commit‐ tee in Washington examined these various reports. Some applications were rejected and the applicants were so notified promptly. The bal‐ ance became a "bank" of applicants ready for further consideration when and as vacancies might develop or be anticipated.

The third screening step consisted of interviews in the National Office in Washington, D. C. Travel expense was paid by the Service. Those selected for National Office interviews spent an entire day in the interview process. Normally, man-to-man personal interviews were arranged with the Director, the Deputy Director, the Disputes Direc‐ tor, and the Director of Administrative Management. Each of these four officials tended to concentrate on somewhat different lines of in‐ quiry, but no rigid subdivision of subject matter was observed. All other available members of the Washington staff who had had media‐ tion experience joined in a group interview. Each applicant appeared before the group alone. While this group interview was not intended to be a "torture chamber" experience, it was designed to test an indi‐ vidual's intellectual and emotional responses "under fire."

For reasons to be noted elsewhere, the FMCS normally hired new mediators in groups or classes of about six to 12 individuals per class.

The final screening step was a National Office staff meeting. About six weeks prior to the EOD (entry on duty) date of a class, a staff meeting was held. The persons present at the staff meeting were the individuals at the Washington office who had participated in the in‐ terview process for all or any of the applicants being considered.

Each staff member, in random rotation, announced his list of appli‐ cants in a "would hire" group and a "would not hire" group with numbered priority order for the "would hire" group. This occurred before any group discussion.

A rather quick consensus normally developed immediately at both ends of the spectrum. If there was virtually unanimous agreement not to hire, there was little further discussion of that applicant. Con‐ versely, it was quite common to find early favorable consensus on a small number of individuals at the top of the group. Extensive discus‐ sion then occurred about the applicants lower down on the list. Nor‐ mally, this staff selection process resulted in job offers to about one fourth of the persons who had been interviewed in Washington.

Under the statute, it is the Director's responsibility to select new mediators. However, under the procedure outlined, it is apparent that many persons had participated actively. What was technically a decision by the Director was, in reality, a group consensus developed after careful inquiry. This selection process consumed a very considerable amount of staff time and energy. It was more than worthwhile in view of the fact that the quality of the mediation staff determines both the present and future usefulness of the agency.

MEDIATOR-TRAINEE PROGRAM—FMCS

As indicated in the main text, most mediator-trainees have been applicants who have lacked the requisite combination of labor relations experience and education to qualify for immediate employment as mediators. However, they have been individuals who have evidenced keen interest in mediation and who have convinced the FMCS staff that they have a combination of motivation and personality that will overcome limited experience after a special training period.

Most of the mediator-trainees were hired at the GS-9 pay level. The training began with assignments at the Washington office for a period of time varying from six months to about one year. They were then assigned to a regional office and subsequent training was essentially the same as for other newly hired mediators.

Table B-1 shows profiles of each of 14 trainees as of January 1, 1969. One of the "graduates" was already a "trouble shooter" mediator at the Washington office, one of four men selected from the entire staff for these difficult assignments. Informal information indicates that some of these former trainees have further improved their mediator grade status since early 1969.

MEDIATORS WITH IMPARTIAL EXPERIENCE JUST PRIOR TO FMCS

As indicated in the main text, a total of 92 FMCS mediators on the staff as of January 1, 1969 came to the Service directly from employment that could be considered as impartial. Table B-2 shows the detailed distribution of such employment.

MEDIATOR SALARIES

Answers to questionnaires by 18 states and Puerto Rico, all the states employing one or more full-time nonsupervisory mediators, and similar data from the FMCS and the NMB provide a basis for comparison of salary scales as of January 1, 1969.

Table B-1

Mediator-Trainees, Federal Mediation and Conciliation Service

(Hired 1961-1969)

Mediator Trainee	Date of Hire	Age Date of Hire	Collective Bargaining Experience, If Any — Labor, Management, or Other	Years	Educational Attainment	Length of Time in Washington Office Training (months)	Employment Status With FMCS as of January 1, 1969
A	July, '61	30	Labor	3¾	BS	8	Mediator, GS-15
B	May, '62	27	Labor	3¾	BS	12	Resigned Dec. '67[1]
C	Apr. '63	28	Wage-Hour	1½	LLB	12	Resigned Oct. '66[1]
D	Mar. '64	32	State Mediator	½	MA	15	Mediator, GS-13
E	Mar. '64	28	State Mediation Assistant	3¾	AB	13	Mediator, GS-14
F	Apr. '65	31	Management	6	BBA	13	Mediator, GS-13
G	June '65	26	None		MA	12	Mediator, GS-13
H	Apr. '66	29	Labor	1½	LLB	14	Mediator, GS-13
I	May '66	34	Labor	6½	2 yrs. college	10	Mediator, GS-13
J	Oct. '66	34	Labor	3½	AB	8	Mediator, GS-13
K	Sept. '67	29	Management	½	MBA	6	Mediator, GS-13
L	Nov. '67	29	NLRB Examiner	1¾	MBA	13	Mediator
M	Feb. '68	33	NLRB Examiner	¾	AB	7	Trainee, GS-11
N	June, '68	33	Wage-Hour	3	MLR	8	Mediator, GS-12

[1] Both resignations were voluntary to accept very substantially higher paying jobs with management in labor-relations work.

Source: FMCS Personnel files.

Table B-2

Basically Impartial Employment Background of Certain Members of
Federal Mediation and Conciliation Service Staff as of January 1, 1969
(last job held prior to FMCS employment in a position to mediate)

Employment Background	Numbers of Mediators
State Mediation Agencies	15
National War Labor Board or Wage Stabilization Board	4
National Labor Relations Board	8
Department of Labor	7
Department of Defense (Labor Relations)	5
Department of State (Labor Attaché)	2
Administrative Assistant (FMCS)	7
Labor Arbitration	3
Teaching (Economics or Labor)	2
Trainees (FMCS)	14
Other	
Labor relations oriented	7
Not labor relations oriented	18
Total	92

Source: FMCS Personnel files.

All the agencies reported one or more grades of mediators. In all
instances, each salary scale begins with a minimum annual salary,
and the maximum for that grade is also shown. No data are available
as to distribution of actual rates of pay within each scale. An individual's position within a scale normally is governed by his length of
service in that grade and, in some instances, by merit increases.

For purposes of this analysis, only so-called journeymen mediators
are included. In other words, only the salary scales applicable to mediators beyond the probationary period are utilized, and trainee or
probationary mediators are excluded from the employee count.

Since the FMCS and NMB salary scales and classifications are substantially identical, only one set of federal calculations need be made.

State agencies have been grouped by size in the same manner as in
Appendix A. Appendix A shows the states in each grouping, and that
information need not be repeated here. Footnotes to Table A-2 also
show the detailed composition of each group.

Table B-3 shows in the first column the lowest applicable journeyman mediator salary within each of the agency groups. The highest
available salary within each group is indicated in the next column.
Since this range covers several state agencies in each group, it is substantially wider than the range in any one agency.

The statistical method used to obtain the last column (weighted
average midpoint salaries) needs to be explained. The initial assump-

tion is that all mediators within each classification of journeymen were being paid at the midpoint of the applicable salary scale as of January 1, 1969. The various midpoint salaries were then weighted by the numbers of mediators in each classification. The result is the weighted average of all the applicable midpoint salaries.

It is obvious that the midpoint assumption means that the weighted averages shown in the third column of Table B-3 are not identical to the figures that would be shown if actual salaries of each mediator as of January 1, 1969, were available. Actual salaries in each agency reflect the length of service of the mediators, the methods of administration of the salary scale, and any legislative or budgetary restrictions that may be imposed on such salary administration. By inspection of the data submitted by each state agency, I would speculate that state agency weighted average actual salaries, if available, would be a bit higher than the midpoint figures shown and that the FMCS and NMB actual average salaries would be reasonably close to the figure shown. However, I doubt whether the federal-state salary gap would be closed very much.

In any event, the midpoint method has some merit in addition to the fact that it is the only method of comparison now available to me. It is the salary scales that are fixed by the respective legislators and the midpoint method of comparison does reflect the legislative actions.

Table B-3

Comparisons of Annual Salary Scales Applicable to
Journeymen Nonsupervisory Mediators

Federal and State Agencies as of January 1, 1969[1]

Agencies	Lowest Salary Applicable Within Group	Highest Salary Available Within Group	Weighted Average Midpoint Salaries[2]
Federal (FMCS and NMB)	$14,409	$22,031	$18,461
State[3]			
Four largest Agencies	7,772	19,648	14,803
Next six Agencies by size	7,200	18,924	13,620
Nine smallest Agencies	6,612	13,908	10,327
All State Agencies (18 states and Puerto Rico)	6,612	19,648	13,671

[1] Two increases in the federal salary scales occurred after 1/1/69 and before 9/16/70, the date this table was prepared. Most states anticipated some increases in 1969 and/or 1970.

[2] Assumes that all mediators within each salary scale were being paid at the midpoint of that scale. The resulting midpoint salaries are weighted by the numbers of mediators employed by the several agencies in each salary scale.

[3] See footnotes to Table A-2 for specific composition of the state agency groupings.
Source: Answers to author's questionnaires.

CODE OF PROFESSIONAL CONDUCT FOR LABOR MEDIATORS

Adopted Jointly by the Federal Mediation
and Conciliation Service and the Several
State Agencies Represented by the Association
of Labor Mediation Agencies

Preamble

The practice of mediation is a profession with ethical responsibilities and duties. Those who engage in the practice of mediation must be dedicated to the principles of free and responsible collective bargaining. They must be aware that their duties and obligations relate to the parties who engage in collective bargaining, to every other mediator, to the agencies which administer the practice of mediation, and to the general public.

Recognition is given to the varying statutory duties and responsibilities of the city, state and federal agencies. This code, however, is not intended in any way to define or adjust any of these duties and responsibilities nor is it intended to define when and in what situations mediators from more than one agency should participate. It is, rather, a personal code relating to the conduct of the individual mediator.

This code is intended to establish principles applicable to all professional mediators employed by city, state or federal agencies or to mediators privately retained by parties.

1. The Responsibility of the Mediator to the Parties

The primary responsibility for the resolution of a labor dispute rests upon the parties themselves. The mediator at all times should recognize that the agreements reached in collective bargaining are voluntarily made by the parties. It is the mediator's responsibility to assist the parties in reaching a settlement.

It is desirable that agreement be reached by collective bargaining without mediation assistance. However, public policy and applicable statutes recognize that mediation is the appropriate form of governmental participation in cases where it is required. Whether and when a mediator should intercede will normally be influenced by the desires of the parties. Intercession by a mediator on his own motion should be limited to exceptional cases.

389

The mediator must not consider himself limited to keeping peace at the bargaining table. His role should be one of being a resource upon which the parties may draw and, when appropriate, he should be prepared to provide both procedural and substantive suggestions and alternatives which will assist the parties in successful negotiations.

Since mediation is essentially a voluntary process, the acceptability of the mediator by the parties as a person of integrity, objectivity, and fairness is absolutely essential to the effective performance of the duties of the mediator. The manner in which the mediator carries out his professional duties and responsibilities will measure his usefulness as a mediator. The quality of his character as well as his intellectual, emotional, social and technical attributes will reveal themselves by the conduct of the mediator and his oral and written communications with the parties, other mediators and the public.

2. The Responsibility of the Mediator Toward Other Mediators

A mediator should not enter any dispute which is being mediated by another mediator or mediators without first conferring with the person or persons conducting such mediation. The mediator should not intercede in a dispute merely because another mediator may also be participating. Conversely, it should not be assumed that the lack of mediation participation by one mediator indicates a need for participation by another mediator.

In those situations where more than one mediator is participating in a particular case, each mediator has a responsibility to keep the others informed of developments essential to a cooperative effort and should extend every possible courtesy to his fellow mediator.

The mediator should carefully avoid any appearance of disagreement with or criticism of his fellow mediator. Discussions as to what positions and actions mediators should take in particular cases should be carried on solely between or among the mediators.

3. The Responsibility of the Mediator Toward His Agency and His Profession

Agencies responsible for providing mediation assistance to parties engaged in collective bargaining are a part of government. The mediator must recognize that, as such, he is part of government. The mediator should constantly bear in mind that he and his work are not judged solely on an individual basis but that he is also judged as a representative of his agency. Any improper conduct or professional shortcoming, therefore, reflects not only on the individual mediator but upon his employer and, as such, jeopardizes the effectiveness of his agency, other government agencies, and the acceptability of the mediation process.

The mediator should not use his position for private gain or advantage, nor should he engage in any employment, activity, or enterprise which will conflict with his work as a mediator, nor should he accept any money or thing of value for the performance of his duties—other than his regular salary—or incur obligations to any party which might interfere with the impartial performance of his duties.

4. The Responsibility of the Mediator Toward the Public

Collective bargaining is in essence a private, voluntary process. The primary purpose of mediation is to assist the parties to achieve a settlement. Such assistance does not abrogate the rights of the parties to resort to economic and legal sanctions. However, the mediation process may include a responsibility to assert the interest of the public that a particular dispute be settled; that a work stoppage be ended; and that normal operations be resumed. It should be understood, however, that the mediator does not regulate or control any of the content of a collective bargaining agreement.

It is conceivable that a mediator might find it necessary to withdraw from a negotiation, if it is patently clear that the parties intend to use his presence as implied governmental sanction for an agreement obviously contrary to public policy.

It is recognized that labor disputes are settled at the bargaining table; however, the mediator may release appropriate information with due regard (1) to the desires of the parties, (2) to whether that information will assist or impede the settlement of the dispute and (3) to the needs of an informed public.

Publicity shall not be used by a mediator to enhance his own position or that of his agency. Where two or more mediators are mediating a dispute, public information should be handled through a mutually agreeable procedure.

5. The Responsibility of the Mediator Toward the Mediation Process

Collective bargaining is an established institution in our economic way of life. The practice of mediation requires the development of alternatives which the parties will voluntarily accept as a basis for settling their problems. Improper pressures which jeopardize voluntary action by the parties should not be a part of mediation.

Since the status, experience, and ability of the mediator lend weight to his suggestions and recommendations, he should evaluate carefully the effect of his suggestions and recommendations and accept full responsibility for their honesty and merit.

The mediator has a continuing responsibility to study industrial relations to improve his skills and upgrade his abilities.

Suggestions by individual mediators or agencies to parties, which give the implication that transfer of a case from one mediation "forum" to another will produce better results, are unprofessional and are to be condemned.

Confidential information acquired by the mediator should not be disclosed to others for any purpose or in a legal proceeding or be used directly or indirectly for the personal benefit or profit of the mediator.

Bargaining positions, proposals, or suggestions given to the mediator in confidence during the course of bargaining for his sole information should not be disclosed to the other party without first securing permission from the party or person who gave it to him.

SECOND REPORT

By The

NATIONAL LABOR-MANAGEMENT PANEL

to

William E. Simkin

Director, Federal Mediation and Conciliation Service

Membership of the Panel

Management Members	*Labor Members*
Mr. Wayne T. Brooks	Mr. H. S. Brown
Mr. Joseph V. Cairns	Mr. Jack T. Conway
Mr. J. Curtis Counts	Mr. Cornelius J. Haggerty
Mr. Jesse Freidin	Mr. Thomas E. Harris
Mr. Gerry E. Morse	Mr. John H. Lyons
Mr. J. Paul St. Sure	Mr. Marvin J. Miller

December 30, 1964

The members of the National Labor-Management Panel have stud-ied various plans conceived by managements and unions, sometimes with the assistance of the Federal Mediation and Conciliation Service or other neutrals, designed to continue problem solving in the period between contract negotiations. The increasingly successful use of this technique and its great potential for avoiding industrial conflict have prompted the Panel to inform itself on this development by:

(a) Examining published reports and articles on the subject

(b) Studying documented case histories of this form of labor-management cooperation

(c) Reviewing and analyzing representative cases from the files of the Federal Mediation and Conciliation Service

(d) Direct consultation and discussions with other labor and management practitioners in the field, and

(e) Consultation and discussions with neutral third parties directly involved in this development.

In consequence of this study, the NLMP has reached certain conclusions and has formulated recommendations concerning preventive mediation. They are set forth in this report.

The forward thrust of technological advance and innovation has brought new dimensions to old problems and urgent and new pressures to deal with them. In a very real sense labor and management feel threatened and challenged by the new technology. Both acknowledge that growth and survival are dependent upon the utilization of new techniques of production, service, distribution and sales. Both are concerned with job security and employment opportunities. But while there is agreement that the problems are common, issues arise over the methods of their solution. These issues do not lend themselves, as other issues have in the past, to piecemeal solution for they involve fundamental problems inextricably interwoven not only in the collective bargaining weave but in our total economic fabric.

Crisis bargaining has too frequently ended in a series of temporary accommodations to high visibility conflicts, leaving their underlying causes often untouched, unresolved, and undiminished.

As desirable as is the avoidance of immediate conflict, of even greater value is the fashioning of long-range solutions to basic problems, solutions that take account of the interests of the public as well as those of the immediate parties.

However successful and effective traditional bargaining has been, management and labor today are confronted with bargaining problems far more complicated than ever before. Their very complexities defy the quick and easy solution and more stubbornly resist the pressure tactic of the impending deadline. For such problems time and study are among the essential ingredients needed, and the normal period of contract bargaining, by itself, does not provide enough of either.

The attitude of the parties and their relationship to each other will determine, in the final instance, whether solutions will be earnestly sought and effectively achieved. Time, study and painstaking exploration can create effective attitudes. Time can provide the span for study and exploration; study can provide the facts and explode the misconceptions; exploration can produce the feasible alternatives.

The process of exploring and solving problems before they reach the crisis stage is not a new concept nor a new practice in labor-management relations. Our advancing technology with its attendant problems has, however, added new impetus to this development. The most widely publicized examples of such joint ventures are found in the major industries: The Human Relations Committee and Kaiser Long Range Committee in the steel industry; the Joint Study Committees in the auto and electrical manufacturing industries; the Armour Plan in the meat packing industry; the West Coast Labor Relations Committee in longshore; and the long-established joint committees in the building and construction industry.

These cooperative efforts were in the main initiated by the parties themselves and operate for the most part in the upper echelons of union and executive leadership.

What is not so well known or publicized is the neutral third-party involvement in this development, particularly among the medium- and smaller-size companies. The joint effort here usually operates at the plant level.

Among the significant and successful third-party forces stimulating continuing labor-management dialogue and problem exploration is the Federal Mediation and Conciliation Service, charged by Congress with responsibility for effective mediation, and which has increasingly focused its activities in this area. The FMCS characterizes this phase of its program, with its many facets, as preventive mediation.

The Service feels its preventive mediation program is just getting started. Preventive mediation cases completed and closed by the FMCS rose from 83 cases in fiscal year 1962 to 375 in fiscal 1963 to 478 in fiscal 1964. Continuing labor-management discussion and joint problem exploration in the periods between formal contract negotiations can take many varied forms with a wide choice of ground rules. The venture may be single or multipurpose, it may be formal or informal and called anything from a review committee to a joint study committee or from a labor-management committee to a harmony board.

Because of their many differing forms these cases are hard to break down into specific types. For its own purposes, the FMCS puts them into seven categories. The most notable, including a brief description and the number of cases handled and closed in each, during the fiscal year 1964, are as follows:

Continuing Joint Labor-Management Committee *110*

Such committees are usually multipurpose and continuing, formally organized and structured, hold regularly scheduled meetings and work from a prepared agenda. Subcommittees may be established but must report back to the full committee.

Joint Study Committees—Contract Issues *11*

These are usually single-purpose committees assigned to gather facts, statistics and explore alternative approaches on a given single subject or problem. Its assignment may be to prepare a particularly perplexing problem for settlement in negotiations or it may be an assignment following the completion of negotiations, to deal with a matter left open by the settlement.

Continuing Liaison or Consultation *152*

This is, in effect, long-range consultation to their bargaining relationship. It continues beyond the normal period of contract negotiations. It is used to accumulate information helpful to the parties in subsequent bargaining sessions and to help them resolve some problem.

Approved Training Programs—Stewards
and Supervisory Force *97*

This activity flows from the parties' recognition of the need for further training of their respective representatives in order to improve the over-all bargaining relationship and the day-to-day operations within the establishment.

Miscellaneous Cases *50*

These cases elude easy categorization but include periodic and informal attempts to deal with joint problems and improve the relationship of the parties.

The Appendix to this Report includes brief summaries of representative cases in each of the above categories. They illustrate the nature, diversity, and scope of preventive mediation, the contribution that can be made by competent and resourceful mediation, and some of the obstacles that can impede the preventive mediation effort.

Ninety-five percent of all its preventive mediation cases originate from dispute cases handled by the Service. The FMCS handles over 7,000 such dispute cases each year and is, thus, uniquely equipped and strategically positioned

—to observe the status and viability of the bargaining relationship

—to identify underlying sources of conflict likely to persist

—to assess the need and usefulness of continuing discussion and problem exploration

—to assist in the early and critical stages of such joint ventures

—to make available, when requested, professional and experienced consultation.

The mediator is first and foremost a consultant—a professional specialist dedicated and committed not to either party but only to their relationship. For it is essentially the attitudes of the parties that finally determine the success or failure of the effort to anticipate and to solve problems through continuing dialogue, study and exploration.

By reason of its extraordinary experience and its continuous availability the FMCS can be effective in stimulating and assisting this development.

RECOMMENDATIONS
OF THE
NATIONAL LABOR-MANAGEMENT PANEL

A. We commend to companies and unions the utility, in the intervals between contract negotiations, of a continuing discussion of difficult and persistent problems and where, to promote this effort, mediation is indicated, we recommend the services of the FMCS in the creation and operation of continuing labor-management committees, study committees, or other appropriate devices.

B. We recommend that:

1. The present FMCS preventive mediation program be expanded.

2. The FMCS establish outside the Service a roster of specialists in preventive mediation, similar to its roster of arbitrators, to which parties can be referred for expert help in the highly specialized and complicated areas of collective bargaining.

3. The FMCS continue and expand its Advanced Leadership Training Program for Mediators, with particular emphasis on workshops designed to enlarge their areas of special competence to enable them to deal most effectively with specific bargaining subjects and accelerate their activities in this field of preventive mediation, and

4. Adequate provision be made in the FMCS annual appropriation to finance these expanded services.

INDEX

T

U